# GROUP RIGHTS

# GROUP RIGHTS

## RECONCILING EQUALITY AND DIFFERENCE

David Ingram

University Press of Kansas

Published by the University Press of Kansas (Lawrence, Kansas 66049), which was
organized by the Kansas Board of Regents and is operated and funded by Emporia State
University, Fort Hays State University, Kansas State University, Pittsburg State University,
the University of Kansas, and Wichita State University

Library of Congress Cataloging-in-Publication Data

Ingram, David, 1952–
    Group rights : reconciling equality and difference / David Ingram.
      p.  cm.
    Includes index.
    ISBN 0-7006-1006-5 (cloth : alk. paper) — ISBN 0-7006-1007-3 (pbk. : alk. paper)
      1. Minorities—Civil rights. 2. Minorities—Civil rights—United States. 3.
    Minorities—Legal status, laws, etc.—United States. I. Title.
    JF1061.I54 2000
    323.1'73—dc21                                                   99-053552

British Library Cataloguing in Publication Data is available.

Printed in the United States of America

10  9  8  7  6  5  4  3  2  1

The paper used in this publication meets the minimum requirements of the American
National Standard for Permanence of Paper for Printed Library Materials Z39.48-1984.

To Jenny

# CONTENTS

# ACKNOWLEDGMENTS

I would like to thank Loyola University for funding the paid leave and the Mellon Core Curriculum grant that enabled me to work on this book. Special acknowledgment also must be extended to the staff at the University Press of Kansas, especially to my chief editor, Nancy Jackson, and my copyeditor, Leslee Anderson. I also owe a debt of gratitude to colleagues and friends who gave me feedback on various ideas contained in it. Among them are Olufemi Taiwo, David Schweickart, Tom Wren, Tom Sheehan, Charles Mills, Sandra Bartky, Patricia Huntington, Martin Matustik, Iris Young, Milton Fisk, Rodney Peffer, Gilberto Valdez, James Marsh, Virginia de Oliveira-Alves, Liam Harte, and Laura Hengehold. I am especially grateful to Kory Schaff and other graduate students enrolled in my Philosophy 438 class for their critical feedback on earlier drafts of the book, to Stephen Steinberg and Naomi Zack for suggestions regarding the book's original proposal, and to my assistants Craig Greenman and Brian Bowles for editorial recommendations. But most of all I am grateful to my partner Jennifer Parks, whose keen analytic skills and companionship have helped me to be a better person and philosopher.

# INTRODUCTION

I can recall two experiences that sharply etched in my mind the contradiction in American life pitting love of equality against disdain for the "different" among us. The first stems from my college years as an organizer working with the United Farm Workers Union in Orange County, California, during the grape and lettuce boycotts of the seventies. Passing out literature to prospective patrons of a major supermarket chain, I was frequently harassed by people who did not take kindly to my sympathy for "ungrateful wetbacks." These critics could not understand why migrant farmworkers, who were mainly Mexican and Guatemalan, were not satisfied with their opportunity to earn starvation wages for doing backbreaking labor under dangerous, unsanitary, and dehumanizing conditions.

Significantly, many of the objections I received from patrons of the supermarket were laced with racist epithets. At the time, I had no inkling about the racial complexities of what I was witnessing. Indeed, it was not until a few years ago, while watching NBC's *New Harvest of Shame* (a *Dateline* documentary revisiting themes raised by Edward R. Murrow in his classic television commentary on the plight of the farmworkers in the early sixties), that I realized how complex America's racial divisions were. Here, black Americans and Mexican migrant workers complained about the influx of undocumented Guatemalan refugees who were willing to do their work for a fraction of the depressed wages they themselves had been receiving. Once again I detected an unsympathetic disdain for the unwanted newcomer who was exacerbating an already saturated labor market (the transporation of southern black laborers into predominantly white labor markets in the North during the first half of this century for use as strikebreakers readily came to mind). And once again, the subtext of this tragedy—U.S. support of ruthless military regimes in Guatemala that were killing and expelling thousands

1

of Mayan peasants—brought home the awful dilemma of social justice: acknowledge our responsibility for and obligation to the desperate refugees illegally entering the country or protect the domestic (and legally
documented) workers from wage depression through stricter enforcement
of immigration controls.

My second anecdote speaks less of the connection between race and multicultural immigration than it does about the extent to which multicultural diversity is valued—or, as the case may be, undervalued—in our society. In 1996
the philosophy department in which I am currently employed advertised a
new, entry-level post for someone to teach both undergraduate and graduate
level courses. The qualifications in the advertisement also stressed teaching
and research expertise in the highly specialized area of graduate studies—in
this case, expertise in Immanuel Kant's *First Critique*. After conducting the
initial round of interviews for the job, three candidates were invited to present papers to the department—two white men and one Asian-Canadian
woman. Speaking in favor of hiring the woman were the following points: evidence of stellar teaching at the undergraduate level, broad expertise in Kant
scholarship and philosophy in general, and multicultural considerations (a
large percentage of our undergraduate student body is of Asian descent and
most of our students are women, but our department of thirty-six full-time
faculty has only five women and no one of Asian descent). Despite the fact
that our female candidate had expressed an interest in teaching some Asian
philosophy (thereby providing our students with an opportunity to appreciate non-Western thought) and despite the fact that she might have symbol-
ized, in the eyes of many of our Asian students, the department's recognition
of *their* culture's contribution to philosophy, she was passed over in favor of
one of the male candidates, ostensibly because he was better qualified or more
closely fit the requirements for graduate research and teaching.

Happily, the male candidate we hired has turned out to be an excellent
teacher and colleague. Still I cannot help but think that my department
missed a golden opportunity to recognize our growing Asian student body
and enrich the cultural horizons of our non-Asian students.

Doubtless it was concern over qualifications rather than cultural insensitivity that explained my department's decision not to hire the Asian candidate.
Yet cultural and racial insensitivity has been—and continues to be—a major
feature of American life. A recent study by Donald Kinder and Lynn Sanders
bears this out. They conclude that race and racial resentment are the most reliable predictors of opinion on a wide range of social issues, including immigration and multiculturalism. As one might expect, racially resentful whites

are not only likely to oppose affirmative action and public assistance, but they are also likely to support stringent restrictions on immigration and oppose multicultural curricular reform.

The relationship between race, ethnicity, class, and cultural difference in the American experience is complex. On one hand, America is a country of immigrants who have added tremendously to the intellectual, cultural, and economic capital of the nation as a whole. On the other hand, nativist fears about "the other" have continued to fuel suspicion and resentment toward non-English immigrants. The first wave of Irish immigrants coming to this country in the middle of the nineteenth century were regarded by many Americans as second-class citizens—even racially inferior—because of their Catholicism and working-class background. The same could be said for the subsequent wave of Italian immigrants. Jews from Eastern Europe faced even more virulent discrimination. In many cases, the kind of segregation and exclusion they encountered mirrored the experience of blacks living in the South.

Because so many white Americans are of immigrant stock, one would think that they would be more sympathetic to the plight of blacks. But this response has not occurred. White Americans of immigrant stock wonder why blacks have not been as successful as they have been in raising themselves out of poverty. Although one might respond to them by pointing out that Americans descended from slaves experienced a uniquely brutal form of discrimination, immigrants counter—with some justification—that they or their ancestors have also encountered hostility, if not outright discrimination.

Today hostility against immigrants is propelled by the effects of a global economy that pits American workers against their counterparts from the depressed regions of the Third World (including our neighbors to the south). As Pat Buchanon's unsuccessful bid for the 1996 Republican presidential nomination amply attests and as the flowering of white supremacist groups throughout the land sadly confirms, this hostility has racial overtones. A substantial number of white males—many of whom have lost their unskilled or semiskilled nonunion jobs because of plant relocation abroad—bitterly resent the influx of desperate immigrants who are willing to compete for scarce jobs at a lower wage.[1] The fact that many of these immigrants enter the country illegally, speak a different language, share a different culture, and are nonwhite to boot adds to the racial siege mentality of these resentful whites. Elected officials at state and federal levels have been only too willing to play upon the fears of these whites. Judging from the recent spate of laws and referenda restricting illegal immigration and cutting benefits to *both* illegal and legal aliens, their jeremiad against the "invading horde" of immigrants has paid off handsomely.

Where does this leave us today? Legislators and judges throughout the land are preparing to launch what can only be described as an all-out war on affirmative action, racial redistricting, immigration rights, multicultural curricular reform, and group rights pertaining to Native Americans. We are told by the Republican nominee for the 1996 presidential race that, despite the absence of equal opportunity for blacks, so-called preferences and quotas are "a source of polarization pitting one group against another group" that have accomplished "absolutely nothing" for 99 percent of all blacks.[2] Meanwhile, in a proposal directed against children born in the United States of illegal immigrants, the platform adopted by his party endorsed the abolition of the guarantee of citizenship extended by the Fourteenth Amendment to "all persons born or naturalized in the United States." And throughout the country, one hears radio commentators and journalists attacking multicultural curricular reform as a kind of left-wing subversion of Western civilization.

Numerous examples of this sort can be cited, from restrictions on immigration and the rights of immigrants to due process and social entitlements to attacks on "preferences" granted to a wide range of minorities (including women). The motivations behind this "backlash" range from overt feelings of racism and nativism to reasonable concerns about racial and cultural polarization, shortages in public services due to increasing population, and social injustice. The aim of this book is to examine—and at least partially lay to rest—the reasonable concerns.

Years of teaching political philosophy have taught me that conservatives, liberals, and radicals generally agree on the most basic principles of justice but disagree on the facts. For example, almost everyone endorses the principle that all should be treated equally and be given equal opportunity, that each is owed certain things (rights, resources, and so forth) just for being a person, and that individual desserts should be based upon some combination of achievement, effort, and need. At the same time, people disagree about the specific meaning of these platitudes, and much of their disagreement stems from disagreement about facts. Few conservatives would deny that social equality in possessions and property is a noble ideal to strive for. In this respect they are one with progressives. However, they disagree with progressives in thinking that capitalism (or more precisely, a relatively unregulated market in goods and services) is the most efficient way to achieve this end—a view with which I strongly disagree.

So it goes with most of our disagreements concerning affirmative action, immigration, and the rights of religious, ethnic, and national minorities. For this reason, I have found it judicious in this book to spend less time working out the deep, philosophical foundations of moral and political principles and more time elaborating the facts—histories and data—by which those principles are variously interpreted.[3]

For instance, in defending affirmative action, I relate the history of oppression endured by African Americans in the past to statistically confirmable cumulative disadvantages that work to oppress them in the present, even after overt discrimination has subsided. Likewise, I further show that affirmative action is an efficient but partial remedy in eliminating this injustice. Finally, I argue that affirmative action is not reverse discrimination but coheres with the predominant conception of equal protection embedded in the U.S. Constitution.

These and other similar arguments contained in *Group Rights* exemplify a kind of philosophizing that I designate as critical social theory. It situates concrete social dilemmas within the framework of contemporary views of justice and their prevalent legal applications. Here, social and political ideals are located within a historical narrative incorporating economics, politics, social science, and cultural anthropology. By infusing these ideals with historical facts, the book generates a perspective that is sufficiently concrete to support criticism and prescriptions for reform. It is also, I believe, objective—albeit not in the way of reflecting a God's-eye view of social reality for no such objectivity exists (indeed, "facts" are always framed in terms of a nonfactual horizon of linguistic meaningfulness and personal significance).

I have cast my net widely here. The topic of group rights is indeed broad, ranging from welfare and disability rights to the multicultural rights that are the chief focus of my study.[4] That focus encompasses many themes and issues—multiculturalism, affirmative action, proportional group representation, minority rights, immigration, race and culture—that have been dealt with by others on an individual basis. If I cannot claim to have provided much depth and originality in my treatment of them, at least I can claim to have brought them together in a mutually illuminating way, for my purpose here is not to edify scholars but to provide a sourcebook for citizens and students.

In Chapters 1 through 4, I engage theoretical issues concerning such notions as rights, equality, liberalism, democracy, and group differences. I discuss important tensions within liberal thought regarding the rights of groups versus the rights of individuals (Chapter 1) and then examine different kinds of oppressed groups and social injustices as well as affirmative and transformative strategies for rectifying them (Chapter 2). Chapters 3 and 4 conclude with a conceptual analysis of racial and cultural groups, conceived as aggregates and affinities. These chapters defend the idea that some group identifications are more legitimate than others (racial categories being highly suspect but not necessarily illegitimate). In Chapters 5 through 10, I apply these preliminary insights to contemporary debates concerning the rights of Native Americans and immigrants, affirmative action, racial redistricting, and multiculturalism. The concluding chapter revisits some of the theoretical issues addressed in the first chapter. While developing a general theory of rights, it reexamines the problem of social injustice within a global setting, assessing the negative impact of free trade policies on group rights to subsistence, security, political self-determination, and cultural integrity. It closes with a brief meditation on the sorts of group differences any ideal society would seek to foster.

# PART I.
# JUSTICE FOR GROUPS AND INDIVIDUALS:
# THEORETICAL FOUNDATIONS

# 1
## EQUALITY AND DIFFERENCE
## IN DEMOCRACY AND LAW

If you believe in equal rights, then consider the following cases: The city of Pawtucket, Rhode Island, and its downtown merchants' association traditionally sponsored a Christmas display that included a Christmas tree, a Santa Claus, reindeer pulling a sleigh, and a creche scene with the usual figures depicting Jesus and the Holy Family—topped with a banner proclaiming "Seasons Greetings." A suit was brought against the city on the grounds that it violated the First Amendment's clause prohibiting government establishment of religion. In a split decision, *Lynch v. Donnelly* (1984), the U.S. Supreme Court upheld the constitutionality of the creche display.

Writing for the majority, Justice Warren Burger argued that, although the creche "advances religion in a sense," it does so in a way consistent with other legitimate precedents, such as the statutorily prescribed motto "In God We Trust," which appears on American money. In his opinion, the founders of the constitution intended to "accommodate" religious belief, so long as it did not explicitly endorse any particular denomination of belief. Dissenting, Justice William Brennan noted that the display was "insulting to those who insist for religious or personal reasons that the story of Christ is in no sense a part of 'history' nor an unavoidable part of our national heritage." In his opinion, "the effect on minority religious groups, as well as those who may reject all religion, is to convey the message that their views are not similarly worthy of public recognition nor entitled to public support."[1]

Here is the second case: Until 1985, the Monroe-Woodbury Central School District in New York had provided Kiryas Joel, a village of Satmar Hasidic Jews, with publicly funded special education for disabled students. Citing legal precedents concerning the separation of church and state, the school district stopped sending teachers into the village's private parochial schools and placed the students in public schools. However, complaints

9

from the students' parents about the district's insensitivity toward the religious and cultural practices of their sect soon surfaced. One child went on a class trip and ate non-Kosher food at a McDonald's drive-in; another had his sidelocks cut off by another student; others experienced teasing about their unusual dress; and all were exposed to school activities revolving around Christmas and other holidays that many of the students' parents found threatening to their faith.

In order to accommodate the sect's fears about religious intolerance and insensitivity, Governor Mario Cuomo signed a 1989 law creating a separate public school district for it. However, six months later, the New York State School Boards Association sued the village district, saying that public money should not be used to support private religion. The suit has been upheld by both the state supreme court and the U.S. Supreme Court (the most recent occurring in April of 1998).[2] So far, efforts by New York legislators to draft a law—neutral with respect to religion—allowing any municipality to create its own school district *if* it satisfied five population and tax-base criteria have failed. Because only one other municipal district besides Kiryas Joel satisfies the criteria (out of some 1,546 municipalities), State Supreme Court Justice Joseph C. Teresi concluded that "there can be no doubt that [the statute] is a clear, unequivocal, but impermissible favoritism, promotion, preference and endorsement by the state of the Satmar community of Kiryas Joel."

Both of the above cases concern equal treatment for different religious sects. The First Amendment's opening statement that "Congress shall make no law respecting an establishment of religion, or prohibiting the free exercise thereof" is normally understood as guaranteeing such treatment. Prohibiting the state from passing laws that have a religious purpose is the most obvious way in which the amendment prevents government from establishing religion. However, prohibiting government acts that advance or inhibit religion (as in the case of the Pawtucket creche) or foster excessive government entanglement with religion (as in the case of the Kiryas Joel school district) also prevents it from favoring one religion over another (*Lemon v. Kurtzman* [1971]).

In the Pawtucket case, plaintiffs argued that the creche scene not only served a religious purpose—the official promotion of the dominant, Christian faith—but also had the effect of advancing it, thereby inhibiting nondominant faiths. Plaintiffs in the Kiryas Joel case, which included liberal Jewish organizations, similarly argued that creating a special school district run by members of the Satmar Hasidim also involved government favoritism—this time on behalf of a minority religion.

The differences between the two cases are also notable. Because the Kiryas Joel case involved favoring a minority religion struggling to preserve its sectarian cultural identity amidst an overwhelmingly secularized Christian culture, equal treatment might seem to involve compensating it for its disadvantage, much as we handicap better golfers in order to "even the playing field." The Pawtucket creche scene, by contrast, involved favoring an already dominant religion, thereby increasing its advantage. Furthermore, the Kiryas Joel case involved a remedy designed to protect a minority culture from discrimination and harassment, so government protection of this culture's equal freedom to practice its faith by setting up a special school district on its behalf might seem justified.

Thus, in addition to raising questions about government establishment of religion, the Kiryas Joel case raises questions revolving around the equal protection of religious freedom. In recent legal decisions, the freedom of religion clause has been interpreted to mean that all religious sects should have equal access to basic resources of education, including fire and police protection, public transportation, textbooks, and special education. Requiring religious sects to pay for these state-mandated services seems to impose an unfair financial burden on them that hinders them from freely educating their members.[3]

It would seem, then, that the establishment and freedom of religion clauses of the First Amendment present us with competing views about the meaning of religious equality. The establishment clause mandates religious equality by prohibiting government entanglement in religion—including, it would seem, the public financing of a school district run by a religious sect. By contrast, the freedom of religion clause mandates religious equality by endorsing some government entanglement. If the defendants in the Kiryas Joel case are right, the disabled students of the village cannot receive an equal education in the larger, integrated public school because of harassment and insensitivity. They need their *own* public school for the disabled, staffed by teachers who speak Yiddish and respect their traditions and run by members of their own community.

The conflict between the two religion clauses in the Kiryas Joel case presents us with competing models of equality. Those who invoke the establishment clause requiring government "neutrality" generally feel that secular public school districts, which *integrate* children from different religious, ethnic, and racial groups, are the best hope for ensuring that each student gets the *same* education—neither better nor worse—as all the others. By contrast, those who appeal to the freedom of religion clause requiring modest government entanglement feel that sectarian public school districts, which segregate children of one group from another, are the best hope for ensuring that each student is treated with *equal concern* and respect for his or her cultural *differences*.

The debate over religious equality exemplifies a much larger conflict in our legal treatment of difference. In the United States today, certain religious sects are exempt from statutes that affect others. Institutions of higher education have established special programs designed to highlight the struggles of women, gays, and minorities but not straight white males. Government agencies have mandated the use of quotas and other forms of preferences exclusively targeting women and minorities in employment, promotion, and placement. Native American tribes have been granted limited sovereignty and immunity from civil suits. Poor, indigent, and disabled people receive special benefits not available to others. And government has guaranteed the election of African Americans and other minorities in racially mixed regions by redrawing political boundaries on the basis of racial demographics. In short, the law treats different groups of persons differently.

But should it? Should differences between citizens have an impact on the way they are treated? If so, should there be different rights for different people?

These questions—so central to the purpose of this study—can be answered affirmatively. But in order to see how, we must first examine the relationship between rights and equality. Beyond understanding how differential treatment furthers equal rights, we must see how rights embody fairness and impartiality—the cornerstones of liberal democracy.

## *Equal Rights and the Common Possession of Humanity*

Let us begin by examining the relationship between rights and equality. Most of us believe that persons possess both moral and legal rights.[4] Leaving aside their exact specification (see Chapter 11), such rights are supposedly possessed by one and all equally. When asked why this should be so, morally speaking, we usually point to our common humanity. Each of us, we say, embodies an equal potential—if not actual manifestation—of humanity, which supposedly distinguishes us from the rest of the animal kingdom. We—not animals—have rights because only we can deploy reason in choosing our ends and the means appropriate for attaining them.[5] Only we can reason that persons should be respected in their freedom to go about their proper business so long as doing so does not infringe upon the freedom of others to do the same. Only we can understand the moral principle of justice requiring mutual respect for each person's interest in his or her own well-being.

Of course, simple reflection tells us that the possession of equal rights can be based as little on potential as on actual reasoning capacities. Severely retarded people, for example, are normally thought to possess a right to life equal to any other, despite their lack of reasoning potential. What matters, then, is not that this or that *individual* possesses the potential to reason, but that he or she belongs to a *social species,* or *community* of essentially *interdependent* and *interrelated* individuals, whose adult members reason as a normal condition of their existence.[6] For involved in this species-specific competency is not only the ability to think in a logical and calculated manner, but also to identify with (and care for) others as centers of experience—an identification that is tacitly presupposed whenever we communicate or interact with one another.

Despite the fact that membership in a social species—rather than individual possession of reasoning ability—grounds our most basic moral rights to security and subsistence, individual differences in reasoning ability do influence the way we assign other basic rights. Either by law or by moral reason infants, children, and severely retarded people do not have a right, enjoyed by normal functioning adults, to sign contracts, drive automobiles, or vote in elections. Possession of these legal rights is made contingent on acquiring a certain minimum level of rational functioning, and this legal requirement, in turn, captures our belief that moral rights to civil and political liberties come with responsibilities whose effective discharge presupposes the attainment of a minimal degree of maturity, rationality, and intelligence. Having satisfied this minimum threshold (whose age and competency criteria vary from legal system to legal system), the moral principle of equality again kicks in (that is, we do not confer greater civil, property, and political rights on persons who happen to possess above-average reasoning skills).[7]

Conversely, nonpossession of certain rights owing to rational incapacity is compensated for by possession of others that are not extended to normally functioning adults. Because children and mentally handicapped people are made vulnerable owing to their incapacity, they possess rights to social services and programs not granted to the rest of us.

In sum, apart from being born with an equal right to life, we acquire additional property, civil, political, and social rights (such as signing contracts, voting, and unemployment insurance) commensurate with our attainment of a minimum threshold of rational functioning. This means that children and mentally disabled people do not have the same rights as normally functioning adults, or that they have them in different ways. In order to secure the same equal right to life, children and mentally disabled persons need access to social services, whereas normally functioning adults need access to property, civil freedom, and political power.

### Social Differences and Equal Treatment

When we extend rights to persons, we normally extend them to all persons equally. That is, we do not discriminate among different groups of persons in the assignment of basic property, civil, and protection rights (for example, we do not give Catholics more religious freedom than we give Muslims). More precisely, because membership in the human species entitles any individual to possess the same basic rights, these rights are assigned first and foremost to individuals as individuals, not to individuals as members of groups. Thus, we say that each and every individual has a universal right to associate, to contract with others, and so on.

By contrast, when we assign special rights to persons belonging to one group but not another, we discriminate between individuals—treat them unequally (or differently)—depending on their actual inequalities and differences. Hence we say that mentally disabled children have an exclusive right to special education services not available to others. This right is group-specific rather than universal, or proper to individuals as individuals.

Social differences affect our understanding of equality no less than differences in rational competency and as such also demarcate group-specific rights. By social differences I have in mind both differences in well-being and differences in status. Differences in well-being (or standing) call for social entitlements to government aid that protect against disadvantages born of hunger, homelessness, and other forms of deprivation.[8] By contrast, differences in status owing to race, class, ethnicity, religious orientation, gender, sexuality, and disability call for recognition rights that protect against domination.

Because social entitlements and recognition rights protect only groups suffering oppression and domination, they seem to enforce a policy of unequal treatment. However, the unequal treatment they permit aims at eliminating social inequalities that prevent individuals from equally developing and exercising their human potentials. So these group-specific rights ostensibly advance the principle of equal treatment. But how is this possible?

To understand how, we must first examine two notions of equal treatment. For some, treating citizens equally means treating them exactly the same way.[9] Sameness of treatment is precisely what citizens demand of their laws; otherwise, not all would consent to them as equally benefiting their interests. In order for this to happen, laws must be impartial,[10] that is, they must advance only universal interests held by any rational individual, in complete abstraction from all the particular interests that differentiate one individual from another. Since our particular interests very often stem from our attachments to religious, ethnic, racial, gender, sexual, regional, and economic groups, impartial laws must articulate rights that apply to individuals as individuals, not as members of particular groups. That explains why the First Amendment's establishment clause prohibits government entanglement with religious groups: equal protection of religious freedom can only mean protecting individuals' freedom to practice (or not practice) their faith as they see fit, independent of official aids and endorsements.

Others, however, argue that treating persons equally means treating them differently, in a way that respects their individual distinctness no less than their common humanity.[11] Their reasoning is this: Not all persons find themselves in social circumstances that are equally conducive to the full cultivation and exercise of their humanity, and some—including members of the Satmar sect—have suffered discrimination at the hands of other, more numerous and dominant groups because of their particular differences. These persons have a unique interest in counteracting their disadvantage and vulnerability. However, because their disadvantage and vulnerability stems from their particular differences, treating them with equal respect is only sometimes best promoted by treating them the same way we treat others. In the case of gays and lesbians, for instance, antidiscrimination statutes—which forbid taking differences into account in hiring and the like—suffice to ensure their enjoyment of the same rights enjoyed by others. However, antidiscrimination statutes might not suffice to guarantee the Satmar sect such rights, thereby requiring for this purpose the statutory creation of special exemptions and arrangements—that is, special group-specific rights—not granted to other groups.

Is difference-regarding equal treatment legally coherent? A cursory glance at the American legal code suggests that it might be. This code pays homage to both sameness and difference-regarding views of equality. For example, the Fourteenth Amendment to the U.S. Constitution famously asserts that no state shall "deny to any person within its jurisdiction the equal protection of the laws." Here the literal reference is to individuals, not groups.

Its notion of equal protection harkens back to early constitutional law, which began as a defense of religious freedom (or "freedom of conscience") during the seventeenth century. This freedom, we believe, extends to all individuals universally, irrespective of their differences, and thus imposes limits on what any group can rightfully do.

By contrast, the Fifteenth Amendment—which expressly addresses the problem of racial discrimination in its assertion that "the right of citizens of the United States to vote shall not be denied or abridged by the United States or by any State on account of race, color, or previous condition of servitude"—suggests a somewhat different interpretation of equal protection, albeit one that, upon closer inspection, is also implicit in the Fourteenth Amendment.[12] Here, instead of referring to all individuals in abstraction from their group affiliation, the amendment singles out for protection a specific group of citizens consisting mainly of former slaves, their descendants, and persons of color. It leaves open the possibility that special measures—such as the group-specific "affirmative action" rights mandated by the Reconstruction Congress in its Freedman's Bureau Act—might have to be adopted in order to ensure that the more basic rights of *this* group are not "abridged."

Again, if we turn our attention to specific categories of law, we see that sometimes one or the other view of equality predominates. Take criminal law. We assume that persons charged with crimes should be processed by the law in exactly the same way, regardless of differences in race, gender, and class. Criminal justice, we think, should be color-, gender-, and class-blind. Although criminal statutes may affect different groups differently[13]—and may even carve out special sanctions for rape and hate crimes perpetrated against women and minorities—the law, we feel, should not use the race, gender, or class of the victims and the accused to draw distinctions between criminal acts and punishments. These categories should be irrelevant for determining the culpability of defendants and the severity of their crimes.

To be sure, the requirement of difference-blindness in criminal law is often honored in the breach. The color, gender, and economic class of defendants and victims still matter to jurors and judges, despite all the legal procedures that have been introduced to minimize the impact of such factors. Meanwhile, as I noted above, statutes regulating hate crimes, rapes and abortions, and substance abuse (just to mention a few categories) explicitly or implicitly single out minorities, women, and poor people for special protection or special discrimination, depending on one's point of view. All of this discussion goes to show how difficult (if not impossible) it is to maintain the view that, in criminal due process, equal treatment means being treated simply as an individual, in exactly the same way as all others are treated.

Although we think that equality-as-sameness should prevail in the area of criminal law,[14] we generally believe that a difference-regarding equality ought to govern social law. Cities seeking to hire counselors for rape clinics might reasonably prefer women over men, while admissions officers for medical schools seeking to place doctors in understaffed minority community clinics might reasonably prefer minority students with average test scores over white students with higher test scores (especially when special linguistic and cultural aptitudes are required).

More strongly, the "sameness" approach to equality does not describe current policies designed to protect the rights of particularly vulnerable groups. Welfare entitlements enable poor children to be raised in a secure family environment; affirmative action rights enable women and minorities—who, statistically speaking, suffer *systematic* institutional discrimination in hiring, promoting, and educational advancement—to compete for a fair share of scarce positions. In these cases, we compensate persons for disadvantages that would otherwise prevent them from *equally* exercising the *same* basic rights that the rest of us enjoy.[15]

In sum, the demand for equal treatment means different things depending on the context in question. In the area of basic civil rights, equal treatment typically means being treated the same way. Here, sameness of treatment is often enforced by limiting government intervention. For instance, we generally think that government should intervene as little as possible in the regulation of political speech, guaranteeing to one and all the same universal right to express themselves as they see fit. Likewise, we feel that government should not become entangled in religious matters, lest it show undue favoritism toward one or another (usually dominant) religion. However, in cases involving social and recognition rights that are granted to differently situated groups, equal treatment will require different treatment. Targeting children living in poor families with special medical and welfare benefits treats them with the same respect and concern bestowed on children living in rich families. The same might be said for affirmative action policies designed to protect oppressed minorities.

*Liberalism and Equality: Individuals Versus Groups*

In discussing the case of the Satmar sect, I left out a crucial detail: The dominant group controlling Kiryas Joel prevented a dissident group from serving on the school board and even prevented the children of this group from attending the public school! Because creating the school board was intended to secure the religious freedom of the group, which then acted to suppress some of its own members, it might seem that this government intervention showed religious favoritism. Although plaintiffs suing the school district made note of this favoritism, the courts held that it was irrelevant to deciding the issue of religious establishment.

This conflict raises another issue: the protection of individuals versus the protection of groups. The First Amendment protection of religious freedom applies to both. On the one hand, it protects the right of individuals to practice their faith independently of interference by religious groups. Thus, when a majority of the Satmar community denies an individual within the community the right to send his or her child to the public school, it interferes with his or her freedom of religion. To secure this basic right, government must intervene in the internal affairs of the religious community on behalf of the individual's right, or the individual must be allowed to exit the community in a way that permits him or her to continue exercising that right.

On the other hand, the First Amendment protects religious groups from interference by other groups and the state. In the Kiryas Joel case, the state intervened in order to protect the Satmar Hasidim from "interference" by the dominant culture. But did it also "interfere" in the internal affairs of that group? Did setting up a public school for the community invite the possibility that the dominant group in the community might use the school board to oppress a minority group? And what about the children in the community? The ultraorthodox religious regimen forceably inculcated in them by their teachers conditions them to accept rigid gender roles that emphasize the domestic subordination of women to their husbands. Does this kind of education (which the liberal state seems to be subsidizing) not restrict the "equal" right of girls to develop a robust sense of their freedom to choose who they want to become in later life?[16] In short, did the state here uphold the religious freedom of the Satmar group in violation of the religious freedom of some individuals within that group?

The conflict between individual and group rights sketched above is symptomatic of a general tension within liberal philosophy that undergirds our understanding of rights. That philosophy favors individual freedom, but it also favors tolerance of religious groups and other ideologically centered sects.

Why individual freedom? Because historical changes beginning in sixteenth-century Europe, most notably those revolving around the rise of capitalism and the Protestant Reformation, valued the individual (or private) cultivation of religious faith and the individual acquisition and disposition of property. These changes, in turn, were accompanied by the dissolution of an all-embracing religious worldview, Catholicism, and an equally all-embracing economic and political system, feudalism. Since both Catholicism and feudalism upheld the justice of a hierarchical order wherein individual freedom was subordinated to the maintenance of inherited occupations and roles, the valorization of individual freedom also entailed a valorization of equality. No longer would access to divine revelation, economic wealth, and political power be based on the accidental privileges of birth. Instead, each individual would be equally permitted to strive for these goods, commensurate with his or her own free actions.

Initially, despite their egalitarian promise, Protestantism and capitalism promoted an individualism predicated on differences, not on commonalities. Protestant sects fought among themselves as well as with the Catholic Church for dominance; and market systems premised on private ownership of the means of production exacerbated social inequalities between peasants and workers, on one side, and landowners and factory owners, on the other. In short, instead of encouraging respect for other persons as embodiments of the same common humanity, the new individualism ignited contempt for their cultural and social inferiority.

By the end of the seventeenth century, however, a new liberal philosophy emerged—exemplified by the writings of John Locke—that sought to pacify the new individualist order by appeal to the egalitarian and humanistic concept of a social contract. According to this notion, society is a voluntary association of individuals who agree to abide by laws for the sake of mutual protection and mutual cooperation. In order to command the voluntary consent of all individuals, such laws must satisfy two conditions. First, they must be relatively impartial with respect to religious and class differences. They must treat each person equally. Second, equal treatment must be seen as following from the fundamental equality of all persons as "equal" embodiments of a common humanity. As noted at the outset of this chapter, such humanity was identified with membership in a species whose distinguishing capacity resided in the ability to rationally discern right from wrong. Indeed, it was possession of a common faculty of reasoning that supposedly enabled different individuals to agree on basic rights. In keeping with this view, Locke believed that any individual who consulted his innate reason would see that all persons must be free to pursue their self-preservation and religious salvation as they saw fit, so long as it did not infringe on the freedom of others to do the same.[17]

Leaving aside Locke's own particular interpretation of the social contract doctrine (with all its racist, sexist, and classist assumptions),[18] we here note that religious and ideological tolerance—at least when it was applied to those deemed sufficiently rational—follows *necessarily* from the basic freedom and equality accorded to all individuals by liberal contractarian theory. Although nonliberal (e.g., theocratic) regimes may tolerate minority ideologies, they are not compelled to do so, and certainly not for purely secular reasons concerning the inherent worth of individuals as rational choosers. However, it is precisely here, in its individualistic foundation, that the liberal principle of tolerance appears most problematic. Typically, the right to believe in and practice one's own set of convictions is interpreted as a right that individuals have as individuals. This conforms to the Protestant belief that individual conscience (faith) is the royal path to salvation, not participation in group-based sacraments. However, freedom of religion is also interpreted as a right that individuals have as members of groups. Because one's faith (and the faith of one's progeny) is normally cultivated within a religious community, protection of one's religious freedom as an individual is seldom separable from protection of the religious group to which one belongs.

Although liberalism requires that the state both tolerate and protect the freedom of different religious groups, doing so might inadvertently infringe on the rights of dissident individuals within those groups—the problem of "double minorities." Furthermore, it might also infringe on the rights of women and children within those groups, to the extent that tolerating the group involves tolerating an authoritarian and patriarchal culture that severely restricts their opportunity to think and act freely, in short, to develop a sense of themselves as autonomous choosers of their own identity, be it religious or otherwise. This seems to be what happened when the State of New York set up a separate school district for Kiryas Joel. To some outside observers and dissidents, this action amounted to government-sponsored religious favoritism, a clear violation of the principle calling for equal respect for individuals.

The Kiryas Joel case presents a real dilemma for classical liberalism. Its primary intent is to protect individual freedom against encroachment by state institutions and social groups. But what happens when these institutions and groups are themselves instrumental for freedom's cultivation?

Today, few people would deny that at least some state-supported education, health services, and welfare programs are necessary in order for certain (maybe most) citizens to cultivate their potential for making rational and informed decisions on which they can then effectively act. Ensuring everyone an equal opportunity to cultivate their freedom, however, requires state involvement and, some would argue, interference. For example, permitting individuals an unlimited right to acquire property inevitably generates social inequalities that wrongly constrain some of them. Specifically, an unlimited property right will allow some individuals to acquire a monopoly in the sale of certain goods, thereby enabling them to charge consumers exhorbitant prices. It will also generate a class of desperately poor persons who will be forced to accept subhuman working and living conditions, in which their freedom to act will be severely constrained.[19] So the state restricts the right of individuals to acquire property for the sake of equalizing the social conditions under which they exercise this right, subordinating it to the right of a group—the group of citizens—to exercise this right equally.

As I noted above, there are cultural subgroups within the state that also apparently contribute to the cultivation of freedom. For example, it has been argued that religious groups enable their members to cultivate the spiritual (metaphysical and moral) motivations requisite for responsible citizenship. Here again, groups such as these limit the freedom of their individual members in matters of faith and ritual observance. Liberalism acknowledges this limitation. But in some of these cases—and unlike the case of restricted economic freedom—limiting an individual's freedom does not obviously seem to enhance freedom overall.

To take our earlier example, how does allowing the majority of the Kiryas Joel community to exclude a dissident minority enhance the religious freedom of either the majority or the minority? How does its authoritarian, patriarchal social order enhance the freedom of the women and children who are subjected to it? Take the problem of dissent. It might be that the majority's religious freedom is enhanced by being free from outside interference, here represented by the dissent of the minority. Excluding the minority is freedom-enhancing for the majority, for if the minority were included, it would frustrate the majority's aims.

This is all well and good, but how is being excluded freedom-enhancing for the minority? It might be that, having been excluded, they are now free to set up their own dissident community. Exiting the dominant group allows the minority to practice its faith freely, without intimidation. Conversely, so long as exiting the group imposes no hindrance to their faith, remaining within the group constitutes no violation of it. For instance, no violation occurs when the Catholic Church excommunicates those of its members who renounce its basic tenets, for these individuals can still practice whatever tenets they subscribe to openly and freely outside the church (indeed, they can found their own church should they choose to do so). By parity of reasoning, no violation of their religious freedom occurs when these same members choose to remain within the church and voluntarily refrain from expressing their heretical opinions, for they are simply exercising their right to associate, contingent on accepting the rules of association.

So long as exclusion from a group constitutes a prelude to a freedom-enhancing (or at least freedom-preserving) exit for those being excluded, liberal theory can have its cake and eat it too. That is, it can protect the freedom of religion of minority groups threatened by disruption from individuals both outside *and* inside the group. And it can protect the freedom of religion of these same individuals, so long as they exit the group whose freedom they are disrupting.

Unfortunately, liberalism's dilemma cannot always be so easily resolved. What happens when the dissident minority refuses to exit? If such an exit is possible, surely it cannot refuse. However, exit is not always possible. Perhaps the dissident minority within Kiryas Joel could not leave the community without seriously jeopardizing its own religous aims. (Perhaps they were too small to establish a self-sustaining community of their own.) On the other hand, even if they had no real recourse but to remain in the community, would their exclusion from the school board amount to a violation of a basic civil liberty?

A few examples drawn from nonreligious contexts might help us answer this question. The first concerns the Rotary Club's exclusion of women from its membership. The U.S. Supreme Court ruled that this exclusion was unconstitutional since it prevented those excluded from engaging in networking practices essential to the conduct of their businesses and thus essential to the full exercise of their basic right to contract freely.[20] The second concerns the Boy Scouts' exclusion of homosexuals. Unlike the first case, the California Supreme Court upheld the constitutionality of the exclusion, arguing that those excluded could join other "private" organizations or form their own clubs.

The Kiryas Joel case involves an act of exclusion that falls somewhere in between the acts engaged in by the Rotary Club (a public institution) and the Boy Scouts (a private organization). Like the Boy Scouts' act of exclusion, the exclusion of the dissident minority did not obviously deprive them of a basic civil liberty. They were technically free to exit the old community and establish their own, new community.[21] (By contrast, women business owners could not exit the business network—which comprises significant Rotary Club contacts throughout America—without giving up their right to do business.) Yet like the Rotary Club's act of exclusion, the exclusion of the dissident minority at least indirectly hindered their exercise of a basic right. At the very least, it forced them to choose which of their basic rights to forgo. Even if leaving the community would have enabled them to practice their faith in some technical sense, doing so might have cost them their jobs, their property, the education of their children, and protection from hate groups.

Liberal theory, then, does not always provide easy solutions to conflicts between the rights of individual dissidents and the rights of the groups to which they belong. It cannot because the line separating external from internal threats to a group's religious freedom is not always clear. At some point, dissident individuals within the group will be perceived by it as outsiders, external threats against whom the group needs special protection. Unfortunately, the only remedy liberal theory provides for protecting both the group and the dissident individual is opportunity for voluntary exit on the part of the dissident individuals—an option that may strike them as unfair and oppressive. And this option, it should be noted, hardly exists for children and other dependents and exists only as an abstract option for wives and mothers, who will be reluctant and unprepared to abandon their families and strike out on their own. Hence, even if a right to exit enabled group rights to function in a freedom-enhancing manner for orthodox members of a group without jeopardizing the freedom of individual dissidents, it would not prevent group rights from denying the freedom of women and children.

### Individual and Group-Specific Rights Versus Democratic Equality

The liberal conception of equal rights derives from a belief in common humanity. It is a conception, therefore, that principally endows individuals with liberties that cannot be overridden for the sake of allowing groups to freely regulate their members. Stated differently, the liberal state does not tolerate the right of groups to violate the basic rights of their members, even if doing so is necessary for the group's survival.

Communitarian critics of the liberal conception of rights charge that privileging the rights of individuals above the good of the community is both politically disastrous and philosophically incoherent.[22] It is politically disastrous because it encourages a "me first," self-centered attitude that leads to the breakdown of families, neighborhoods, religious groups, and overall lack of commitment to others. It is philosophically incoherent because the very rights it bestows on individuals to act against the good of the community exist for the sake of individuals who must cooperate with one another as a community. More precisely, rights are morally justified because they make possible a certain kind of communal reciprocity that a certain kind of community deems to be good, both for itself and for each of its individual members. Hence, contrary to liberalism, the good of the individual—as encapsulated in those most valuable freedoms and entitlements we claim by right—is scarcely separable from the good of the community, as conceived and valued by the community.

The communitarian critique of liberalism is right to insist that the good of the individual, when referring to a *specific* set of freedoms and entitlements rather than a *general* account of human necessities, is inseparable from the good of the community as conceived and valued by it. The "natural" rights of individuals may indeed be arrived at through rational deliberation, in abstraction from the particular conventional prejudices we happen to share with members of our parochial community; but whatever concrete, prescriptive meaning they happen to possess at any given time and place cannot be so determined. Rather, this meaning largely (if not entirely) devolves upon them in light of the particular concerns, values, and perspectives by which persons, participating in specific communities shaped by specific historical traditions (cultures), understand them.

Be that as it may, the communitarian critique is mistaken in arguing that liberalism always privileges the freedom of the individual over the good of the community. It is true, of course, that most liberal societies are too pluralistic and multicultural to constitute a single culture possessing a single good (except perhaps the abstract humanistic faith in the inherent goodness of freedom and equality, which of course is not shared by religious fundamentalists or ideological racists). Yet liberal societies do constitute a plurality of cultures, each with its own conception(s) of the good, and these cultures are not only tolerated but sometimes protected. Liberal societies protect the rights of corporations and groups as well as the rights of individuals to act independently of external constraint. Included among these rights is the right to associate freely. Whenever dissidents within an association exercise their freedom in ways that endanger its cultural identity as viewed by the majority in the group, they appear to threaten the individual rights of the other members. In cases like this, the state often upholds *these* rights against the conflicting rights of dissidents. Likewise, liberal states will uphold the right of parents to educate their children in accordance with the narrow ideological dictates of the group to which they belong as long as doing so is not deemed to be too incompatible with providing them with an education capable of bestowing the same opportunities to develop themselves as fully capable citizens as that afforded other children.

Liberalism, then, sometimes limits the rights of individuals for the sake of upholding the rights of the group (or rather, the rights of the most numerous adults within the group). It reminds us that the exercise of individual rights must be *limited* for the sake of ensuring to each an *equal* exercise (compatible with a like exercise for all). Indeed, if we turn our attention away from the right to associate in groups to the right to participate in their governance, an even more profound egalitarian limitation of individual rights by the group comes into view: the right of a democratic majority to impose its will on a dissenting minority.

Democracy has traditionally been understood as a way of protecting ordinary citizens from the tyranny of unaccountable rulers. During the nineteenth century, the emerging conflict between wage workers and propertied classes redefined the function of democracy further: as a tool for restraining the economic power of the rich and enhancing the effective rights of the more numerous poor. By the twentieth century, when political equality for the poor became increasingly linked to their social equality, democracy served to further limit the economic freedom of the business class in the name of social justice and the public good. The result was the social welfare state, which created a new tier of social rights, some of them specifically targeted toward the elderly, the disabled, the poor, children, and other vulnerable or disadvantaged groups.

Briefly, defenders of the social welfare state have sought to justify the democratic subordination of individual freedom to the egalitarian needs of the community—now legally enshrined in the form of group-specific rights—in two ways: by appeal to the inherent goodness or rightness of the majority's will or by appeal to the fairness of the procedures by which that will is regulated. The former justification has a long and distinguished history. In its classical form, dating back to ancient Greece,[23] it presumes that the public (or electorate) is sufficiently knowledgeable and virtuous to put aside its private interests and support policies (or candidates) that promote what is good and just for all (including the dissenting minority). A variation of this theory holds that the leaders elected by the majority possess sufficient knowledge and public goodwill, even if those who elect them do not.

Given the unlikelihood that the majority (or its representatives) are as knowledgeable and virtuous as the classical model assumes, another, economics-based justification of democracy is often recommended.[24] Making a virtue out of a vice, it assumes that voters converge on policies that advance

the public good unintentionally, even when they know and seek only their
own selfish advantage. The idea that conflicting interests cancel each other
out, leaving behind a common interest, sounds appealing. But the likelihood
of a public good arising from the unrestrained competition among selfish interests is about as great as the likelihood of the poor being made rich by the
market (as though by an "invisible hand," to use Adam Smith's phrase).[25]
For in any market economy, it is the effective demand of those wealthy and
powerful few who influence what gets done, which is almost always to
their—and not the public's—advantage.

Perhaps the most striking "goodwill" defenses of democracy argue that
individual self-interest and ignorance can be overcome by imposing procedures on the democratic process that ensure wise and impartial decisions.
The most famous of these was advanced by Jean-Jacques Rousseau in *On the
Social Contract* (1762). This treatise begins with the liberal idea that a rational individual is morally obligated to obey only those laws to which he has
freely consented. In order for all to consent, however, the laws must express
what each wills. Because each wills what is to his own particular advantage
as well as what is to the advantage of all, special procedures must be established in order to filter out the former. Without this safeguard, laws would
end up advancing but a partial interest and so would morally bind only those
who shared that interest. Imposing laws on those who did not share the interests it advances would then amount to a form of tyranny—the tyranny of
the majority over the minority or, if you prefer, the tyranny of the group
over the individual.

The safeguards that Rousseau proposed for avoiding the conflict between
individual and group were strikingly bold. Unanimity of agreement was to
be assured by making all citizens equal—or the same. Sameness not only required equality in social class (there are no dependent wage laborers in
Rousseau's ideal society, only small independent farmers) but equality in
tastes and manners as well. Cultural homogeneity, in turn, demanded the
suppression of particular corporate associations that might distract citizens
from their undivided loyalty to the general good of the state. At the very
least, it demanded the presence of official censors who could instill the unified sentiments (or public opinion) of "the people" in the individual citizen.

Rousseau's attempt to harmonize modern individuality, with its emphasis
on justice and rights, and ancient democracy, with its emphasis on self-ab-
negating virtue and the public good, struck subsequent liberal democrats
like John Stuart Mill as a travesty of both principles. For him, the suppression of individual and group differences is illiberal, while the suppression of

partisan association and communication is undemocratic. Indeed, fearing that religious sectarianism would create antagonisms among the citizens and distract them from their unitary love of country, Rousseau placed a severe constraint on religious freedom: it must comport with a civil religion mandating worship of the state. For this reason, his democratic ideal would have offered the Kiryas Joel community neither protection from public harassment nor state tolerance.

It comes as no surprise that subsequent liberal democrats have dispensed with the Rousseauian requirement of egalitarian sameness. Today, most base their defense of democracy on the assumption that individuals are equal only in their common possession of humanity. Equality in this sense endows individuals with the same basic rights, but possession of these rights is regarded as compatible with (and even protective of) social and cultural difference. Taken together, such rights make up constitutional limits on what any democratic majority can force a dissenting minority to do.[26]

The premise underlying limited (or constitutional) democracy is that valid laws must not only express the good that the majority wants but also harmonize with the justice that morality requires. Contrary to Rousseau's defense of absolute democracy, the good desired by the majority and the justice demanded by morality cannot be made to coincide through any conceivable procedure; hence, the importance of basic rights as checks on the *unequal* treatment of individuals by the majority and its governmental agencies.[27]

As noted earlier, the constitutional imperative to treat everyone equally—desisting from favoring one individual over another—cannot always be acted upon by treating everyone the same way. Thus, leaving aside the Satmar community's suppression of dissidents and its patriarchal authoritarianism, that community's equal right to practice its religion free from outside constraints arguably required treating it differently. But remember: it was not moral reason alone—in total abstraction from knowledge of the peculiar historical, cultural, and political circumstances surrounding the Satmar community and its relations with outsiders—that justified safeguarding this community's religious freedom by conferring upon it a special group right to have its own public school district. Rather, it was moral reason as filtered through the democratic will of the citizens of New York and their knowledgeable legislators that did so.

We seem to be arguing in a circle. Initially, we insisted that appeal to universal reason was necessary in order to justify basic rights that constitutionally limit the power of the majority in its treatment of minorities. Yet we now see that universal reason is too abstract a principle for deriving specific rights

and duties.[28] What gives concrete meaning and morally binding force to our
right to freedom of religion as Americans and, more specifically, as members
of oppressed minority sects is a specific history of democratic legislation (beginning with the First Amendment and continuing through other religion-
regarding statutes) and a specific history of judicial interpretation
(culminating in *Grumet v. Pataki* [1998]). Thus, the basic moral rights to
which the minority appeals in claiming that they have been treated unfairly
by the majority are largely meaningless and without determinate force when
considered in abstraction from the specific meaning and force that the majority (or their government) attaches to them. Paradoxically, then, it is the
group that democratically determines the concrete scope of rights claimed
by individuals against the group.

We are back to Rousseau—and the problem of majoritarian tyranny.
Rousseau proposed a totalitarian procedure for circumventing this problem;
we must find a liberal one. Specifically, we must justify the right of the majority to impose its will on the minority without assuming that will is always
impartial with respect to competing interests and conceptions of the good.
In short, we must find a purely *procedural* justification of majoritarian rule
that explains why a dissenting minority is conditionally obligated to obey the
majority, even when the majority is mistaken about or indifferent to the public's interest.[29]

The idea behind a purely procedural justification of democracy is simply
this: If the rules governing the competition for influencing public opinion and
electing officials are impartial with respect to all competitors, then even the
losers will abide by partisan results, so long as the results do not strike them as
profoundly bad or unjust (in which case their recourse to nonviolent civil dis-
obedience might be justified). The rules in question concern not only voter
registration and voting procedures, methods of tallying results and assigning
seats, schemes for drawing up electoral districts, systems of checks and bal-
ances, and laws concerning campaign financing, lobbying, and term limits.
They also include institutional opportunities that enable citizens to take advantage of these rules effectively. Thus, even if the rules governing registration,
voting, tallying results, assigning seats, and so forth treated everyone equally,
the prevalence of unequal education and unequal economic opportunity
would permit some persons to take advantage of these rules more effectively
than others (in general, those who possess more education, wealth, and leisure
time participate more—and with greater effect—than those who do not).

The important thing about the rules and institutional opportunities regulating a procedurally just democracy is not that they are *neutral* with re-

spect to all interests, but that they instantiate the ideal of treating everyone *equally*. A procedurally just democracy, for instance, would ensure that women and racial minorities were treated with equal respect by according them basic rights that could never be overridden by racists and sexists, no matter how numerous they might be. Indeed, the more that constitutional safeguards ensure the political equality of everyone, the less likely that citizens will pass unjust laws.

Having examined the basic concept underlying procedural justifications of democracy, the next topics to consider are the different procedures of voting and representation that have been institutionalized by democracies in order to protect minorities from the tyranny of the majority. The first (and least acceptable) is the one James Madison and other Founding Fathers designed for the United States. It equates procedural fairness (equal treatment) with giving each citizen the right to cast a ballot for the candidate of his or her choice. Unfortunately, even when supplemented by judicial review, this procedure does not adequately check majoritarian tyranny. For example, during the sixties the Supreme Court invoked the Bill of Rights and other constitutional guarantees to ensure that southern blacks would be given the right to vote and elect representatives of their choice. But white legislators continued to alter the boundaries of legislative districts so that blacks would remain a permanent minority in all of them, thereby depriving them of a right to elect *black* candidates of their choice. The federal courts then had to redesign these districts in ways that permitted blacks to exercise this right.[30]

The second model of democratic proceduralism (famously defended in John Stuart Mill's *Considerations on Representative Government* [1861]) addresses the weakness of a majoritarian system by providing for some form of proportional group representation. Unlike the first model, it does not view democracy as a mechanism for summing up individual preferences as expressed in vote tabulations. Instead, it views democracy as a mechanism for fairly representing different groups. Taking this model, a politically organized group comprising 12 percent of the population (roughly the percentage of blacks in the total U.S. population) would be ensured of electing 12 percent of all federal legislators.

Although this model goes a long way toward rectifying majoritarian tyranny, it does not ensure that minority representatives—when elected—will exercise significant influence in counteracting the oppressive legislative designs of the majority. In order for them to exercise such influence, they might need the additional aid of special veto powers, or perhaps supermajoritarian voting procedures, that strengthen their votes. Although such

procedures give *individual* members of a minority more political power than
their majority counterparts, they do not treat the latter unfairly; rather, they
equalize the power between the minority and majority by offsetting the latter's overwhelming numerical advantage—an advantage, one need scarcely
add, that in the United States has been used by whites to oppress blacks.

Unfortunately, even when appropriately supplemented by supermajoritarian procedures, the model of proportional representation usually protects
only the most numerous and powerful of minority groups. Furthermore, it
might not adequately protect "double minorities" within those groups, for
it seems to presume that individuals of the same race and ethnicity stereotypically think alike or have the same interests.[31]

The third model of democratic proceduralism, recently advocated by
African-American law professor Lani Guinier, attempts to rectify the unequal, stereotypical treatment of individuals by replacing the proportional
representation of groups with the proportional representation of interests.[32]
According to this latter model, voting districts would be represented by several—and perhaps many—representatives. Voters would then have an opportunity to cast multiple ballots, enabling them to elect candidates
representing a wide variety of group interests. Thus, instead of being
grouped within a black district as a black person with stereotypical black interests, a black lesbian businesswoman might find herself in a multiseat district whose several candidates include a homosexual, a woman, a black, and
a businessman, each of whom shares some (but not all) of her interests.

The third model has another advantage, and it is this advantage that
points in the direction of a fourth, dialogic model. In the current winner-
take-all system of electing representatives, candidates need only consider the
narrow interests of their own constituency. This system does nothing to
break down the current pattern of racial and ethnic polarization that sepa-
rates America's communities or to facilitate dialogue between them. By contrast, in multiseat districts with plural voting, candidates will have to speak
to a diverse range of constituencies, which in turn will encourage dialogue
and alliance-building between them.

### *Dialogic Democracy, Difference, and Equality*

The dialogic (or participatory) model of democratic proceduralism advocated by Jürgen Habermas and others goes beyond the previous models in
stressing the importance of public opinion formation in the setting of the
legislative agenda.[33] The model makes two assumptions: First, legislative

agendas must respect the interests of common citizens by addressing issues and arguments that originate in public opinion; second, public opinion must grow out of an all-inclusive dialogue in which citizens communicate their needs to one another for the sake of reaching a mutual agreement on what is in their rational best interest.

The first assumption requires expanding our conception of democratic participation. To the extent that we allow our representatives to set the legislative agenda according to their own whims (and the whims of well-financed lobbyists), we abdicate political control over our lives. Real participation involves organizing and speaking out, not merely voting.

The second assumption addresses the nature of this participation. In order for people's expanded involvement in the formation of public opinion to be carried out in a way that exemplifies equal respect and equal concern for all, it must first permit every citizen—and every significant political community of interest—an equal chance to participate. This stipulation means not only that the rich and powerful should be prevented from spending their money to monopolize the media, but also that poor and marginalized citizens should be provided economic resources and educational opportunities for informed and effective participation.

Formation of public opinion should be as free as possible from the pressures of life as from the distorting and constraining influences of prejudice, rhetorical manipulation, and the like. Citizens should be able to critically analyze the information they receive through the media, which, in turn, should reflect a full range of opinion, free from domination by corporate-sponsored publicity.

Citizens might also be motivated to exercise civic virtue—or impartial, public-spirited reason—in the course of communicating with one another. Even if they are not generally predisposed to seeking the public good and justice for all, the need to persuade others with arguments having broad appeal might incline them to do so. By placing themselves in the shoes of others, they might come to understand the harmful consequences of their own and others' lifestyles, which, in turn, might lead them to transform not only their lifestyles, but also their basic needs. Perhaps, they might even reach agreement on common interests. In any case, the transformative potential of genuine dialogue might work to mitigate conflicts of interest, thereby generating common support for democratic reform.

The transformative potential of democratic dialogue is scarcely imaginable apart from the presence of different voices. Indeed, difference and dissent lie at the very core of political life generally, inciting the dialogic search for a mutual understanding in the first place. But how can the aim of mutual agreement be reconciled with the retention of differences? And how can there be communication of differences absent prior agreement on the terms of dialogue?

These questions go to the very heart of our initial concern: the possibility of treating different groups equally. Indeed, if Habermas and other discourse ethicists are correct, this possibility merges with the possibility of genuine communication. It is because we must communicate with others in order to reach mutual understanding that we treat them with equal respect and accord them full rights to speak freely. And because this orientation toward equality and reciprocity already anticipates an orientation toward fairness and impartiality common to all cultures, we think of it as the very hallmark of rationality.[34]

If participating in potentially conflict-ridden cooperative ventures calls for a readiness to engage in consensus-oriented discussions, and if participating in these discussions forces one to consider one's own as well as one's interlocutor's interests, values, and perspectives impartially, then one can scarcely avoid (except upon pain of contradicting one's cooperative conduct) respecting the other as an equal and autonomous agent. But, as I have repeatedly stressed, such commitments to impartiality (abstract ideals of justice and individual rights) that constrain dialogue are meaningless apart from being concretely and collectively interpreted in dialogue.

But what kind of rational impartiality best captures the essence of genuine dialogue? Is it the impartiality of generally agreed-upon rules of fair engagement? Is it the impartiality of difference-blind neutrality? As John Rawls has forcefully argued, in order for reasonable and civil discussion to occur, citizens inhabiting modern democracies must learn to converse across the conflicting "comprehensive doctrines" that divide them.[35] First and foremost, they must agree on rules of civility—the constitutional framework mandating tolerance and equal respect for all.

Contrary to Habermas, Rawls believes that reasonable citizens will subscribe to the same terms of civil and rational discourse for different (and quite possibly conflicting) reasons.[36] So, even if persons speak the same language and consent to a common framework for civil debate, their use of the language and their understanding of the framework are still colored by their conflicting comprehensive doctrines and distinct ways of relating to the world around them. Thus, the Kiryas Joel community might well endorse the First Amendment's establishment and freedom of religion clause as grounding a framework of mutual tolerance and freedom. But they will probably do so for reasons different from those given by atheists. (The former will endorse it as an expression of their belief in the divine and the need to have that belief respected. The latter, by contrast, will endorse it as an expression of rational neutrality.)

Rawls suggests that this "overlapping consensus" among different groups might become more stable to the degree that citizens exercise public reason in refraining from arguing in ways that will undermine the effort at reaching agreement about basic rights. In such a case, civility requires not introducing any reason into an argument that might not persuade all of one's potential interlocutors. In other words, in the company of fellow citizens who do not—and will not—share one's particular metaphysical, religious, and ethical outlook (or, for that matter, one's particular way of life), it is advisable to avoid referring to these outlooks in one's arguments.

The difficulty with Rawls's proposal, it seems, is that the very background of culturally diverse lifestyles that grounds and lends meaning to our constitutional consensus also colors our understanding of it in ways that are both potentially divisive and resistant to conscious bracketing. Although we sometimes can consciously filter out our comprehensive metaphysical and moral beliefs from the reasons we give for our claims, we cannot filter out the comprehensive cultural background—the worldview, lifestyle, and embodied linguistic comportment—that goes along with it. And this background will continue to influence the way we understand and communicate. For this reason, the free and equitable expression of differences undertaken in the hope of reaching compromise through mutual understanding may well be a more realistic (albeit more modest) expectation of rational dialogue than consensus, which is not (contrary to Habermas) necessary for mutual understanding.

What is at issue is not merely the style but the very substance of what people take to be civil and rational dialogue. Philosophers trained in logical analysis will have a hard time accepting biographical narratives as foundational principles of moral reason; similarly, social workers who have been exposed to the relativity, contingency and complexity of moral decision-making will have a hard time accepting abstract principles as concretely compelling. Again, what counts as civility for one person may strike another as the epitomy of rudeness. For many blue-collar workers, loud, profanity-filled speech is a necessary prerequisite for intimate and civil conversation; for many staid, upper-class Episcopalians, it is a sign of rudeness.

Because different groups will inevitably understand conversational civility differently, one must exercise caution in excluding those who are "uncivil." Dominant groups, for example, have imposed their understanding of conversational civility in order to marginalize (or even exclude) participation of subaltern groups in democratic dialogue. For instance, during the Vietnam war, nonviolent street demonstrations were viewed by authorities as "disturbances of the peace" rather than as political arguments. In suppressing them, the government denied the participants (many of whom lacked formal education and the decorum of academic civility) a public space in which to be heard.

However, even if persons could reach an "overlapping" consensus on the basic rules of civil discourse that was sensitive to different interpretations, this would not suffice to establish the neutrality of the terms of discourse. Indeed, in some cases it seems impossible to achieve such neutrality. For example, because Native Americans are forced to defend their territorial claims in the alien language of property and contract bequeathed to them from English common law, they are prevented from genuinely and convincingly defending their belief that their land designates a spiritual locus of communal identity.[37] By effectively denying cultural groups an equal right to assert their claims in their own language, damage is done to their sense of identity and self-worth (hence the self-alienation so many forceably assimilated minorities claim to experience). Deprived of a forum for rationally articulating their claims, frustrated minorities may rightly feel compelled to resort to other means for "arguing" their case, including violence.

When the terms of dialogue are slanted in favor of the dominant group, the subaltern group has a morally compelling reason for exiting the discussion. Dialogue can be restored only if the dominant group expands the terms of discourse to include the linguistic horizon of its subaltern counterpart. In general, fair terms of discourse must be flexible enough to allow for differing languages and rhetorical address while being rigid enough to exclude hate speech and other forms of verbal violence that undermine the ability of others to speak.

In this chapter, I have argued that equal citizenship is compatible with the differential treatment of groups and individuals. I have argued that liberalism allows groups to limit the freedom of dissenting individuals so long as freedom-enhancing exit from the group is possible, or the limit in question is regulated by fair democratic procedure. Liberal, multicultural democracies, I have argued, should embody procedures of conversational impartiality that confer on minority groups an equal right to be heard. Conferring such a right in turn might require guaranteeing such groups some kind of proportional representation as well, in conjunction with other supermajoritarian privileges. In the next chapter I hope to show that a just democracy would transform and overcome certain differences while preserving others.

# 2
## DIFFERENCES MADE LEGAL:
## OPPRESSION AND DOMINATION

Differences made legal can sometimes protect groups, which was the case with the Kiryas Joel public school district. But consider the following case: A California statute excludes normal pregnancy from its list of disabilities that warrant workers' compensation. However, it includes male-only procedures, such as circumcision and prostate surgery, as well as elective operations, such as cosmetic surgery. The statute's unequal treatment of women and men was eventually challenged in a sex discrimination suit, which was invalidated by the U.S. Supreme Court in 1974. Writing for the majority in *Geduldig v. Aiello,* Justice Potter Stewart concluded that the statute did not discriminate since it benefited nonpregnant women, who—owing to reduced coverage costs—ended up paying lower insurance rates.

*Geduldig v. Aiello* is one of those landmark cases that raises troubling questions about the unequal treatment of different groups. In the previous chapter, I suggested that the unequal treatment of unequally situated groups might be justifiable to the extent that such treatment is required to ensure that everyone is treated with equal respect and concern. Indeed, the Supreme Court has acknowledged as much.[1] In this case, however, it seems that the unequal treatment of pregnant women does not advance equal respect and concern.

Why? The question cannot be answered easily. Justice Stewart thought that the pregnancy exclusion did not discriminate against women *as such,* only pregnant women. Presumably, this exclusion could be justified—like so many other medical insurance exclusions—by a consideration of the overall savings that would accrue to both men and women. Indeed, some pregnant women were benefited by the exclusion: those who were supported by their husbands.

Yet two serious objections can be raised against this line of reasoning. First, it would countenance discriminating against any number of groups on the

35

grounds that some members of the group might benefit from the exclusion. Why not, for example, disallow coverage for prostate cancer? Although an increasingly large percentage of males will contract this "disability," the percentage that does not will surely benefit from lower premiums.

Second, the fact that the pregnancy exclusion directly hurts only one class of pregnant women—namely, working mothers—suggests that the underlying motivation behind the statute is to discriminate against women who buck the traditional role of homemaker. If so, the statute indirectly hurts all women, for the unequal treatment of women in nontraditional roles acts as a prior restraint on the freedom of all women to choose these roles.

California's pregnancy exclusion, then, commits an injustice against women *as such*. Eliminating the exclusion rectifies it, but it does not rectify *all* the injustice that women suffer. The injustice of the exclusion is but a part of a complex system of injustice. In order to eliminate *this* injustice, reformers will have to gain a better understanding of injustice in general.

Injustices come in many forms. Some befall individuals for reasons that have nothing to do with where they work and live and who they happen to be. A pedestrian who just happens to be crossing the street at the very moment when a drunk driver runs a stoplight suffers a criminal injustice that could have happened to anyone. By contrast, some injustices befall persons because of legally sanctioned deprivation or domination. Unlike the injustice befalling the pedestrian, their rectification requires changes in the law rather than simple applications of it.

For simplicity's sake I shall focus on two sorts of social injustice: oppression and domination.[2] Oppression is caused by a failure to distribute basic goods in ways that promote the equal development of each person's human capacities. Domination, by contrast, is caused by a failure to recognize all citizens as free, responsible human beings worthy of equal respect.

Oppression occurs whenever persons are not provided decent food, shelter, education, and other resources essential to overall well-being, which typically happens whenever they are confined to undesirable and poorly paid work (or denied access to work altogether). Here, injustice consists in not receiving one's fair share of the goods that one's labor has created (or in not receiving one's fair share of the total, societal output). Lacking a fair share of goods, one is then denied resources and opportunities—granted to others—requisite for leading a minimally decent life.

Domination, by contrast, typically involves hierarchies of decision-making and power that prevent some persons from exercising control over their lives.

Domination can be economic (as in slavery), political (as in dictatorship), legal (as in racial segregation of public facilities), social (as in familial patriarchy), and cultural (as in monolingual education in a multilingual society).

Typically, the five forms of domination mentioned above mutually accompany and support one another. For example, economic oppression of blacks in the South during the era of Jim Crow was reinforced by legal segregation, political disenfranchisement, social subordination, and cultural marginalization. This example also illustrates the close connection between being dominated and being denied recognition as a full human being. Those who are dominated economically, politically, and legally feel diminished in their capacity as rational decision-makers. Those who are dominated socially and culturally feel diminished in their self-esteem (i.e., they are taught to believe in their inferiority). In general, exclusion from economic and political power means exclusion from the administration of education and culture. Exclusion from the latter, in turn, entails dependence on others for the constitution of one's identity.

The distinction between domination and oppression is not absolute. One could, I suppose, just as easily describe domination as a maldistribution of power (as if power were a basic good).[3] We do, after all, talk about the distribution of votes, electoral districts, parliamentary seats, and so on as decisive for determining who rules whom. But such talk of distributing power obscures the more basic nature of political life, which is a matter of *doing* (or *relating to others*) rather than of *having* (or *personally possessing and consuming*).[4] That is why I earlier characterized democracy as a form of communicative interaction. Here, the tallying up of votes for distributing seats is but a mere formality that conceals the real, nondistributive work of politics: the collective formation of political opinion.

Distinct though they are, oppression and domination do condition one another. Oppression conditions domination. Extreme starvation does not just stifle one's ability to learn, think, and choose; it cripples the body, thereby preventing any action whatsoever. A deprived population is a compliant one that is easily dominated.

This supposition applies as well to subtler forms of oppression involving cultural deprivation. I have in mind both deprivation of culture in general and deprivation of culture in particular. By "deprivation of culture in general" I mean the denial of basic knowledge and skills. Cultural oppression might entail enforced illiteracy for a subjugated population. More often it involves enforced ignorance. Even if a subjugated population has access to language, art, and religion, it might not have access to the higher functions of linguistic, artistic, and philosophic creativity. For example, if it expends most of its time and energy in laboring to satisfy its (and the ruling classes') needs, it would not have the leisure or inclination to engage in much reflection.

Denying a subjugated group culture in general is distinct from denying it its own culture. It is conceivable that a subjugated group will have access to its own culture—but in a way that prevents it from articulating it in a fully reflective and literate manner. For instance, a group might be permitted to practice its culture without having the general knowledge or reading and writing skills to theoretically elaborate upon it. Conversely, it is conceivable that a subjugated group might have access to higher, literate forms of education while being denied the right to practice its own culture.

Oppression conditions domination, but does the reverse hold true? Certainly. Persons who are denied opportunities to make and act upon basic decisions that affect their lives are usually dependent on others. These others—let us call them the ruling elite—usually feel entitled to consume a disproportionately large share of the available goods, even though they often constitute a small percentage of the population. (In the United States today, the top 1 percent of the population has a total net worth greater than that claimed by the bottom 90 percent.) In order to perpetuate this state of affairs, the ruling elite must ensure that the subjugated remain dependent. And the best way to do that is to keep them materially, culturally, and spiritually impoverished.

Earlier I raised a question about the kind of injustice suffered by women as a whole. We are now in a position to answer that question provisionally: Women suffer from both oppression and domination. Women as a group are oppressed: they occupy a disproportionate percentage of those living in poverty and holding down part-time, unskilled, and low-paying jobs; and they continue to suffer legalized job-related discrimination related to childbearing and raising children. Educated women still earn less on average than their male counterparts with similar credentials. Moreover, women continue to carry an unfair burden of household chores, and housewives' labor remains largely unremunerated.

Women as a group are also dominated: although they comprise a majority of the population, they constitute but a small fraction of elected officials and business leaders. Their minority status in political life explains the unequal treatment they receive at the hands of the law. Pregnancy exclusions are but the tip of the iceberg (think, for example, of the legal restrictions imposed on a woman's right to have an abortion). Furthermore, Western culture portrays women as possessing diminished capacity to make rational choices.

They are frequently depicted as being emotional, fickle, passive, and help-less—in short, dependent. What they say is often not taken seriously; and worst of all, they are portrayed as sex objects to be violated and dominated.[5]

## Systemic Versus Identity-Based Injustices

Women suffer from both oppression and domination. But why? The answer is complicated. In order to see why, we need to distinguish between two *sources* of injustice: systemic and identity-based.

Systemic injustices can affect any group of persons (men, women, mi-norities—you name it). In a capitalist society like ours, they generally have their source in the workings of the economy. From there, these forms of op-pression and domination radiate out to all areas of political, social, and cultural life. For example, unskilled wage earners receive poor wages and benefits; they are more vulnerable to layoffs owing to recession, replace-ment, and so forth. Their general state of insecurity and want makes it dif-ficult for them to concentrate on little else but survival (hence their low rate of political involvement). Lacking material and cultural resources, they are oppressed; lacking power over their lives, they are dominated. This is the meager inheritance they are likely to bequeath to their progeny as well.

The injustice born of systemic poverty, then, consists in its befalling "in-nocent" persons who have little control over their condition. Perhaps they were born into a broken family with parents who could not nurture them or instill in them a desire to achieve. Perhaps they were raised in an urban ghetto whose schools were little more than prisons. Perhaps they lacked the educa-tion to secure a decent job, or their community had no jobs to offer them. Perhaps they secured a job but were laid off due to no fault of their own.

Interestingly, the Supreme Court regards systemic inequalities such as these as "natural" outcomes of what are otherwise "neutral" market distri-butions rather than social injustices.[6] In fact, market distributions are neither natural nor neutral; they are directly influenced by governmental decisions, including the determination of the prime interest rate, which is set by the head of the Federal Reserve Bank. Raising interest rates in order to deter borrowing and investment slows economic growth and lowers the demand for labor, an inflation-decreasing measure that is good for financiers who want to get the full return on their fixed-rate loans, but bad for blue-collar types struggling to hold on to low-paying (often temporary) jobs. In essence, their misfortune is our gain; we get the benefits of low inflation while they get the boot.

But even a booming economy with low unemployment is no guarantee of increased labor demand and higher (inflationary) wages, as is evidenced by the recent trend to replace costly full-time employees with cheaper part-time workers. Indeed, federal and state workfare programs that replaced welfare for the poor during the last decade of this century have actually encouraged companies (with the aid of government subsidies and other corporate welfare incentives) to replace their full-time employees with temporary and part-time workfare recipients, who sometimes work for free and sometimes receive in return less than what they would have under minimum-wage statutes.[7] Hence, even government efforts to rectify market injustices inflicted on the poor often have contradictory, punitive effects that magnify the original injustice inflicted upon them.

Identity-based injustices also befall innocent persons. But instead of having their source in the system (the so-called cycle of poverty), they have it in sexist, racist, and homophobic discrimination.[8] Here persons suffer injustices because of who they are. It is because they are identified as belonging to an inferior class of persons that they are oppressed and dominated, not because they find themselves occupying a disadvantageous position within the system. A few examples will suffice to clarify this distinction. Take, for example, the injustice suffered by gays and lesbians. Gays and lesbians compose a cultural subgroup whose suffering stems almost entirely from being stigmatized by others as threatening. Because many members of this group are well-educated, financially secure, and own their own businesses, we would not say that they are systemically oppressed. It is true, of course, that federal, state, and municipal governments seldom protect them against arbitrary job dismissal or provide them with the family health insurance and welfare benefits normally extended to married heterosexual couples. However, it is clear that such systemic injustice originates in prejudice. Were this prejudice to be eliminated, virtually all of the social injustice perpetrated on them as a group—including the systemic—would disappear.

By contrast, workers constitute a group whose suffering stems principally from systemic causes, although we cannot deny that they also suffer from discrimination owing to their working-class identity. Unskilled wage laborers are often denied the dignity and respect they deserve. Yet (arguably) the stigma of working-class brutishness could best be rectified by eliminating the systemic causes underlying brutish working conditions rather than by simply reforming cultural prejudices. (Some types of work are intrinsically dirty and brutalizing, no matter what we think.)

Finally, we note that some groups suffer from both identity-based and systemic forms of oppression in ways that are mutually supportive and co-original. Take the case of women. Part of their oppression and domination stems from sexist prejudice. Western culture rewards traits that traditionally have been associated with masculinity—such as aggression, competition, individualistic detachment from family, and devotion to career advancement. Conversely, it devalues traits that traditionally have been associated with femininity—such as caring for others and commitment to family and community.

But sexist prejudice does not explain all of the injustice borne by women. The systemic need for a marginally employed (un- and underemployed) reserve labor pool that can be employed during periods of growth and laid off during times of stagnation explains why women remain concentrated in the household economy, performing unremunerated labor associated with child-rearing and the like. If there were no equivalent to this reserve labor force, one would have to be invented.

So the systemic and identity-based sources of women's oppression are irreducible and co-original. They are co-original in that gender discrimination explains women's disadvantageous position within the system and vice versa. They are irreducible in that elimination of gender discrimination alone will not irradicate the systemic lack of decent-paying jobs that condemn so many women to poverty and dependence, just as elimination of a gendered division of labor along with all the other systemic injustices suffered by women will not irradicate the sexual objectification, denigration, and violence perpetrated against women as women.

Oppressed racial groups such as Latinos and African Americans also suffer from a combination of systemic and identity-based injustices. As in the case of women, these injustices are simultaneously co-original and irreducible. The connection between racism and economic exploitation finds ample testimony in the importance of slavery in contributing to the primitive accumulation of investment capital that anchored European capitalism's earliest growth. After the elimination of slavery in the southern states the exclusion of African Americans from unions, universities, and many professions continued to produce economic benefits for whites as a whole. Today, the accumulated effects of discrimination continue on even after overt discrimination has subsided. Like women, a disproportionate percentage of African Americans are consigned to the reserve labor force. Indeed, the legacy of systemic racial oppression and domination is virtually global, pitting wealthy nations of predominantly European ancestry against their poor Asian, African, and South American counterparts.

However, the usefulness of racism for generating and stabilizing a class-structured capitalist economy and the usefulness of a class structure for perpetuating cultural distinctions between racially superior and inferior groups should not blind us to the irreducibility of racist and systemic injustices perpetrated on African Americans. Eliminating racist attitudes and securing for African Americans the respect and dignity they deserve will not substantially affect the systemic cycles of economic segregation and poverty that afflict so many of them. Likewise, eradicating these cycles will not eradicate racial prejudice. No matter how economically successful African Americans become, they will still suffer the indignities of prejudice, discrimination, exclusion, and marginalization.

### Aims and Remedies for Rectifying Injustice

Reformers intent on eliminating oppression and domination must design their remedies to fit the underlying causes, be they systemic or identity-based. If the cause is systemic, the remedy should address the economic structures that generate poverty, exploitation, and a hierarchical division of labor. These structures produce systemic effects at the levels of social, political, and cultural life as well, as the chronic, systemic underemployment of today's urban underclass also consigns them to political powerlessness and social oppression (crime, malnutrition, and so forth). Hence, eliminating systemic injustice involves abolishing the distinction between social classes.

The elimination of social classes appeals to equality as sameness. Ideally, everyone would have the same economic resources, opportunities, and powers; these, in turn, would equalize resources, opportunities, and powers in other areas of life as well.[9] By contrast, the elimination of identity-based oppression and domination appeals to difference- as well as sameness-regarding conceptions of equality.

The elimination of identity-based injustice sometimes appeals to equality as sameness. For instance, most theorists believe that the remedy for eliminating racial discrimination is racial integration, or assimilation. In an ideally just society, skin pigmentation would be as insignificant as eye pigmentation in determining one's well-being and freedom. In other cases, however, the elimination of identity-based oppression appeals to difference-regarding conceptions of equality. What gays and lesbians want is legal recognition of their distinct lifestyles. Although they want to be treated the same way as other citizens, they do not want this treatment to depend on their assimilating into the mainstream heterosexual lifestyle, which parallels the earlier case involving the Satmar Hasidim of Kiryas Joel: They want the law to treat them as equals while recognizing their difference.

In most cases, however, the elimination of identity-based oppression and domination will require remedies that draw on both sameness- and difference-regarding conceptions of equality. Many women, for example, want to be treated exactly the same way as men, especially when it comes to an appreciation of their basic humanity and rational agency. They want the same rights as men—the universal rights that accrue to individuals as individuals. Ideally, the just society they envisage is a gender-blind one, in which gender differences are as insignificant as differences in eye pigmentation.

However, women also want their gender differences to be respected and legally recognized. For example, some women want to positively emphasize aspects of their gender-specific socialization that lead them (more than men) to care for others. Rather than be like men, they want men to be—at least in this respect—more like them. Admittedly, this latter aim still comports with the model of gender sameness. But other aims do not. For example, the fact that only women bear children is cited as a reason for giving them special legal privileges. Women—either singly or collectively—should have sole control over decisions affecting their bodies (including the freedom to abort). They should have special rights to paid maternity leaves, and their hitherto unpaid work as homemakers should be recognized (and possibly remunerated by the state).

## Conflicts Between Different Remedies

My discussion of sex discrimination suggested that the elimination of identity-based oppression and domination sometimes pulls us in the direction of two seemingly incompatible remedies: one promoting equality as sameness, the other promoting equality as difference. Are these remedies necessarily opposed?

There are two ways to answer this question. The first recalls my discussion of equal treatment in Chapter 1. There I noted that our legal system endorses either a sameness- or difference-regarding approach to equality, depending on the context in question (e.g., sameness-regarding equality prevails in criminal law, difference-regarding equality in social law). We might say the same about the equal treatment of men and women. In some areas—for example, in the area of job promotion—we want men and women to be treated more or less the same way. However, in the area of workplace laws regulating safety conditions and paid leaves, we may want the law to legally recognize biological differences between men and women.

The second way to answer the question is to note that the remedy for an injustice might invoke a conception of equality that is at odds with the ideal it is intended to realize. For example, let us suppose that an ideal society will be "blind" with respect to gender and race. That is, it will instantiate equality in the form of sameness, in which persons are seen simply as individuals and not as members of a particular race or gender. Achieving that society, however, might require temporary remedies that recognize racial and gender differences. Thus, affirmative action preferences granted to women and minorities might be unavoidable means for equalizing social conditions, the existence of which guarantees that gender- and race-neutral laws will treat everyone with equal respect. (Conversely, civil liberties granted to gays and lesbians not only recognize them as human beings like the rest of us but also promote their right to be different from us.)

### Affirmative Versus Transformative Remedies

The discussion of affirmative action raises yet another question about the effectiveness of difference-regarding remedies for achieving difference-blind aims. Because these remedies typically work within the structures of an unjust society that generally affirms difference, they cannot fully achieve their aims.

In order to clarify what I mean, let me first explain the distinction between affirmative and transformative remedies. I designate as affirmative those remedies that work within the systemic and identity-based injustices of our current society.[10] Such remedies take for granted the existence of a capitalist economic system and a fixed order of racial and gender identities; thus they mitigate—but do not eliminate—the social injustices that arise within this system and order. In short, they perpetuate differences of class, race, and gender.

Transformative remedies, by contrast, aim to radically transform the capitalist economic system and the fixed order of racial and gender identities. Transformation of the capitalist economy aims to eliminate the system of private productive property and private investment capital. It strives to create a classless society in which economic and political organizations are structured in democratic ways. Transformation of the identity order aims at deconstructing false biological (or essentialist) conceptions of race and gender. It strives to create a society in which race and gender—as social categories—disappear.

A few examples will suffice to clarify the distinction. Affirmative remedies to systemic injustice typically address oppression, not domination. As such, they work to redistribute social goods rather than equalize (democratize) relationships of power. Redistributing tax revenues in the form of social welfare transfers is one such remedy, which is affirmative because it mitigates the inegalitarian outcome of a capitalist market economy without transforming the underlying structure of private ownership. But altering market outcomes does not begin to eliminate the class distinction between those who are bosses and those who are workers, those who are employed and those who are unemployed, those who are paid for their work and those who are not.

Transformative remedies, by contrast, severely curtail private property ownership, replacing it with some form of (democratic) community ownership. These remedies aim to eliminate both oppression and domination; they redistribute social goods and replace hierarchies with democracies. (Indeed, not only are investment decisions subject to democratic oversight, but—at least in market socialist schemes—so are decisions in the workplace.)[11]

As for the identity order, affirmative remedies, such as affirmative action, affirm the dominant ideology of racial and gender differences. That ideology holds that racial and gender differences designate real, culturally if not biologically determined, differences. It holds, in other words, that each African American (or woman) possesses some definite set of values, interests, and characteristics which he or she shares with all other African Americans (or women).

The assumption that there is a single African-American (or female) identity with which all African Americans (or women) necessarily identify reflects the sort of stereotypical reduction inherent in any form of racism or sexism. That is why it is so dangerous to make sweeping generalizations about differences between blacks and whites, women and men; and it is dangerous even when done for the sake of combating racism and sexism.[12]

A transformative remedy, by contrast, questions the metaphysical assumption on which this notion of "identity politics" rests. That is, it questions racial and sexual generalizations, even to the point of denying that there are distinct races and gender roles. Thus, it challenges the coherence of gender and racial distinctions by arguing that we are all androgenous and racially mixed.

Which strategy best accords with the aims of social justice? Affirmative strategies, on the whole, reinforce gender, racial, and class differences even if their aim is to dissolve them. For example, the manner in which welfare is distributed and administered (as a form of charity begrudgingly doled out and rigorously policed) reinforces the image of welfare recipients as mentally and morally defective. Instead of considering the systemic causes underlying their poverty, we think only of their laziness, irresponsibility, and hedonism.

Accordingly, we think it entirely appropriate for the government to treat them in a sternly paternalistic manner as if they were naughty children. Unfortunately, given our racial and gender stereotypes about "welfare queens" and the like, these images of moral defectiveness and dependency only serve to fuel our racism and sexism.

The same could be said about affirmative action programs designed specifically to combat racism and sexism. Despite the best intentions of their advocates, these programs reinforce the image of inferiority that many people have in thinking about minorities and women. Again, consider California's exclusion of pregnancy as a "disability" warranting worker's compensation. The affirmative remedy to this discrimination involves classifying pregnancy as a disability covered by the act. But notice that in describing a perfectly normal condition (pregnancy) as an abnormal disability, it reinforces the stereotype of women as "deviant" from the prevailing norm of masculinity. It also reinforces the image of them as needier than men in general and thus dependent on (male) protection. Remedies providing maternity—but not paternity—leaves also reinforce the impression that women are naturally different (in the sense of being needier) and naturally domestic in a way that men are not.[13]

But perhaps one of the most serious objections that can be brought against affirmative remedies is that they work at cross-purposes to one another. For example, protection of job seniority, which mainly safeguards white males from being laid off, collides with affirmative action retention of less senior women and minorities. Here, the affirmative remedy for systemic injustice (protection of job seniority) cannot be fully implemented without obstructing the affirmative remedy for identity-based injustice (affirmative action preference) and vice versa. The only way to avoid this conflict (which pits one oppressed and dominated group against another) is to adopt transformative remedies that eliminate the need for layoffs.[14] Such remedies would involve, for instance, redistributing the salaries of top management downward, reducing weekly shifts for all workers, and compensating downsized workers with equivalent jobs (pay and seniority) in other industries or providing them with full financial remuneration coupled with reeducation.

### The Dialectic of Affirmation and Transformation

It is one thing to endorse radical transformation in theory, another to implement it in practice. Given the current state of the world, it is highly unlikely that many transformative policies will be implemented; the maintenance of racial, gender, and class divisions has simply proven to be too congenial a method for controlling the masses. That being so, we had better reexamine what was just said about affirmative remedies. Are such remedies more effective for transformation than I have so far suggested?

To begin with, what I said earlier about remedies that embody one conception of equality for the sake of realizing another applies here as well. Just as securing the same civil rights for gays and lesbians that the rest of us enjoy functions to protect their different lifestyles, so, too, affirming differences between groups in the short run sometimes proves necessary for eliminating them in the long run.

For example, in order to struggle against the use of racial categories as stigmas of inferiority, racial minorities might first have to organize themselves solidaristically in accordance with them. If the struggle against anti-black racism is to be principally initiated by blacks, they must identify themselves as the group so designated by this kind of racism.

This way of affirming group differences treats them as "necessary evils" that would disappear in an ideal society. However, why couldn't they also be affirmed in a more positively transformed manner? African Americans might express pride in their historical identity as descendants of proud slaves who freed themselves from bondage; and as W. E. B. DuBois once noted, this identification could form the basis for identifying with oppressed peoples all over the world. Racial identity would then designate a difference transcended.

But the discussion here is about affirmative remedies, not affirmative identities. As we shall see in the next chapter, affirmation of certain kinds of cultural differences may be entirely compatible with a transformed (classless, raceless, and genderless) society. But can we achieve transformative ends using affirmative means?

Perhaps. Take the example of multicultural education. While it certainly promotes the mutual affirmation of distinct and diverse cultures, it does so only by encouraging their mutual communication; and that communication, in turn, sets in motion a process of mutual transformation whereby each informs the other, so to speak. In this sense, groups in communication are never fixed and closed off from one another in some pristine state of self-generated identity, but are always contaminated by the outsider and hence are complex, multivalent, and "mixed."

Transformative ends can also be achieved affirmatively in restructuring work environments to accommodate gender differences; instead of excluding one gender or the other, jobs can be transformed to affirm both genders (for example, where jobs require upper-body strength, technology can compensate for women's relative disadvantage). But although gender differences need to be recognized, they must not be regarded as biologically fixed. Biology can be altered technologically and interpreted differently. Women can redefine who they are (as determined by their needs and experiences) in an ongoing act of collective reflection.

In conclusion, some differences should be retained in any transformative democracy of the sort envisaged by our ideal of social justice; for transformative dialogue is scarcely imaginable apart from them. But which ones? That is the question addressed in the following chapters.

# PART II.
# A THEORY OF RACIAL AND CULTURAL GROUPS

# 3

## GROUPS AND INDIVIDUALS:
## THE RACE CONTROVERSY

Groups can oppress their individual members. When there is no chance of exit, they can violate their right to equal protection. Legal classifications can also have this effect. Thus pregnant women are denied their freedom to work by male legislators who classify them indiscriminately—regardless of their individuality and occupation—as "disabled."

Something similar happens when persons belonging to the same race are presumed to have the same interests. The African-American philosopher Cornel West accordingly notes that "although all black Americans have some interest in fighting racism," any talk of an "authentic" black identity is "contingent on one's definition of black interest and one's ethical understanding of how this interest relates to individuals and communities in and outside black America."[1] We cannot assume, in other words, that African Americans share any overarching interests that uniquely distinguish them as a political community. Nevertheless, this kind of racial stereotyping is precisely what is assumed when African Americans are grouped into voting districts for purposes of ensuring the representation of some supposedly common racial interest. To cite Supreme Court Justice Sandra Day O'Connor:

A reapportionment plan that includes in one district individuals who belong to the same race, but who are otherwise widely separated by geographical and political boundaries, and who may have little in common with one another but the color of the skin, bears an uncomfortable resemblance to political apartheid. It reinforces the perception that members of the same racial group—regardless of their age, education, economic status, or the community in which they live—think alike, share the same political interests, and will prefer the same candidates at

51

the polls. We have rejected such perceptions elsewhere as impermissible racial stereotypes.[2]

It does not take much imagination to see how this attack on racial classifications (prejudging individuals' interests by the color of their skin) might be extended to include other groups as well. (In fact, O'Connor's colleague on the Court, Justice Anthony Kennedy, reasoned that treating individuals as "components" of a "religious, sexual, or national class" is equally wrong.)[3] But notice what this assumption implies: if classifying individuals into groups on the basis of race, religion, sex, and national class wrongfully presumes that each member of the group shares something in common with all the other members, then groups so classified are misleading fictions whose very existence ought to be challenged.

Furthermore, by presuming that each member of a group shares something in common with all the others, such classifications gloss over individual differences, thereby encouraging us to treat each member of the group the same way. But treating in the same way persons who are in fact different in relevant respects is unjust. Therefore, instead of treating individuals as members of groups, we should (so it seems) treat them simply as individuals. That is, we should respect their individual rights even if this means, for example, refusing to grant African Americans a special group right to have their own voting districts wherein they can elect representatives of their choice.

Unfortunately, respecting the rights of individuals without at the same time respecting the rights of groups also seems to violate the principle of equal treatment. As I noted in Chapter 1, some individual rights can be exercised only by participating in groups. Unless groups like the Kiryas Joel Hasidim are protected from internal and external interference and provided security and other resources, they will perish—along with the rights of individual members to continue practicing their respective religious cultures freely and securely. Similarly, under our current system of political representation, unless African Americans are allowed to group themselves into their own legislative districts, they will not be able to elect representatives of their choice who will agressively defend their rights.

### Affinal and Aggregate Groups

Defending the rightful existence of social groups requires drawing several distinctions. First, we must distinguish groups that are generated by external methods of aggregation (such as random voting patterns, formally defined criteria, and statistical correlations) from those that are generated by internal affinities between persons who consciously identify with one another. I shall argue that, while the presumption of a common group attribute is often acceptable in cases involving aggregates, it is less so when extended to affinal groups. That does not mean, however, that such an assumption cannot be made when talking about affinal groups. Even if it did, that would not mean that affinal groups do not rightfully exist, for such groups might possess their respective affinities in the manner of overlapping, rather than common, identifications.

Second, I argue that affinal groups who evolve their own sense of solidarity must be distinguished from those for whom this sense was externally imposed through domination. The relevant contrast cases here are religions and races (insofar as the latter are understood as designating affinities rather than aggregates). In contrast to religion, race designates an affinity that is originally imposed by one group on another for purposes of domination, which would normally speak against its legitimacy as a legal classification. However, in the course of struggling against racial domination, racial groups have come to evolve their own, quite legitimate sense of racial affinity; and this identification can be reappropriated by individuals in a manner that is at least partly voluntary and noncoercive.

Let me begin by distinguishing between aggregate and affinal groups.[4] By "aggregate group" I mean any group that is constituted by some formal procedure. Take voting, for example: it groups together all the voters who happened to vote for a particular candidate. The group designated by the expression "all those who voted for candidate X" is real enough, even if its individual members should happen to have no knowledge of one another's existence. Furthermore, by formal definition each and every member of this group shares some interest in common with all the others—getting candidate X elected.

Again, take the group of persons living below the officially designated poverty line. This group is formally constituted by a different procedure: a quantitative means test. As in the case of voting, it is conceivable that none of the members of this economic class even know of one another's existence. They are not the ones who have organized this class out of some sense of solidarity. Rather, they have been grouped together on the basis of a criterion (procedure) that has organized them.

Finally, take the example of race. Anthropologists have stipulated—in ways that are biologically, if not socially, arbitrary—that certain physical traits associated with skin pigmentation, hair texture, body type, physiognomy, and the like can be used to classify individuals into one race as opposed to another.[5] Here, the criterion for classification is not as formally precise as marking a ballot or meeting a financial means–based test. We cannot assume, for instance, that all members of a racially designated population share a single property. Physical characteristics that have been deemed racially relevant are not only numerous—including, say, facial features as well as skin pigmentation—but at best statistically probable (albinos are born to people designated as racially black). Given the fact of racial intermarriage, race as a statistical probability becomes even less salient as a predictor of shared attributes.

Be that as it may, persons designated as racially black are more likely than whites to pass down the cumulative disadvantages of oppression and domination, just as they are more likely than whites to pass down the cumulative genetic dispositions that produce dark skin pigmentation and sickle-cell anemia. What explains these correlations is not race, conceived as some interlocking set of physical traits, biological determinations, and behavioral dispositions, but years of legally enforced segregation, which made it difficult (and illegal) for blacks to marry whites. So, even though skin pigmentation is becoming less salient as a predictor of economic, social, and political standing, the enduring presence of segregation and discrimination continues to justify the use of this external marker for statistically demarcating racial aggregates; and it does so regardless of whether the individuals grouped within any given racial aggregate consciously identify with one another.

In contrast to aggregates like those cited that have been formally constituted with reference to some arbitrarily selected external characteristics, affinities comprise groups whose identifications are at least partly generated by a consciousness of belonging and solidarity. Religious sects, for example, exist only to the degree that they are consciously maintained by their members in solidarity with one another. The same can be said of political parties and numerous other voluntary associations. But examples of affinities that are either externally imposed or involuntarily sustained come to mind as well. People do not voluntarily choose to be speakers of their native language; yet affinities based on native linguistic inheritance can become important for galvanizing nationalist political struggles, as in the case of French-speaking Canada. Likewise, persons who have been discriminated against because of their skin pigmentation, gender, or other inborn characteristic identify with others like themselves out of social and political necessity.

## Aggregates and Stereotypes

Now that we have distinguished aggregates from affinities, we are in a position to answer one of the objections posed by Justices O'Connor and Kennedy. To begin with, aggregating individuals into groups need not entail a violation of their individuality. When individuals are classified as a group according to some property each of them by definition possesses (e.g., supporting candidate X or having financial assets below X dollars), nothing is implied about their other, distinguishing characteristics.

Likewise, no stereotyping need occur when scientists treat racial groups as coalescing around statistical correlations linking physical and social characteristics (skin pigmentation and low income, for example) that crop up in varying degrees and frequencies in relatively segregated populations. Logically speaking, these characteristics imply nothing whatsoever about moral and intellectual competence. Moreover, as mere statistical frequencies, they allow for plenty of exceptions and considerable individual variation. Thus, the statistical underrepresentation of "blacks" in certain occupations relative to their overall percentage of the population (combined with the high statistical probability that persons designated as black have suffered cumulative disadvantages owing to legally sanctioned job discrimination in the past) suffices to designate them as a legal class of persons who merit affirmative action preference. Doing so, however, implies nothing about them as individuals.

Of course, it might be argued that statistical correlations linking possession of dark skin pigmentation with occupational discrimination are different from those linking blacks with those meriting affirmative action preferences. Although statistical correlations linking occupational discrimination to skin pigmentation that justify including blacks among the benficiaries of affirmative action do not as such stigmatize individual "blacks" as morally or intellectually deficient, the same, it might be argued, cannot be said of statistical correlations linking affirmative action preference with lower performance on standardized tests. (In fact, many black beneficiaries of affirmative action score significantly lower on standardized college admissions tests than their white counterparts.)[6] Hence, the statistical correlation linking affirmative action preference with lower-than-average performance on standardized tests creates the impression that blacks as a group are less able (needier) than whites, and that individual blacks are on average less able (needier) than individual whites.

What are we to conclude from statistical correlations linking skin pigmentation and low performance on standardized tests? Without knowing the causes underlying this correlation (ranging from the existence of unequal, racially segregated schools to cultural bias in the construction of standardized tests), one does indeed get the erroneous impression that blacks as a group are less able than whites because of some innate, racial deficiency. Hence, it would seem that, *in the absence of any further explanation,* the statistical aggregation of individuals into racial groups does in fact stigmatize them.

The failure to explain statistical correlations encourages racial stereotyping in other areas as well. Simply knowing that young black males are incarcerated at an alarmingly high rate in proportion to their percentage of the overall population might lead one to wrongly infer that this group is more prone to criminal behavior than the group composed of young white males. In order to dispel this impression, one would have to appreciate the enormous amount of racism that continues to permeate the U.S. criminal justice system. Therefore, although statistical methods for aggregating racial groups do not as such stereotype the individual members of such groups, deploying them without an accurate understanding of their underlying causes does.

The danger of stereotyping arises in a more direct way in the designation of affinal groups. Take the case of racial redistricting (reapportionment), which groups individuals who are racially designated the same way in order to ensure their right—as a minority group—to elect candidates of their choice. Doing so, however, seems to presume that most individuals in the group want to elect representatives who are only like themselves, racially speaking. But this is a false stereotype, and one that promotes racial divisiveness. Equally questionable is the presumption that persons of the same race all share exactly the same interests and values; this, too, is an illegitimate stereotype.

### *Interests, Values, and Perspectives: Essentialist and Nonessentialist Conceptions of Group Affinity*

As I have just discussed, presuming that each member of a given group shares some interest, value, or belief that uniquely binds them together is not always justifiable. Unlike members of the American Cattle Breeders Association, who share a unique interest in furthering the breeding of cattle, members of the group racially designated as African American share no unique interest that distinguishes them from other groups. Although they might share some overarching interests and values—such as ending racial discrimination for the sake of advancing the universal dignity of all persons—these interests and values do not uniquely define them as a group, because almost everybody, with the exception of a few racists, wants to end racial discrimination.

At first glance, it seems that what constitutes the affinity of a group is some interest or value (or set thereof) that is held by all and only members of that group. In keeping with standard philosophical nomenclature, I will designate such an affinity *essentialist*. Accordingly, a group possesses an essentialist affinity if and only if there is some set of beliefs, values, and interests whose possession by any person is both necessary and sufficient for membership.

It is relatively easy to discover a set of beliefs, values, and interests that all African Americans would necessarily (or universally) share simply because they are African Americans. For example, if a person is African American, it more or less follows that he or she has an interest in living a good life (which, we assume, he or she values). This interest, while being a necessary (or universal) condition for membership in the group designated as African American, does not suffice to establish membership in it. I, like most Americans, have an interest in living a good life (which I, like most Americans, value), but that does not make me African American.

It is also relatively easy to discover a set of beliefs, values, and interests whose possession would suffice to ensure one's being an African American. For example, if one possessed the set of beliefs, values, and interests that only Jesse Jackson possesses, then that would make you Jesse Jackson (and you would be African American). But being Jesse Jackson, of course, is not a necessary (or universal) condition for being African American.

The question then arises whether there is any set of beliefs, interests, and values whose possession is essential to being African American.[7] I shall argue that there is, but only if we define this set to include, in addition to beliefs, interests, and values, experientially based perspectives.[8]

By "interests" I mean *specific* goals and instrumental means. My desire to eliminate racial discrimination is a specific interest of mine and so is my support for affirmative action as a means for attaining it. By "values" I mean judgments about right and wrong, good and bad. My opinion that persons ought to be respected equally in their capacity as autonomous agents is an example of a value I cherish.

By "perspectives" I mean, in contrast, ways of understanding and being in the world. Perspectives are the background presuppositions, sedimentations of habit, and embodied repertories of practical know-how that condition the way we perceive ourselves and others; they lay out a frame (or horizon) of possible meaningfulness, interest, and value as well as structure preconscious

body images and postures.[9] For example, the language I speak and the socially conditioned body I inhabit open up a definite space for perceiving,
conceiving, and identifying the things and events I experience. This psychic
space might differ from that opened up by another language and embodied
cultural habitus (for example, what I see as two distinct inanimate things—
a tree and a river—might be experienced by an Australian Aborigine as but
different manifestations of a single spirit).

Perspectives, like interests and values, are acquired through experience.
However, whereas interests and values can become objects of conscious
choice, my embodied perspective cannot, at least not entirely. Although I
can become conscious of some of the presuppositions that condition my perspective, I cannot become conscious of all of them; to be conscious of anything at all is to be conscious of it against the background of some
taken-for-granted habits and assumptions (for example, just try to become
conscious of all the habits and presuppositions underlying speech, gesture,
and movement).

So my perspective is not only acquired through experience, it is like experience. That is, I have a perspective the same way I have an experience—
both come to me more or less independently of my conscious control. This
applies even when I choose to broaden my experience and, by so doing,
broaden my perspective (as when I decide to visit a country whose culture
is very different from my own and become habituated to its way of life, its
marking of social space and time, its embodied cadences and rhythms). For
unlike any belief, interest, and value, an experience cannot be consciously rejected; it forever remains as memory trace and habitual affect, tacitly shaping one's perspective on life.

To return to the original discussion, it might well be that what constitutes
the essential affinity uniting African Americans is not some set of interests
and values, but a common perspective accompanied by feelings of corporeal
vulnerability and perhaps corporeal alienation. For example, Jesse Jackson
and Clarence Thomas are famous African Americans who disagree about
how to interpret certain basic values, such as the importance of treating persons with equal respect and concern (Thomas, who is conservative, thinks
that treating persons with equal respect means according them the same
basic individual rights to property, protection, political participation, and so
forth, but *not* the same economic, educational, and health care provisions;
Jackson, who is progressive, thinks that treating persons with equal respect
also means equally providing them with these provisions). Jackson's and
Thomas's respective political interest in turn reflect their different value

judgments (Jackson supports government aid in correcting market-based inequalities, Thomas does not). Yet despite their different interests and value judgments, both Jackson and Thomas have spoken poignantly about the discrimination and hardship they as blacks have had to endure. In other words, Thomas and Jackson share, along with virtually every African American, a general perspective on race, an understanding unique to blacks of what it is like to grow up as a "black" person in a "white" society.

The perspective and understanding Thomas and Jackson share, of course, are very general. No single black person's experience and understanding of racial discrimination are exactly like another's. So Thomas's and Jackson's perspectives on this score will differ, but only somewhat. Both will possess to some degree the "double consciousness" of which the great African-Dutch-American sociologist W. E. B. DuBois spoke in *The Souls of Black Folk:* "this sense of always looking at one's self through the eyes of others, of measuring one's soul by the tape of a world that looks on in amused contempt and pity." Thus, even if it is wrong to stereotype African Americans as sharing common interests and values that merit special political representation, it is not wrong to impute to them the perspective that comes with having involuntarily acquired a "double consciousness"; and *that* perspective is one that undoubtedly should be guaranteed political representation.

It might be objected that my describing African-American affinity in terms of a uniquely shared perspective based upon their having experienced themselves through the eyes of white people begs the question. The description seems circular in that having this experience is almost part of what it means to be African American; and it seems to beg the question because adducing an essential affinity binding African Americans—which is equivalent to adducing some truly informative facts about them—is not equivalent to defining the meaning of "African American." However, speaking against this objection is the fact that nothing in the bare idea of being an American of African descent logically implies possession of a double consciousness; indeed, some light-skinned Americans of African descent largely lack it, while some dark-skinned Americans of Asian or European descent possess it.[10]

However, even if the attempt to adduce an essentialist account of African-American affinity begs the question in the manner indicated above, the defense of African-American affinity can proceed along a different track. We can, in short, conceive this affinity nonessentialistically. The idea that most but not all members of a group share some uniquely distinguishing beliefs and understandings with one another represents the most familiar example of a nonessentialist conception of group affinity. Another, less familiar one concerns what we might call family resemblances. Here, we assume that there is no single belief or affinity that each member of a group shares with all the others. Instead, we assume only that any two members of a group will share something in common. Thus, if A, B, and C belong to a group, what A and B have in common may be very different from what B and C (or A and C) have in common.

For example, let us suppose that A, B, and C identify with one another as Latinos. A (who is Afro-Cuban) and B (who is Mayan Mexican) speak Spanish but little English; C (who is a U.S. citizen by birth) does not speak much Spanish but identifies strongly with her mixed Mexican-Cuban cultural heritage. C will identify with both A and B, but for different reasons; and A and B, in turn, will identify with C for reasons other than those they have for identifying with each other.

What makes overlapping affinities so important for purposes of political representation is that they elude standard objections against essentialist conceptions of group identity. In speaking of Latinos as composing a group with overlapping affinities, we do not assume any stereotypes about the cultural, racial, or linguistic identities of individual Latinos. Nonetheless, we do assume that many of them will be Spanish-speaking, of indigenous, Castilian, or African descent, and so on. We also know that these affinities will translate into a nexus of overlapping concerns revolving around general support for such things as bilingual education, lax (rather than strict) immigration and nationalization policies, rigid enforcement of antidiscrimination laws, and so forth. Some of these overlapping interests and concerns in turn will doubtless reflect overlapping experiences of discrimination based on not speaking English fluently or not being racially white.

*Externally and Internally Generated Affinities*

Let us suppose for a moment that the perspectives, values, and interests shared by African Americans were not ones that they themselves generated. This assumption is not entirely far-fetched. African slaves brought to America were often forbidden to speak their native tongues and practice their native cultures. Instead, they were forced to speak the language of their oppressors and practice Christianity. Would the perspectives, values, and interests developed by African slaves as a result of forced acculturation from outside be as authentic and legitimate—in short, as worthy of representation—as ones these groups were originally born into?

Today, many African Americans resist being identified as black or even

African American, for that matter, simply because these racial points of reference were not ones they themselves generated but were (and still are) imposed on them by the dominant majority. In their opinion, to consider oneself as being black—or being racially designated—tacitly buys into a classificatory hierarchy that reinforces stereotyping and racial subordination because that is how the scheme was (and still is) understood by many whites. For them, whether or not race designates a real locus of affinity is irrelevant. As long as racial affinity is the outcome of external imposition (such as slavery and discrimination), it has the same status as an ideology that has been brainwashed into a captive population.

### Digression: A Brief History of Race

In order to appreciate the argument against race, one needs to have some appreciation of its history. Skin pigmentation and other physical characteristics that we today associate with race have been observed since the beginning of recorded history. However, these differences were not originally conceived as racial differences and did not function to divide and rank social groups according to intelligence and ability. This is not to deny that a belief in the natural differences between persons existed and even played a role in justifying slavery. In antiquity, for example, Greeks captured in war were enslaved by other Greeks, and at least some of them were regarded by no less an authority than Aristotle as naturally inferior in moral virtue. In general, we find that throughout antiquity, when "natural" rankings were drawn, they were more likely to be based upon gender (with men dominating women), culture (people finding their own way of life naturally superior to other ways of life), or social class.

Perhaps an incipient kind of racial thinking already makes its appearance along with concern about the purity of legitimate descent in ancient times. If so, then racial thinking might well be conascent with the emergence of class and gender oppression as well. Patriarchs of noble "blood" had to exercise scrupulous vigilance over their wives (as well as over men of common stock) in order to ensure the purity and nobility of their lineage. Even as recently as the twentieth century, the ever-present need to preserve the purity of bloodlines as an integral feature of racial ideology and domination led to the gradual suppression of interracial coupling in the colonies; and in Europe and America it led to the passage of laws prohibiting miscegenation, prostitution, abortion (for white women), and unregulated birth (for women of color).[11]

Although a kind of racial thinking lies at the root of gender and class domination, racism as we know it today is of more recent provenance, having
emerged alongside the European conquest of the world.[12] Perhaps, as Lum-
bee Indian legal scholar Robert A. Williams Jr. suggests, racism grew out of
Europeans' obsession with their own exceptionalism; beginning with the
Crusades, they aggressively distinguished themselves as defenders of the
"true" Christian faith from the rest of the "heathen" world.[13] Although "in-
fidels" were not always treated as subhuman and bereft of rights, they were
regarded as morally inferior.[14] During the Spanish conquest of America, this
distinction later legitimated the enslavement of indigenous people by their
"culturally superior" conquerors.

Religious exceptionalism, however, proved to be an unreliable basis for
slavery, since the heathen could convert to Christianity and thereby demonstrate their moral and cognitive worth. Gradually, the religious distinction
was replaced by a distinction (of Roman origin) between the civilized and
the barbarian.[15] By the middle of the eighteenth century, this distinction had
hardened into the quasi-biological distinction between savage and human.
Ironically, the emergence of humanist political doctrines stressing the universal "rights of man" provided an indirect justification for this distinction,
since they explicitly linked full humanity with rational competencies that
only white European men were thought to possess. Although the stamp of
racial inferiority had by then been philosophically ratified by one of the
greatest humanists of all time, Immanuel Kant (1724–1804),[16] it would take
another fifty years for the doctrine of race to be fully articulated as a full-
blown theory of biological racism (which occurred mainly in America, where
the need to legitimate a still thriving but endangered African-American slave
economy became urgent).

Not surprisingly, the most trenchant form of racism appeared in the
United States, where the children of slaves were regarded as the property of
their owners. Traditionally, skin pigmentation had served as a convenient
way of keeping track of the slave population. But this was by no means a
proven method, as children born of mixed-race couplings between master
and slave could pass as white. In order to ensure that such children would
continue to be regarded as black, thereby guaranteeing the increase of the
slave population, a new theory of race had to be invented: the so-called *blood
quantum theory.*

According to this theory, racial characteristics are carried in one's blood,
with each member of a sexual coupling contributing half of his or her blood-
line to the offspring. Furthermore, since possession of any amount of "black"

blood was regarded as a dilution of "white" blood—that is, as a kind of corruption of racial purity—persons who descended from several generations of mixed coupling (miscegenation) were still regarded as "black."[17] Thus, in the landmark case upholding Jim Crow segregation in the South, *Plessy v. Ferguson* (1896), a light-skinned Creole named Homer Plessy, who was "seven-eighths white," was denied his appeal that he should not have to give up his train seat to a white man. (The blood quantum theory was also imposed on Native Americans in determining the extent of their tribal proprietary rights under the reservation system.)

Today, the blood quantum theory stands discredited by modern genetics. Physical characteristics are passed down through genes, not blood (there is no correlation between the four blood types and any set of racial characteristics). Such characteristics in any offspring are the result of combining the distinct genetic materials of the parents in such a manner that these materials are neither diluted nor retained in the same way but recombined to form a totally unique set of genes. Thus, while the blood quantum theory would have us believe that an offspring born of a mixed-race marriage will possess racial characteristics that appear to be midway between the extremes represented by the parents, the genetic theory allows for surprises: albino offspring of dark-skinned parents; tall offspring of short parents, and so forth.[18]

The preceding history lends support to those who would reject racial identifications as inherently racist—and without scientific basis. Indeed, when scientists today talk about races, they have nothing more in mind than self-contained "breeding populations" that have a higher percentage of individuals possessing certain physical characteristics than other similarly self-contained populations. But no such populations in fact exist; or rather, in sharp contrast to animal species, such populations exist at best in part, and only then because of an "unnatural" history of legally sanctioned racial segregation.[19]

Such, then, is the sordid history of what the Jamaican-born philosopher Charles Mills calls the "racial contract." This contract justified the expropriation of indigenous people, the enslavement of Africans and their descendants, and the colonization of non-Europeans throughout the world. It was a contract among whites that, in effect, created a unified European (ostensibly "civilized") sensibility contrasted with an equally unified "oriental," African, or indigenous (ostensibly "exotic" and "primitive") sensibility. In the years that saw the biological articulation of this contrast in terms of light-skinned and dark-skinned races, the simple black/white scheme would undergo considerable moderation, allowing for finer discriminations among both whites and nonwhites. Thus, among persons of European descent,

Slavs, Mediterraneans, Jews, and Irish were initially viewed as darker than, and therefore racially inferior to, archetypically white-skinned Anglo-Saxons and Nordics.[20] It would take decades for each of these groups to be recognized by the dominant Anglo-Saxon/Nordic majority as full-fledged members of the white community.

Conversely, among those nonwhites classified as savages (for whom no chance of admission to the club of civilized white folk was ever envisaged), Africans and Australian Aborigines generally ranked lower than Native Americans. They, in turn, were ranked lower than Asians, who were conceded the possibility of acquiring Western civilization. (By contrast, in Latin American countries that had experienced considerable race mixing—especially in countries like Brazil, where the offspring of slaves were accorded the status of freemen—"black" and "white" eventually came to designate distinctions of economic class rather than of heritable moral and cognitive distinctions.)[21]

If today most whites seem ignorant of the historical existence of the racial contract and its enduring aftereffects, it is because, in the words of Charles Mills:

> In a racially structured polity, the only people who can find it psychologically possible to deny the centrality of race are those who are racially privileged, for whom race is invisible precisely because the world is structured around them. . . . The fish does not see the water, and whites do not see the racial nature of the white polity because it is natural to them, the element in which they move.[22]

### A Possible Defense of Racial Identifications

Given the powerful argument against racial identifications, one might wonder why anyone, except maybe a racist, would be interested in defending them. As Naomi Zack notes, "black" and "white" have no descriptive value whatsoever, only moral value—namely, the moral denigration of those classified as "non-white." In liberal society, where individuals are respected in their freedom to choose their own identities, racial identifications such as these inevitably "limit individuals in their subjectivities, even when they take up the designations themselves."[23] African Americans especially would seem to have the least reason for identifying themselves racially, since doing so merely perpetuates the denigration of their universal humanity and individuality.

But is racial affinity among blacks merely an outcome of external imposition? No doubt, African Americans would not share a racial affinity had they and their ancestors not been born into a racial (and racist) system of European and American invention. But the racial affinity African Americans have for one another is also partly one that they themselves have elaborated in response to this system. Most obviously, they have identified themselves as those who have been racially designated, for racist purposes, as "black," and they have done so precisely in order to organize themselves solidaristically in fighting for a color-blind society.

Moreover, African Americans have undermined the racial system by freely appropriating it in ways that invert its hierarchization (recall, for instance, the "Black Is Beautiful" and "Black Power" slogans of the sixties and seventies). Indeed, no less an antiracist than W. E. B. DuBois thought that "the badge of color" could be legitimately appropriated by all peoples—regardless of color—insofar as they suffered from oppression (hence, the strong affinity that many Jews felt toward blacks during the civil rights struggles of the sixties). To cite DuBois on expanding black consciousness to include nonblacks:

> The actual ties of heritage between the individuals of this group vary with the ancestors that they have in common with many others: Europeans and Semites, perhaps Mongolians, certainly Marican Indians. But the physical bond is least and the badge of color relatively unimportant save as a badge; the real essence of this kinship is its social heritage of slavery; the discrimination and insult; and this heritage binds together not simply the children of Africa, but extends through yellow Asia and into the South Seas.[24]

By the time he wrote this passage, published in *Dusk of Dawn* (1940), DuBois understood the perils of retaining race—conceived as a biological category—for galvanizing resistance to racism. Even color seemed inadequate to him as a basis of political identification, given that African Americans of extremely diverse skin pigmentation had established their own hierarchies based upon what they perceived to be the desirability of "passing" as white in white supremacist society.[25] In fighting against both biological and color-based conceptions of racial identity, he himself referred repeatedly to the fact of an "integration of physical differences."[26] But he did not want this fact to be misinterpreted as a prescription for biological assimilation, since "whitening" merely perpetuated color-based hierarchies while obliterating what he took to be the positive significance of race "as the vastest and most ingenious invention for human progress."[27] Consequently, he sought to develop a sociohistorical (or sociopolitical) account of race that would transcend physical differences altogether. This account, as his earlier quote makes clear, even transcends cultural differences, since its locus of identification is the heritage of "insult and discrimination" shared by persons of widely differing geographical, cultural, and historical backgrounds.[28]

As Tommy Lott and others have observed, the problem with this purely political conception of racial identity is that it does not sufficiently distinguish the peculiar color-based discrimination formative for the racial identity of African Americans from the ethnic- and religion-based discrimination formative for, say, the racial identity of Jews; for even among Jews, blacks experienced a special form of discrimination.[29]

On the other hand, DuBois was right to note that color was but one, in itself relatively insignificant, among many signs of racial stigma. Thus, no matter what their color, Jews and persons of partial African "blood"—indeed, virtually everyone excepting persons of Anglo-Saxon and Nordic descent—were regarded at one time or other as racially inferior and subject to a common regimen of "discrimination and insult." Although each of these groups endured its own unique version of this regimen, that suffered by African Americans being the most difficult to surmount, they all shared a common history of having their identities forged through the external imposition of race consciousness.

This history suggests an additional reason why its origin in an act of external imposition need not render black racial affinity wholly illegitimate: many nonracial group affinities that are currently recognized as legitimate at least partly originated the same way. Recall, for example, the emergence of racial distinctions out of religious and class distinctions. Most religious sects probably originated from acts of expulsion and exclusion committed by some dominant religion (and, of course, most dominant religions began as so-called "infidel" sects). Again, the affinities uniting members of ethnic groups often refer back to acts of expulsion and exclusion by the nationalities into which they have been forceably incorporated. In many cases, excluded ethnic groups and nationalities adapted to their situation by transforming a negative experience into something positive. Denied admission into mainstream society, they withdrew into themselves; suffering the stigma of racial and ethnic inferiority, they rejuvenated among themselves a sense of racial and ethnic pride.

In sum, one of the reasons why certain members of oppressed racial and ethnic minorities embrace racial and ethnic identities that they otherwise regard as too restrictive is because the dominant, mainstream culture continues to exclude them. Thus, some Native American women continue to identify with their tribal nationality and defend their tribe's right to self-governance even when doing so might subject them to a form of patriarchal domination they personally loathe. Although they might think that the dominant, liberal culture affords them greater freedom and equality as women, they might also feel that, being subservient to the interests of a hostile Anglo majority, it is closed to them as Native Americans. Indeed, they might feel freer living on the reservation than living off of it, since "white" society provides fewer resources for—but many hindrances to—the practice of their native lifestyle. Likewise, some African Americans who prefer to be identified merely as individuals might continue to identify with blacks as a group as well as defend blacks' rights to affirmative action simply because the dominant white society to which they would like to assimilate has prevented them from doing so. But what about members of racial and ethnic groups who are prevented from identifying with the universal identity of liberal humanism and participating in mainstream liberal society not because of discrimination by the dominant group, but because of the restrictive socialization patterns of their own racial or ethnic group?

## Individuals and Groups Reconsidered

It would seem that the racial and ethnic affinities of groups can be legitimate even if they were originally imposed by other groups. This is possible to the extent that members of racial and ethnic groups have come to positively valorize their affinities. To be sure, dominant groups also had their affinities positively valorized during the course of establishing their dominance over other races and cultures, but this positively valorized affinity is illegitimate insofar as it depends on a self-attribution of racial and ethnic superiority. As a general rule, we may say that racial (and very possibly ethnic) identities are legitimately affirmed only to the extent that they reflect a positive reaction to a genuine (and not merely fabricated) experience of racial and ethnic oppression. This means that racial (and very possibly ethnic) identities, as well as the protective rights claimed on behalf of the groups that identify with them, are contingent on the continued threat of racial and ethnic domination and thus provisional vis-à-vis the eradication of racism and ethnocentrism. In the words of Gerald Doppelt, "the worse-off the group's status in the dominant culture, the stronger its claims to its own right of cultural self-expression and thus group rights; with the proviso that the group is not one which discriminates against its own members, or against non-members."[30]

To Doppelt's rule I would add several other provisos. First, the majority of any group may be permitted to discriminate against a dissident minority within the group if, by exiting the group, the dissident minority can exercise its rights fully without suffering undue hardship. Second, the nature of the discrimination cannot involve any violation of a vital, fundamental right, such as the right to life, property, and bodily freedom and inviolability. Third, a group illegitimately discriminates against its own members when it prevents them from developing capacities that normatively speaking should follow from any fully human process of acculturation and socialization. These capacities include the capacity to critically reflect on and voluntarily choose one's identity.

Our understanding of how fundamentalist religions can restrict the education of children and the occupational roles of women thus forces us to raise an additional question: How can we defend the legitimacy of groups whose affinities, while internally generated, are coercively instilled in individual members? Wouldn't the affinity have to be voluntarily accepted by each member in order to be legitimate? The problem is that membership in affinal groups gravitating around family, friends, linguistic culture, religious and higher-order belief systems, and the like is indispensable for cultivating a robust sense of individuality and free agency. However, it is also not entirely voluntary.

When I talk about my individuality I mean many things: my interests and values, occupations and roles, and the experiences that I have had (and that have partly made me who I am). It is this individuality that provides the background for my choices; indeed, my having choices (freedom) is scarcely imaginable without my also having a repository of experiences, habits, orientations, and understandings lending direction and meaning to those choices.

The important thing to note here is that nothing that each of us individually attributes to his or her individuality would be possible without socialization. The primary community (and affinal group) into which we are socialized is our family; as children we learn habits of thought and behavior from our parents as soon as we are born. We unconsciously model ourselves after our parents, whose recognition and approval in turn strengthens this identification.

Significantly, our parents' habits (on which we also model ourselves) mirror in many ways the language, thought, and behavior of their wider community. Thus, our parents, as models, give us ways of understanding and behaving that are shared by others in their group. But we tailor these ways of understanding, evaluating, and behaving to fit our own needs and experiences, and in the course of growing up, we expand our group identifications beyond kith and kin. These additional identifications (be they vocational, ideological, and so forth) come to modify our earlier identifications in unique ways.

The important point to stress here is that we need habits, just as we need preconscious perspectives, in order to consciously deliberate and act. Both habits and perspectives are initially acquired through socialization into groups, and both are individually tailored by our ongoing relations with others. At the same time, they are largely involuntary. Although as mature adults we can and should critically reflect on (and thereby take responsibility for) our habits and perspectives, we cannot do so entirely, because at any given moment our conscious thoughts will be tacitly framed by some largely unconscious presuppositions (such as the embodied grammar and vocabulary of the various groups we inhabit).

In conclusion, identification with any group is never entirely voluntary and is less so when the group in question is the outcome of racial or ethnic domination. However, beyond questioning the degree to which any oppressed group internally valorizes its identity as something positive, we must question the degree to which its individual members are permitted to criticize, reformulate, and even reject that identity. Again, to take the example of race, the double-consciousness that goes with having been raised black in white supremacist America constitutes a racial affinity that can be an object of voluntary choice only in a limited sense. But this sense is crucial. In the words of the great African freedom fighter Frantz Fanon: "There is no Negro mission; there is no white burden. . . . I have one right alone: That of demanding human behavior from the other. One duty alone: That of not renouncing my freedom through my choices—I am not a prisoner of history. I should not seek there for the meaning of my destiny."[31] Perhaps, as Noel Ignatiev and John Garvey remind us, white people, too, can come to voluntarily renounce their complicity in upholding white racial identity, to denounce their whiteness by expressly identifying themselves as nonwhite in the company of white racists.[32]

In this chapter, I have sought to defend the legitimacy of racial groupings. Racial aggregates designate legitimate racial generalizations to the extent that the statistical correlations on which they are based are not assumed to be explanatory apart from deeper sociological accounts relating them to institutionalized norms of segregation and discrimination. Racial affinities, by contrast, designate legitimate loci of group identity only to the extent that they evince a positive valorization; coalesce around shared perspectives or overlapping beliefs, interests, and values related to genuine experiences of racial oppression; do not reflect racist or supremacist aspirations; *and* are voluntarily appropriated and individually interpreted. Because white racial affinity is not grounded in a genuine experience of oppression, it cannot be the legitimate locus of even a nonracist identity.

Race is probably the most important affinity that African Americans have in common, but it is not the only one. Culture (or ethnicity) is almost as important and raises important questions about the relationship between culture and group identity that I will explore in the next chapter: Can cultures also arise from external imposition? If so, under what circumstances does this render them illegitimate?

# 4

## CULTURES AND GROUP AFFINITIES

Here is a view of the deaf community that might surprise you: Today, the dominant view among most deaf speakers of American Sign Language (ASL) is that deafness is not a disability but a distinct linguistic culture. Although ASL founds a cultural community, it is atypical. ASL is seldom passed down from parent to child (indeed, 90 percent of deaf children are born to hearing parents), and so deaf children acquire their cultural identity from their peers (like homosexuals). Because ASL has its own unique grammar, puns, and poems that are very different from English, and because English is difficult for congenitally deaf children to learn, up until now these children have not integrated well into the dominant hearing culture (indeed, they score poorly on tests of English skills).[1] However, now that cochlear implants that enable them to hear are available to deaf children, defenders of deaf culture (or DEAF) feel that their community is being threatened with extinction, or "cultural genocide," and are asking that the government stop research on such implants.[2]

DEAF advocates raise questions that are familiar to us by now: How far should government go in assisting groups in exercising their right to exist? With whom should it side when this right conflicts with the freedom of individuals? Like the majority in the Kiryas Joel community, DEAF advocates want the government to intervene on behalf of preserving their culture, and they want this despite the fact that it restricts the freedom of a dissident minority: the *hearing* parents of deaf children. Indeed, they want this intervention despite the fact that it restricts the freedom of deaf children generally.[3]

Not surprisingly, deaf parents of deaf children overwhelmingly support DEAF's goals—so important to them is ASL as an affinal bond that they cheer when finding out that their babies are deaf. Understandably, like all parents, deaf parents want to pass down their language and culture to their

71

children, because doing so makes possible the closest communication and mutual identification between them and their children. But what happens when doing so entails denying their children the opportunity to fully assimilate into mainstream society? Should the desire of parents to maintain intimate communication with their children (sharing their deaf cultural identity with them) override their children's right to choose assimilation in later life?

The case is roughly analogous to some religious sects, such as the Old World Pennsylvania Amish and, to a certain extent, the Kiryas Joel community. Members of these communities want to raise their children in a traditional manner, in accordance with their own cultural beliefs and practices, even if doing so denies them the benefits of a high school education (as in the case of the Amish) or broader exposure to different value systems and cultures. Such communities therefore pose a serious challenge to liberalism's attempt to reconcile toleration (allowing groups to transmit their culture to their descendants as they see fit) with individual freedom (protecting children's right to choose).[4]

In other respects, however, the case of DEAF is disanalogous to cases involving religious freedom. Here, the minority whose freedom is being threatened also comprises hearing parents of deaf children, who are decidedly not members of the ASL community. Thus, DEAF's attack on cochlear implant research arguably amounts to coercing these parents into having their children join DEAF's community rather than their own. Furthermore, denying deaf children access to cochlear implants entails a more serious restriction of their freedom to choose than denying them a secular education (which is what traditionalist religious communities do), because children do not have the freedom to choose whether and when they will learn a natural language. Unless they hear at an early age, their chances of ever learning a natural language with any degree of facility are remote.[5]

The charge of denying children their basic freedom may sound harsh in light of DEAF advocates' legitimate concerns about the oppression and domination of deaf people. From 1880, when the Congress of Milan voted to banish sign language from education, until the early 1960s, deaf children were forbidden to speak ASL in classrooms. Some managed to assimilate into English-speaking culture, but the vast majority did not (and those who did not suffered the consequences). Deprived and dominated by the majority, they began to organize themselves and form their own small communities. But political divisions within the deaf community soon emerged, and now those who prefer to speak English (in order to communicate with their hearing parents) are occasionally ostracized for not being "genuinely" deaf.[6]

This resistance to "mainstreaming" is virtually unique among advocates for the disabled. Advocates for every other disabled group have insisted that the disabled want to be treated just the same way as everyone else; hence, they have demanded universal access to public buses, schools, and the like rather than separate accommodations. DEAF advocates, however, insist on affirming their difference from the mainstream and have generally resisted remedies, such as cued speech and total communication, which they feel concede too much to English.[7]

But they have not resisted all such remedies. Like the mainstreamers, they also want access to technologies such as TV captions, flashing alarms, phone lights, and keyboard devices for telephone communication. Ironically, this desire creates a problem for their belief that ASL constitutes a separate cultural community. Such technologies undermine the distinction between the "authentically" and "inauthentically" deaf; indeed, they do not appear to be significantly different from cochlear implants (both, in their own way, involve substituting English for ASL). The mere fact that these technologies are not implanted in the individual seems irrelevant, since (to take a somewhat different example) eyeglasses appear to alter the "authentic" identity of blind persons as little or as much as corneal implants and contact lenses.

Hence, besides raising questions about the rights of groups to demand government assistance in preserving their cultures (does *any* culture that arises from a disability have a legitimate claim in this regard?), the case of DEAF also raises questions about what it means to be a cultural group possessing its own distinct (or authentic) identity. Is deaf culture inherently contaminated by English-speaking culture to the point of losing its distinctness and authenticity? If so, does it still count as a genuine culture?

*Preliminary Observations on Culture and the Deaf Community*

One way to begin answering this question is by consulting a dictionary. Merriam-Webster's Collegiate Dictionary (fifth edition) defines "culture" as: (1) action of developing by education, discipline, or training; (2) the enlightenment refining of taste, acquired by intellectual and aesthetic training; (3) a particular stage of advancement in civilization or the characteristic features of such a stage or state; as primitive, Greek, Germanic *culture*. The first definition emphasizes the close relationship between culture, tradition, and knowledge: a culture consists of knowledge (beliefs and skills) and instilled behaviors that are passed down from one generation to another. This knowledge falls into four broad categories: *beliefs, practices, linguistic idioms,* and *artifacts.* Examples of cultures characterized primarily in terms of belief are the great religions, where doctrinal principles usually surpass rituals and artifacts in degree of importance. Cultures defined in terms of practice, on the other hand, emphasize behavior over belief. Consumer culture, corporate culture, and gay and lesbian culture exemplify the practical sense of knowing how something is done as distinct from knowing that something is true. Linguistic cultures, by contrast, presuppose only a minimal practical skill (knowing how to speak and/or write) and virtually no commitment to any specific beliefs. Finally, cultural knowledge is directly embodied in material artifacts, such as texts, artistic works, computers, and the like. DEAF advocates maintain that ASL constitutes a culture in at least the third sense and possibly also in the second sense.

The second definition stresses the manner in which culture, as a more or less habitual (or unthinking) manner of understanding and comportment, can be thought about, articulated, and refined. There is low (popular) culture and high (refined) culture. Initially inculcated in the learner by way of training and discipline, culture that is passed down from generation to generation as tradition also bears the stamp of timeless authority, which is especially true for the customs and languages of everyday life. (Think about the way in which children never question the proper, authoritative use of a word when spoken by an adult.) However, once someone has mastered a culture, he or she can begin to critically reflect on it so as to improve (or refine) it. He or she can invent new words or phrases or even a whole new way of talking (think of the poetry of jive, rap, and other forms of African-American vernacular). Indeed, traditions that we designate as high culture—which usually center around canonical literatures of a sacred nature—are never simply accepted without question (as dogmatic authority) but instead preserve their lasting vitality and authority through critical and often imaginative interpretation.

ASL signers, who lack a *literary* (high) culture, share this capacity as well; they compose poetry, make puns, and critically reflect on the limits and possibilities of expression and understanding peculiar to ASL. ASL signers who read, speak, and write English carry this process of reflection even further, by comparing ASL with other linguistic cultures.

In the third definition, "culture" has a certain normative meaning. Already, the distinction between unrefined and refined (low and high) culture suggests a value ranking. High culture artfully develops the expressive and cognitive potentials implicit in low culture; it is richer and, in some sense, more developed.

Those engaged in the production of high culture typically make another comparison as well. They rank *different* cultures according to their expressive and cognitive qualities. In the nineteenth century especially, it was common among persons of European descent to rank their culture ("Western civilization") as superior to all others. Eventually, the assumption of European superiority was linked to a theory of racial descent, in which each culture was seen as expressing the biological tendencies of a distinct "people." As French defender of European colonialism Jules Harmand (1845–1921) so bluntly put it, "It is necessary . . . to accept as a principle and point of departure the fact that there is a hierarchy of races and civilizations, and that we [Europeans] belong to the superior race and civilization."[8]

Ever since E. B. Tylor wrote his pioneering study on civilizations and Franz Boas and Ruth Benedict argued that cultures constituted incomparable systems of self-contained meaningfulness, cultural anthropologists have almost unanimously rejected the racialization and ranking of cultures.[9] Today, going beyond even these earlier researchers, they are more likely to emphasize the hybrid impurity of all cultures, now conceived as social adaptations to environmental challenges.

The defense of cultures as artificial adaptations to environmental challenges would seem to harmonize well with the demands of DEAF advocates. After all, they have been maintaining for some time that ASL is the equal of any linguistic culture, its lack of literature notwithstanding. However, on closer inspection it becomes clear that things are not quite so simple. Some DEAF advocates still assume that deaf culture is relatively self-contained and "authentically" expressive of a certain biological group: congenitally born deaf children whose parents are also deaf.

Like European cultural racists of the previous century, these advocates distinguish between ASL speakers of "pure" and "mixed" lineage. Those whose parents hear (and communicate in English) have had their lineage corrupted; because they have had to compromise their commitment to ASL by learning English, their credentials as genuine members of the ASL community are tarnished. Hence, within some ASL circles, those with mixed biological (and linguistic) lineages are ranked lower in esteem.

But the specter of cultural racism is not the only problem with which DEAF advocates must contend. They also must defend the legitimacy of their culture as something having intrinsic merit; that is, as something worth preserving despite whatever costs it might inflict on young deaf children.

Here we observe another discomfitting similarity between the views of some DEAF advocates and cultural racism. During the late eighteenth century, it was common for many ethical idealists to distinguish culture, conceived as a freely created artifact of the human spirit, from nature, understood as a domain of physical and biological necessity. However, this dualism was replaced by a crudely reductive materialism. Nineteenth-century imperialists took the concept of race (i.e., the concept that people's phenotypical differences were caused by biological differences) and wedded it to the idea of culture. The product was cultural racism; or the assumption that race determines cultural (cognitive, moral, and expressive) achievement.

As noted in Chapter 3, the untruth of cultural racism is compounded by its illegitimacy—its being "invented" by one group, mainly Europeans and their descendants, and imposed on all other groups in order to justify the domination of the latter by the former.[10] For those who are dominated and oppressed, external imposition means that their cultural identity, no less than their racial identity, ceases to be a matter of free, rational choice. Racial categorization takes a group's sense of self (and self-worth) out of their own hands and places it under the control of their oppressors; cultural racism takes away their native language, religion, and way of life and replaces it with another: the language, religion, and way of life deemed worthy by the group's oppressors.

Although no DEAF advocate seeks to forceably replace the hearing culture of deaf persons who have already learned to speak, a few seek to suppress it among those who have not (at least, this is the outcome if not the intent of their proposal). In this respect, they come close to promoting the oppression of congenitally deaf children: they want to halt government funding of cochlear implant research in order to externally impose *their* cultural identity on them (since, absent cochlear implants, such children more or less will be compelled to join the ASL community).

It is also important to remember that the biological condition of congenital deafness that generates ASL culture acts as a kind of external imposition as well. After a certain age, deaf children who begin to hear for the first time have a much harder time acquiring spoken English than those who begin to hear at an earlier age. Thus, full immersion in the ASL culture at an early age—without benefit of hearing—might well prevent exit from that culture in later life.

Of course, DEAF advocates deny that being born deaf is a disabling constraint; hence, they also deny that it constitutes an external imposition on deaf children's freedom to choose their identity. But surely, were it not for the fact that being born deaf has forced the creation of sign language, no one would deny that it was a disability. Therefore, the fact that the survival of ASL culture depends on the persistence of a correctable disability (and eliminative constraint on the freedom of those who suffer from it) distinguishes it even from fundamentalist religious cultures like that of the Kiryas Joel community, whose origin and preservation still depend mainly on the volition of its adherents, however stultified that volition might be.

### The Legitimacy of Deaf Culture and the Deaf Community's Right to Self-Preservation

If fundamentalist religious groups such as the Satmar Hasidim—but not the ASL deaf community—had a legitimate claim not to be threatened with cultural extinction by government acts or omissions, this could only mean that members of the former retained greater freedom than members of the latter to reject their culture, despite peer pressure and rigidly dogmatic indoctrination. Assuming that dissidents, oppressed women, and children (once grown) were not denied the will or opportunity to exit the group without undue hardship and that the group itself did not seek to discriminate against other groups, we might even say that the Satmar Hasidim constituted a fully legitimate cultural community.

By fully legitimate community I mean any community whose origin and preservation depend mainly on the reasonable, voluntary choices of its adherents rather than on external constraint. The deaf community is no doubt legitimate for those who had no choice but to learn ASL or face discrimination. Their desire to preserve this community is reasonable in at least this sense: without the community, they would be denied important cultural resources for understanding their world and making choices. Yet reasonable though it is, their decision to remain in this community is nonetheless constrained by their disability.

More problematic is the desire of deaf parents to acculturate their deaf children in the ASL community; for although it is reasonable for them to want to forge strong ties with their children (which might not happen if their children were raised in the dominant hearing culture), denying them the opportunity to hear severely limits their freedom to assimilate into mainstream culture in later life. Given the hardship that this restriction of freedom will impose on them, it cannot be said that the decision of deaf parents to deny their children the opportunity to hear is reasonable. But if it is not reasonable to deny them this opportunity, it also is not reasonable to deny them the opportunity to learn English, an opportunity that, once made available, will almost certainly have the predictable effect of undermining deaf culture.

It is now apparent why the ASL community is not fully legitimate. Because it is morally desirable (and perhaps even legally imperative) for deaf children to have the same freedom and opportunity to succeed as hearing children, they should not be forced (against their own best interests) to join the ASL community. This would not be the case if the ASL community were fully legitimate, for then we would allow parents this right of coercion,[11] as we do and perhaps should in the case of the Old World Amish and the Satmar Hasidim.

DEAF advocates, of course, deny any fundamental difference between these religious communities and the deaf community; in both cases, a culture will be imposed on children against their will that "limits" their options in later life. Likewise, they deny that there is any difference between demanding that the congenitally deaf correct their physical disability and demanding that African Americans "whiten" their skin pigmentation; in both cases, a physical condition is presumed to be a handicap for assimilating into the mainstream.

As I noted earlier, this counterresponse ignores the fact that acculturation in deaf culture restricts the choice to assimilate more radically (and irreversibly) than does acculturation in a religious sect; and it confuses a naturally disabling physical trait (deafness) with one that is not (skin pigmentation). Be that as it may, the counterresponse does provoke further reflection on the relationship between race and culture. For DuBois, at least, the racial affinity linking African Americans cannot be dissociated from their sharing a unique culture. The question remains whether this culture—whose own formation owes as much to religious inspiration as it does to racial discrimination—is also a product of external imposition and, as such, illegitimate.

## Kinds of Cultural Groups

In order to determine whether African-American racial identity is linked to a distinctly African-American culture, and whether, as such, this linkage renders that culture illegitimate, we must first examine the role of culture in constituting affinal groups generally. At first glance, the affinal group "African American" has a racial identity defined by the perspective of having lived as a "black" in white supremacist America. Nothing in this identity—conceived in terms of the lived experience of being "black" in white supremacist America—tells us anything about what common (or overlapping) cultural affinities African Americans might share. It is thus a matter of empirical fact whether such affinities exist and, if so, whether they condition (and in turn are conditioned by) African Americans' racial identification.

One way to begin to answer this question is by noting that virtually all affinal groups possess an affinity that is at least partly, if not mainly, cultural in nature. For purposes of convenience, we can classify such groups in terms of whether their affinities are strongly or weakly cultural with respect to one or more of the four cultural elements mentioned earlier.

Perhaps one of the most overarching kinds of cultural affinity pertains to persons who identify themselves as belonging to one of the great world religions: Christianity, Islam, Judaism, Hinduism, Buddhism, Taoism, and Confucianism. The faithful identifying with any one of these religions inhabit different parts of the globe, speak different languages, practice different customs, and express themselves in different artifacts. Yet they commonly share the general *beliefs* of their religion, however much they disagree on doctrinal details and rituals.

Next we have national (or geographic) affinities, which very often are associated with language and somewhat less often with religion. For example, the Russian national identity is solidified by both a common language (Russian) and a more or less dominant religion (Russian Orthodoxy). However, national (or geographic) affinity sometimes exists in the absence of one or the other of these affinities. For example, the cultural affinity uniting the indigenous peoples of Guatemala is not mainly linguistic (counting Spanish, there are twenty-four languages spoken there, twenty-one of them Mayan). Religion is a more important bond, since the overwhelming majority of indigenous peoples continue to practice a common form of nature spirit worship, which they have grafted onto Catholicism.[12] However, owing to the recent upsurge of evangelical forms of Protestantism among many indigenous people, the religious bond has weakened. Counteracting this religious schism, indigenous peoples (especially Mayans) are organizing themselves politically, as a nationwide interest group, in order to defend their right to land, education, and the secure practice of their separate cultures. Thus the new affinity among Guatemalan indigenous people is being forged along multiple (economic, political, and cultural) paths that are as much based on geographic proximity as on religion and ethnic culture.[13]

National and geographical affinities can be quite complex. Immigrants, for example, often continue to identify strongly with their native land, even while assimilating into their new society. They retain their ancestral cultural ties but evolve new, culturally mixed ethnic identities. For example, some second-generation Mexican Americans acquire distinctive Chicano sensibilities associated with such popular dialects as "Spanglish," which are distinct from the ancestral cultures of their native Mexico.

Cultural affinities also include lifestyles, practices, and codes of behavior. For example, we can talk about gay and lesbian cultures, working-class cultures, corporate cultures, consumer cultures, and the like. These cultures transcend religious and other belief commitments, just as they transcend national-geographic ties. At the same time, cultural practices such as these are at least indirectly influenced by the more encompassing religious and national-geographic cultures that surround them.

Physical differences between people pertaining to "race," "gender," and "disability" also map onto cultural differences. Admittedly, this assertion seems to contradict my emphatic insistence on sharply distinguishing culture and nature. In order to avoid any pretense of reducing culture to nature (the fallacy of cultural racism), I suggest that we think of the relationship between these terms as strictly socio*logical* rather than socio*biological*.

So construed, the deaf community's ASL culture is properly understood as one among many possible social responses (adaptations) to a natural disability. Similarly, gender-coded occupational roles, styles of dress, and comportment must not be regarded as naturally predestined but as socially constructed. Indeed, we can go farther and insist, along with Judith Butler, that even the so-called "biological" sex differences onto which gender codes map are also, at bottom, nothing more than social constructs.[14] This assumption applies as well to ethnic cultures that are commonly ascribed to "racial" groups. Supposing that African Americans (if not persons designated as "black") share some overlapping cultural traits, this is because race itself is a social (or cultural) construct to which these traits are an adaptive response.

In addition to the above cultural types, there is what Will Kymlicka calls a "societal culture." According to him, societal culture means a meaningful way of life that extends across "the full range of human activities, including social, educational, religious, recreational, and economic life, encompassing both public and private spheres."[15] Groups that possess such a culture normally constitute "an intergenerational community, more or less institutionally complete, occupying a given territory or homeland (and) sharing a distinct language and history."

Kymlicka's notion of societal culture has two virtues: first, it describes the complex interlocking and mutual conditioning of cultural elements that we find with national cultures, such as the Japanese culture; second, it designates a cultural inheritance that is largely acquired and retained involuntarily. However, it also has two vices: it applies to very few cultures (only those whose designated groups have undergone nation-building and modernization); and it presumes an institutional completeness, linguistic and historical distinctness, and all-encompassing closedness that today are being challenged by certain global economic, political, and multicultural tendencies.

Despite its limitations, the notion of a societal culture is useful in designating cultural communities that are relatively freestanding and distinctive. What we now need to ask is whether African-American communities, understood ethnically rather than racially, might be plausibly characterizable as having such a culture.

### Do African-American Communities Possess a Societal Culture?

African-American identity appears to be simultaneously racial and cultural (ethnic) in ways that are not easily distinguishable. To begin with, color-based categories (white and black) and geographically based categories (Asian-Pacific Islander and American Indian–Alaskan Native) appear indiscriminately on the U.S. government's official "racial" classication scheme, which appears on census forms and other documents requesting demographic information. Admissions and employment forms used by institutions of higher education also list "Hispanic" as an additional racial category, despite its ambiguous reference to either language or nationality.[16] Here, persons of mixed descent are invited to view their cultural and racial identifications interchangeably. Thus, a Native American of African-Cuban ancestry could potentially be identified as either black, Hispanic, or Caucasian, depending on his or her cultural affinities.

Another reason why race and culture seem to merge in the African-American identity is that racial discrimination and segregation isolated African-American communities and forced them to elaborate their own distinctive cultural responses to their oppression. African slaves and their slave descendants often were prevented from openly speaking their native language and practicing their native religion. At the same time, however, they were frequently denied access to Christian churches; indeed, by the second decade of the nineteenth century, some southern states had prohibited them from learning how to read and write. Under these conditions, it is not surprising that, beginning with the mass conversions in the mid-eighteenth century, African-American slaves would evolve their own distinctive brand of spiritual Christianity, along with their distinctive music, cuisine, dialect, and familial culture.

African Americans thus fashioned their own culture in response to slavery and segregation. Even after they were legally emancipated, African Americans were concentrated in (and forceably acculturated into) the brutal sharecropping economies of the rural South. Following the post–World War I migrations, their social and economic existence remained restricted in ways that, after three decades of civil rights legislation and moderate integration into the mainstream, continue to shape the "black" urban underclass culture.

According to African-American Harvard sociologist William Julius Wilson, African-American communities have evolved two sorts of cultural adaptations in response to their oppression: one positive, the other negative. The positive response revolves around "basic institutions in the inner city (including churches, stores, schools, recreational facilties)" that promoted "a sense of community, positive neighborhood identification, and explicit norms and sanctions against aberrant behavior." Key to maintaining these institutions was "the presence of stable working- and middle-class families" who provided "mainstream role models that reinforce[d] mainstream values pertaining to employment, education, and a family structure."[17]

The second response is negatively enshrined in the dissolution of the family—once a product of slavery and migration, now a function of unemployment. Wilson observes that the absence of viable jobs decreases the pool of "'marriageable' (that is economically stable) men," thereby increasing the percentage of "out-of-wedlock births and female headed households."[18] Accompanying this economic decline is a mass migration of stable, middle-class families—and along with them, jobs, resources, values, and role models—to the suburbs.

Focusing on culture rather than race, conservatives naturally blame "welfare dependency" for undermining the work ethic that once prevailed in the black ghetto.[19] In Wilson's opinion, however, faith in individual self-help as the panacea for poverty ignores the manner in which cultural attitudes reflect chronic economic deprivation (the cycle of poverty) rooted in years of racial oppression:

Cultural values emerge from specific circumstances and life chances and reflect an individual's position in the class structure. They therefore do not ultimately determine behavior. If ghetto underclass minorities have limited aspirations, a hedonistic orientation toward life, or lack plans for the future, such outlooks ultimately are the result of restricted opportunities and feelings of resignation originating from bitter personal experiences and a bleak future. Thus . . . inner city social dislocations (joblessness, crime, teenage pregnancies, out-of-wedlock births, female-headed families, and welfare dependency) should be analyzed not as cultural aberrations but as symptoms of racial-class inequality. It follows therefore that changes in the economic and social situations of the ghetto underclass will lead to changes in cultural norms and behavior patterns.[20]

Wilson is critical of approaches that blame individuals rather than unjust economic structures for moral failings of a cultural nature.[21] His analysis, however, makes two crucial assumptions: ghetto culture is a kind of societal culture, and (contrary to the views of DuBois and others) African-American cultural affinity is distinct from African-American racial affinity.

My acceptance of Wilson's assumptions by no means indicates my endorsement of his conclusions. Stephen Steinberg and others have rightfully objected to Wilson's tendency to blame the problems of the black ghetto on nonracial factors, such as urban deindustrialization, and to indict the cultural effects of underemployment, rather than persisting white racism, for the failure of blacks to acquire education and employment opportunities. They also have correctly noted that Wilson's own "myth of the black middle class" exaggerates the degree to which middle-class blacks have abandoned the urban ghetto and surmounted obstacles of racism in their working lives.[22] That argument aside, let us accept Wilson's depiction of the black ghetto (however excessively hypernegative it might be). As Wilson describes it, ghetto culture constitutes (in Kymlicka's words) a way of life "extending across a full range of human activities, including social, educational, religious, recreational, and economic life," encompassing both family and community. Like any societal culture, it corresponds to "an intergenerational community, more or less institutionally complete, occupying a given territory or homeland (and) sharing a distinct language and history."

Most important, however, as a societal culture it represents an interlocking nexus of beliefs, attitudes, and practical habits that is involuntarily acquired through experiential conditioning. Contrary to the conservative mantra of self-help, cultural attitudes toward work, consumption, and family planning are not "beliefs" that can be individually isolated, pried off of bodily habits, and simply discarded on a moment's reflection; rather, they are deeply engrained psychological and physical dispositions that require years of economic and social reconditioning in order to be "remade." Restoring community pride and the work ethic to the societal culture of the ghetto thus requires massive economic and social reengineering of the sort recommended by Wilson—job creation, job training, federally funded day care, federally funded child and family support, and so forth.

Perhaps of greater significance than the societal status of ghetto culture is the existence of an intergenerational community necessary for sustaining it. So

far, residential and occupational segregation has made it possible, indeed necessary, for African Americans to live in such intergenerational communities,
but this situation could—and I would argue, should—change. Hence, in an
ideally integrated world, African-American societal culture would probably
disappear, despite the fact that isolated elements of that culture (music, cuisine, and religion) might continue to survive as distinctly African American.

Let us assume that African-American societal culture exists. Should it be
the heart of African-American racial affinity? Ever since DuBois wrote "The
Conservation of Races" (1897), black leaders espousing a pan-Africanist,
Afrocentrist, Black Muslim, or Black Power philosophy have thought so. For
them, the struggle against racism must be community-based, rooted in the
societal culture of that community, and premised on gaining full control
over its economic, political, educational, and religious institutions.

Others, however, would demur. Collapsing African Americans' racial and
ethnic identities makes it seem as if the struggle against racism were identical
to the struggle for multicultural recognition. Because the latter is a struggle
for recognizing cultural differences between groups, this identification would
suggest that the struggle against racism is really nothing more than a struggle on behalf of African Americans to assert their ethnicity as "blacks," perhaps even to the point of supporting the kind of racial segregation defended
by Black Muslims and other advocates of black community sovereignty.

The collapse of race and ethnicity, I believe, is misguided. As I noted in
Chapter 2, racism straddles the line separating two kinds of social injustice:
cultural misrecognition and economic maldistribution. Affirmative strategies
for short-term reform allow one to defend black community sovereignty in
the form of racial redistricting; and part of this defense hinges on the need
to recognize the distinctly institutional nature of African-American societal
culture. However, achieving full justice for African Americans will require
their integration into the economic mainstream, where they will finally receive their fair share of resources. Economic integration, in turn, is virtually
inconceivable apart from residential and occupational integration. Thus, although the affirmation of cultural separateness for African-American communities might be justifiable in the short term, it cannot be reconciled to
the transformation of social and economic institutions in the long run.

In the final analysis, to the extent that race and culture merge in the
African-American community, it is because culture has been shaped by race—
or rather, by racial oppression—which again raises questions about the legitimacy of that culture. For while there is no reason to perpetuate the culture
of poverty, there is every reason to perpetuate the culture of spiritual uplift

(if only there were viable communities that could do so!). This belief, however, does not dispel our initial concern that even the culture of spiritual uplift arises from a disability (socially imposed, to be sure) that renders its legitimacy , like that of ASL, suspect.

*Two Challenges to the Legitimacy of Cultural Groups*

Those who challenge the legitimacy of ASL and African-American cultures do so on two grounds: their failure to exist as fully independent and distinguishable communities; and their origination through a form of external imposition. This section addresses the former charge.

The charge of failing to exist as a fully independent and distinguishable culture has often been leveled against African-American ethnic life. Aside from the familar objection that there are no distinctive cultural attributes shared by all African Americans in a given community, the claim has been made that even if such attributes did exist, they would be marked so thoroughly by the imprint of "white" American culture as to be indistinguishable from it (in other words, it would be impossible to be "authentically" African American in a manner that was not also "authentically" white American). One could go even farther and say that American culture is as much African American as African-American culture is American, so that talk of distinct "white" and "black" American cultures is meaningless.

The same charge can be made of ASL culture in relation to the dominant English-speaking culture: because ASL culture is partly parasitic on written English (its practitioners rely on TV captions and keyboard devices for telephone communication), it is *not* distinguishable from it. But because ASL culture is not distinguishable from English-literate culture, it is virtually impossible to be authentically deaf without also being authentically English-literate. Granting that, it would seem that DEAF advocates should stop criticizing the use of cochlear implants (which are but alternate means of gaining access to English language culture) and stop insisting on the continued preservation of deaf culture as if it were fully independent and distinct.

What are we to make of these objections? To begin with, objections against cultural purity (independence and distinctness) parallel objections against racial purity. Virtually no culture today is an island unto itself, cut off from communication with other cultures. Indeed, anthropologists who once sought to protect the so-called "pristine" cultures of indigenous peoples from outside influences have long since conceded that the very act of "discovery" irreversibly alters them.

But does the fact of cultural mixing undermine the idea of cultural distinctness and autonomy? In order to answer this question, we must distinguish between three sorts of mixing: assimilation, fusion, and contamination. Assimilation occurs when one culture becomes so dependent on another, and so internally informed by it, that it becomes absorbed into it. For example, the forced acculturation of Native American children into Anglo-American culture (in combination with the suppression of their native languages and religious customs) resulted in the absorption of many indigenous cultures into the cultural mainstream. By contrast, when fusion occurs, *both* cultures lose their distinct identities in the course of blending into one another. The fusion of Roman and European cultures thus reconfigured both in the form of new hybrid cultures that we today associate with the Romance languages. Finally, cultures can contaminate one another without losing their identities.

Of the three kinds of cultural mixing, only contamination seems inevitable. Part of the reason why, as paradoxical as this might sound, is that the long-term survival of any culture depends upon it. We can appreciate this situation better once we realize that cultures must adapt to changes in their environment in order to survive. Not all cultures are equally adaptable; oral narratives and rituals, which are dependent upon relatively static modes of existence for their setting, are more vulnerable to the disintegrating effects of migrations, dislocations, and invasions than literary texts. Unlike speech, literature is detachable from the specific context of its authorship; its readership and audience are open-ended. Beause it is so "decontextualized," it can be reinterpreted in different ways by differently situated readers.

The mere passage of time guarantees that the meaning of literary texts will be understood differently (contaminated, if you will, by the expectations of readers whose understanding of the world is very different from the authors').[23] The likelihood of migration, invasion, dislocation, and so on increases the chances of contamination further by allowing readers from alien cultures to reappropriate these texts as well (witness, for instance, the Greco-Roman appropriation of the Hebrew Bible or the Roman-Islamic-European appropriation of Plato's dialogues and Aristotle's writings on metaphysics).

As Alasdair MacIntyre notes, a culture can develop an "identity crisis" when exposed to another that can be successfully managed only by its incorporating aspects of the first culture.[24] In order for incorporation to occur without assimilation or fusion, the cultures in question must communicate with one another. Recalling my discussion of democracy in Chapter 1, communication is truly meaningful only if those communicating have significant differences to discuss, *and* these differences are not so overwhelming as to undermine a common framework of discussion. Speakers speaking out of different cultures will have to learn each other's languages (or some third language), thereby gaining a feel for expressions in the other language that cannot be translated literally into their own. However they manage to communicate, one thing remains certain: each speaker's cultural horizon will have been expanded and transformed by encountering the other, and this transformation will be all the more genuine and mutual to the degree that communication approximates equal and open dialogue.

If the normal state of most cultures is one of cross-cultural contamination, it cannot be held against the distinctness of ASL and African-American cultures that they are intermeshed with and partly dependent on other cultures. At the same time, this dependance on other cultures cannot be held against the "authenticity" of those members of theirs whose cultural credentials—like the English speakers within the deaf community—are not pure and uncontaminated. Thus, although the use of cochlear implants doubtless presents an unprecedented possibility for contamination that will likely lead to assimilation, this risk is no different from that faced by any culture once its members expose themselves to outsiders.

*Culture and Domination: The Racial Ideology of Nationalism*

Perhaps, then, it is expecting too much to demand that liberal governments protect cultural groups from risks of contamination and assimilation that normally arise when their members freely expose themselves to other cultures. But cultural groups also provide the background conditions for personal identity and agency, so protecting individuals' rights to participate in cultural groups will sometimes require protecting the rights of these groups to maintain themselves against the threat of assimilation and fusion. Unfortunately, it is sometimes hard to determine at what point cross-cultural communication ceases to be merely contaminating and becomes assimilation or fusion. Thus, a dilemma arises: dissident members of cultural groups who choose to be contaminated by other cultures are often indistinguishable from outsiders who threaten the independent identity of the group; but threatening the identity of the group is tantamount to threatening its very existence.

I suggested in Chapter 1 that allowing dissident individuals an opportunity to exit the group can often (but not always) solve the dilemma. The dilemma is not so easily resolved, however, when, as in the case of ASL, and perhaps certain fundamentalist religious communities, the very process of acculturation virtually removes any possibility of exit in later life (again, if deaf children have not acquired hearing early on, it is unlikely they will ever successfully assimilate to mainstream society). DEAF advocates respond to this seeming peculiarity of ASL culture by pointing out that it is not really different from how other cultures (such as the Amish) acculturate their members, since acculturation into a traditional form of life without benefit of a full, liberal arts high school education will also limit opportunities for assimilation. Indeed, acculturation in any culture opens up possibilities for understanding and behaving only by closing off other possibilities. If it is then objected that deaf culture arises from an external imposition (a disability), DEAF advocates can again respond, with some justification, that all cultures arise in this manner, at least to some degree.

Like the external imposition of a racial scheme, the external imposition of a culture on unwilling persons renders the culture in question suspect, or illegitimate, unless some extenuating factor can be adduced showing that the culture is *also* internally generated and freely embraced. In fact, the argument could be made that ASL culture—no less than African-American culture—is *in part* internally generated and *in part* freely embraced by its practitioners. Be that as it may, the suspicion remains that these cultures, indeed all cultures, are coercive to some degree.

Why? Because of the coercive nature of acculturation and the way in which this process is structured by relations of power and domination. As noted in the previous chapter, culture is inculcated into children through discipline, training, and with threat of punishment if need be. Norms of speech and behavior are instilled in the body as unconscious habit; beliefs are programmed into the mind as authoritative command and prejudice. Only in later life do children come to possess the critical skills necessary to reflect on and change these habits and prejudices. But change is at best selective and partial, since habits and prejudices once attained function as the necessary background conditions for thinking and acting.

Also coercive is the way in which power and domination shape culture.[25] While domination takes the form of a (more or less deliberate) top-down control of the beliefs and practices of the "governed" by their governors, power is more insidious and anonymous. For example, in a society where some persons are better educated than others, those who are better educated will often take charge of conversations involving the less well educated. In certain situations (e.g., in a political debate at the local PTA meeting), their superior command of the language will enable the better educated to conduct the conversation in the direction they desire, and this will happen regardless of whether they consciously intend it to happen. Hence, despite confronting one another as equals in the formal sense (perhaps each is given the same amount of time to talk), the cultural qualifications of the better educated will permit them to exercise a certain power over their less educated interlocutors.

It is apparent, then, that power relations are built into the very linguistic fabric in which culture is woven. Assuming that these relations unavoidably structure communication and that domination has, up until now, been a fact of social and political life, it is hard not to reach the conclusion that all culture is to some degree externally imposed, coercively inculcated, and constrained by power in ways that vitiate its presumed claim to legitimacy. And that claim is at least partly contingent on the assumption that culture is capable of being accepted freely and with reasoned justification (that is, justification that is free from the constraints of authority, domination, and power).[26]

Be that as it may, I will allow that any culture is legitimate to the extent that it does not discriminate against members of other groups and does not overly hinder its own individual practitioners (men, women, and children) from acquiring capacities to critically revise, reject, and, if need be, exit the culture in question, including any of its prescribed social roles, beliefs, and practices. Significantly, cultures that inculcate uplifting, freedom-enhancing moral values worthy of protection might at the same time inculcate freedom-diminishing gender roles and authoritarian practices that are not so worthy of protection. Unfortunately, it is often difficult (if not impossible) to separate out the former from the latter since values can be interpreted and lived out in various ways. In general, the determination of cultural legitimacy must remain sensitive to the complexity of cultural phenomena; for within any cultural group there are subcultures that gravitate around distinctive beliefs, practices, and gender codes.

### Digression: Nationalism and Racism

I have already discussed the possible illegitimacy of ASL and African-American cultures, but now I would like to examine the legitimacy (or lack thereof) of national cultures. The idea of a national culture seems the closest approximation to what Kymlicka calls a societal culture. Unlike the microcultures of indigenous peoples, whose consolidation predates the kind of modernization associated with European nation-states, societal cultures as Kymlicka describes them seem coterminous with the rise of nineteenth-century nationalism.

Nationalism represented a new attempt by the state to wrest control from feudal principalities. Its driving force was mainly economic: the accumulation of capital and consolidation of markets over as wide a territory as possible. Its guiding ideology, however, was political: the demand for national independence. Struggles for national independence during the nineteenth century, the period that saw the first great wave of nation-building, differed depending on whether they were inspired by the emancipatory ideals of the Enlightenment or the anticolonial aims of racially subjugated peoples. European nationalism was strongly influenced by the rational natural law doctrines informing the former, which emphasized the universal "rights of man" (i.e., of "civilized" white men of European ancestry). Latin American nationalism, by contrast, was mainly inspired by an anticolonial reaction to European monoracial sensibilities, so its appeals to Enlightenment ideals were always made on behalf of a racially and culturally heterogeneous people.[27]

Although European nationalism was strongly influenced by the French Revolution—the paradigm of an emancipatory Enlightenment project—it was also, somewhat paradoxically, motivated by the Romantic, counter-Enlightenment ideals of ethnic and racial particularism (especially in Germany). More specifically, the demand for national sovereignty was premised on the existence of a people united by a common language and culture. National peoples, in turn, provided just the ideological middle term necessary for linking the particular concrete identities of cultural and regional subgroups with an abstract, all-encompassing identity premised on democratic citizenship and respect for universal rights, both of which were indispensable for generating a broad political consensus. Yet initially, such nationalistic preconditions for democratic community did not exist. Germans, for instance, were divided on religion; Italians were divided geographically and culturally; Poles were divided linguistically and ethnically. Virtually all of these "nations" contained subnationalities possessing distinctive dialects and traditions.

Lacking a preexisting people (heterogeneous or homogeneous) on which to base their demands for sovereignty, nationalist ideologues in Europe and Latin America created one. In Germany, for example, the Grimm brothers fashioned a national folk literature; Goethe's writings became the standard for a "high" German culture; and philosophers like Herder, Fichte, and Hegel forged the concept of a distinctive German Spirit. Inspired by cultural idealism and political realism, German historians like Leopold Ranke linked the destiny of the German people to the existence of a German state that would safeguard its geopolitical and cultural integrity. In this manner, diverse

German-speaking communities began to identify themselves as part of an overarching German nation. By the time Bismarck finished consolidating the German Reich in 1870, something like a national affinity united formally antagonistic Catholics and Protestants.

Of course, in order to get persons of widely differing regions, religions, cultures, and dialects to identify with one another, it was necessary that their national affinity be conceived metaphysically, not empirically. The metaphysics that proved most convenient for establishing this affinity was that of race. "Race" in this context did not always refer to phenotypical characteristics necessarily possessed by persons of common descent; more often, it designated moral and cognitive tendencies that most members were presumed to exhibit in varying degrees. As Matthew Arnold put it in *Culture and Anarchy* (1869):

> Science has now made visible to everybody the great and pregnant elements of difference which lie in race, and in how signal a manner they make the genius and history of an Indo-European people vary from those of a Semitic people. Hellinism is of Indo-European growth, Hebraism of Semitic growth; and we English, a nation of Indo-European stock, seem to belong naturally to the movement of Hellinism.[28]

Arnold here invokes "race" (or blood descent) to explain the cultural differences between the English and the Jews. But Arnold's racialism is not racism, for he goes on to observe that the "strength and prominence of the moral fiber" that makes the English "so great a power" stems from their inheriting the "genius and history of the Hebrew people"—an inheritance, to be sure, that has been passed down through culture, not blood. For Arnold, this cultural mixing does not disprove the importance of race in determining cultural tendencies; it merely qualifies it.

Arnold was not a racist; indeed, he clearly esteems the moral genius of the Semitic "race." Other nationalists, however, were of a different mind. Why? A cursory glance at German nationalism suggests an obvious explanation. The German "nation" was an imperfect union, an ideological fiction invented to mask over real cultural differences between Catholics and Protestants. Irredentist (nationalistic) German-speaking communities in Poland and the Austro-Hungarian empire were not included in it, a fact that would later be construed as justification for Germany's expansionist policies entering World War II. Within Germany, however, there were groups—most notably Jews—whose German identity was suspect.

Simply put, Jews lacked the Indo-European (Aryan) descent demanded
by German nationalism. Having been historically vilified by German
Catholics and Lutherans as the people who murdered Jesus, they provided
just the scapegoat nationalists needed to close ranks among German Christians of all stripes.

The same racial (and racist) pattern of anti-Semitism repeated itself
throughout Europe wherever nationalist ideologies took hold: Jews and
Gypsies were vilified as inferior and alien races. The link between nationalism, racialism, and racism also played a pivital role in the consolidation of the
United States. Although the United States was expressly founded on the
principles of universal freedom and equality for all human beings, its conception of citizenship—which involved liquidating, enslaving, or excluding
all those who were not of European descent—was not. Thus, what appears
to unite American nationalists with their Latin American counterparts—the
un-European idea of the nation as a melting pot—was interpreted by the
former in a decidedly European manner so as to exclude the latter.

National identities, like the racial (and racist) identities that supposedly legitimated them, were thus born of exclusion and were externally imposed on
peoples of widely differing cultural affinities. Yet their logic forbade any inclusion of difference, which is why the very notion of a multinational state
seems absurd; hence the need for nationalists to successively dominate, suppress, and then liquidate Jews, Gypsies, and other "alien" subnationalities
within their territories. The fascist movements that came to prominence in
Italy, Germany, and Spain in the twenties and thirties (and which found avid
supporters throughout Europe, Japan, and the United States) culminated
this logical succession. Unfortunately, as evidence of "ethnic cleansing" in
Bosnia-Herzegovina and mass genocide in Rwanda amply testifies, such
movements did not exhaust the deadly potential of nationalist ardor.

Can we retrieve a legitimate, nonracist concept of nationalism in the same
way we retrieved a legitimate, nonracist concept of racial affinity? That all
depends. Of course, defensive nationalist movements that are not premised
on feelings of national superiority can function legitimately to combat colonialism, imperialism, and other forms of unjust external intervention. Just as
those who have been racially oppressed ought to unite as a race to combat
racism, so those who have been regionally marginalized and culturally oppressed ought, at least sometimes, to unite as a nation (or democratic community) to combat nationalism (of the predatory kind). We certainly can
envisage patriotic loyalties that make no appeal to national affinities. Citizens of multiracial, multiethnic, and multicultural democracies like the

United States and Canada might well end up identifying with one another as mere citizens, or copartners, of a fair and mutually beneficial venture.

But patriotic loyalty to a regional community of mutually interdependent individuals, even when governed by liberal democratic procedures, is not always legitimate. When liberal democracies seek to dominate weaker regimes for economic and political gain, professing loyalty to the state, which includes a willingness to advance its narrow interest, is clearly illegitimate. Moderate (legitimate) expressions of patriotism, like moderate (legitimate) expressions of racial identification, are generally premised on a collective experience of oppression, which suggests that such legitimate expressions of patriotism coincide with a defensive nationalism of the sort mentioned earlier.[29] Be that as it may, a "nationalism" or patriotism expressing nothing more than loyalty to procedures of liberal democracy—in complete abstraction from any sense of attachment to a geographical community of interdependent individuals—would be a contradiction in terms. Because the basis for identifying with these procedures is so abstract and universal, there is no reason (short of maintaining internal security) for excluding anyone from enjoying them. (Indeed, since Kant, it has been the hope of many liberals that such a community of abstract rights bearers, once established, could logically evolve into a global state, or a federation of states, under the unitary rule of constitutional law.)[30]

However, it is far from clear whether such an arrangement would adequately safeguard the regional democratic sovereignty of particular political communities. Furthermore, as we shall see in Chapter 6, even if there are universal moral constraints on the manner in which communities exercise their national sovereignty (including with respect to would-be immigrants and noncitizens), there may well be some communitarian arguments that favor a plurality of quasi-autonomous nations. Hence, we may tentatively conclude that whatever international economic and political institutions evolve in response to globalization, they will have to permit some form of national identification commensurate with the legitimate desire of regional communities to govern substantial portions of their lives without undue outside interference.

These ruminations will be addressed further in Chapters 5 and 11, where I shall argue that the classical liberal model of the state developed by Mill and advocated more recently by neoliberal developmentalists as a universal paradigm for nation-building in Third World countries is neither culturally nor economically well-suited for this purpose. Suffice it to say, under the reign of liberal constitutionalism nationalism would cease to be a principle for organizing states. Of course, citizens inhabiting such states might retain distinctive national identifications, but such identifications would no longer exist in the divisive, racist manner prescribed by nationalism. For persons whose primary loyalties were to liberal humanism, national identifications would be treated like mere cultural (ethnic) affinities. For those whose primary loyalties were to some incorporated subnation (as in the case of Native Americans and First Nation Peoples inhabiting the United States and Canada), national identifications would likewise be treated as ethnic affinities—but affinities nonetheless linked, as I will explore in the next chapter, to legitimate demands for partial, territorial sovereignty.

In summary, I have argued that cultural groups worthy of being accorded group rights must satisfy the following conditions. First, they must be clearly distinguishable from other groups. Second, they must not discriminate against members of their own group unless doing so respects vital rights and is compatible with exit opportunities that enable dissidents to enjoy their rights fully and without hindrance outside the group. Third, they must not discriminate against members of other groups. Fourth, they must be in need of special governmental protection against predatory threats posed by other groups. Fifth, they must coalesce around affinities that are at least internally generated and maintained (if also externally imposed). Finally, they must allow each of their constituent members to develop the capacity to reflect upon, revise, and even reject the social roles, beliefs, and practices around which these affinities gravitate. As long as children who are socialized into deaf culture suffer a form of deafness that could have been corrected by their deaf parents had they wanted to, we cannot say that that culture satisfies the second or last conditions. The same goes for authoritarian and patriarchal religious groups that diminish the rights of women and stunt the moral development of children, neither of whom have viable opportunities of exiting their families and communities.

# PART III.
# NATIONAL SOVEREIGNTY
# AND THE RIGHTS OF MEMBERSHIP

# 5

## LIBERALISM AND THE RIGHT OF
## INDIGENOUS PEOPLES TO SELF-GOVERNANCE

Members of indigenous nations sometimes identify themselves as belonging to a "race" distinct from that of "white" people. They do so not because they wish to buttress their demands for national self-determination with specious claims about their biological uniqueness, but in order to affirm their participation in a societal culture that they think is incompatible with modern values.[1] For example, writing about her own Mayan culture, Guatemalan Nobel Prize winner Rigoberta Menchú observes that governments "have tried to take our things away and impose others on us, be it through religion, through dividing up the land, through schools, through books, through radio, through all things modern."[2]

When Menchú was dictating these comments to Elisabeth Burgos-Debray in 1982, Guatemala was embroiled in a cruel civil war between the miltary government and a guerrilla movement that represented students, workers, and indigenous peoples (who compose 85 percent of the population). Several of her younger brothers had already died of malnutrition and pesticide poisoning, and her father, mother, and younger brother had been murdered or tortured to death by the military.[3] However, her criticism of "imposing" modern ways on indigenous people extends beyond her criticism of the Guatemalan government's reign of terror and addresses philosophical concerns.

For example, Menchú observes that among the "modern" ideas the Guatemalan government tried to impose on her people was the idea of "capitalism and getting on in life."[4] Mayan culture, she repeatedly emphasizes, places the community ahead of the individual: "Each child is taught to live like the fellow members of his community."[5] Before marrying, young couples vow to "reproduce the earth and the traditions of the ancestors," defending "the rights of our ancestors to the last." After taking this vow, they "ask forgiveness for any occasion on which they may have abused traditions" and "offended the laws of the natural kingdom." Finally, they swear to "be true to their race," with their parents responding that "generations and generations will pass but we will always be Indians."[6]

Menchú, who describes herself as an "Indianist," defends these communal traditions. Indeed, she asserts that "middle class Indians who have abandoned their traditions" are no longer considered Indians; and she rejects family planning "as an insult to our culture."[7] Yet on closer inspection of her autobiography, it becomes plain that she accepts a great deal of the "white man's" modern ways, even to the point of rejecting some Mayan customs. For instance, as a teenager she herself became a catechist working on behalf of "Catholic Action"—a concession to "modern" European civilization that seemed perfectly acceptable to her given that "there was already the mixture of our culture with the Catholic religion."[8] More important, she rejected traditional Mayan gender roles by becoming an educated and well-traveled political organizer. In fact, Menchú criticizes the traditional, paternalistic sheltering of girls and the male domination of women, or machismo (which, however, she thinks would only be worsened if women formed their own separate liberation movement).[9]

Menchú's autobiography was an important catalyst in generating support for the *Agreement Concerning the Identity and Rights of the Indigenous Peoples* that was signed by representatives of the Guatemalan government and the URNG guerrilla movement on March 31, 1995. This document is important because it allows Guatemala's indigenous people to govern their internal affairs so long as they respect "fundamental rights defined by the national judicial system [and] internationally recognized human rights."[10]

The "fundamental" and "internally recognized human rights" refer to those universal rights that all individuals are presumed to possess as rational human beings. As such, they are the rights that liberalism esteems. However, they are also the rights that first came to prominence with the advent of modern Enlightenment culture, which Menchú tells us is incompatible with indigenous culture.

Thus, the agreement to protect the *premodern* "identity" and "culture" of Guatemala's indigenous people through the legal mechanism of *modern* rights exhibits the same tension that was presented earlier when talking about the Kiryas Joel Hasidim. These rights are preeminently rights of individuals; they protect the freedom of the individual against interference from both the state *and* the broader community to which he or she belongs. But the cultural "identity" of indigenous people reverses this priority: it places the preservation of the community above the freedom of the individual.

The agreement, then, protects two freedoms: individual (human) rights and group-preserving rights. As I have already discussed, these rights sometimes collide with one another. Here the possibility for collision increases, however, because the groups in question are indigenous peoples whose communal culture is ill-suited to modern individualism.

The agreement thus reflects the same tension between modern and indigenous ways that informs Menchú's own self-understanding. Only if we assume that European ideas already contaminate indigenous culture does the tension lessen. I noted that Menchú herself believes this to be the case, at least partly. But what about the agreement?

On the one hand, it takes note of the capacity of the Maya to "resist assimilation" in matters of descent, language, cosmological worldview, collective memory, culture (art, ethics, and science), and self-identification.[11] This premise suggests that Mayan culture is worlds apart from the dominant European culture and its conception of rights. Indeed, the agreement reinforces this impression by emphasizing the distinctness and independence of indigenous cultures as reflected, for example, in their traditional (cooperative, collective, and communal) cultivation of land—a linkage of community, nature, and religious practice that, according to the agreement, must not be subject to modern capitalist privatization and exploitation.[12]

On the other hand, the agreement asserts that "indigenous cultures constitute an active and dynamic factor in the development and progress of Guatemalan society."[13] The dynamic nature of indigenous cultures as something less than independent, distinct, and "self-identified" finds penultimate expression in the very terms of the agreement, which seeks to progressively integrate indigenous communities into a modern judicial system based on individual rights.[14]

Is the accord inconsistent in maintaining both the "self-identified" and "dynamic" nature of indigenous cultures? Can traditional communitarianism accomodate modern individualism? In short, must a liberal theory of rights always privilege individual freedom over group preservation?

*How Liberalism Came to Privilege Individual Rights: A Brief History*

Let me begin by answering this last question. As I noted in Chapter 1, liberalism originated as a defense of individual freedom. However, as early as Locke's *Letter Concerning Toleration* we note a parallel concern: the protection of

groups (specifically religious groups) against governmental and societal interference. Indeed, the need to accord groups rights of protection comparable to those extended to individuals follows from the need to protect
individuals in their rights to associate and to practice their religion freely.
The protection of groups against outside interference, however, sometimes
conflicts with the rights of dissident members to remain in them, at least insofar as their dissenting behavior interferes with the freedom of association
and religion of the majority. So, although group rights are derivative of
more basic individual rights, their enforcement sometimes requires restricting individual rights—all for the sake of protecting the individual rights of
the majority.

By the nineteenth century, liberals confronting nationalism and imperialism were compelled to acknowledge the inherent tension between individual and group rights. Not only did they have to devise new arrangements for
securing mutual tolerance (or peaceful coexistence) between national and
religious subgroups, but they also had to show how majoritarian democracy—the penultimate expression of national sovereignty—could be reconciled with protection of minorities.

Using a scheme suggested by Michael Walzer, we can identify at least five
regimes of mutual tolerance that liberals sought to defend.[15] Aside from defending mutual tolerance between sovereign states in the *international society,* they also defended mutual tolerance between semisovereign nations that
had been legally incorporated into *empires,* which often entailed granting
subnationalities considerable freedom to govern their own territories. Doing
so, however, involved allowing these groups to tyrannize dissident individuals and subminorities.

The breakup of the Austro-Hungarian and Ottoman empires following
World War I gave rise to two other defenses of liberal tolerance, neither of
which was much more successful in protecting individuals against majoritarian tyranny. The first revolved around the older concept of the *nation-state.*
As I noted in Chapter 4, the nationalism fueling the formation of European
states was largely intolerant of subnationalities—indeed, much less tolerant
of them than the more cosmopolitan multinationalism undergirding the empires these nation-states replaced. However, since all European nation-states
contained subnationalities, states with liberal democratic constitutions had
to devise ways for tolerating them. Here—unlike multinational empires—
mutual toleration never involved granting subnationalities territorial sovereignty. At best, it permitted them some degree of self-administration and
official use of their languages.

In short, instead of regarding subnationalities as legally recognized corporate entities with special rights, liberal nation-states treated them as "voluntary" and "private" associations whose individual members were primarily regarded as citizens of the nation. Significantly, this approach meant that, in principle at least, nation-states were committed to being more tolerant toward—and more vigilant in defending—the rights of individual dissidents within these associations than were the old multinational empires. In practice, however, this was seldom the case, since individual dissidents within minority groups (such as assimilated German Jews) were still often treated as second-class citizens.

Another kind of mutual tolerance that emerged after the collapse of the old multinational empires revolved around *consocial (bi- or trinational)* states. Consocial states, which have in fact existed for centuries (witness the case of Switzerland), are premised on "the constitutionally limited dominance of one party or on their rough equality. Offices are divided, quotas established for civil service, and public funds allocated—all on the basis of this limited dominance or rough equality."[16] Consocial states, then, are like the old empires—minus the transcendent, impartial rule of third-party bureaucrats. Because the remnants of racialized nationalism (coupled with demographic shifts and other destablizing factors that upset the balance of power) continually threaten their union, consocial states like today's Bosnian federation of Croats, Muslims, and Serbs are much more fragile than nation-states. These subnationalities tolerate one another not out of mutual respect, but out of mutual fear of being incorporated into some larger, more powerful neighbor.

Like multinational empires, consocial states protect the rights of subnationalities often at the expense of violating the rights of dissident individuals and subminorities. The fifth type of mutual tolerance, *immigrant societies,* reverses this priority, providing what is arguably the greatest protection of individual freedom. Here members of different groups and subnationalities are transplanted from their native territory, dispersed across their adopted homeland, and (unlike colonists) oriented toward assimilating with the dominant culture. To the extent that national loyalties are retained at all (as illustrated by hyphenated ethnic monikers like Italian-American), they function merely as one among many possible associations that individuals can more or less freely choose.

The reader will note that, of all the regimes of tolerance defended by liberals since the nineteenth century, only one of them—immigrant society—offers good prospects for consistently defending individual freedom against competing demands for group preservation; and among immigrant societies (most notably Canada, Australia, and the United States), this defense often ceded pride of place to racist discrimination and segregation. This being the case, how did liberal theorists come to privilege the rights of individuals above the rights of groups?

They did through a most improbable succession of events. By the nineteenth century, liberals were already substituting the regime of assimilation for the regime of toleration, *and* they were doing so, paradoxically, on the grounds of racial and cultural superiority. Simply stated, liberals like John Stuart Mill believed that the culture of individualism and economic liberty were the principal engines of progress; hence, they believed that its global imposition on backward (i.e., communal and conformist) societies would bring about the greatest happiness for all. As Mill succinctly put it: "experience proves it is possible for one nationality to merge and be absorbed in another: and when it was originally an inferior and more backward portion of the human race the absorption is greatly to its advantage."[17] Disseminating the individualistic spirit of modern European liberalism would add another benefit as well: the imposition of a universal language of individual rights would make democracy possible by suppressing (instead of tolerating) divisive linguistic and cultural differences. Again, to cite Mill: "Among a people without fellow-feelings, especially if they read and speak different languages, the united public opinion necessary to the workings of representative institutions cannot exist."[18]

Mill's chauvinistic defense of individual rights met strong opposition from liberal pragmatists who preferred to keep their colonial subjects happy by tolerating their inferior ways. As Kymlicka notes, the supremacy of individual rights within liberal thinking would coincide with the decline of the British Empire coupled with the rise of the Cold War and the prominence of the American civil rights movement.

First, the concept of group-specific rights fell out of favor. The League of Nations' protection scheme for national minorities that was adopted at the conclusion of World War I later presented Germany with a pretext for militarily reincorporating territories occupied by irredentist (unassimilable) German nationals living in Czechoslovakia and Poland, a "protection" of national minorities that precipitated both a world war and a holocaust.

Second, the propaganda war fought between the Allies and the Axis powers during World War II required that both sides close ranks behind antagonistic ideologies: in contradistinction to the fascist collectivism espoused by the Axis powers, the United States and its allies portrayed themselves—

disingenuously, to be sure—as stolid defenders of individuals of all races, religions, and nationalities. This portrayal would change little during the Cold War that followed; indeed, if anything, it would force the United States to confront its own form of racial group segregation and discrimination. The civil rights movement that followed in the wake of this confrontation was universally understood as a struggle for national integration, that is, as a struggle to extend universal human rights to blacks as individuals rather than as members of a despised race. Since the movement made no distinction between racial and national minorities, its equation of emancipation with integration effectively precluded any defense of group-specific rights. Thanks to the unprecedented global prestige and power possessed by the United States as the leader of the "free world," the civil rights movement, and its equation of emancipation with assimilation, became *the* model for thinking about minority rights everywhere.

Since the seventies, however, liberals in the United States and Canada have been confronted with a number of recalcitrant minorities—from Puerto Rican nationalists to Native Americans, Old Order Amish, and French Canadians—who strongly reject the equation of emancipation with assimilation. Not only has assimilation failed them, but it also has deprived them of the one legal device they think *will* emancipate them: the right to defend themselves as distinct communities against the cultural imperialism of the majority.

### *Liberal Rights and Alternative Forms of Modern Law*

My discussion of actual constitutional practice suggests that historical contingency, rather than theoretical necessity, explains liberalism's recent privileging of individual freedom over group toleration. If so, liberal constitutions can (and, as I have argued, must) accommodate group rights.

But my discussion of Guatemala's constitutional protection of indigenous culture raised an additional concern: the compatibility of that culture with modern individual rights. Charles Taylor has recently argued that not all modern polities need rights to regulate their members' behavior.[19] Such polities *do* need to adopt some norms specifying tolerance, freedom of association, and so on, but they need not interpret them as the inalienable rights of culturally deracinated and societally disencumbered "atomistic individuals." Instead, they can interpret them as social obligations that persons owe first and foremost to their communities.

Indigenous peoples like the Maya seem to prefer this interpretation; so too do modern Asian countries such as Indonesia, Malaysia, Thailand, and other signatories to the Bangkok Declaration. Unlike the Maya, however, these societies have integrated themselves into the global market economy and its individualistic conventions regarding contract and property. Hence, even if these countries seem illiberal to us because they have not thought it necessary to incorporate a full schedule of civil liberties and political rights in their constitutions, they are arguably more liberal (in their embrace of capitalism and private property) than the Maya.

Groups like the Maya, who must defend themselves by means of weapons provided by modern constitutional law, thus find themselves in something of a quandary. They can reject some of liberalism's strong defense of individual freedom—for instance, the freedom to enter into contracts and acquire property with minimal government hindrance—but they cannot reject all of it. More precisely, they cannot reject the civil terms of the social contract into which they have entered, which guarantees individual Mayans the right to freely assemble, speak out, and practice the faith of their choice. But Mayans who have chosen to exercise this right—for instance, by converting to Evangelical Protestantism—have sometimes been attacked by other members of the Mayan community.

At this point, a liberal critic of the Mayan right to cultural self-determination might be tempted to say the following: It only seems as if there were a conflict between modern liberal individualism and premodern Mayan communalism. But there is not, because liberal individualism is not a contingent artifact of one historical epoch (the modern). Rather, it is an uncontestable fact about the human condition—the condition, in short, of having to communicate with one another as individuals whose distinct contributions merit equal consideration. Hence, as the good liberals they ought to be, Mayans should tolerate dissenting Evangelical brothers and sisters.

The argument—that persons must respect one another's rights as comembers of a community of communication oriented toward uncoerced agreement—might well be valid, as I argued in Chapter 1, despite the fact that so few have grasped its force (hence, the refusal to allow women, children, colonial subjects, slaves, and all other supposedly "subrational" persons the right to speak out and be heard). But supposing that the argument were sound, would it justify the claim that liberal individualism is a timeless truth about human nature? Unfortunately, a metaphysical fact about the universal necessity of respectfully speaking and listening to one another is just too general and imprecise a thing on which to base a particular doctrine of rights.

Perhaps extensive cross-cultural communication will some day bring it about that people everywhere will come to think of themselves as individuals in the liberal sense. But it will not eliminate all relativity and contingency, for persons who identify themselves as individuals in this sense still disagree about the precise meaning and scope of their rights.

In sum, even if the liberal theory of rights were demonstrably true (or instantiated the endpoint of moral evolution), many devout persons would still reject it in favor of more communitarian value systems; and those who did not would doubtless disagree about its proper meaning and application. For this reason, one must deploy the theory with caution in defending the rights of indigenous peoples whose way of life depends on strong communal attachments.

### *Two Ways of Tolerating Cultural Minorities: Sovereignty and Accommodation*

Now that we understand the tension animating liberalism's historic attempt to reconcile group toleration with individual liberty, let us examine more closely what liberals mean by "toleration": Sometimes toleration means bestowing rights of self-governance on territorial subnationalities; elsewhere it means merely accommodating the cultural practices of religious and ethnic minorities.

I noted earlier that societal cultures—which are frequently but not invariably associated with territorial nationalities—must be distinguished from diffusely scattered subcultures gravitating around religion, sexual preference, race, and disability. Toleration of societal cultures often requires granting their practitioners sovereign control over matters of education, communication, government, religion, and economic life that fall within their territorial jurisdictions. By contrast, toleration of subcultures typically requires guaranteeing their practitioners the same individual civil liberties accorded to everyone else.

Most gays and lesbians, for example, restrict their multicultural demands to just those rights enjoyed by all citizens: the right to practice consensual sex in the privacy of their homes without governmental intrusion and the right to be free from sexual harassment and job discrimination.[20] Some gays and lesbians go farther in demanding that schools teach tolerance of the gay lifestyle as a part of their standard curriculum. In cities like San Francisco, where they constitute a sizable minority, gays have also won the right to be represented on governing bodies, zoning committees, and medical boards that rule on matters directly affecting their interests.

Ethnic immigrants often seek much less than this; having voluntarily up-rooted themselves from their native societal culture, they want nothing more than to be accepted into their new society as equals. Immigrants usually do not settle in areas in sufficiently concentrated numbers where they might be able to exercise limited sovereignty.[21] Integration is therefore the only way they can protect themselves. However, when they *do* lobby for special treatment, it is usually to compensate for linguistic handicaps that prevent assimilation. Thus, many ethnic immigrants support bilingual education for their children, not because they want their children to retain their native culture, but because they want them to do well in school (despite their inadequate mastery of English).[22]

As distinct from oppressed subcultures and immigrants, religious minorities practicing a traditional way of life often resist assimilation. This resistance can lead them to request special accommodations, such as exemptions from workdays that fall on their religious holidays and from dress codes that violate their religious customs. In more extreme cases, as in the Kiryas Joel public school district, accommodation can include provisions for limited territorial self-governance.

Like religious sects, racial minorities straddle the line separating subcultures from societal cultures—hence, the complexity of their demands, which range from assimilation and accommodation to self-governance. For example, almost all African Americans strongly support civil rights and full integration. Many of them also support special accommodations devised for them by the government (such as affirmative action). One of these accommodations, race-conscious redistricting, also seems to provide African-American communities with more self-governance than they otherwise would have.

It is worth noting that granting African Americans their own sovereign territory in the South once seemed as compelling as granting Native Americans title to their ancestral lands: both groups were forceably concentrated into a territory of the United States. But here the similarity ends. Unlike African Americans, Native Americans had always been recognized by treaty as constituting *quasi*-sovereign peoples. Furthermore, although Native Americans were eventually uprooted from their native territories, they (unlike African Americans) retained a sense of their native language and religion.

Yet, in another sense, the situation of African Americans more closely resembles that of Native Americans than of immigrants. Both Native Americans and African Americans were conquered peoples, and both were segregated from the mainstream—voluntarily, in the case of Native Americans, forceably in the case of African Americans. Thus, given current patterns of residential segregation, it is not surprising to hear black nationalists talking once again about wresting control of their communities from white-dominated municipal, state, and federal governments.

### Why the Distinction Between Societal Cultures and Subcultures Is Important

The case of African Americans and religious sects suggests that the distinction between societal cultures and subcultures is at best relative. Guest workers, illegal immigrants, political refugees, and former colonizers, just to name a few examples, straddle the distinction. None of these groups is permitted to assimilate, and none is accommodated or allowed to govern itself.

The distinction between rights of accommodation and rights of self-governance is also not clear, nor does it map neatly onto the distinction between societal cultures and subcultures. Practitioners of African-American and deaf subcultures often seek, in addition to special accommodations, control over their communities. The converse holds true for indigenous people, who are granted self-governance in compensation for the expropriation of their native land. Because the right to self-governance only partly compensates for their loss, indigenous people remain dependent on the state for special economic assistance, medical care, and education.

Why should we retain the societal culture/subculture and self-governance /accommodation distinctions if they are so vague? Kymlicka, for one, insists that they help us to understand what is wrong about simplistic objections to multicultural rights. These objections tend to view multicultural rights as falling on only one side of the sovereignty/accommodation spectrum: as segregating groups from one another instead of assimilating them into the mainstream.

It is easy to refute these objections once we see that different cultural groups merit different rights to accommodation (or self-governance)—and for different reasons. Indeed, many groups often seek protection by combining distinct categories of rights, thereby suggesting that their reasons for seeking protection are not motivated simply by a desire for segregation or assimilation but by a more complex need for self-determination or cultural preservation. The complex demand for self-governance and cultural preservation advanced by many indigenous peoples seems to fit this description. This demand typically seeks accommodation within a larger national economy when it is advanced as a claim for federal assistance. The demand, which is conditional with respect to the availability of government resources, is put foward as a matter of forcing the government to comply with its trustee obligations and also as a matter of procuring the equal protection of Native Americans as citizens, similar in this regard to the Satmar community's demand for a special public school district. By contrast, the demand for self-governance—distinguishable in principle from the demand for total sovereignty or isolation (segregation)—has different justifications, some of which, being grounded in historical title and treaty, are relatively unconditional.

Of course, no mere historical title suffices to legitimate an unconditional claim to self-governance, or to any other group right for that matter. Even Kymlicka concedes that indigenous peoples, annexed nationalities, and original colonial settlers (such as the Dutch Afrikaners in South Africa) have legitimate claims to self-governance within the liberal, multinational societies into which they have been incorporated only if they do not seek to dominate other groups (as the Afrikaners did with respect to the African majority) and do not unjustly discriminate against members of their own group (as the Pueblan tribe in the United States has done with respect to women, children, and evangelical dissidents). This qualification aside, however, the argument that the aims, motivations, and justificatory grounds underlying many and perhaps most demands for multicultural rights are irreducible to simple considerations of accommodation or sovereignty, historical entitlement or independent moral justification, still stands as an adequate response to those who find such rights to be an unequivocal pretext for succession or separation.

### Legal, Psychological, and Political Dilemmas of Multiple Citizenship

In the remainder of this chapter, I will focus specifically on the right of subnationalities to self-governance. This right, as we shall now see, requires that subnationals view themselves as citizens of two or more distinct polities.

In a recent essay on national identity in Canada, Joseph Carens distinguishes legal, psychological, and political dilemmas facing the project of multiple citizenship.[23] In federal states such as the United States and Canada—and increasingly in federations of states such as the European Community—citizens belong to more than one political community. For example, in Canada and the United States citizens are subject to both federal governments and provincial (or state) governments. In addition to these governments, indigenous people inhabiting tribal lands are also subject to tribal governments.

The legal problem of multiple citizenship as it bears on indigenous peoples and other subnationalities is closely connected to the psychological problem of identification and the political problem of representation. Unless subnationalities positively identify with the state in which they are incorporated, there is no reason for them to respect its jurisdiction over their lives—short of economic necessity and fear of military intervention.

The much-discussed example of Canada's long quest to pacify Quebec poignantly illustrates this problem. Recent public opinion surveys show that francophone Quebecers tend to think of themselves as citizens of Quebec first and as citizens of Canada second, despite the fact that in 1982 Canada adopted a Charter of Rights and Freedoms that included provisions for group rights specifically designed with Quebec in mind.

The situation with indigenous Canadians (or First Nation people) is perhaps even more dire, because the cultural differences between them and the rest of Canada are much more acute than the differences between francophone Quebecers and the anglophone population. For example, their support for the Charter of Rights and Freedoms is considerably weaker than the support shown by francophone Quebecers. This reticence is not because they want to deny these rights to other groups; rather, they question the appropriateness of the theoretical and practical framework in which such rights are embedded. Specifically, many of them feel that the theoretical framework of liberal individualism, majoritarian democracy, and judicial review downplays communal obligations and consensual tribal self-determination. Furthermore, on a practical level they know that the Charter of Rights and Freedoms will be "interpreted and applied by particular people (not, need it be said, aboriginal people for the most part), people selected and trained in certain ways (and not others), people attuned to certain considerations (and not others), people taught to regard certain forms of communication (and not others) as intellectually respectable and relevant."[24]

Concern over theoretical and practical bias is the chief reason why the Assembly of First Nations opposes the Charter of Rights and Freedoms. Other aboriginal people, of course, disagree. The Metis (or urbanized aborigines) endorse it subject to emendation by their own charter; the Inuit Tapirisat seem willing to do so contingent on their being able to protect their language and culture through an override provision; some aboriginal women view it as a bulwark against male-dominated Indian leadership. However, even in these instances support for the charter is acknowledged as a "regrettable necessity" in light of the economic and political dependency of indigenous peoples on provincial and federal governments.

This discussion brings us to the third dilemma facing multiple citizenship: the political. In order for indigenous peoples to identify more positively with both provincial and federal governments, they will have to secure better political representation in provincial and federal legislatures and courts, which might require any one of the following:

- increasing indigenous political representation in numbers greater than their percentage of the population;
- acknowledging the legitimacy of nonelected indigenous leaders as spokespersons to be consulted by provincial and federal governments; and
- extending veto privileges to indigenous representatives (or requiring potentially detrimental legislation to be ratified by supermajorities).

Most important, as I argued in Chapter 1, securing better political representation for indigenous people might require altering the terms of political discourse so that concepts of justice, rights, and democracy are open to cross-cultural definition. In return for these additional rights, aboriginal groups might reasonably be expected to surrender some of their right to decide on matters that primarily affect the rest of the nation.

## Aboriginal Peoples and Their Rights

On April 1, 1999, some of Canada's First Nation people took a major step toward realizing the aforementioned aims. Fifty years after luring them from their igloos with promises of warm housing, medical care, and schooling for their children, Canada officially inaugurated a new era for its Inuit people by convening the nineteen-member legislature of its newly created sovereign territory of Nunavut ("our land" in the Inuktitut language), located in the eastern half of Canada's Northwest Territories, which occupies about 20 percent of Canada's total landmass and comprises 27,000 of its inhabitants. The new territory enables the Inuit to preserve their traditional culture while creating a modern economy. A $650 million trust fund and 135,000 square miles of potentially mineral-rich land will be administered by a federal agency in conjunction with the territorial government. More important, the Nunavut legislature and judiciary reflect an interesting fusion of liberal and traditional culture: the legislature revolves around consensus (there are no political parties), while the judiciary interprets Western legal precepts from an anticolonial standpoint that is sensitive to the traditional communitarian aspects of Inuit culture.

So begins postdiscovery North America's boldest experiment in realizing the demands for self-governance pressed by its indigenous peoples. In order to understand the urgency of this claim, we must first appreciate the way in which their cultural life is intrinsically related to habitation on ancestral lands. Next, these claims must be situated within the overall history of legal treaties concluded between them and the states into which they were forceably incorporated.[25]

The history of legal treaties with indigenous peoples in the Americas began in the early sixteenth century. They were partly provoked by the moral concerns of sympathetic white people, like Bartolome de las Casas (a former adventurer in the service of Columbus), who were shocked and dismayed by the systematic slavery, torture, and killing inflicted on Native Americans by Spanish settlers. Bartolome's treatise, *A Brief Account of the Destruction of the Indies* (1542), inspired the development of the papal regulation known as the doctrine of discovery, which recognized native peoples as sovereign nations whose territories could not be transferred to European powers without their consent.

The idea that Native Americans were full-fledged "owners" of their land was never clearly established, since the discovery doctrine only entitled them to transfer it to the European Crown that first "discovered" them. Furthermore, like most well-intentioned treaties, it was more often honored in the breach; but these infelicities would seem minor in light of what was to come.

By the seventeenth century, the English Crown had determined that Native Americans did not own their land. What entitled them to make this stupendous presumption was a curious addendum in English common law (the so-called Norman Yoke doctrine) that made land ownership dependent on cultivation. Henceforth, all "wilderness" lands—including those used by indigenous people for hunting and gathering—were to be regarded as unclaimed and available for expropriation by the first cultivators (or in Locke's judgment, the "industrious" peoples of European stock).[26]

It goes without saying that the Norman Yoke doctrine instigated a period of brutal warfare between English settlers and Native Americans. Things got a little better when, in the eighteenth century, Native Americans found themselves caught in the middle of a war between the French and English, both of whom solicited their support in exchange for guns and provisions—and, of course, recognition of Indian territorial claims. After winning the war, King George II of England sought to end all confrontations with indigenous nations by issuing the Proclamation of 1763, which suspended further settlements west of the line running along the Allegheny/Appalachian ridge.

The peace established by the English could not last. The Proclamation of 1763 angered soon-to-be revolutionaries, many of whom by then possessed titles to land west of the line. In fact, Washington's Continental Army issued more of these titles to its poor recruits. Fortunately for Native Americans living west of the line, the new postrevolutionary government of the United States was too strapped for cash to settle these claims. Desperately seeking peace and recognition from European powers as a legitimate sovereign power, the fledgling government entered into treaties with indigenous peoples under the same provisions as those accepted by European states. These provisions still recognized indigenous peoples as sovereign powers whose land and property (in the wording of the Northwest Ordinance of 1789) "shall never be taken from them without their consent" and whose "property, rights, and liberty . . . shall never be disturbed."[27]

Peace prevailed until 1810, when pressure on the federal government to fulfill its earlier promise of land grants west of the Allegheny/Appalachian ridge required entering into treaties with Native Americans. Thus began a history of duplicity whose trail of broken treaties would continue down to the present day. The first broken treaties were legally sanctioned in a number of opinions rendered by Chief Justice John Marshall (himself a claimant to land occupied by Native Americans) from 1810 to 1830. In effect, these opinions overturned the assumption that had governed international convention (and U.S. and European policy) for almost three hundred years, namely, that indigenous people were independent, sovereign nations—legal equals, as it were—whose land could not be transferred without their consent. According to Marshall, because native nations were "domestic to" (residing within the territory of) and "dependent on" the United States, they possessed less sovereignty than that enjoyed by the United States. In short, Indians were not equal legal subjects who possessed clear title to the land they inhabited but were "wards" of the state, occupying land that was not legally theirs.

Marshall's doctrine (developed in the infamous Cherokee cases of 1830) could only have applied to the Cherokee nation in Florida—and even then only by misrepresenting facts and ignoring treaties. (The Cherokees were "surrounded" by U.S. territory and were dependent on the southern slave economy, circumstances not duplicated in the case of Indian nations living west of the Mississippi.) However, from that point on, native resistance to U.S. invasions of indigenous territory would be regarded as unlawful aggression (on the part of Indians) and dealt with accordingly.

In practice, that meant genocidal extermination of native populations through massacres and confinement of noncombatants (women, children, and the elderly) as well as combatants. It is, therefore, no small wonder that

Adolf Hitler would later proclaim that "neither Spain nor Britain should be models of German expansion, but the Nordics of North America, who had ruthlessly pushed aside an inferior race to win for themselves sail and territory for the future."[28]

Hitler obviously learned his lesson well from "the Nordics of North America." And well he should have. By 1900, the U.S. Native American population of 237,000 was but 2 percent of what it had been at the point of first contact with Europeans; its land holdings were reduced to 2.5 percent of its original territory. The lives of indigenous peoples would henceforth be regulated by a series of statutes designed to severely limit what little sovereignty they still possessed.

The first of these statutes was the General Allotment Act of 1887, which imposed a racist criterion for determining Indian membership based on "blood quantum." This criterion ensured that the number of "pure breeds" entitled to full land allotments on reservations was considerably less than the number of full allotments assigned to the reservation. The remainder of these allotments (those that were not parceled out to Indians) were then made available to white homesteaders and to national parks. Not only were Indians denied their fair share of land (as stipulated by prior treaties), but the allotments assigned to them were generally not of arable quality, further increasing their dependency on the federal government. The act also forced Indians to give up their traditional collective use and occupancy of land in favor of the Anglo-Saxon system of individual property ownership. Finally, it required that those receiving deeds accept U.S. citizenship, a requirement that proved to be the first in a series of steps designed to eradicate any sense of native identity.

The Indian Citizenship Act of 1924 imposed citizenship on all Native Americans whether they consented to it or not. Laws prohibiting the use of native languages and spiritual practices (like the Ghost Dance) were already in force and were supplemented by even harsher measures. The worst of them required the removal of native children from their families and tribes to military-styled boarding schools. The Termination Act of 1953 and the Relocation Act of 1956 sought to complete the process by dissolving 109 indigenous nations within U.S. borders and forcibly relocating reservation residents to urban areas.

This attempt to assimilate Native Americans seemed to contradict the U.S. government's belated decision to once again recognize reservations as semisovereign indigenous territories. Once it was discovered that many reservations sat atop rich mineral deposits, the U.S. government moved to acquire some of this wealth by exercising licensing control over extraction rights, which meant creating a system of tribal councils that would act as puppet governments of the federal Bureau of Indian Affairs (BIA), the power officially delegated the responsibility for negotiating mining leases. Predictably, the creation of tribal councils authorized by the Indian Reorganization Act of 1934 has not worked to benefit the lives of "Indian wards," who receive but 15 percent or less of the market value extracted from their lands while they suffer the environmental degradation that comes with it. (Indeed, some of the reservations have been so contaminated by radioactive refuse that the federal government has designated them "national sacrifice areas" unfit for human habitation.)

The Indian Claims Commission Act of 1946 represented a belated (and woefully inadequate) attempt to compensate—at market prices a century old—a few tribes for the land taken from them, but it did nothing to restore native sovereignty. Attempts by natives to wrest control of their reservations from the government, as evidenced by the American Indian Movement's effort to liberate the Pine Ridge Reservation in South Dakota, have been met with violent resistance by the FBI, the U.S. Marshal's Service, and tribal councils whose loyalty to the government has been purchased with bribes.

But outrages such as these pale in comparison to the Indian Health Service's policy, implemented during the sixties and seventies, of forced surgical sterilization of native women—an action that clearly violated the United Nations conventions on genocide.[29] In defense of these and other policies, the United States and Canada refuse to recognize the UN Universal Declaration of the Rights of Indigenous Peoples as applying to native North Americans, arguing that the "permanent trust" they exercise over them does not constitute colonialism—which, according to the Blue Water Thesis, only obtains when the colony is separated from its colonizer by at least thirty miles of water.

Today, native peoples are the poorest group of Americans based on yearly and lifetime per capita income; they have the highest rates of unemployment, drug and alcohol addiction, infant mortality, teen suicide, domestic violence, incarceration, and death from disease, malnutrition, and exposure; and they have the lowest level of education and of life expectancy (for men, forty-five years; for women, forty-seven). Recent attempts by tribal councils to reverse this state of affairs have generally focused on revenue-generating schemes such as gambling casinos, nuclear waste dumps, and the like. Evidence indicates that, although these projects generate substantial revenues, they also aggravate problems associated with crime, violence, and addiction.[30]

What little right to self-government Indian reservations do possess is threatened by critics who seek to limit their hunting and fishing prerogatives;[31] construction of amphitheaters,[32] nuclear waste sites,[33] and casinos; and immunity from civil lawsuits.[34] The critics gained a major victory with passage of the Indian Gaming Regulatory Act (IGRA) in 1988, which for the first time ever entitled state governments to regulate certain commercial activities on reservations. Tribes ceded more control to states in a 1996 Supreme Court ruling, which struck down a provision of the IGRA allowing tribes to file lawsuits in federal courts against states refusing to bargain in good faith.[35]

### The Rights of Dissidents, Women, and Religious Minorities Under Tribal Governments

Let us now turn from the loss of tribal sovereignty to the theme with which I began this chapter: the implications of tribal sovereignty for the free exercise of individual natives' civil and political rights. Prior to 1968, tribes were exempt from the Bill of Rights, so there was no legal guarantee that individual natives' rights to freely associate, speak out, and worship would be respected by the tribal community. The Indian Civil Rights Act (ICRA) of 1968 ended this exemption. However, it did not require that violations of basic civil and political rights be adjudicated in federal and state courts. Instead, except under special circumstances, individual tribal members seeking redress for rights violations under the ICRA cannot appeal to state and federal courts but must have their cases adjudicated by tribal courts.

Therefore, although individual natives can sue their tribal governments for civil rights violations, the judges adjudicating their cases—who are themselves tribal members—might not be impartial.[36] Be that as it may, my concern in raising the problem of tribal sovereignty is less practical than philosophical. Specifically, it forces us to reconsider some old questions: Is it right for tribal authorities to discriminate against natives whose deviation from tribal practices is perceived to be threatening to the survival of the tribe's way of life? Does allowing dissident natives (and oppressed women and children) an opportunity to exit the tribe resolve this dilemma satisfactorily?

In order to answer these questions, we need to look more closely at the relationship between culture and land. To Native Americans, the loss of their land signified much more than the loss of an economic resource; it signified the end of their way of life. This life is inextricably wedded to the land, which holds the spirits of ancestors and natural beings—animals, plants, rivers, and mountains—with whom they communicate. Land, then, is not individual property, to be sold and used up; it is a spiritual inheritance entrusted to the entire tribe, a fact that is now officially recognized by the Canadian and U.S. governments.[37]

Failure to appreciate the communal nature of native culture and land use might lead one to think that conflicts between tribal self-preservation and individual freedom are capable of being resolved by allowing individual dissidents to exit the reservation or by restricting tribal councils' control over it.[38] To appreciate the naivete of this view, let us look at some cases. The first is described by Leslie Green:

> David Thomas, a member of the Lyackian Indian Band in British Columbia, was forcibly and without consent captured and initiated into the ceremony of "spirit dancing," in the course of which he was assaulted, battered, and wrongfully confined. His captors (all members of other bands) defended their actions on the ground that they had a collective Aboriginal right to continue their traditions of spirit dancing, notwithstanding that this practice violated Thomas's individual rights to personal security.[39]

The second case, involving the Pueblo Indians, is described by Chandran Kukathas:

> Some members of this culture, following conversion to Christianity, chose to withdraw from certain communal functions. The result was the ostracizing of, and denial of resources to, those apostates who had thus violated Pueblo religious norms. Objecting to this treatment, the Christian converts appealed to the "Indian Bill of Rights" (Title II, added to the 1968 Civil Rights Act) for religious protection.[40]

The third case involves the right of Pueblan women who have married persons outside the tribe to have their children declared tribal members. The Supreme Court ruled in 1978 *(Santa Clara Pueblo v. Martinez)* that an all-male tribal council could exclude such children from tribal membership because doing so conformed to the tribe's "tradition" of patriarchal governance and patrilineal descent.

The first case appears to be a straightforward violation of civil liberties. Thomas had not spent much time on the reservation, knew virtually nothing about the spiritual practices of any Indian band, and had no interest in learning about them. Although his captors saw him as subject to generic Indian religious rites, the judge who presided over the case disagreed, citing Thomas's right to "believe in, and to practice, any religion or tradition, if he chooses to do so."

The judge's opinion seems eminently reasonable. Thomas did not spend much time on the reservation, so his refusal to participate in Indian religious practices did not endanger them. Had it endangered them, however, another solution might have suggested itself: Thomas's exiting the reservation for good (on the assumption that he had no ties to it).

The second case, involving the denial of resources to dissident Christians inhabiting tribal lands, is more problematic. Here we are not talking about a violation of basic civil rights, but a denial of less basic communal resources. Furthermore, unlike the case involving Thomas, in this instance we are dealing with many "apostates" who also happened to live on the reservation full-time. These nonbelievers were not merely indifferent to Pueblan religion; some were convicted proselytes of evangelical Protestantism who regarded that religion with disdain.

Our intuitions about how to resolve this case pull us in two directions. To begin with, there are those like Kymlicka who treat this case as a fairly straightforward violation of civil liberties. In denying resources to the dissidents, the tribe was making it difficult for them to practice their religion. In Kymlicka's opinion, allowing the dissidents to practice their religion posed no danger to the survival of Pueblan culture. But even if it had, he doubts whether such a threat would have entitled the tribe to deny the dissidents communal resources.

Interestingly, Kymlicka does not think that allowing the dissidents to leave the reservation would have solved their conflict with the tribe in a manner that would have been fair to them. It would have done nothing to rectify the original injustice of discrimination they might have suffered, nor would it have fairly protected their religious freedom once they had left. For him, the "length, severity, and distribution of burdens" imposed on them in the course of their exile might well have been worse than those imposed on them by the tribe. Here we must recall that even Native Americans who have embraced Protestant beliefs will continue to retain some of their older cultural ties pertaining to daily speech, dress, artifacts, and comportment. Despite renouncing their tribe's ancestor worship and spiritualization of nature, they will still feel a deeply spiritual connection to their family and community.

So, unlike the case of dissident Catholics who are excommunicated from the Church, exit from membership in the Pueblan tribe means exit from one's identity *as an Indian*. Hence, for liberals like Kymlicka—who see cul-ture as a means for exercising individual choice—the only way to resolve the conflict between the tribe and its dissident minority is by favoring the lat-ter's freedom to choose.

This solution, however, has unpleasant consequences. As Green observes, when "religions incorporate as central elements doctrines that are inconsis-tent with respect for the rights of women, children, sexual minorities, and so on . . . to liberalize is to change." Green is concerned about the destruc-tive impact that liberalization will have on tribal culture; Kukathas, by con-trast, is worried about the injustice of imposing European conceptions of individual freedom on indigenous people who do not accept them.[41] In the end, one wonders whether Kymlicka's defense of tribal rights is not rather half-hearted.[42]

Perhaps there is no clear-cut way of resolving the dispute between the Pueblan nation and its dissident members. As Kymlicka himself points out, both seem equally justifiable: "We might say that cultural membership has priority over the rights of individual members, since cultural membership provides the context of individual choice; or conversely that individual rights always have priority over cultural membership, since the value of cultural membership is in enabling individual choice." Given this standoff, perhaps we should conclude that, so long as dissident minorities can exit (or remain in) the tribe without suffering undue hardship, and without actively under-mining its culture, the state should not intervene.

But what if the tribe in question is run autocratically by a select minority of males who seek to prevent women in the tribe from doing something that poses no threat to the culture? The third example, involving a Pueblan tribal council's refusal to allow the children of women (but not men) who have married outside the tribe to become tribal members, touches on just this issue. The Supreme Court upheld the right of the all-male council to enforce this exclusion on the grounds that patrilineal (but not matrilineal) descent was a part of the Pueblan culture. Likewise, it upheld the right of the coun-cil to enforce this exclusion on the grounds that Pueblan culture empowered men (not women) to be members of the council.

Was the Supreme Court's decision in upholding Pueblan patriarchy and patilineage correct? One might plausibly argue that the "tradition" of patri-archal government and patrilineage is not at all indigenous to native culture, as the Court claimed, but in fact represents a European imposition. Ac-cording to Annette Jaimes and Theresa Halsey, "while patrilineal/patrilocal cultures did exist, most precontact North American civilizations functioned on the basis of matrilineage and matrilocality."[44] Evidence suggests that in most native societies, women and men viewed themselves as performing complementary but equal roles in society. It also suggests that women were not, for the most part, politically subordinate and disempowered. For example, Jaimes and Halsey note that the clan mothers who headed each of the fifty extended families composing one of the six nations of the Iroquois Confederacy of New York

> formed a council within the confederacy that selected the males who would hold positions on a second council, composed of men, representing the confederacy's interests, both in formulation of internal policies and in conduct of external relations. Any time certain male council members adopted positions or undertook policies perceived by the women's council as being contrary to the people's interest, their respective clan mothers retained the right to replace them.[45]

The political power of Iroquois women (and women in many other tribes, as well) was further strengthened by virtue of their owning most of the household property. For a Lakota woman, divorce was as simple as placing the few possessions of her spouse outside the door of their lodge (children remained with the mother).

The disempowerment of native women came with the arrival of the Europeans. Eleanor Burke Leacock notes that as Native Americans became dependent on the settlers, they also adopted their patriarchal customs. The Jesuits, for example, imposed monogamy, forbade divorce, and refused to deal with anyone except certain male representatives of the Montagnais-Naskapi nation, thereby forcing this tribe to adopt a patriarchal political structure.[46] Among the Iroquois, the process of patriarchalization occurred in the nineteenth century when the Seneca prophet Handsome Lake promulgated a legal code—one that would be acceptable to the American government—abandoning the clan mother–controlled councils convened in the longhouse in favor of a patriarchal, nuclear family arrangement.

As for the Cherokee, the British had earlier encouraged them to intermarry, attend schools in England, and adopt English religious and legal customs, including the plantation system with its enslavement of blacks and natives from other tribes. So integrated into the European order had the Cherokee become that, by the early nineteenth century, their leaders (Elias Boudinot, Major Ridge, and John Ross) drafted a constitution, modeled on the Constitution of the United States, that disenfranchised women and blacks—all in order to curry favor with the U.S. government and stave off their inevitable removal. The same story was repeated elsewhere:

> In *not one* of the more than 370 ratified and perhaps 300 unratified treaties negotiated by the United States with indigenous nations was the federal government willing to allow participation by native women. In *none* of the several thousand nontreaty agreements reached between the United States and these same nations were federal representatives prepared to discuss anything at all with women. In *no* instance was the United States open to recognizing a female as representing her people's interests when it came to administering the reservations onto which American Indians were ultimately forced; always, men were required to do what was necessary to secure delivery of rations, argue for water rights, and all the rest.[47]

The situation in Canada was no better. In fact, the Indian Act of 1876 expressly classified as "non-Indian" any native woman who married a non-Indian or anyone else outside her tribe, and this classification applied to her children as well. Everywhere in North America the disempowerment and disenfranchisement of native women were accompanied by increased incidents of battery, rape, and incest on the part of native men, who were themselves victimized by shocking rates of unemployment (65 percent).

Native women began to reassert their former political power during the fishing rights movement of the sixties in the Pacific Northwest; in the seventies they played a key role in founding and maintaining the American Indian Movement (AIM). In response to the sexism of their male colleagues, they established their own political organizations, such as Women of All Red Nations (WARN) and the Indigenous Women's Network (IWN). In Canada, beginning in 1952, native women began challenging the patriarchal and patrilineal biases of the Indian Act and, by 1985, revised the act so as to make possible the resumption of traditional matrilineal/matrilocal tribal organizations. Along the way, the Tobique Women's Political Action Group became a potent force in challenging patriarchal tribal councils, in some cases evicting men from offices and occupying tribal buildings. Not surprisingly, native women in Canada—and not the men "officially in charge"—have become their nations' leading spokespersons.

Perhaps we will never know whether patriarchy and patrilineage were features of Pueblan life prior to contamination by European culture. However, we do know that native peoples were often forced to accept these practices by their European invaders. In any case, we cannot assume (as the Supreme Court did) that patriarchy and patrilineage were fully legitimate (i.e., internally generated and freely accepted) aspects of Pueblan culture. Hence, upholding these practices as a way of respecting the rights of the Pueblo Indians to practice their culture as they see fit is highly questionable.

A defender of patriarchy and patrilineage might not be bothered by the fact that these aspects of present-day Pueblan culture were a European supplement. After all, cultures are unavoidably contaminated by other cultures, and indigenous cultures were unavoidably contaminated by European cultures. Hence, appeal to the notion of a matrilineal/matriarchal indigenous culture existing before the European "discovery" seems a bit naive.

In response to the defender of aboriginal patriarchy and patrilineage, one might argue that what is at stake here is not the honoring of a historical title, which is always insufficient to legitimate a cultural practice, nor the restoration of a culture to its original (pristine and pure) state, as if such a state ever existed. Rather, as we have seen, the problem with any attempt to equate one's cultural identity with one's societal culture (in Kymlicka's sense) is that it "masks the fact that persons typically are provided with multiple identities by a shared culture, and gain different identities and statuses within it—based on distinctions of gender, race, class, religion, etc."[48] The issue at hand, then, involves respecting more fundamental political values regarding freedom, equality, and democratic governance shared by both indigenous and European cultures. Men *and* women should collectively decide the rules regulating membership in their tribe. Indigenous women understand this concept, which is why they have appealed to constitutional principles in resisting a form of patriarchy that finds increasingly less support in either European or indigenous culture.

In conclusion, the dilemma with which I began this chapter—reconciling Mayan cultural self-determination within a modern constitutional framework—is less insuperable than it first seems. Indigenous cultures designate dynamic practices and belief systems that have long since been contaminated by European ideals. Some of these, such as patriarchy and patrilineage, find increasingly little support among practitioners of both indigenous and European cultures. The very fact that these practices were first imposed on women by men and later on indigenous peoples by Europeans strongly counts against their legitimacy. However, even had they been original features of indigenous culture (a questionable supposition), their rejection by so many women today would render them illegitimate.

The questionable legitimacy of patriarchy and patrilineage stands in stark contrast to the democratic ideal, which reflects a venerable tradition extending across cultures and epochs.[49] Other aspects of indigenous culture of more recent, European origin—such as individualism—are more problematic. Possessive individualism, which places the individual above the community, cannot be harmonized with indigenous culture, but respect for individual civil and political rights can be—up to a point. That point is reached when these rights threaten the survival of the community. Under these circumstances, dissident minorities may be forced to exit the tribal community, so long as doing so does not overly restrict their freedom of religion and association. However, should exiting the tribe prove excessively burdensome, both they and the community will have to reach some other accommodation in which both sides agree to limit their rights.[50]

In the next chapter I will continue probing the limits of national sovereignty with respect to another individual right: the right to immigrate. Although Indian tribes occupying small parcels of land and possessing limited material resources are unlikely targets of immigration, their right—which they claim as a group—to exclude outsiders might conceivably conflict with the universal rights of needy immigrants to settle on land that can provide them a basic subsistence. Indian tribes base their right to exclude outsiders not simply on the self-preservation of their inhabitants but also on the preservation of a distinctive religious culture whose practice is intimately interwoven with the sanctity of the land they inhabit. This argument—that preservation of a distinctive cultural identity requires restricting the access of outsiders into a particular community—might carry some weight in the case of monocultural nations whose identity and solidarity as a group are embedded in worship of the land. But does it carry weight when applied to large, multicultural nations like the United States and Canada? Does the kind of loyalty and patriotism that infuses these countries gravitate around a distinctive national culture comparable to that informing the identities of indigenous people? If not, can these large, affluent countries justifiably deny entry to starving and otherwise desperate persons whose only fault lies in not being born in a rich, liberal democracy?

# 6

## CITIZENSHIP AND THE RIGHTS OF IMMIGRANTS

My discussion of the Maya illustrates well the challenges facing indigenous people in preserving their culture in the modern era. My own experience in working with them also has taught me much about the brutal poverty and exploitation they have had to endure at the hands of Guatemala's ruling elite. This experience in some ways paralleled my work with migrant agricultural laborers in California in the seventies. These workers, some of whom were Mayan and most of whom were of indigenous Mexican and Guatemalan descent, were trying to eke out a living under equally brutal circumstances. Working long hours of backbreaking manual labor under conditions that can only be described as hellish, they endured a litany of deprivations (heat exposure, dehydration, starvation, pesticide poisoning, unsanitary waste disposal, ramshackle housing, physical injury, and abuse)—all for the sole "privilege" of earning less than a minimum wage.

It was only later that I became aware of the profound contradiction in the lives of these workers: having fled as refugees from the political and economic oppression of their native land, they were increasing the number of farmworkers in California to the point where the supply of cheap, available labor had exceeded demand, thereby effectively depressing wages and working conditions even further. As someone who had once organized for Cesar Chavez's United Farmworkers Union, I could not but sympathize with the plight of farmworkers who were fighting to stem the tide of Guatemalan immigrants; however, as someone who had known some of these refugees personally, I equally supported their right to immigrate.

In order to appreciate my dilemma, one must first understand that as an American citizen I felt a certain moral responsibility for the plight of these refugees. In 1954, the U.S. government actively colluded with disaffected members of Guatemala's ruling elite to overthrow the democratically elected regime of President Jacobo Arbenz. Arbenz had just forcibly expropriated vast, uncultivated landholdings from United Fruit Company for a purchase price equivalent to what the company had estimated its taxable value to be worth. This land was to be redistributed to a starving population of indigenous people (the vast majority of whom were of Mayan descent) for their personal cultivation, thus ending centuries of colonial and imperial domination by outsiders and wealthy Ladinos (Guatemalans of mainly European ancestry).

The military dictatorship installed by the U.S. government halted land redistribution and quickly moved to suppress labor and student organizations, opposition leaders and journalists, and all other progressive democratic forces. From 1960 until 1996, the Guatemalan government fought a brutal civil war against a popular front representing the interests of peasants, workers, and students. With full financial and military backing from seven U.S. administrations, the government initiated a counterinsurgency policy of systematic torture and killing that left upwards of 150,000 dead and missing (mostly Mayan civilians) and another 750,000 homeless.

These homeless refugees fled first to Mexico and then to the United States. The State Department under the Reagan administration (1980–1988) refused to recognize them as political refugees, since they were fleeing from a government the administration actively supported. In response to this policy, a number of churches and legal organizations in the United States formed the Sanctuary Movement. Like the old Underground Railroad that helped refugee slaves escape their masters, the Sanctuary Movement prevented Guatemalan refugees from being deported back to their oppressors by hiding them in churches and homes.

Today, Guatemalan refugees still enter the United States illegally. With unemployment in Guatemala running as high as 45 percent, these refugees are desperately looking for any job that will prevent them and their families from starving to death. Their willingness to work for starvation wages has had the predictable effect of depressing wages and working conditions among all farmworkers. Labor organizations have pushed to restrict their immigration but have encountered stern opposition from growers and other representatives of U.S. agribusiness, who argue that such workers are needed to fill jobs that most Americans find undesirable.

How does one choose between resident farmworkers seeking to improve their living standards and Guatemalan refugees fleeing economic and political oppression? Are there any legal and moral principles that will help us to resolve this dilemma in a manner that is fair for everyone?

Few would deny that immigrants have made the United States the rich, dynamic country it is today. Yet awareness of economic and environmental limits coupled with anxiety over the fast pace of cultural change has provoked a sharp reaction to the recent upsurge in immigration.

No doubt some of this anxiety flows from xenophobic and racial prejudices that have been part of a legacy of nativism dating back almost two hundred years. But much of it does not. In some sectors of the economy, immigrants who are willing to work for subminimum wages have driven down earnings. Immigrants who have been unable to find adequate employment due to language and educational handicaps—or just plain prejudice—place an additional burden on public social and medical services. Even immigrants who possess highly needed technical skills acquire jobs that might have gone to qualified citizens.

Then there is the environment. In a continent that has become increasingly conscious of the environmental costs of population growth, the on-average larger families of immigrants can be seen as accelerating ecological crises. Finally, the somewhat higher than average crime rate of immigrants in comparison to the rest of the population—due in large part to the desperate economic circumstances in which many of them find themselves—fuels the mistaken impression that immigrants have less respect for the moral values shared by the rest of "us." Leaving aside this misapprehension, many political scientists voice concern about the disintegrative effects of cultural pluralism with respect to a democratic politics premised on solidarity and consensus.

The debate over immigration raises a number of issues about the rights of immigrants. Most basically, it forces us to consider what moral grounds states might have for restricting immigration (and emigration) and according immigrants different rights than those enjoyed by citizens.

### American Immigration Policy from 1790 to the Present

As we Americans debate these questions, it would be well to recall the history of our country's immigration policy, which has reflected both racial prejudice and economic necessity. Although the Naturalization Law of 1790 had declared only "white" immigrants fit for immigration, the westward expansion of the United States and the need for cheap, unskilled labor made it possible and desirable to permit unrestricted immigration of Asians and Pacific peoples, who, however, were officially classified as "nonwhite" and thus as ineligible for citizenship.[1] This situation persisted until the passage of the Chinese Exclusion Act in 1882, which essentially cut off all immigration from Asia. However, by the turn of the century, the demand for cheap, un-skilled labor in the industrialized urban centers of the Northeast called forth a new wave of immigrants from Europe.

Once again, race played a role in immigration policy—but in a surprisingly different way. In 1895 the great agronomist and African-American leader Booker T. Washington had pleaded with northern industrialists to hire the available pool of southern black laborers then chafing under oppressive con-ditions of Jim Crow and its economy of sharecropping.[2] They preferred to hire white Europeans instead, thereby postponing indefinitely the integra-tion and advancement of American blacks.

By 1910 the percentage of the population that was foreign-born peaked at 14.6 percent and would continue to decline to 4.7 percent by 1970. This increase, coupled with the nationalist fervor generated by World War I, fu-eled a nativist backlash that eventually led to the passage of the 1924 Na-tional Origins Act. This act—which imposed a low annual immigration ceiling of 154,000 and explicitly discriminated against Jews, Italians, and Eastern Europeans while favoring Western and Northern Europeans—led to the tragic exclusion of thousands of Jews seeking refuge from Hitler's geno-cidal regime. (In the meantime, the racial exclusions directed against Chi-nese immigrants were expanded to include immigrants from Japan, India, and the Philippine Islands and would not be lifted until 1952.)

The restriction of immigration might well have been one among many factors that contributed to the overall increase in blue-collar wages and unionization to the point where, by the late sixties, the earnings of Ameri-can households achieved the greatest equalization in U.S. history. Then the Cold War and the rise of the civil rights movement in the sixties forced the government to abandon the racist immigration policy that had been in place since the twenties (the ban against homosexuals was lifted in 1990). The Immigration Act of 1965 replaced the old preference system based on na-tional origin and labor resource concerns with one that emphasized "family unification," reserving 74 percent (amended to 80 percent in 1980) of all visas for family members of current residents. Most important, it gave statu-tory recognition to refugees for the first time in American history.

Defenders of the Immigration Act did not anticipate a significant rise in immigration. However, that is precisely what happened, owing in part to the act's failure to punish employers who hired illegal workers and its later inclu-sion (as of 1980) of persons seeking asylum, who—unlike refugees—are screened only after they arrive in the United States. In exchange for granting amnesty to some three million qualified illegal immigrants, the Immigration and Reform Act of 1986 eliminated the first loophole by imposing stiff criminal sanctions on employers who knowingly hired illegal immigrants. However, it did not alter the provision for persons seeking asylum. Although 40 percent of all illegal immigrants have entered the country through work visas that have expired, it has been the expansion of persons eligible for asylum—including women fleeing from cultures that practice female circumcision and HIV-positive gay men seeking escape from discrimination—that has mainly contributed to the increase in immigration.

According to a recent report issued by the INS Center for Immigration Studies, the total number of foreign-born in the United States has practically tripled since 1970 (increasing from 9.6 million to 26.0 million, or about 10 percent of the population). Counting illegal immigrants (who now number over five million), the flow of newcomers has exceeded a million per year since the early eighties, 65 percent of whom have settled in a few major states (California, New York, Florida, Texas, and Illinois) and a few major cities (Los Angeles, New York, Miami, Chicago, and Washington, D.C.). Immigrants from Asia and Latin America account for 80 percent of the post-1965 immigrants, and more than half of the combined Asian-Hispanic labor force in the country are foreign-born.

The education and income profile of immigrants is strikingly bimodal, the highest concentration occurring at the lower end of the spectrum with a lower concentration occurring at the upper end.[3] The concentration of immigrants at the lower end has probably contributed somewhat to the widening of the wage gap between rich and poor. Since the seventies, American manufacturing and heavy industry, the economic sectors that had previously absorbed most of the unskilled immigrant workforce, have declined precipitously in the face of stiff foreign competition. American companies have shifted their production units abroad to take advantage of cheap labor. In addition, the number of unskilled jobs has not kept pace with the number of available unskilled workers. The entry of women and African Americans into trades and unions following the passage of the Civil Rights Act (1964) also expanded the labor pool.

The resulting glut of unskilled laborers has had a particularly chilling effect on wage increases in a number of areas—agriculture, domestic work, and construction, to name a few. In turn, wage depression has discouraged native-born workers from seeking jobs in these areas (thereby increasing unemployment among native-born unskilled workers). Meanwhile, the number of professional, administrative, managerial, and technical jobs in the service sector has grown so quickly that those educated enough to take advantage of them—natives and nonnatives alike—have seen their incomes rise. Indeed, amidst charges that it allowed foreigners to take jobs that might otherwise have gone to Americans (many of them blacks and Latinos who are poorly represented in high-tech fields), Congress in 1998 expanded the number of temporary work visas available for recruiting foreign (mainly Asian) engineers and programmers, all for the sake of improving the computer industry's global competitiveness.

There is considerable disagreement about the overall impact of immigration on the economy. No scientific instrument has been developed that would enable one to measure the extent to which immigrants have taken jobs from native-born workers. Anecdotal evidence shows only that the influx of immigrants into certain labor markets has brought along wage depression and a subsequent disinclination on the part of native workers to remain in these markets.

However, given the record low levels of unemployment in recent years, wage depression cannot be attributed solely to glutted labor markets and is partly to be explained by factors that have nothing to do with the current influx of immigrants, such as the weakening of organized labor, the preference among many baby boomers to choose job security in favor of risky but potentially more lucrative job opportunities, and the tendency among businesses to replace higher-paid permanent staff with lower-paid temporary (or part-time) employees. In any case, wage depression translates into lower inflation, which is good for consumers.

Nevertheless, leaving aside the ambiguous causes and effects of wage depression, what statistical data we have show that immigrants are unemployed at a higher rate than their native-born counterparts (9.4 percent for immigrants compared with a national average of 6.5 percent), are 50 percent more likely to live in poverty than their native-born counterparts, and, according to a recent study by George Borjas of Harvard University, are more likely to receive welfare payments than their native counterparts (as of 1994, 21 percent of immigrant families received some form of welfare as compared with 14 percent of all citizens) and at a higher rate (immigrants constitute 9 percent of the population but receive 14 percent of the total outlay in welfare costs).[4]

Offsetting these negative statistics, however, are more positive ones. The Immigration and Naturalization Service (INS) reported a decline in the number of legal immigrants of 9.3 percent in 1996, the largest drop in fifteen years. Other studies by the Cato Institute (a libertarian Washington-based think tank), the National Academy of Sciences (NAS), and the Urban Institute show that immigration (legal and illegal) positively impacts the nation's economy. According to a study released in December 1995 by the Cato Institute, California annually spends $3,818 in public services (health, education, transportation, and so on) for each citizen while spending only $2,590 for each immigrant. And while each immigrant family on public assistance receives $1,404, each citizen receives $2,279.[5]

The NAS report issued in 1996 concedes that each taxpaying family living in states with large concentrations of immigrants must pay between $232 (New Jersey) to $1,178 (California) per year for their maintenance. However, the same report notes that immigrants make a *net* annual contribution of close to $10 billion a year to the U.S. gross national product. The Urban Institute was even more optimistic in its estimate, claiming that immigrants (legal and illegal) add $70.3 billion in annual tax revenues while drawing out only $42.9 billion in services.

The conflicting evidence on immigration's economic impact was largely lost on the public thanks to anti-immigrant media hype. The passage of Proposition 187 in California, which denied public education and health services to undocumented children, was but the first in a series of laws reflecting this hostile sentiment. Proposition 187 was eventually declared to be in violation of the Supreme Court's earlier ruling in *Plyler v. Doe* (1982), which upheld the right of children of undocumented parents to equal protection. In the meantime, responding to overwhelming public support for reduced entry and benefit levels for immigrants,[6] Congress has moved quickly to restrict the flow of legal immigration and curtail social benefits to all noncitizens.[7] Republicans have also proposed eliminating the Fourteenth Amendment's clause granting automatic citizenship to anyone born on U.S. soil.

Recent changes in immigration and welfare laws do not bode well for immigrants seeking entry or accommodation in the United States. The Illegal Immigration Reform and Immigrant Responsibility Act of 1996 (IIRIRA) reduces the total number of documented immigrants that can be admitted annually to the United States from 775,000 to 542,000;[8] it also limits the number of admissible refugees to 50,000 and the number of special work visas for technically trained immigrants and their families to 90,000. Just as significantly, the law redefines the system of preferences and criteria for admission.[9]

The Immigration Act of 1965 replaced national origin with familial relationship as the basis for ranking applicants for immigration; the IIRIRA qualifies the act further by privileging certain familial relationships over others. The IIRIRA prohibits legal residents from doing what any citizen can do: sponsor his or her siblings and older children (twenty-one years and older) for immigration. Not only does the IIRIRA make it more difficult for legal residents to reunite with some members of their family, but it introduces stricter income requirements for sponsors. As specified in the Immigration and Nationality Act (INA), sponsors must be eighteen years old and earn 25 percent above the poverty level for each relative sponsored (INA, sec. 213[a]). Thus a family of four must earn at least $19,500 to sponsor a single relative. Other persons besides the sponsor may sign a declaration of support in order to help meet this income threshold, but under the new rules, all signed affidavits will be held legally binding until the immigrant becomes a citizen or has worked for forty quarters (or ten years).

The antiterrorism legislation signed by President Bill Clinton in April 1996 also tightens the INA's rules for admitting refugees and persons seeking asylum. Undocumented persons who have just arrived are subject to immediate deportation unless they explicitly request religious or political asylum. For example, a Nicaraguan-born wife of an American citizen who had her green card stolen before arriving in the United States was immediately sent back to Nicaragua without any hearing. Persons who have resided in the country illegally for up to two years will also be treated like newly arrived asylum seekers. When arriving at ports of entry, such persons must convince a low-level INS official that he or she faces "extraordinary circumstances" in his or her current country of citizenship or else be subject to immediate deportation.[10]

Any asylum seeker who fails this summary hearing—conducted without benefit of legal counsel, translator, or family member—has just seven days in which to prepare an appeal to a special INS judge. That judge's decision is then final and not subject to review by any federal or state court. Even refugees who pass the asylum test, such as a Jewish refugee from Russia seeking to be reunited with American relatives, can be deported to another "safe" country (for example, Israel) with which the United States has a bilateral agreement.

Last but not least, the IIRIRA severely limits the right of immigrants to have their rejected solicitations for asylum and amnesty reviewed by a federal court. Class action suits—such as those made on behalf of some 100,000 to 400,000 immigrants who claimed that the INS prevented them from obtaining amnesty under the provisions specified in the 1986 Immigration Reform Act due to misinformation and processing improprieties— are no longer considered actionable. Individuals who currently are not being subjected to deportation procedures of certain kinds (for having committed crimes and the like) can sue the INS, but only if they can afford to hire expensive legal counsel.

Penalties for those who are subject to deportation are severe: if an immigrant has resided illegally in the United States for more than 180 days but less than one year, he or she will be disbarred from reentering the country for three years; the penalty is increased to ten years for those whose stay has exceeded one year (INA, sec. 212[a][b]).

Deportation proceedings against an illegal immigrant will be canceled only if he or she (1) has lived in the country for at least ten years (three years longer than was required under the old law), (2) possesses good moral character, and (3) can prove that deportation will impose "exceptional and extremely unusual hardship" on a relative (citizen or legal resident) who is under his or her care (INA, sec. 240[a][b]). Under this provision, an undocumented eighteen-year-old Mexican boy who had been caring for his grandmother in the United States for seven years could be deported for not having satisfied the new ten-year residency requirement.

Last but not least, the new welfare law enacted by Congress and signed by President Clinton in September 1996 (the Personal Responsibility and Work Opportunity Reconciliation Act)[11] substantially reduces the number of benefits available to noncitizens in order to "assure that aliens will be self-reliant" (sec. 400).[12] Excepting children, illegal residents will be ineligible for federal, state, and local benefits. These include grants, loans, licenses, benefits (retirement, welfare, health, unemployment, and disability), public housing, postsecondary education, and food assistance. With few exceptions, legal immigrants who had been receiving food stamps, supplemental security income (SSI), nonemergency medical aid, and public assistance (Temporary Assistance to Needy Families [TANF]), formerly known as Aid to Families with Dependent Children [AFDC]) will no longer unless the states in which they reside should decide to allocate some of their own federal block grants and state revenues for these purposes (secs. 401[c,] 403[c], and 411[d]).[13] Newly arrived immigrants will be ineligible for receiving any federal, means-tested assistance for at least five years, at which time they may qualify for just twelve months of assistance—assuming, of course, that their sponsor is financially incapable of providing a minimum level of support.

There are few exemptions to these benefit exclusions: refugees and asylum seekers (for their first five years of residence); aliens who have been paroled into the country for at least one year (sec. 431[b]); legal immigrants and their families who have served or who are currently serving in the armed forces (sec. 402[a]); legal immigrants who lack sufficient means because they have separated from physically abusive spouses (sec. 501); and legal immigrants who have contributed forty quarters' (ten years') worth of Social Security withholdings (sec. 402[b]).[14]

Altogether, 44 percent of the total savings ($55 billion) in reduced benefits sought by the welfare reform bill come at the expense of legal immigrants, who comprise just 5 percent of the welfare rolls. According to the Congressional Budget Office, approximately 500,000 legal immigrants—half of whom will have been in the United States for more than ten years—will lose SSI benefits (extended to low-income individuals who are sixty-five or older, blind, or disabled), and 900,000 will lose food stamps.

After some well-publicized suicides, horror stories, and pleas from critics of the new immigration and welfare legislation, Congress and the president appeared ready to soften some of its harshest features and by 1997 had moved to restore food stamps to some 250,000 legal immigrants. In the meantime, states with large immigrant populations have taken it upon themselves to restore other benefits cut by the federal government.[15] Such changes, however, do not address other aspects of the reform bill that make it almost impossible for legal immigrants to prove job discrimination and for illegal immigrants to report crimes without being subject to immediate identification, arrest, and deportation.

The new welfare reform poses serious questions of justice: Is it right for the government to deny benefits to a legal immigrant whose taxes have helped finance them? Is it right for it to suddenly and drastically change the "rules of the game" in midstream after so many legal immigrants and their families have planned their lives around the old rules?

### *Immigration and the State*

These questions cannot be answered until we establish the right of states to decide who is—and who is not—a member in good standing. In order to answer this question, we must first determine why states exist. According to liberalism, states exist in order to protect individuals. Although protection agencies that hire out bodyguards could fulfill this function, they could not do it as well as territorial states. Once protection is extended to include the provision of food, shelter, and other economic necessities, the territorial monopoly exercised by states becomes quite decisive.

If states are necessary for securing survival, then individuals should be entitled to claim citizenship in *some* state. But what kind of state? Three options present themselves. To begin with, there is the state as we know it today: a legal order that regulates entry into its territory. Next is the state that permits unrestricted immigration. Finally, there is the global state, whose members would include all of the world's inhabitants.

According to Michael Walzer, the global state and the territorial state with open borders both suffer from an irremedial defect: they dispense with the sentiment of patriotism, or communal identification that is a prerequisite for persons caring about one another: "It is only if patriotic sentiment has some moral basis, only if communal cohesion makes for obligations and shared meanings, only if there are members as well as strangers, that state officials would have any reason to worry especially about the welfare of their own people (and of *all* their own people) and the success of their own culture and politics."[16] Walzer here suggests that liberal theory—which sees the state simply as an agency that guarantees the physical and economic protection of its inhabitants—does not satisfactorily explain why "state officials would have any reason to worry especially about the welfare of their own people." The explanation, according to Walzer, is that they, like the rest of us, are motivated to worry especially about certain persons and not others. In other words, because we cannot extend our concern to all of humanity without seriously diluting it—which is what global and borderless states are compelled to do—any special concern we show for others must be limited to those few with whom we identify as belonging to our immediate or extended family, including our community and nation.

If we examine in detail Walzer's argument for territorial states that restrict membership and immigration, we notice that he gives two reasons for the importance of group membership as a basis for loyalty and special concern. First, like other so-called communitarian thinkers, he assumes that individuals must identify with particular groups and communities in order to achieve a sense of psychological belonging and security. As noted in Chapter 3, we need recognition from a relatively closed circle of consociates whose opinions we especially value. Strangers cannot provide this recognition, since they neither know us intimately nor care deeply about us. However, family, friends, neighbors, coworkers, coworshippers, and significant others care about us, and we reciprocate in kind. Second, the affective basis underlying interactive recognition is a sense of belonging, or communal membership, in which our concern for others is motivated by a sense of affinal identification (loyalty or patriotism) rather than by self-interest or abstract moral duty to respect universal humanity.

Further extending this insight into the affective dynamics underlying stable identity, Walzer invites us to think of the state as a large family rather than as a neighborhood, which by definition lacks "an organized or legally enforceable admissions policy."[17] Neighborhoods can pass zoning laws that sometimes maintain class segregation; they can occasionally be inhospitable to newcomers; but they have no institutional apparatus for legally excluding strangers who wish to move in. Indeed, the more residents move from place to place looking for employment in today's dynamic economy, the more they relate to one another like strangers.

Walzer's strong contrast between neighborhoods and families is no doubt overwrought: stable neighborhoods often display a remarkable sense of communal esprit de corps, while members of families can be quite alienated from one another. Even if it were true that neighborhoods increasingly are becoming temporary residences for today's alienated job seekers, it might be that states are becoming more—rather than less—like neighborhoods. After all, today's global economy has placed increasing pressure on states to open their markets with respect to goods and services; and this pressure is being applied to labor markets as well, as can be seen with the consolidation of the European Union.

But that openness is not happening in the United States, which—to use Walzer's other metaphor—is behaving more like an exclusive club. According to Walzer, the risks to persons at both ends of the immigration highway are too great for it to be otherwise. On one hand, the psychological risks associated with dislocation are so great that we hesitite to emigrate unless economic and political hardship absolutely compel us to. On the other hand, these same psychological anxieties (at times bordering on the xenophobic) make us hesitant to open up our communities to strangers. So powerful are these communitarian needs that critics of unrestricted immigration like Walzer feel confident in concluding that "if states ever become large neighborhoods, it is likely that neighborhoods will become little states."[18]

For Walzer, then, it makes perfect sense for states, like clubs, to have formal admissions policies that—in keeping with Walzer's other analogy—typically stress family reunification.[19] Family reunification means different things depending on context. In the United States, it has long been recognized that the luxury of having cheap laborers who are willing to do the sorts of menial jobs that most of "us" do not want to do comes with a social price. As Walzer eloquently puts it, "Since laborers are men and women with families, one cannot admit them for the sake of their labor alone without accepting some commitment to their aged parents, say, or to their sickly brothers and sisters."[20] In other contexts, however, familial reunification reinforces communal solidarity, rather than labor policy.

As I noted in Chapter 5, tribal membership is crucial for determining residential rights on Indian reservations. Again, citizens inhabiting states formed by nationalist sentiment typically think of themselves as a race or family apart from other peoples. Germany, for example, has an open admissions policy with regard to all ethnic Germans regardless of their economic viability. Israel has adopted a similar policy with respect to Jews. Likewise, Greeks who feel persecuted in Cyprus or Turkey find safe haven in Greece, just as Turks who feel persecuted in Cyprus or Greece find safe haven in Turkey. And even so-called immigrant states like the United States have at various times in their history thought of certain nationalities (the English, for instance) as "family."

### The Right to Restrict Entry

It is easy to see how residents of a state who consider themselves to be "family" or "club members" might justify their right to restrict entry to foreigners. Patriotic loyalty entitles one to discriminate between members and nonmembers and to favor the former over the latter. Since we have few qualms about dispensing with moral impartiality when it comes to choosing the beneficiaries of our charity—we privilege those with whom we are closest and only begrudgingly extend our beneficence to strangers—why should we have any when it comes to choosing whom we admit into our society?

Yet for those of us who have grown up in a liberal state like Canada or the United States, the decision to dispense with impartial justice is not so simple. The mandate to evaluate immigration and aid policies in terms of impartial justice—that is, in terms of universal human rights—competes with our partial loyalty to kith and kin. Indeed, one such right—the right to associate freely—seems to pull us in opposite directions, sometimes justifying the right to exclude others from membership, sometimes not. Hence, to complicate matters further, the right to free association as well as the right to immigrate—or, as the case may be, the right to exclude—are susceptible to being applied and interpreted in different ways.

Walzer understands this dichotomy, which is why he proposes that we base our evaluation of the justice (or injustice) of restrictive immigration policies on something other than vague appeals to universal rights. This approach should not surprise us; after all, he insists that what is most crucial for our moral psychology is identification with some definite community of persons, and even those who profess love of humanity above all else still need the security and recognition that come with belonging to a particular family, however "extended" it might be. Since our thinking about justice is inevitably shaped by our membership in some definite community, Walzer concludes that any critical evaluation of a state's immigration policy should respect how the inhabitants of that state frame their own understanding of that policy. In other words, instead of imposing our country's views about what justice requires in this area, we should instead look to the views of the inhabitants of the country whose policies we are evaluating.

Yet even Walzer acknowledges at least one rule of morality—universally binding in all cultures—that limits the extent to which communal ties can restrict immigration: the principle of mutual aid. As John Rawls once put it, we have a general obligation to help persons in distress, and "not only to definite individuals, say to those cooperating together in some social arrangement, but to persons generally."[21] In short, the principle of mutual aid says that countries are obliged to allow entry even to total strangers, at least whenever doing so "is . . . urgently needed by one of the parties and . . . if the risks and costs of giving it are relatively low for the other party."[22]

The principle of mutual aid, then, acts as a kind of external limit on the admissions policies of states; it obligates them to allow entry to persons who are suffering from some sort of dire distress so long as doing so does not impose too great a burden on the host state(s). Of course, in many situations what constitutes "dire distress" and "too great a burden" is not easily agreed upon. Common sense tells us that, all things being equal, poor countries already suffering from overpopulation will be less obligated to allow entry to starving people than rich countries. Unfortunately, things are almost never equal between countries. According to Walzer, even inhabitants of rich countries might justly balk at the prospects of a mass immigration of starving foreigners if they have good reason to believe that the new immigrants will significantly lower their standard of living or undermine their sense of community.

Walzer is no doubt right in arguing that questions concerning standards of living and political bonds are relevant to the question of immigration: if allowing persons in dire distress to enter a territory poses grave security risks for the current residents—to the point where they can no longer exercise their basic rights to protection, subsistence, and political self-determination—then it can hardly be disputed that they have a right to refuse entry to such persons. But Walzer is wrong in neglecting another moral principle, inherent in the liberal culture he happens to share with most of his readers, of impartial justice. That principle says that no one's basic rights to subsistence and security, including the rights of would-be immigrants in dire distress, can be sacrificed for the mere sake of preserving a way of life. States can refuse entry to persons in dire distress for the sake of maintaining law and order, basic health and welfare, and democratic sovereignty, but they cannot do so for the sake of maintaining a high standard of living, a pristine environment, or an elite or distinctive ideal of political and cultural attainment (unless, as in the case of Indian tribes, the culture in question revolves around religious worship of the land).[23]

Before discussing how the liberal principle of impartial justice qualifies Walzer's argument in support of restrictive immigration, let us first examine the argument itself. The argument hinges on the communitarian assumptions that (1) individuals need to identify solidaristically with some definite and distinctive community in order to feel secure psychologically and (2) definite and distinctive communities flourish only when their memberships are restricted.

The first premise might very well be true. However, it tells us little about the need for people to live in restrictive communities, which is what the second supposition asserts. Of course, our need to belong to particular groups, to identify with persons with whom we share a special affinity, might require that we join private clubs and other organizations that admit only persons possessing the proper credentials. Our freedom to associate with persons who share our religious and ideological convictions, for example, cannot be fully realized unless we and our fellow consociates are allowed to exclude persons who do not share these convictions: Orthodox Jews, for example, should not have to admit non-Jews into their congregations. But the need to belong to particular groups like this does not justify restricting movement across political borders. In principle, we could live in a global state—or in a world without restrictive political boundaries—and still retain our exclusive memberships in churches, clubs, and the like.

A somewhat different but related point is made by Joseph Carens, who argues that restrictive political boundaries are neither necessary nor sufficient for a community's possessing a distinctive identity or esprit de corps. As he notes, cities

> are formally organized communities with boundaries, with distinctions between citizens and non-citizens, and elected officials who are expected to pursue policies that benefit members of the community that elected them. They often have distinctive cultures and ways of life. Think of the differences between New York City and Waycross, Georgia, or between California and Kansas. These sorts of differences are often much greater than the differences across nation-states. Seattle has more in common with Vancouver than it does with many American communities.[24]

Cities as diverse and distinct as New York and Waycross thus constitute well-defined communities—whose respective inhabitants solidaristically identify with one another as New Yorkers and Waycrossers—despite permitting the unrestricted entry of outsiders who share widely varying attachments. People can identify with—and care for—one another simply because they inhabit the same place, which functions as the primary locus of their mutual concern for one another. Conversely, the cities and towns strewn along the northern and southern borders of the United States constitute communities that are not always so well-defined in contrast to their contiguous counterparts in Canada and Mexico, although access from one side of the border to the other is highly restricted. Thus, open immigration across political jurisdictions like New York and Waycross is no obstacle to their maintaining distinctive identities, just as restricted immigration across political jurisdictions like National City, California, and Tijuana, Mexico, is no guarantee of the same.

The fact that cultural and political solidarities sometimes straddle relatively closed territorial borders while cultural and political divisions fall within them disproves Walzer's notion that the main reason closed territorial borders exist is to secure communal solidarity. Of course, Native Americans inhabiting reservations might plausibly limit the number of nontribesmen living and working in their communities for this reason, for their right to religious association—and their right to participate in a distinctive worship of the land conferring ultimate value on their way of life—takes precedence (in their minds) over all other rights. This cannot be said, however, of citizens inhabiting most multicultural polities, least of all those inhabiting liberal societies, in which communal attachments are highly fluid, diverse, and weak.

A more plausible—liberal rather than communitarian—explanation for retaining closed borders appeals to the importance of maintaining political control over matters of common concern pertaining to the shared enjoyment of security and economic well-being. This reason was cited by former governor of California Pete Wilson in support of Proposition 187, whose denial of benefits to illegal aliens was premised on the assumption that such aliens constituted a severe drain on the state's financial resources. We need not agree with Wilson's support for Proposition 187 to accept its underlying principle: in a climate of economic scarcity and insecurity, citizens can act solidaristically to protect themselves and their community by restricting entry.

How much weight should be given to these claims to territorial sovereignty? A lot, if we accept Walzer's analogy between states and private clubs. However, as Walzer's own account makes clear, states are not really like private clubs at all. Individuals cannot exit and enter states as easily or safely as they can private clubs. Indeed, as I remarked in earlier chapters, the exclusion of persons from private clubs is morally tolerable only insofar as it is easy and safe for those excluded to form their own club or to enter another one. But what makes exclusion acceptable in the case of private clubs—easy exit and entry—does not obtain in the case of states. For this reason, perhaps it would be better if states behaved in a less restrictive manner and more like the Rotary Club discussed in Chapter 1, whose functions are public: the provision of basic conditions of life.

## The Argument for Open Borders

The right of citizens to restrict entry for the sake of maintaining control over their lives thus needs to be qualified by at least two principles: the principle of mutual aid and the principle of impartial justice. Be that as it may, many arguments in support of restrictive immigration simply ignore this latter principle entirely. For example, it is often assumed that the sheer accident alone of having been born in a wealthy democracy justifies one's right to certain exclusive privileges—as if freedom, security, and subsistence were goods to which only the privileged few are entitled.

Or perhaps our modern-day aristocrat feels that his country is a rightful inheritance over which he has a legitimate property claim. If so, the claim is very weak: North America was stolen from its original inhabitants, and property rights are themselves derivative of a more fundamental right to self-preservation—the very right that would-be immigrants urge us to acknowledge on their behalf. Such rights supposedly constitute natural endowments of individual human beings that precede artifical institutions such as the state, which means that the state can protect the right but cannot diminish its exercise. Because the rights to self-preservation and to private property have typically been understood as entailing a right to purchase or sell goods and services, including the labor of foreigners, it would seem that no state has any moral authority to prevent foreigners from freely entering domestic labor markets at their own or others' behest. In short, the natural right to property allows me as an individual to exclude people from my own property, but it does not allow others, acting as a group, to force me to do so should I choose not to.

In response to this argument, one simply might deny that anyone has a natural right to self-preservation or, assuming that such a right exists, that it either entails an unlimited freedom to go about one's business or imposes strong obligations on others to provide assistance. My own view of the matter is that a right to self-preservation, while not entailing an unlimited freedom to move about and transact business as one likes,[25] does impose strong obligations on others to provide assistance.

Persons possess a right to self-preservation that prohibits us from wrongfully impeding them in their exercise of it—hence laws against killing and the like, which only permit exceptions involving cases of justifiable (reasonable and measured) self-defense. Furthermore, like all so-called natural rights, the right to self-preservation—the most basic of all rights—devolves on persons equally and impartially in their human capacity as potentially rational, purposive agents. It therefore follows that persons normally should be allowed to move freely from place to place in order to procure their basic subsistence, so long as their doing so does not endanger the self-preservation of others. Stated differently, the right to immigrate should be regarded as a natural right whose normal exercise can only be restricted for the sake of self-defense (in other words, contrary to Walzer, those who seek to restrict immigration—not those who seek to expand it—carry the main burden of proof). Therefore, refusing entry to persons in dire distress (or refusing to provide them with comparable foreign aid and other assistance) normally amounts to violating their rights[26]—which is a more serious moral infraction than merely being uncharitable or selfish in lending aid.[27]

Let us review this argument in more detail. Justice urges impartiality, which requires that we regard the assignment of rights from an unbiased point of view—that is, from a point of view that does not allow us to appeal to peculiar aspects of our social standing that might influence our thinking in these matters. Justice makes this requirement because much of what determines who we are and what we possess is a function of natural endowments, social circumstances, and other accidents of birth over which we have no control. Since none of us deserved to be born rich or poor, well-endowed or handicapped, a well-fed citizen of the United States or a starving Guatemalan, we are not entitled to appeal to these accidents in deciding who has a basic right to what.[28]

John Rawls has devised the following thought experiment to aid citizens inhabiting a single state in determining what an impartial distribution of rights might look like. Extending the scope of his experiment, suppose we imagine ourselves to be party to a social contract involving all the world's inhabitants. In order to ensure impartiality and agreement, we know nothing about our particular identities or social status (for all we know, we might be starving Guatemalans).

As Carens points out, anyone deliberating under this "veil of ignorance" would agree with others on an assignment of rights that would maximally protect the most vulnerable of the world's inhabitants. Because the poor greatly outnumber the rich and our chances of numbering among the former are very high, self-interest combined with a rational aversion to risk-taking would lead impartial contractors to agree on social arrangements that would likely maximize the well-being of the worst off. In principle, freedom to immigrate would maximize the well-being of the worst off by allowing them access to regions rich in resources and job opportunities. Of course, it would not maximize the well-being of those who are better off, however, since they would be forced to compete for scarce resources with the newcomers. Nevertheless, it is likely that eventually the world's population would be distributed in a manner that would yield a maximally efficient consumption of the world's resources: a modest living for all minus the superfluous wastefulness of extreme wealth and poverty.[29]

Ideally—that is, in abstraction from all knowledge about existing geopolitical realities that might bias moral deliberation—impartial contractors would choose a rule permitting unlimited freedom of movement. But would they still do so once this knowledge were made available to them? What if unrestricted immigration in the current situation led to a massive breakdown of law and order, endangering everyone's lives? What if, in the short run, it led to a drastic lowering of economic gains across the board, threatening the worst-off members of a given society with starvation?

In a just world—in which social inequalities were limited, political oppression nonexistent, and immigration less urgent—these questions, frequently raised by today's "lifeboat" ethicists, would be moot.[30] In the real—and far from just—world, we have to concede that the right to immigrate cannot be absolute.

To begin with, considerations of self-defense (or national security) warrant the exclusion of would-be invaders, criminals, and subversives, albeit not the exclusion of large numbers of political and economic refugees that is currently in force. More strongly, such considerations do not warrant racist and ethnocentric quotas; given what we know about past waves of immigration from Asia, Africa, South America, and Eastern Europe, current concerns about foreigners threatening our public order seem highly exaggerated.

A more pressing worry is the economic and environmental impact of massive unrestricted immigration. Let us assume that unrestricted immigration would result in a huge influx of immigrants into the United States that would likely reduce the economic well-being of current citizens, especially those who lack education and technical skills. The principle of justice, which recognizes the equal right of all persons to self-preservation, would allow persons in dire distress to immigrate so long as doing so did not endanger the lives of U.S. citizens. It is possible that permitting immigration in these circumstances would be obligatory even if doing so depressed the standard of living in the United States to a level approximating that found in the immigrants' own native countries. As unemployment in these countries diminished and the influx of earnings from expatriates to families back home increased, the standard of living there would rise. Once the world achieved economic and political parity with the United States, everyone would enjoy a modest standard of living capable of sustaining democratic institutions, thereby eliminating the main incentive to immigrate (see note 29).

Of course, if achieving high levels of per capita income were necessary for bringing about the educational and cultural prerequisites for sustaining democratic institutions—which are so fundamental for procuring basic rights[31]—considerations of justice might justify restricting immigration (but only if admitting higher numbers of immigrants would saturate available labor markets and depress wages below tolerable levels). However, contrary to the communitarian position defended by Walzer, justice does not permit sacrificing the lives of would-be immigrants merely for the sake of avoiding inconveniences or preserving a distinctive sense of community.[32] In the words of Carens, "If freedom of movement within the state is so important that it overrides the claim of local political communities, on what grounds can we restrict freedom of movement across states?"[33]

In a world full of starving and oppressed people, restrictive immigration might be tolerable if basic goods and freedoms were more equally distributed; but achieving equality would require transforming the global economy. Capitalism exacerbates uneven development between rich and poor countries by concentrating ever greater wealth in the hands of rich countries. Poor countries are already at a tremendous disadvantage, since they have to accept the terms of exchange that are dictated to them by the rich countries' lending institutions. Typically, these terms allow rich countries to extract raw resources cheaply from poor countries in exchange for expensive technologies. The result is a net drain of wealth from poor to rich nations.[34]

Capitalism also promotes uneven development within countries. In the global market, those who possess the requisite technical skills win, while those who do not—well over 80 percent of the world's population—find themselves living in increasingly impoverished and degraded conditions.[35]

Under these circumstances, which are typically exacerbated by growing class conflict and political oppression, it is no wonder that people immigrate. Global capitalism as we know it will not transform itself. Poor citizens of all countries must act to take control over their local economies, banding together across national borders to protect their nonrenewable resources, if need be. They should use restrictive immigration policies only as a last resort for protecting fragile labor markets. Indeed, the best affirmative labor strategy involves the creation of international labor federations and the consolidation of fragmented or single-export businesses (which are either dependent on foreign markets or controlled by foreign companies) into export cartels or self-sustaining regional economies.

Only when the inhabitants of rich countries realize that the world's resources and waste capacities are limited—that what befalls the inhabitants of undeveloped countries in terms of environmental degradation and human exploitation ultimately affects them as well—will they elect leaders who will promote a different economic agenda.[36] We who live in rich countries must understand that illegal immigration is the price we pay for global injustice, and that the solution to both injustice and illegal immigration is radical transformation of the economy.

### Priorities for American Immigration

Until the global economy is transformed in the manner already suggested, states will continue to have justifiable reasons for regulating immigration. Severely underdeveloped and overpopulated states will have the most reason for doing so, while developed, sparsely populated countries like the United States and Canada will have the least. However, because even these countries will have some justifiable security reasons for restricting immigration, the question arises as to which immigrants they should admit first.

Giving priority to well-educated and wealthy immigrants over less-educated and poor immigrants—the Canadian model toward which the United States is moving—strikes me as wrong. In most instances, admitting the well educated and wealthy ahead of the less educated and poor is unjust, for it improves the lot of those who are better off at the cost of worsening the lot of those who are less well off. Specifically, it worsens the lot of the less well off still residing in the community vacated by the wealthy and educated, for they now are deprived of skills and capital that otherwise could have been used to improve their lives.

Immigrants seeking to reunite with their families should be given higher priority. The United States and Canada owe those who have already immigrated and contributed to the well-being of their adopted country the same opportunity—to live with their families— that they extend to their own citizens. Because the principle of contribution is decisive here, the current U.S. policy of allowing citizens but not legal residents to sponsor older siblings and children seems arbitrary. Likewise, it seems wrong for both the United States and Canada to link sponsorship to income qualifications that favor the wealthy over the poor.

Although family reunification fairly compensates those who have uprooted themselves from their families in order to work abroad, it should not be given the highest priority on our list of immigration criteria. Indeed, because U.S. and Canadian immigration policies do not regard family reunification as an end in itself but only as just compensation for sacrifices endured in the course of working abroad, it need not be an integral part of these policies. For instance, the United States and Canada could probably rely on their own citizens to perform whatever unpleasant jobs need to be done (assuming that these countries could entice their citizens with competitive wages). However, once we eliminate immigration for purposes of filling economic needs, we eliminate the need to reunify immigrant workers with their families.

Our obligation to reunify families through immigration is thus conditional. Less conditional—and more important—is our obligation to provide political asylum and economic assistance to persons whose lives are in immediate danger. Of course, instead of providing them with asylum and jobs here, we can undertake to ensure that their economic and political rights are respected abroad.

Our obligation to refugees varies depending on circumstances. We have the highest obligation to those political and economic refugees whose distress our government and business establishment has caused. Unfortunately, the U.S. government has not consistently lived up to this obligation. Special exemptions granted to Cubans, Vietnamese, and Nicaraguans who fled regimes that our government actively opposed have not been extended as readily to Guatemalans, Salvadorans, and Haitians, whose governments our leaders actively supported.[37] Likewise, our leaders refuse to acknowledge that many illegal immigrants from Mexico were made homeless, landless, and jobless by our business establishment.[38]

Must we choose between the right of resident farmworkers to a decent wage and the right of Mexican and Guatemalan campesinos to immigrate? Perhaps not. If the U.S. government were to own up to its contribution in generating the economic and political oppression in Mexico and Guatemala, it might find it within its moral conscience to provide a massive infusion of aid—combined with diplomatic support for significant agrarian, labor, and political reform—capable of stemming the tide of immigration from that region. Otherwise, it could relocate refugees from this region to sectors of the economy with tighter labor markets. However, whatever it chose to do for them, it would be morally obligated to do for other Americans as well.

### Obligations with Respect to Guestworkers

Affirmative strategies for reforming our immigration policies must also extend to the treatment of immigrants who have been admitted into the country. Should citizens have greater rights than immigrants to basic social services such as health, education, and welfare? Should they have greater political rights?

To begin with, no immigrant should be denied the right to become a citizen with full political rights. It is immoral for a community to profit from the labor of persons while legally tyrannizing them. It is—as Walzer puts it—to treat them as inferior beings. Likewise, it is immoral to deny the title of citizen to children who have been born on native soil. In some instances, denying them this title is equivalent to denying them the only viable claim to citizenship they will ever have. Absent citizenship, and the equal protection of laws, their right to self-preservation remains insecure at best.

However, in some countries (most notably Germany), so-called guestworkers, who have been brought in to do unpleasant jobs, are denied the option of becoming citizens (and this option is denied their children as well). The idea of exploiting a whole population of workers without extending to them the full protection of the law granted to other citizens—including the right to elect legislators—seems arbitrary. Yet, as I have already discussed, recent changes in U.S. immigration and welfare law have this very effect.

Permanent residents who contributed tax revenues are now being denied benefits that their tax revenues generated. Furthermore, some members of the business community have sought to bring back the old Bracero program that existed in the United States from 1942 to 1965. This program, which involved transporting Mexican farmworkers into the United States for temporary periods during harvest time, also denied them basic rights enjoyed by most immigrants.

Defenders of the new immigration and welfare reform argue that its harsh provisions deter illegal immigrants and reward hard workers. But there is little evidence that such measures will stem the tide of illegal immigration.

Desperate people—who, in any case, have little familiarity with immigration and welfare law—will migrate for the sake of acquiring even the poorest of employments. As for rewarding hard work, only the most naive spectator would believe that the welfare cutbacks befalling legal residents had anything whatsoever to do with encouraging them to work, since the vast majority of them had already contributed substantially more in taxes than many citizens who retained their benefits.

To conclude, restrictive immigration policies should aid states in protecting the basic rights of their inhabitants to self-preservation. In traditional indigenous societies, these rights might include a right to maintain a distinctive cultural identity and sense of community, as Walzer argues. However, in liberal, multicultural societies that lack such an identity and sense of community, such rights should extend only to the preservation of security, subsistence, and political self-determination. This is not to deny that patriotism and loyalty—or special concern for one's fellow citizens—are also important for maintaining solidarity in liberal states. However, the *partial* concern we show our fellow citizens, which extends beyond our impartial moral duties to strangers inhabiting other countries, is here a function of inhabiting a shared environment and political space—a solidarity based upon devotion to a territorily delimited regime of mutual cooperation and *impartial* self-governance. Therefore, despite the fact that neither communitarian bonds of loyalty nor impartial duties of justice taken separately suffice to capture the complex rationale governing restrictive immigration policies in liberal states, it is the latter—impartial duties of justice—that take precedence. These duties require that developed countries like the United States and Canada either adopt less restrictive immigration policies or redistribute some of their wealth to poor nations containing distressed populations. More urgently, these duties require both desisting from policies that harm poor nations and compensating the inhabitants of such nations for whatever distress has been caused to them.

# PART IV.
# RACIAL OPPRESSION AND AFFIRMATIVE ACTION IN THE UNITED STATES

# 7

## AFFIRMATIVE ACTION
## AND THE LEGACY OF RACISM

One day, while driving my friend to a social agency located in what the U.S. Department of Housing and Urban Development describes as "the most distressed small city in America" and what the St. Louis *Post-Dispatch* once dubbed "America's Soweto,"[1] I found myself lost in the middle of what looked like an enormous trash heap, surrounded by piles of tires and collapsed buildings. Suddenly, from out of nowhere, there arose before me a magnificent Victorian mansion so majestic and starkly contrasted with the polluted wasteland that I literally froze in dumbfounded astonishment. As I looked closer at this apparition, I noticed something even more surprising: beneath the rolls of plastic covering the paneless windows were boxes full of brightly colored pansies and geraniums. Here, amidst the worn and dreary monument to a once prosperous and distant past, was a glimmer of Zion— that blessed utopia vouchsafed for humanity's redemption from pain, suffering, and hatred.

The city in which this revelation occurred, East Saint Louis, has 50,000 inhabitants, 98 percent of whom are black. Of these, 75 percent live on welfare, while a third of its families earn less than $7,500 a year.[2] The city is so bankrupt that since 1987 garbage pickups have virtually ceased. Surrounding it are chemical, sewage, mineral-ore processing, and hazardous-waste incineration plants that fill the city with poisonous fumes, toxic waste from spills, and raw sewage from floods. Besides its destitute public sector, brothels, liquor stores, and drug dealing make up the bulk of the city's economy, which has one of the highest unemployment rates of any city in the United States. Add to this the fact that East St. Louis ranks first in fetal deaths, first in premature births, and third in infant mortality among sixty-six cities in Illinois,[3] and one can readily understand why a teacher from the University of Southern Illinois describes the city as "a repository for a non-white

149

population that is now regarded as expendable."[4] Safir Ahmed, reporter from the *Post-Dispatch* who finds disturbing parallels between his native Calcutta and East St. Louis, leaves us with this grim tally of wasted lives:

> The decimation of the men within the population is quite nearly total. Four of five births in East St. Louis are to single mothers. Where do the men go? Some to prison. Some to the military. Many to an early death. Dozens of men are living in the streets or sleeping in small, isolated camps behind burnt-out buildings.[5]

So marginalized is East St. Louis that it was recently left off the Illinois map and virtually excluded from Southern Illinois Bell's telephone listings.[6] It has become, in short, a shameful indictment of this country's professed commitment to equality of opportunity for all citizens.

## A Society Separate and Unequal

In the heat of the race riots that burned the nation's cities during the spring of 1967, President Lyndon Johnson appointed a commission headed by Governor Otto Kerner of Illinois to examine the causes and potential remedies for the violence. The opening line of the commission's report issued what has since become the rallying cry for a generation of reformers: absent aggressive government intervention, the United States will continue moving "toward two societies, one black, one white—separate and unequal."[7]

East St. Louis confirms this diagnosis as convincingly as any example possibly could. But how accurately do these symptoms describe the rest of the country? Despite some recent gains in their quality of life,[8] a third of all black families live in poverty as compared with 11.6 percent of white families. Currently, only a third of all black families earn middle-class incomes of $20,000 or more.[9] Data provided by the U.S. Census Bureau show that the median income for black families *fell* from $18,378 in 1970 to $18,098 in 1987, while during that same period the median income for white families *increased* from $29,960 to $32,274. Today, the average white household commands more than *ten times* the financial assets of the average black household. The rate of unemployment among blacks (10 percent in 1995) is more than twice that among whites, with black youths currently registering a whopping 34 percent unemployment rate.

In 1995 the Glass Ceiling Commission reported that, although blacks currently constitute about 13 percent of the U.S. population, they occupy less than 1 percent of senior managment positions (defined as vice presidents and above), while white men, who constitute 43 percent of the population, occupy 95 percent of such positions. White women, who have benefited most from affirmative action, now hold 40 percent of middle management jobs, but black women and men hold only about 9 percent. In general, whites comprise a disproportionately higher proportion (between 87 and 95 percent) of professionals, technicians, managers, sales personnel, and crafts-people, while a third of all employed blacks occupy minimum or low-paying jobs as laborers or service workers.

Inequalities in economic power are reflected in political inequalities. Despite the fact that more blacks and Latinos have been elected and appointed to political offices than ever before, they remain (as do women) grossly underrepresented in legislative, executive, and judicial bodies. For example, only 2 percent of elected officials in the United States are black.

Disparities in educational opportunity and achievement no doubt account for many of the economic and political inequalities dividing whites and blacks. Although the high school completion rate for blacks between the ages of eighteen and twenty-four had gradually climbed to 77 percent by 1994 (as compared with 83 percent for whites and only 57 percent for Hispanics), the total percentage of blacks attending college—about 59 percent—still remained relatively low compared with the percentage of whites (68 percent). Furthermore, test scores show that most black children are not receiving nearly the same quality of education as their white peers and so are less well prepared to compete with them at the college level.[10] Equally distressing is a recent study by the Commerce Department's National Telecommunications and Information Administration showing that as of 1998 only 12 percent of black households and 13 percent of Hispanic households had home Internet access (as compared with 33 percent of white households). Interestingly, the disparities in personal computer ownership between whites and Asians, on one side, and blacks and Latinos, on the other, narrows as income rises.

These facts must be interpreted against the background of educational and residential segregation patterns that have remained virtually constant for the past thirty years. Although it is true that the percentage of blacks living in neighborhoods that are 90 to 100 percent black has declined from 35 percent to 31 percent, fully 80 percent of blacks in most cities would have to relocate in nonblack neighborhoods in order to achieve racial balance.[11] The inability to relocate is partly caused by economic hardship, which has steadily worsened during the twenty-year decline of manufacturing and heavy industry experienced by U.S. cities. But even well-educated middle-class blacks who have moved to the suburbs tend to locate in predominantly black enclaves.

Discrimination in securing mortgages, real estate redlining, and racial hostility have conspired to render patterns of residential segregation all but intractable. One need only look at the results of scientifically designed studies, polls, and surveys showing the prevalence of persistent patterns of discriminatory treatment favoring whites over equally qualified blacks in securing jobs,[12] loans,[13] salaries,[14] houses,[15] fair prices on selected merchandise,[16] decent health care, affordable insurance, and fair treatment from law enforcement agencies. Apposite here is a recent study showing that 15–19 percent of all eligible white voters would not vote for a qualified black candidate for governor or president under any circumstances.[17]

As for education, a 1992 Harvard survey found that public schools across the nation were more segregated than they were in 1967. In the public school systems of larger northern cities, the percentage of white students enrolled ranges from 9–11 percent in Chicago, Detroit, Newark, and New York, 16–17 percent in Baltimore and Philadelphia, and 32–35 percent in Boston, Cincinnati, and Milwaukee.[18]

These gloomy statistics confirm William Julius Wilson's negative diagnosis of urban ghettos as socially isolated concentrations of poverty that are pathologically bereft of social support networks, responsible collective supervision, and formal and informal organizations (churches and political parties as well as block clubs and parent-teacher associations). Even if, as some critics have argued, this diagnosis reflects mainstream middle-class biases, there can be no disputing the fact that poverty, unemployment, segregation, powerlessness, and lack of education have together transformed what were once stable working-class neighborhoods into war zones contested by fractious drug lords.[19] Blacks are incarcerated at a rate seven times that of whites—and in a country that incarcerates a higher percentage of its population (373 per 100,000) than any other nation, excepting the former Soviet Union. In 1991 it was estimated that 42 percent of all black men between the ages of eighteen and thirty-five living in Washington, D.C., were either in prison, on probation, awaiting trial, or being sought by police. In Baltimore, the comparable figure for this period was 56 percent. According to a 1993 Justice Department report, 22 percent of male students attending inner-city schools reported owning a gun, and nearly 70 percent of all students stated that guns were present in their homes. Not surprisingly, homicide is now the leading cause of death among young black men.[20] Even more startling, two-thirds of black male teenagers can expect to die before reaching the age of 65 (and they are less likely to reach the age of 45 than their white counterparts are of reaching 65) because of cardiovascular disease, cancer, and other chronic illnesses that medical researchers attribute to the daily stress of having to cope with poverty, discrimination, and the threat of violence.[21]

## Divided by Color

Who (or what) is to blame for this tragic state of affairs? A recent study by Donald Kinder and Lynn Sanders shows just how divided blacks and whites are on this question. Although most whites concede that blacks as a group have faced and continue to face discrimination and hardship—there is a considerable discrepancy between whites and blacks in assessing the extent of that discrimination and hardship—a substantial majority of them say that government should no longer try to remedy these harms. As might be expected, blacks disagree quite strongly with whites on this score.[22]

On the positive side, Kinder and Sanders note that the incidence of *biological* racism—the view that blacks are genetically inferior to whites in intelligence and moral character—has dramatically declined since the thirties. On the negative side, they observe that biological racism has been replaced by a more subtle, *symbolic* form of racism: a majority of whites think that blacks are solely responsible for their problems. They resent blacks for being pushy and lazy—in short, for wanting a free government handout without having to work hard for a living (as they have done). The belief that blacks *as a group* are less morally reponsible than other groups varies somewhat in relation to class and income, but even affluent suburban whites whose schools, neighborhoods, jobs, and incomes are not "threatened" by blacks subscribe to this negative stereotype.[23]

Is such a stereotypical view of black moral failing tantamount to a racist prejudice? It would seem so, at least insofar as whites remain unwilling to give up their racial resentment in light of disconfirming sociological data, including knowledge of the social causes underlying welfare dependency, teen pregnancy, and crime. As things currently stand, conservative political leaders have been only too willing to play upon the largely unfounded fears of resentful whites, while the mass media have done little to dispel—and much to reinforce—current racial stereotypes.

Unfortunately, the available evidence indicates that most resentful whites will hold on to their stereotypes no matter what social scientists say. First,

the pervasive belief in the Protestant work ethic among resentful whites inclines them to the view that individuals, not social institutions, are responsible for what happens to them.[24] The widespread presence of crime,
ignorance, and poverty among a substantial segment of the black urban "underclass" will therefore be perceived by resentful whites as a tendency toward moral and intellectual failing among blacks generally, which
distinguishes them as a class from whites.[25] Second, the need to come up
with a nonsocial scientific explanation for the black underclass that goes beyond mass individual moral failing (or absence of willpower) predictably
leads some sociobiologists to posit natural inheritance as the reason why
blacks score lower than whites on IQ tests. Richard Herrnstein and Charles
Murray's recent best-seller, *The Bell Curve,* shows just how alarmingly fashionable this scientifically unsustainable racism has become once again among
some conservatives.[26]

Finally, the treatment of blacks in the criminal justice system indicates that
discrepancies in criminalizing behavior, processing cases, and sentencing are
explicable only on the basis of white racial resentment. Although young
blacks compose only 15 percent of the U.S. population, they constitute 26
percent of arrests, 32 percent of court referrals, 36 percent of those formally
charged, 41 percent of those detained pending trial, 46 percent of those incarcerated, and 52 percent of those who are transferred to adult court
(meanwhile, young Latinos are 60 percent more likely to be in jail than their
white counterparts).[27] Contrasted with the incarceration of "predatory"
urban blacks and Latinos, middle-class white youths who commit crimes are
regarded as merely "troubled" and "in need of therapy." The long-term effects of this dual justice system also merit observation: over 500,000 black
ex-felons have permanently lost their right to vote, thereby further weakening the political power base of black communities. Significantly, despite the
fact that in 1992 Congress passed the so-called "disproportionate minority
confinement" mandate requiring states to analyze "minority overrepresentation" in juvenile prisons and take steps to reduce it on pain of losing millions of dollars of federal delinquency prevention funds, the Senate is today
debating a bill (S. 254) that would eliminate the mandate and allow children
over thirteen years of age to be tried and incarcerated as adults. Even the
criminal code reflects racial bias. For example, 88.3 percent of federal defendants convicted of selling crack (cocaine that has been cooked with bak-
ing soda) are black, while 73 percent of those convicted of selling pure
cocaine are white. Could one plausibly argue that the one hundred times
more severe, federally mandated penalties assessed for possession of crack

(five years for a first-time offender possessing just five grams) in comparison to those assessed for trafficking in cocaine (five years for possession of five hundred grams) stem from the gang violence typically associated with the former drug and have nothing to do with race? Perhaps. But then one can only hope that recent research showing the roughly comparable behavioral effects of crack and pure cocaine will induce Congress to reduce the existing discrepancy in sentencing guidelines.[28] Unfortunately, Congress, with President Clinton's approval, recently rejected a 1995 recommendation by the U.S. Sentencing Commission to eliminate that gap, despite the commission's warning that the guidelines reflected a most serious form of racial discrimination (incidentally, this gap was upheld as constitutional by the Supreme Court in its ruling in May 1996, which argued that the discrepancy did not sufficiently prove evidence of racial discrimination).

Skeptics of the federal government's selective prosecution of blacks, however, must still confront the by now well-documented evidence of racial profiling used by state law enforcement agencies in stopping vehicles driven by blacks and Latinos and in issuing citations.[29] The savage beating meted out to Rodney King by the Los Angeles Police Department and the damning testimony in the O. J. Simpson trial concerning Detective Mark Fuhrman's planting of evidence in order to convict blacks only confirm that harassment for "driving while black" often is a prelude for much worse treatment. One need only mention the much praised study of Georgia's sentencing procedures by University of Iowa professor David Baldus, which showed that between 1973 and 1979, blacks who killed whites were seven times more likely to be sentenced to death than whites who killed blacks, while white-victim cases were eleven times more likely to result in a death sentence than black-victim cases.

### Race and Caste: The Uniqueness of the African-American Dilemma

Conservatives often blame the black underclass for its plight, arguing that immigrants of ethnic stock, who also were discriminated against, managed to raise themselves up from poverty and powerlessness through dint of hard work and without the aid of government preferences.

Rebutting this claim requires showing that the kind of discrimination meted out to African Americans is qualitatively distinct from that visited upon ethnic immigrants. It is unique in that no ethnic group experienced a form of oppression remotely as vicious as the slavery, Jim Crow segregation, and widespread prejudice to which African Americans were subjected. Although

Native Americans experienced the incomparable horrors of government-sanctioned genocide, they were never subjected to the same degree of systematic dehumanization to which African slaves and their descendants were subjected.

Nothing comparable to this catastrophe ever befell any other ethnic group. True, racism runs deep in the American psyche. Many ethnic groups —Irish, Jewish, Polish, Italian, Mexican, Chinese, and Japanese—have experienced virulent forms of racial discrimination. But the discrimination meted out to these groups has been of a lesser degree and duration. Their lighter skin enabled them (or their children) to shed their ethnic racial identity. More important, many Jewish, Irish, Italian, and German immigrants benefited from racism; they were awarded good jobs previously held by blacks and, in some instances, formed ethnic trade unions, such as the Greek furriers' local, the Italian dressmakers' union, and the Jewish waiters' organization, that were explicitly closed to blacks.

Many recent immigrants today continue to enjoy a competitive advantage over urban blacks. In particular, many enter under INS guidelines that give preference to persons already possessing capital assets or desirable skills. Modestly affluent families in Korea and India, for example, provide substantial financial support to family members who immigrate to the United States and set up businesses.

Conservative critics of affirmative action like Nicholas Capaldi cite Thomas Sowell's[30] controversial sociological study of African Americans who emigrated from the West Indies: "African Americans who immigrated to the United States voluntarily from the West Indies have been remarkably successful despite facing the same obstacles as those who were descendants of slaves."[31] Although subsequent studies have shown that West Indians face racial discrimination in housing, employment, and other areas of life comparable to that experienced by the descendants of American slaves, they hardly confirm Capaldi's claim that these immigrants have been "remarkably successful."[32] The census data for 1980 show that West Indian household incomes and the earnings of West Indian males remain significantly lower than similar statistics for comparably situated whites.[33] The extent to which West Indians have been more successful than American blacks in advancing along the path toward upward mobility may be accounted for by significant disanalogies in their situation. (Haitians, for example, overthrew their white slave masters two hundred years ago and so managed to avoid much of the oppression endured by American blacks.) To cite Gertrude Ezorsky,

The virtual absence of a white working class in the West Indian home-land, where blacks held majority status, facilitated their acquisition of skilled trades. According to immigration records in the 1920's, West Indians had advantages in literacy and skills, advantages that are con-ducive to an achievement orientation and that would tend to be repli-cated in their children.[34]

Despite the persistence of overt discrimination, the real key to under-standing America's racial caste system is the prevalence of *unintended* insti-tutionalized racism. Institutionalized racism occurs whenever procedures for admissions, hiring, promoting, and contracting that are racially neutral in wording and intent work to exclude a disportionate percentage of minori-ties. For instance, a high percentage of job openings (possibly as high as 86 percent) are advertised through word of mouth rather than through classi-fied ads, so personal acquaintance with the employer, or living in close prox-imity to his or her business, becomes a necessary condition for obtaining employment.[35] Given the undeniable reality of residential segregation—ex-acerbated by "white flight" to the suburbs—and the large concentration of businesses of all sizes in the hands of white employers, word-of-mouth hir-ing alone serves to exclude a sizable percentage of inner-city blacks from even being considered for employment.

Referral unions that recommend candidates for good-paying jobs in con-struction, printing, and transportation also rely heavily on personal contacts, but these, too, have been controlled by whites. Patronage remains an im-portant feature of government life, and most elected officials, who are pre-dominantly white, will fill government posts with persons whom they trust: acquaintances, family members, and associates. Finally, studies have shown that, because blacks and whites rarely interact outside the workplace, blacks are systematically excluded from personal connections.[36] This exclusion con-tinues to handicap well-educated blacks looking for good jobs even after they have relocated to job-rich suburbs.

Another form of institutionalized racism is the seniority system. It has only been in the past twenty years or so that blacks have gained admission to occupations controlled by formerly all-white labor unions. Unfortunately, blacks' lack of seniority has made them especially vulnerable to layoffs dur-ing times of recession. Given the cyclical frequency of recessions, being "last hired and first fired" means that many blacks will always find themselves at the bottom rung of the economic ladder.

Institutionalized racism has a profoundly crippling impact on the capacity of African Americans to succeed economically—hence, the great disparities noted earlier between income levels and total family assets that exist between whites and blacks. Market mechanisms magnify these inequalities further by generating a cumulative effect over time. As noted economist Lester Thurow has remarked, 66 percent of the improved fortune of succeeding generations is explained by the intergenerational transfer of assets, and "approximately half of all great wealth is inherited."[37] Fully one-third of all black families have only cash on hand, and only those few who possess enough assets to invest in high-yield CD accounts, stocks and bonds, and other capital-generating ventures will manage to accumulate significant savings once inflation is factored in.

The castelike nature of oppression facing most blacks—the combination of race and economic deprivation—would not be complete without factoring in a third element: political powerlessness. Political powerlessness is endemic to poverty generally. It is not simply that the wealthy have the resources to curry favor with candidates, and that governments must appease them with favorable tax policies in order to ensure that they continue to invest in the domestic economy. It is rather that the poor lack the education and the time to inform themselves about public policy debates, and in some instances are even discouraged from voter registration by municipal and state governments.[38]

This powerlessness applies to wealthier blacks who occupy positions of authority. Despite the fact that blacks as a whole have increased their political involvement overall in comparison to whites and have seen a fourfold increase in the number of black elected officeholders since 1970, the money-driven nature of American democracy and the economic and racial demographics of American political life place severe limits on the capacity of blacks to acquire meaningful power: Blacks constitute only 12 percent of the population; whites are disinclined to vote for black candidates unless they are running for lower office or are otherwise perceived as nonthreatening to their interests; and most black candidates sympathetic to the needs of the black community who do succeed in being elected typically serve in districts mainly inhabited by poor black populations. Unable to amass the war chests available to white candidates serving wealthier constituents, the most successful of these black officeholders are elected to marginalized congressional seats or the mayoral offices of financially strapped, impoverished cities. Beholden to white governors and state representatives who control the cities' purse strings, their power to effect policy reforms on behalf of their constituents is severely limited.

Power is also a scarce commodity even for "successful" blacks. A significant number of black executives feel that their "token" positions give them symbolic but not real power over company policy. The same can be said of black principals of inner-city schools, who—ironically—often lose their positions to white school administrators when school districts are *de*segregated.[39] We may conclude, following Jennifer Hochschild, that "inequalities of race, class, and power accumulate, that cumulative inequalities worsen the inequalities of each dimension alone, and that blacks are more constrained than whites in translating achievement in one dimension into further achievements in that or other dimensions."[40] What all this means is that blacks in the United States have suffered—and continue to suffer—the cumulative disadvantages of a unique form of overt and institutionalized racism that no other ethnic minority in the United States has had to bear.

### The Current Status of Affirmative Action

Despite suffering from the cumulative disadvantages of racism, some African Americans have managed to improve their lot over the last thirty years. Since 1970 the percentage of African-American households recording yearly earnings of more than $50,000 in constant dollars has grown from 11.6 percent to 21.2 percent.[41] During this period, blacks more than doubled their representation among telephone operators (from 2.6 percent to 21 percent), firefighters (from 2.5 percent to 7.5 percent), accountants (from 1.6 percent to 7.0 percent), secretaries (from 2.0 percent to 7.7 percent), retail salespersons (from 2.4 percent to 9.7 percent), electricians (from 2.2 percent to 6.1 percent), and lawyers (from 1.3 percent to 2.7 percent).[42] As for women, they now constitute 54 percent of all persons receiving bachelor's degrees (up from 43 percent in 1970 and 35 percent in 1960), and their share of managerial, executive, and administrative positions has climbed from 16 percent in 1970 to 43 percent today. Meanwhile, white men—who now make up less than half of the entire workforce—have ceded much of their dominance to Asians and women except in two blue-collar occupations: electricians and sheet metal workers.[43]

What explains this monumental shift in the composition of the workforce? From the few data that we have, Asians have increased their representation among engineers, computer analysts, physicians, and college faculty largely owing to their possession of skills that are in great demand. Asians who immigrate to the United States are among the most highly motivated and well-educated members of their native country; excelling in school and willing to relocate in less desirable areas of the country, they have not had to rely on affirmative action to accomplish their gains.

The case of women is more complicated. On the lower end of the earnings scale, many women (single or married, with or without children) have been forced by recent changes in welfare law or by sheer economic necessity to accept minimum wage jobs. On the upper end of the scale, women are outperforming men in school, and this fact, combined with their willingness to work for less pay than men, may well explain why they have made such impressive inroads into the business world. Aside from these factors, affirmative action undoubtedly provided a vital catalyst for initially boosting the representation of women in the professions, even if their advances have been restricted by a "glass ceiling."

Only African Americans and Latinos seem to have relied heavily on affirmative action for their gains, although they now comprise less than 50 percent of its beneficiaries. A recent study published in the *Chronicle of Higher Education* explains why. The percentage of blacks and Latinos admitted to the University of California at Los Angeles in 1994 was 7.1 percent and 20 percent respectively; without affirmative action—basing admissions solely on academic criteria—that figure becomes 1.2 percent and 5 percent.[44] A recent national study of law school admissions found that basing admissions solely on test scores and grades would return law schools to their former, overwhelmingly white status (currently 26 percent of black applicants and 32 percent of Latino applicants are admitted; without affirmative action that figure reduces to 3 percent and 9 percent respectively).[45]

In light of the reduced number of blacks and Latinos among the applicants and admissions to the University of Texas Law School and the University of California system following the abolition of affirmative action programs at those institutions in 1995, it is sobering to recall that in 1968, using only test scores, grades, and interviews, the School of Medicine at the University of California at Davis admitted no blacks or Latinos. Thanks to the abolition of affirmative action, this remarkable feat of exclusion is being reduplicated: out of 268 first-year students currently enrolled at the law school of the University of California at Berkeley for 1997, only one is black—in stark contrast to the period from 1970 to 1992, when 5 percent of the first-year enrollment was black and 10 percent was Latino.[46] (To appreciate the enormity of this statistic, consider that over 40 percent of the prison population consists of black males.) The full impact of affirmative action in higher education becomes most apparent when one realizes that even black and Latino students whose families earn between $60,000 and

$70,000 still achieve only average scores of 800 and 887 respectively on the SAT test in contrast to scores of 1,011 and 959 recorded for Asians and whites.[47]

My point in citing these depressing statistics is not to reinforce racial prejudices regarding the cognitive deficiencies of blacks and Latinos, since whatever cognitive deficiencies they possess are likely attributable to the innumerable effects of chronic discrimination. Rather, my point is that affirmative action is the principal reason why blacks and Latinos have increased their representation in the professions and trades; without it they would likely be excluded to a degree not witnessed since the early sixties.

All of this is but a prelude to our present concern. Affirmative action may not be the most useful litmus test for gauging the legitimacy of group preferences, but it certainly has become the lightning rod around which Americans have debated this issue. As we approach the millennium, the declining popularity of affirmative action among jurists and laypersons seems part and parcel of a general conservative reaction against government intervention on behalf of persons who find themselves economically and politically marginalized. Kinder and Sanders report that 85 percent of white respondents oppose "preferential hiring and promotion of blacks"; fewer than half of them think that government ought to redress unfair treatment of blacks in the job market. Significantly, opposition to affirmative action diminishes to as little as 31 percent when women and minorities—rather than blacks—are mentioned as the beneficiaries of preferential treatment.[48] This discrepancy testifies to a widespread sentiment among whites that blacks as a group, or at least poor blacks, are morally undeserving of governmental assistance of any kind. The discrepancy also underscores the confusing complexity of affirmative action itself.

### Affirmative Action and Multicultural Preference

Affirmative action was originally designed to compensate African Americans for the peculiar disadvantages of past and present oppression by granting them preferential treatment in education and employment. The preferences bestowed on them, however, were eventually extended to a substantial majority of the population, encompassing women, Native Americans, Aleuts, Eskimos, South Sea Islanders, and persons of ethnic immigrant stock, a situation that sometimes pits one preferred group against another in competing for scarce positions.[49] Certainly, many in this majority who were singled out for preferential treatment could justifiably claim that they had suffered discrimination. Others in this group—for instance, immigrants from Sri Lanka—might have received preferential treatment simply for the sake of increasing diversity.

To compound the confusion, groups that have benefited from affirmative action in certain situations have been harmed by it in others. Some colleges and universities extend preferential treatment to persons of Asian background in order to increase their representation among the faculty and student body; others, such as the University of California, do not, ostensibly on the grounds that such persons are already adequately represented among the faculty and student body.[50]

The confusion over affirmative action stems not only from its multiple rationales and beneficiaries but also from its multiple applications, which range from weak preferential treatment, the voluntary recruitment of women and minorities for placement in schools and businesses, to strong preferential treatment, such as setting aside a fixed percentage of government contracts earmarked for women- and minority-owned businesses. Despite this confusion, I think it is legitimate to distinguish between the primary and secondary aims of affirmative action, especially as regards the aim of diversification, which it shares with multicultural reform.

Proponents of multiculturalism view diversification as an end in itself. Ensuring the representation of different cultures and groups in education, for instance, ostensibly enriches our understanding of ourselves and others while at the same time recognizing the positive value of distinct lifestyles and belief systems. By contrast, proponents of affirmative action see integration, rather than diversification, as the chief aim. Affirmative action preferences are not aimed at preserving group differences; instead, they function to eliminate differences (i.e., racial and class distinctions that hinder individuals from achieving the basic and universal qualifications of citizenship). Because affirmative action has its roots in the civil rights movement that sought to end discrimination against racial minorities and women, its aim has always been to bring about a society in which differences in gender and race no longer matter.

For this reason, it is misleading to think of affirmative action as a policy of diversification. Unfortunately, educators and policy-makers frequently make just this mistake. They fail to notice that admitting and hiring African Americans in higher education is mainly intended to procure them equal opportunity citizenship, while admitting and hiring Asians is mainly intended to enrich the cultural and experiential diversity of the whole student body while also showing respect to Asian students.

Of course, the aims of inclusion and diversification are by no means exclusive. Admitting and hiring African Americans in higher education also serves the secondary function of exposing the student body to different perspectives and experiences, even if these perspectives and experiences, largely born out of the legacy of racial oppression, are ones that we hope will disappear some day along with the passing of racism. Conversely, admitting Asians in higher education also serves the secondary function of ensuring that Asians in general are guaranteed the same degree of access to doctors, lawyers, and teachers enjoyed by the rest of the community.[51]

### The Limits of Affirmative Action in Remedying African-American Oppression

Leaving aside for now the role of affirmative action in promoting diversity, I would like to focus instead on its original aim: compensating African Americans for past oppression and counteracting present discrimination. The question frequently asked these days is: Is affirmative action really necessary for compensating African Americans and counteracting discrimination? Underlying this question is the suspicion that white Americans owe African Americans nothing and that whatever oppression African Americans endure today is largely of their own making.

This suspicion is well confirmed by numerous studies that show that the fate of affirmative action, especially as it applies to blacks, is closely tied to that of welfare. Many whites erroneously believe that recipients of welfare are overwhelmingly black. They also believe that welfare recipients are largely responsible for their own condition due to moral failing. This stereotypical impression finds parallel expression in the negative impression many whites have about beneficiaries of affirmative action. Not only do they mistakenly believe that most beneficiaries are black, but they also believe that beneficiaries are morally less deserving than the white men whose positions and contracts they have supposedly robbed.[52] Thus, one often hears (from white men, especially) that affirmative action simply discriminates in reverse by awarding positions on the basis of race rather than qualifications—despite findings by the Department of Labor that only six of the more than three thousand discrimination cases filed in federal district courts from 1990 to 1994 ruled in favor of white plaintiffs claiming "reverse discrimination."

Be that as it may, the common consensus today seems to agree that blacks' failure to be economically integrated into mainstream American society is not a function of past and present discrimination but of a simple lack of willpower to do what every other ethnic group who "immigrated" to this country has managed to do: internalize the work ethic of self-discipline and individual achievement. Defenders of affirmative action must counter this diagnosis with an alternative one, which must first show that the possibility for exercising willpower—and therewith the possibility for internalizing a work ethic of self-discipline and individual achievement—is not a metaphysical given, internally planted in the soul of each individual from birth. It must show, in other words, that these possibilities are dependent for their cultivation on economic, political, and educational opportunities, both legally mandated and federally implemented. Without decent jobs, schools, housing, child and health care services, *and* opportunities for advancement, "working" families—especially those living in gang- and drug-infested slums—will have a hard time raising their kids to be self-disciplined individual achievers.

Second, the alternative must show that the continuing presence of family breakdown in the black urban ghetto and the failure of blacks to be fully integrated into all strata of economic life (from middle management on up) are not caused by individual moral deficiency or (as some critics claim) by welfare and affirmative action programs that breed passive dependence and disincentives to achieve. Even allowing for the disincentive effects of welfare programs, the defense of affirmative action must show that the main reason for the failure of black families to be fully integrated into American life is the continuing effects of past and present discrimination.

I think the case for both assumptions is strongly supported by social scientific data, some of which I have already noted. Conservative critics of affirmative action, of course, disagree. They argue, correctly, that statistical data are subject to interpretation and that strong statistical correlations linking racial discrimination, economic deprivation, and social and political subordination do not conclusively demonstrate a simple and exclusive causal relationship between these factors. Still, among mainstream social scientists there is much less disagreement regarding the correct interpretation of these data than conservatives care to admit. In any case, the standard of proof demanded by conservatives would be impossible to meet even among biologists.[53] Confronted with this truth, conservatives sometimes resort to slinging ad hominem arguments, criticizing mainstream social scientists as ideologically motivated radicals and dismissing social science as pseudoscience.[54] More often than not they cite a small minority of ideologically conservative social scientists whose causal explanations for the failure of black integration—ranging from the dysfunctional tribalism of Afrocentric culture to the genetic inferiority of blacks generally—are a great deal more speculative than any adduced by their so-called "radical" counterparts.[55]

But defenders of affirmative action must not only show the presence of institutionalized racism; they also must show that affirmative action efficiently and fairly counteracts it. Indeed, given the perception that affirmative action violates our ideal of a just society—wherein, as the Reverend Martin Luther King Jr. once put it, one is judged by "the content of one's character" and not by "the color of one's skin"—one must show that it is the *only* viable remedy.

First of all, defenders of affirmative action must concede that as currently implemented it remedies only part of the underrpresentation of blacks in the economy. Affirmative action mainly benefits blacks who already possess sufficient skills and education to own their own businesses or apply to professional and trade schools (or positions requiring degrees and licenses testifying to advanced secondary education). However, it also benefits unemployed or unskilled blacks by providing them with a preferential advantage in job training programs and the like.[56] Although affirmative action could (and perhaps should) be extended to enhance minority job placement in all occupations, its current implementation was never intended to rectify the so-called injustices of the marketplace.

Second, defenders of affirmative action must concede that it might not be the most direct method for remedying the underrepresentation of blacks in skilled vocations. A more direct approach would ensure that black children living in inner-city ghettos receive the same quality of education (*and* educational support) as children living in affluent white suburbs. Unfortunately, most Americans would find this approach to be either too costly or too egalitarian (because the values of properties are directly linked to the quality of school districts). In any case, no one contemplating educational reform can plausibly expect it to work without the equalization of educational support systems—decent employment, housing, education, safety, health, food, clothing, and the like. Such an all-out assault on urban and rural poverty would be very costly, indeed so costly that it might have a recessionary effect on the economy. Given the structural limits that capitalism imposes on the taxing and spending capacity of the welfare state,[57] the general disinclination of Americans to sacrifice their incomes for the sake of rectifying social injustice, and the persistence of overt and institutionalized racism in the occupational sphere, educational reform seems a very distant hope on which to pin one's resistance to affirmative action.

*Some Standard Criticisms of Affirmative Action*

Critics of affirmative action argue that it
• produces inefficiency by promoting the unqualified ahead of the qualified;
• increases racial tension;
• unjustly deprives white males of positions they have earned;
• stigmatizes its beneficiaries as inferior and undeserving; and
• reinforces the very dependency and laziness that is the principal cause of a failure to achieve on one's own.

In my opinion, none of these charges is defensible. Clearly, some are more serious than others, and some are more easily assessed. Those that are less easily assessed address the psychological impact of affirmative action. Take, for instance, the charge that affirmative action increases racial tension. It is impossible to confirm or deny this charge, for whites who disagree with affirmative action may not feel hostility to blacks as such. Likewise, the real increase in racial tension, indexed to a rise in Klan membership, racially motivated hate crimes, and the like, might be caused by factors besides a simple opposition to affirmative action.

Doubtless, many blue-collar white males feel resentment toward blacks who compete against them for scarce jobs. Such resentment, which predictably increases during times of recession, is often directed against affirmative action hiring and promoting. Yet if whites report feelings of hostility to blacks who are hired or promoted ahead of them because of affirmative action—instead of blaming, say, the union's history of racially closed shops or the company's exportation of jobs abroad—then this might simply reflect their long-standing prejudicial scapegoating of blacks. An increase in racial tension caused by opposition to affirmative action would indeed be cause for alarm, but it would not justify abandoning affirmative action anymore than racist opposition to civil rights for blacks justified abandoning these rights.

Of course, it is entirely possible that affirmative action has reduced racial tension or might do so given more time. The supposition being unprovable, we consider the next charge, that affirmative action stigmatizes its beneficiaries as inferior and reinforces bad behavior. This charge likewise resists confirmation or denial. True, some whites think that beneficiaries of affirmative action are less qualified, and some beneficiaries of affirmative action resent this fact. However, lacking affirmative action, which has demonstrably increased the representation of blacks in the skilled vocations and professions, many whites would still think that the absence of significant black representation in these areas proved that blacks were unqualified. Furthermore, the underrepresentation of black role models in the professions would likely send a signal to many blacks that educational and economic advancement are closed off to them, thereby discouraging them from even pursuing these paths.[58]

Likewise, the charge that affirmative action encourages laziness and dependence seems more a figment of racial prejudice than of reality. If anything, the evidence indicates that blacks who have been awarded affirmative action positions have put themselves in that favorable position against all odds. Lower performance on standardized tests (whatever their reliability for gauging future performance) is no indication of laziness, since many blacks who have acquired sufficient knowledge and skill to be admitted or hired had to work mucher harder than their white counterparts and under much less favorable conditions. As studies confirm, once having been admitted or hired, affirmative action beneficiaries generally continue to work harder than their white peers in order to make up for whatever educational handicaps they were burdened with.[59] Without black role models, however, it is unlikely that many economically and educationally handicapped blacks would have any incentive to work hard to gain admission to an elite club that they perceive to be exclusive.

### Affirmative Action and the Demand for Justice

We should not, then, allow ourselves to be overly concerned about the alleged psychological effects of affirmative action; the evidence here is either inconclusive or disconfirming. This leaves two other accusations: that affirmative action favors the unqualified over the qualified (the argument from efficiency) and that it is unjust.

Let me first comment on the latter accusation. The question of justice can be divided into two separate issues. The first issue involves the question of compensation. Affirmative action is sometimes justified as a way of compensating African Americans for harms done to them in the past by whites. The second issue involves the question of procedural justice. Here, affirmative action is justified on the grounds that it is necessary for ensuring that the "rules of the game" treat everyone fairly, including African Americans, who suffer distinct disadvantages stemming from institutionalized racism.

Issues of compensatory and procedural justice are related but distinct. Defending affirmative action on procedural justice grounds need not assume anything about the causes of *un*equal opportunity in today's society. Yet without addressing the racist causes of unequal opportunity—and without seeing affirmative action as compensating for past injustice—this policy loses much of its moral urgency. All things being equal, harms that are deliberately inflicted by certain persons on others are more grievous and needy of rectification than harms that arise from structurally induced inequalities of opportunity.

Thus, the most powerful defense of affirmative action shows that blacks are owed preferential treatment as compensation for past injuries deliberately inflicted on them by the white majority. There are several ways in which this might be done. First, it might be argued that beneficiaries of past discrimination against blacks, which arguably includes all whites, ought to compensate blacks by restoring them or their progeny to the condition they would have been in had they not suffered discrimination. Even if it is unrealistic to monetarily compensate blacks for the total harm inflicted on them and their descendants—a sum that could well exceed the entire wealth of the United States[60]—it is not unrealistic to compensate them at least in part for economic opportunities lost through discrimination. Supposing that blacks are as naturally talented and motivated as whites, it is not unreasonable to assume that, had there been no discrimination, they would have been represented in most desirable occupations in numbers roughly proportionate to their percentage of the American population.

In the next chapter, I will discuss how disanalogies between the concept of compensation operant in tort law—its original field of application—and the concept of compensation appealed to by defenders of affirmative action render the latter concept somewhat problematic. Granting this, defenders of affirmative action also appeal to principles of procedural justice.

Following John Rawls, I distinguish three senses of procedural justice: perfect, imperfect, and pure.[61] Perfect procedural justice occurs when procedures are designed that invariably guarantee a specific outcome that one has decided in advance is just. Suppose that dividing a pie equally is just. Perfect justice is ensured by requiring that the person who slices the pie take the last piece (here the procedure limits greed by exploiting it). Imperfect justice, by contrast, occurs when procedures are designed that only approximately guarantee a just outcome. Trial procedures, for example, do not guarantee that all and only malfactors will be found guilty and punished. Finally, pure procedural justice differs from both perfect and imperfect justice in that there exists no independent criterion of a just outcome prior to the actual workings of the procedure. Games embody pure procedural justice insofar as the fairness of the rules determines the fairness of the outcome, regardless of who wins.

Most of us believe that the economic and political institutions of our society should embody pure procedural justice. We believe that a fair democracy should enable each citizen to exercise as much influence on politics as anyone else. But merely allowing everyone an equal chance to participate does not ensure that decisions reached will be just according to some predetermined standard of perfection, such as the equal advancement of each person's welfare. The same applies to truly competitive markets; we think that everyone should have an equal opportunity to compete for scarce jobs and assets. If everyone started out with different but equal resources, free exchanges between ideally rational persons would result in outcomes about which no one would have just cause to complain.

Existing forms of democracy and market economy are highly imperfect instantiations of pure procedural justice. The procedures regulating both can be distorted in their functioning by social, political, and economic inequalities. The concentration of wealth in the hands of a few lends them disproportionate bargaining leverage in both political and economic spheres; they can threaten governments with investment strikes just as they can threaten the working poor with loss of jobs. Racism distorts the workings of democracy and economy too, so affirmative action can also be understood as an attempt to align political and economic institutions with the demands of pure procedural justice.

Few would deny the importance of achieving procedural justice in political and economic life. But critics charge that affirmative action quotas and set-asides (government quotas specifying a certain percentage of contracts with women- and minority-owned businesses) do more than merely ensure equal opportunity for everyone. They argue that such quotas go beyond securing pure procedural justice by dictating (perfectly or imperfectly) a pre-given outcome: the perfect representation of minorities and women in exact proportion to their percentages of the total population. This outcome, they correctly note, is not mandated by social justice.

The critics seem to have a point. Pure procedural justice might not be achievable without first establishing what looks like perfect (or imperfect) procedural justice. For example, let us assume that procedural justice requires that each group in society have equal access to basic resources. Next, let us assume that equal access to basic resources is partly defined in terms of perfect procedural justice—for instance, adequate access to medical care correlated with a certain ratio of doctors to patients. By generating a pool of black doctors who will be more likely to live and work in black communities in numbers roughly proportional to the black population as a whole (somewhere around 12 percent of the U.S. population), affirmative action produces a perfect (or imperfect) ratio of doctors to patients in these communities. Likewise, through set-asides, it produces a similar ratio with respect to jobs and capital assets.

Thus, affirmative action seems to be an example of perfect (or imperfect) procedural justice, just as the critics maintain. However, seen from another vantage point, it functions in a purely procedural manner. Although affirmative action policies sometimes aim at increasing the representation of women and minorities commensurate with some numerical percentage, it is not because that distribution is thought to be inherently just. In an ideal society that had eradicated all vestiges of racism, there is no good reason why persons of one skin color would necessarily be dispersed throughout all sectors of society in any particular proportion. Even under ideal circumstances, African Americans might continue to be disproportionately overrepresented in professional basketball and disproportionately underrepresented in professional hockey.

Of course, if such a distribution were partly caused by racism, *that* would render it morally suspect. Because defenders of affirmative action in fact believe that the distribution of jobs is at least partly (if not largely) tainted by racism, they propose to alter that distribution by increasing the representation of African Americans in certain key fields where they are grossly underrepresented. This aim is purely procedural: to counterbalance the effects of racism in order to give each citizen an equal opportunity to compete for scarce political and economic resources.

Affirmative action set-asides and placements thus aim to bring about equal opportunity, not some (perfect) proportional representation of minorities, as critics maintain. Be that as it may, affirmative action seems an imperfect device for achieving that aim. Some black professionals helped by affirmative action move away from urban black communities that need their services. Even minority set-asides that allocate jobs and assets to black businesses do not necessarily help the black community. Black-owned businesses, for instance, sometimes hire nonblacks to perform the government-contracted jobs.

In response to these criticisms, one might reply that the mere presence of black professionals and business owners provides the black community with role models that encourage black children to succeed in walks of life that were formerly denied their parents and grandparents. Here again, increasing the ratio of black professionals and business owners does not satisfy any perfect or imperfect conception of justice, for there is no predetermined criterion for deciding how many black role models are necessary for encouraging black children to succeed. However, we do know that without role models, black children will not be encouraged to succeed; and that alone will mean they have not been given equal opportunity to cultivate their ambition.

Defenders of affirmative action also appeal to procedural justice in order to show why blacks who score lower on tests or who otherwise appear to be less qualified than whites should still receive preference in admissions, hiring, promotions, and contracting. The argument here is that better qualified whites do not deserve to benefit from their qualifications—at least to the extent that their qualifications were acquired unfairly, through participation in a system of public education that favored them even as it discriminated against blacks.

### Digression: Efficiency, Justice, and Qualifications

Most liberals think that justice should not be compromised for the sake of efficiency (or happiness) unless doing so is absolutely necessary in order to avoid a great harm. Defenders of affirmative action agree. However, governments, businesses, and schools are generally unwilling to sacrifice efficient job performance simply for justice's sake.[62] Therefore, defenders of affirmative action must show that hiring qualified women and minorities ahead of men who are better qualified (on the basis of experience, test scores, or grades) need not result in a decrease in efficiency.

To begin with, defenders of affirmative action rightly note that efficient job performance is not always linked to the possession of testable qualifications. Indeed, many important positions are not awarded on the basis of qualifications. For example, college admissions' slots granted to students of former alumni and jobs awarded on the basis of cronyism only partly depend on qualifications. Yet few critics of affirmative action question the fairness or efficiency of Princeton University's policy of admitting 40 percent of its alumni applicant pool in comparison to 15 percent of the regular applicant pool.[63]

Second, defenders of affirmative action note that qualifications are not always a reliable predictor of job performance. Although pronounced differences in grade point average and test performance may reliably predict differences in job performance, less pronounced differences often do not. Yet, the differences in qualification between qualified affirmative action candidates and better qualified white (male) candidates are invariably minor. Hence, generally speaking, picking a less qualified affirmative action candidate over a better qualified white (male) candidate does not result in decreased efficiency in job performance.

Third, defenders of affirmative action argue that some qualifications that are used to predict job performance are simply irrelevant to this purpose. Sometimes it is the level of attainment rather than the qualification that is irrelevant. Possession of a college degree is relevant to teaching sixth-grade history in most public schools. But there is no reason to think that a black teacher with a B.A. in history cannot teach a sixth-grade course on American History as well as (or even better than) an eminent white historian with a Ph.D.

In other cases, the qualification itself is irrelevant. In one famous case, *Davis v. Washington* (1976), the Supreme Court upheld the right of the District of Columbia's police department to assess applicants for jobs by administering a test (Test 21) designed to evaluate verbal ability, vocabulary, and reading comprehension. Agreeing with plaintiffs that the test had a disproportionately exclusionary impact on blacks, the majority on the Court nevertheless ruled that, because there was no evidence of discriminatory intent and the test was rationally related to job performance, it did not constitute a violation of the Equal Protection Clause.

This conclusion seems too hasty. As Justice John Paul Stevens remarked, "the line between discriminatory purpose and discriminatory impact is not nearly as bright" as the Court had assumed.[64] More relevant to my purposes here, Test 21 is not as racially neutral as it appears. While the mastery of standard English is important for communicating with middle- and upper-class white citizens, it is useless for communicating effectively with poor urban blacks who speak a street dialect. Test 21 thus selects skills that are useful to white officers seeking to maintain their racial dominance and useless to black citizens seeking to obtain less-threatening law enforcement by members of their own community.

Tests such as these may be biased in other ways as well. Many require cultural background knowledge that suburban whites, but not inner-city blacks, are likely to possess. Other qualifications—of a more subjective nature—invite examiners to unconsciously project their racial stereotypes on applicants in evaluating their character, collegiality, or capacity to "fit in." These stereotypes are especially pernicious in evaluating the cognitive and behavioral capacities of black children, who often find themselves "tracked" into classrooms designed for low achievers and behavioral misfits.[65]

Fourth, defenders of affirmative action note that some jobs require racial, gender, or ethnic qualifications for their efficient performance. For example, a black police officer might be preferred over a white officer to work a beat in a predominantly black neighborhood that has been repeatedly wracked by racial unrest owing to confirmed instances of police brutality by whites. Here, preference has nothing whatsoever to do with affirmative action, since consideration of race is based solely on the requirements of successful job performance—keeping the peace—and not on any factors relating to compensation or diversity.

Having examined the role of qualifications in predicting efficient job performance, it becomes apparent that awarding jobs and positions to competent affirmative action candidates ahead of better qualified white (male) candidates need not—and usually does not—result in a decrease in job efficiency, a fact that is confirmed by recent studies of affirmative action admissions policies at selective universities and colleges.[66] Nevertheless, critics still maintain that affirmative action is too imperfect a device for establishing equal opportunity for all.

Affirmative action seems to benefit those who need it the least while not benefiting those who need it the most. It helps middle-class blacks who have not suffered profound educational deprivation (and who therefore have enough skills to advance beyond high school) but it seems to neglect poor blacks who have. Moreover, if procedural justice is the only justification for affirmative action, there seems to be no reason to restrict it to blacks or other groups who have suffered discrimination.

Indeed, procedural justice requires that affirmative action also be extended to poor whites who have suffered demonstrable economic (and educational) handicaps. However, given the special nature of discrimination suffered by African Americans as a group, and the special obligation to compensate them as a group, preferring an economically disadvantaged white person over a less economically disadvantaged black person still seems indefensible. And it seems more indefensible in light of the fact that increasing the percentage of blacks in the professions and skilled trades indirectly benefits all blacks.

Defending affirmative action requires showing that it does not favor undeserving blacks over whites. Arguments based on compensatory and procedural justice can demonstrate this result, but only if the rights of white men are factored into the equation. These rights will be discussed in the next chapter.

# 8
## THE LEGALITY AND MORALITY
## OF AFFIRMATIVE ACTION

I noted in the preceding chapter that African Americans face both deliberate and institutional forms of discrimination that have consigned them to
the status of an oppressed caste deserving of remedial state intervention. I
further observed that affirmative action at least has succeeded in partly remedying the effects of such discrimination. Yet critics doubt whether affirmative action achieves its results in a manner that comports with our legal
traditions and moral intuitions. Their concern culminated in the following
landmark decision.

Between 1866 and 1942, only one black had ever graduated from the University of California's medical school. In response to California's flagrant history of segregation at all levels of public education, the medical school at the
University of California at Davis implemented a program in 1970 setting
aside sixteen seats (out of one hundred) for "disadvantaged" minority applicants (including blacks, Asians, Latinos, and Native Americans), who were
evaluated by criteria that placed less emphasis on entrance test scores than on
interviews. Allan Bakke, a thirty-seven-year-old white engineer, had applied
for admission to the school in 1973 and 1974 but was rejected on both oc-
casions, despite the fact that his test scores were higher than some of those
admitted under the special program. A year later he sued the university,
claiming that the set-aside violated his rights as guaranteed by the Fourteenth
Amendment, the California state constitution, and the Civil Rights Act.

In a bitterly divided opinion, four justices of the Supreme Court upheld
the lower court's ruling that the set-aside violated Bakke's right not to be
discriminated against on account of his race. Four dissenting justices, led by
Justice Brennan, argued that the set-aside violated neither the Civil Rights
Act nor the Fourteenth Amendment's guarantee of equal protection. Justice Powell, who cast the deciding vote in favor of the lower court's ruling,

delivered a compromise opinion. Although he agreed that the set-aside violated Bakke's right to "individualized consideration without regard to race," he added that race could be taken into account as one factor among many in furthering the traditional academic goal of enriching "the training of its student body" through exposure to diverse "experiences, outlooks, and ideas."

Powell's decision hinged on interpreting the Fourteenth Amendment's guarantee of equal protection as a universal moral principle, extending to all persons individually and not specifically to blacks as a group. This interpretation enabled him to argue that preferences aimed at helping minorities were as suspect as preferences aimed at oppressing them; both used racial classifications that violate the rights of individuals to be treated as individuals. In effect, Bakke was blamed for discriminatory acts for which he, as an individual, was not responsible. Meanwhile, each minority who benefited from the set-aside was stigmatized for being "unable to achieve success without special protection."[1]

In order to surmount the Court's suspicion that the university's racial set-aside was just discrimination in reverse, the set-aside would have had to pass "strict scrutiny." That is, it would have had to be shown that the set-aside was both necessary for and narrowly tailored to satisfying a compelling state interest.[2] However, the interests cited by the university—increasing the percentage of traditionally excluded groups in the professions, countering the effects of societal discrimination against racial groups, increasing the number of physicians practicing in underserved minority communities, and enhancing the diversity of the student body—were deemed by Powell to be uncompelling or too broadly tailored.

Powell noted that the university's first interest was unconstitutional because it amounted to preferring a particular group "merely because of its race or ethnic origin." He argued that the second was also unconstitutional because only individuals, not groups, were guaranteed equal protection. Although Bakke could prove that he had been intentionally discriminated against, UC–Davis provided no proof showing that the minorities who had benefited from its set-aside had suffered a similar harm. By contrast, Powell agreed that the university's third and fourth reasons served compelling state interests but denied that the set-aside was necessary for satisfying them. He noted that nonminority physicians will just as likely have an interest in serving minority communities as minority physicians. He also observed that race and ethnicity do not exhaust the scope of diversification sought by universities—hence, his preference for Harvard's admissions process, which compared individuals across a wider spectrum of factors including (besides racial and ethnic identity) place of residence, family background, possession of special talents, and income status.

Powell's reasoning in *Regents of the University of California v. Bakke* (1978), subjecting all race-conscious policies (however benignly intended) to strict scrutiny, later guided the Supreme Court's increasingly conservative majority in its increasingly hostile review of affirmative action legislation. That majority would strike as unconstitutional consent decrees aimed at protecting recently hired minorities from recessionary layoffs on the grounds that they violated the seniority rights of individual white plaintiffs,[3] a position it recently reaffirmed in upholding a lower court's decision to overturn the Piscataway, New Jersey, school board's attempt to retain a black teacher ahead of a white teacher in a layoff plan.[4] In *City of Richmond v. Crosen* (1989), the Court further ruled that set-asides authorized by state and municipal governments also fell under the provisions of strict scrutiny. Such set-asides were deemed illegal unless proven necessary to rectify a chronic history of discrimination. Writing for the majority, Justice O'Connor contested Richmond's 30 percent set-aside for minority construction contractors despite evidence showing that blacks, who constituted 50 percent of the city's population, received only 0.67 percent of municipal contracts. In her opinion, the low percentage of contracts to black-owned enterprises could be explained just as plausibly by disinterest among blacks in the construction industry and by "deficiencies in working capital, inability to meet bonding requirements, unfamiliarity with bidding procedures, and disability caused by an insufficient track record."[5]

Recent decisions by the Supreme Court have only reconfirmed its opposition to strong forms of affirmative action. In *Adarand Constructors, Inc. v. Pena* (1995), the provisions of strict scrutiny that proved so deadly for state and local set-asides were extended to the federal government as well. In November 1997 the Court upheld the constitutionality of California's Proposition 209 (1996), which ended racial, gender, and other kinds of preferences in education, employment, and contracting by state and local governments. In *Hopwood v. State of Texas* (1996), the U.S. Circuit Court of Appeals for the Fifth District went even further by declaring unconstitutional the use of different criteria and different subcommittees for reviewing applications from African Americans and Latinos to the University of Texas Law School. Going beyond Powell, Justice Jerry Smith proclaimed that even diversification fuels "racial hostility" by treating "minorities as a group, rather than as individuals."[6]

## The Early History of Affirmative Action

In order to assess these recent court decisions, a familiarity with the early history of affirmative action is helpful. The words *affirmative action* were first used by President John F. Kennedy in 1961 when he issued Executive Order 10952 creating the Equal Employment Opportunity Commission (EEOC). This order required persons contracting with the federal government to take "affirmative action to ensure that applicants are employed without regard to race, creed, color, or national origin." Kennedy's order hardly expanded upon the scope of a similar injunction (Executive Order 8802) issued by President Franklin D. Roosevelt twenty years earlier banning employment discrimination by the federal government and defense contractors. Indeed, it merely provided apprenticeships and on-the-job training opportunities to members of discriminated classes.

The Civil Rights Act of 1964 did not expressly enjoin anything more. The vagueness of the act, however, emboldened President Lyndon B. Johnson in 1965 to order the Department of Labor to establish the Office of Federal Contract Compliance, which required firms conducting business with the federal government to establish "good faith goals and timetables" for employing "underutilized" qualified minorities (Executive Order 11246). In 1967 the Department of Health, Education, and Welfare issued further guidelines for implementing Title VI of the Civil Rights Act prohibiting discrimination in any federally assisted program. Recipients of federal funding were required to take affirmative action, including recruitment of minorities, "even in the absence of . . . prior discrimination." The rationale behind minority recruitment aimed at expanding "participation of a particular race, color, or national origin" in order to provide "members of a particular racial or nationality group" with "more adequate service."[7] Thus was born the rationale underlying the first significant affirmative action program, President Richard Nixon's Philadelphia Plan of 1969, which required federal contractors to show that they were hiring blacks.[8]

Initially, the EEOC required that companies who voluntarily elect to do business with the government actively recruit underrepresented minorities.[9] Because the success of this weak form of affirmative action depended on the good faith of companies to carry their recruitment efforts to the end, there was no way to monitor whether a company's failure to hire minorities was due to a lack of qualified applicants or simple resistance on the part of the company—hence, the turn toward "goals and timetables."

Under these stronger guidelines, companies were required to prove that failure to meet specific goals and deadlines was caused by an insufficient number of qualified minority candidates. This problem could then be remedied by establishing special minority training programs. However, in cases where resistance to integration or the lack of qualified competitive minorities was beyond immediate repair, the use of a stronger form of affirmative action was recommended: numerical set-asides that reserved a specific number of positions for women and minorities only.

The movement toward preferences and quotas gained further momentum when the U.S. Commission on Civil Rights issued its 1971 report detailing the failure of the Civil Rights Act's nondiscriminatory provisions to protect minorities against discrimination. Under these provisions, individuals bore the burden of proving that they were intentionally discriminated against. Court decisions in the early seventies reversed this burden of proof by expanding the concept of discrimination to include statistically demonstrable institutionalized racism. Thus, in *Griggs v. Duke Power Co.* (1971), the Supreme Court ruled that "practices that are fair in form, but discriminatory in operation"—such as possession of a high school diploma or performance on general intelligence tests—are prohibited unless they "bear a demonstrable relation to successful performance on the jobs for which they are used."[10]

The issue over discriminatory intent resurfaced in the landmark case *United Steelworkers v. Weber* (1979). Brian Weber and other white workers brought suit against the United Steelworkers Union for voluntarily agreeing with Kaiser Aluminum and Chemical Corporation to reserve 50 percent of the openings in a training program for blacks aimed at increasing their representation in skilled craft jobs from 0 percent to 39 percent (their percentage of the local workforce). The plaintiffs noted that Section 703(j) of Title VII of the Civil Rights Act expressly stated that employers and unions could not be required to correct racial imbalances without proof of past discrimination. They further argued that the aim of the act was to compensate individuals who had suffered demonstrable discrimination, not to remedy imbalances between racial groups.

In a divided opinion, the Supreme Court ruled that significant racial imbalances in the workforce could be sufficient to prove a pattern of past discrimination. More important, the Court ruled that Title VII not only does not prohibit the use of quotas but actually encourages voluntary agreements designed to remedy racial imbalances. Indeed, the Court had already ruled (in *Fullilove v. Klutznick* [1977]) that nonminority businesses had to "share the burden" for past acts of discrimination from which they had "innocently" benefited. Not only could innocent beneficiaries of injustice be expected to compensate the victims of such injustice, but they also could be expected to compensate even those who were not victims so long as those compensated belonged to a minority whose members had suffered discrimination as a group.

From 1970 until 1978, the courts consistently upheld the right of government bodies to pursue policies of preferential treatment and quota hiring. Other decisions in the eighties reaffirmed the use of quotas for expanding employment opportunities for minorities and women. In these instances quotas were validated as temporary measures designed to achieve (but not maintain) racial balance in traditionally segregated areas of employment, so long as they did not bar the advancement of white male employees.[11]

*Affirmative Action and the Constitutional Principle of Equal Protection*

The principal disagreement between proponents and opponents of affirmative action occurs over the proper interpretation of the Fourteenth Amendment's Equal Protection Clause. Beginning with *Bakke,* opponents have argued that the principle of equal protection extends only to individuals and not to groups, as proponents maintain. However, considerable disagreement reigns with respect to who these individuals are.

Defenders of affirmative action claim that the Equal Protection Clause was originally intended to protect blacks and other groups suffering from discrimination. It is a perverse kind of reasoning, they argue, that invokes this clause to protect the rights of white men, when doing so merely perpetuates the advantages of past discrimination. Ironically, by invoking the principle of equal protection in this manner, unequal protection will almost certainly be guaranteed, since white men will continue to benefit from the effects of unjust discrimination—and at the expense of those who have been discriminated against.

For this reason, defenders of affirmative action argue that it is wrong to construe "equal protection" to mean "treat the same way." Treating persons the same way—as if they were colorless and genderless—would be appropriate in an ideal world where no one was ever racially or sexually discriminated against. But treating them the same way in our world ignores the reality of discrimination. Opponents of affirmative action respond to this argument by insisting that "equal protection" must apply exclusively to individuals as embodiments of the same humanity; otherwise it ceases to be neutral and impartial with respect to their particular group attachments. To suggest that this clause targets only oppressed groups for special protection would have the implication of politicizing its meaning, since what would count as an oppressed group would then be a matter of political contestation. But just as it is wrong to establish special set-asides for politically powerful white males who feel oppressed by women and minorities, so too it is wrong to establish special set-asides for politically powerful women and minorities; it makes upholding the rights of some contingent on violating the rights of others.

### Equal Protection and the Problem of Constitutional Interpretation

Because the debate over affirmative action revolves around the meaning of the Equal Protection Clause, its proper resolution can scarcely avoid touching on the nature of meaning and interpretation. To begin with, many conservative critics of affirmative action view the meaning of law as relatively fixed and unchanging. Some of them, such as Justices Antonin Scalia and William Rehnquist, prefer an "originalist" viewpoint that equates a legal document's meaning with the original intentions of its framers. Their reason for limiting the scope of judicial interpretation in this manner is to avoid judicial tyranny—the power of appointed jurists to nullify the will of the people as exemplified in the legal enactments of democratically elected legislators.

Originalism has been roundly criticized by conservatives and liberals alike. It reduces the meaning of law to whatever the majority and its elected representatives happened to want at the moment the law was enacted. Given this reduction, the illegality and injustice of Jim Crow segregation vis-à-vis the higher law of the land—the Constitution as amended by the Equal Protection Clause—could never have arisen. The framers of that amendment thought segregation was compatible with equal protection (for instance, they allowed segregated schools in the District of Columbia). Likewise, legislators in the southern states thought that equal protection meant providing blacks with the same access to public resources enjoyed by whites—education, transportation, political life, and the like—but only in special places and under special conditions. In this decision federal and state legislatures across the land acquiesced, as did the Supreme Court in *Plessy v. Ferguson* (1896).

If originalism allows no room for judicial intervention in checking majoritarian tyranny, it demands it whenever new cases arise that existing law has not explicitly addressed. Originalism requires that judges infer the meaning of law only from what can be logically deduced from its express wording. But laws apply to an indefinite number of unforseeable cases that cannot be mentioned expressly in their statutory wording. Hence, according to originalism, judges will have indefinite discretion to determine these "hard case" applications as they personally see fit.[12]

The law's vagueness and generality aggravate this problem further. Legislators deliberately formulate their laws in vague, general terms precisely in order to allow future generations of judges interpretative discretion. Implicit in this intention is the idea that future generations should not be absolutely limited by the time-bound understanding and intentions of past generations, for being bound in such a manner would conflict with the generally accepted fact of progress in moral and scientific thinking.

The complexity of what legislators intend renders originalism even less workable. In democracies, laws typically assume the form of compromises in which legislators hope to achieve many different, often incompatible, ends (only some of which are expressly stated). Indeed, any single framer typically intends the law to fulfill a variety of hopes and expectations, and even these need not cohere with one another.

The failure of originalism to capture the inescapably interpretative nature of legal practice has led most conservatives and progressives to adopt a principled approach to law. According to this theory, the meaning of law transcends the particular intentions of its framers to include deeper reasons (of a philosophical nature) that lend law coherence and moral legitimacy. Part of the coherence and legitimacy of a judicial decision is its fitting well with legal precedent, including the original intentions of framers. However, there are times when this criterion of fit fails, because the precedent in question is out of step with the evolving conceptions of justice. As a coherent system of moral principles, law provides judges with at least some guidance in rejecting as well as reinterpreting past precedents, as evidenced by the court's overruling of *Plessy*'s "separate but equal" interpretation of the Fourteenth Amendment.[13]

One important strand of principled moral interpretation, the natural law approach, has gained increasing popularity among conservatives like Justice Clarence Thomas. According to the modern version of this theory that descends from John Locke, basic constitutional principles possess an unchanging meaning—specifiable in terms of "inalienable" human rights—intuitable by reason alone.

The advantages of natural law interpretation are one with its disadvantages. On the one hand, natural law provides a transcendent moral basis for criticizing the injustice of particular statutes. Rationally intuitable moral ideals possess a meaning that cannot be equated with any time- and place-bound tradition. Their sheer generality opposes them to statutes that discriminate against individuals on the basis of race, ethnicity, and gender; and generations of abolitionists, suffragettes, and civil rights crusaders have appealed to them for this very reason.

On the other hand, natural law principles are too abstract to provide sufficient criticism of the status quo. In fact, even segregationists have thought that the Equal Protection Clause's famous injunction that no state shall "deprive any person of life, liberty, or property, without due process of law; nor deny to any person within its jurisdiction the equal protection of the laws" accords with natural law. In their opinion, if the state took the interests of blacks as well as whites equally into account and then reasonably concluded that the greatest happiness for both groups was best advanced by segregation, then segregation was as good an interpretation of equal protection as any other. Proponents of natural law doctrine like Justice Henry Brown thus argued with some justification that segregation accorded with the natural science of his day, which tended to view the races as biologically, socially, and morally distinct.[14]

By the time *Brown v. Board of Education* (1954) was decided, the dominant scientific understanding of race had radically changed. Biological racism was no longer rationally defensible and was rejected by most Americans. Moreover, the Supreme Court invoked sociological and psychological data showing that "separate educational facilities are inherently unequal." Without appealing to a new "natural fact"—that segregation as such stigmatized blacks as an inferior race—the justices might not have declared the old "separate but equal" interpretation of the Fourteenth Amendment unconstitutional.

Although the "color-blind" interpretation of the Fourteenth Amendment favored today by many natural law theorists is compatible with contemporary natural science, I think another rationale, more favorable to affirmative action, is equally justifiable. This other rationale—which, following Ronald Dworkin, I call the "banned sources" approach—better accords with our modern understanding that moral and scientific reasoning changes (or evolves) over time.

The banned sources approach interprets the Equal Protection Clause in terms of the best reasons (sources) available at any given time. Unlike natural law theory, it presumes that the meaning of law progressively evolves commensurate with changes in morality, science, and historical circumstance. It bans racial classifications motivated by racist rationales, because these are false and immoral by today's standards; but it accepts racial classifications motivated by antiracist rationales, because they are not false and immoral by today's standards. Thus, contrary to natural law theorists like Justice Thomas, the rationale underlying affirmative action is not "reverse discrimination" (as if white men, instead of minorities and women, were now being stigmatized as inferior beings who could be treated inhumanely) but equal respect and equal concern for those harmed by racial and gender discrimination.

Of course, one could object that the best reasons for affirmative action are still not good enough: because racial classifications are based upon factors beyond one's control, and because factors beyond one's control are not morally relevant for deciding how one should be treated, racial classifications should be banned. (Bakke did not choose to be born white, so why should he be penalized for it?) This objection is too sweeping. The law unavoidably classifies us according to genetically and environmentally determined criteria. Thus, the disabled and the infirm are entitled to certain health benefits that are routinely denied to those who are able-bodied, just as those (like Bakke) who possess sufficient native intelligence are entitled to rights normally denied to those who are mentally challenged.

Perhaps racial classifications should be banned because only individuals, not groups, have rights that can be equally protected. Suppose this were true, that the law protects only individuals, because only individuals can be discriminated against. How would we know that individuals were being discriminated against if those discriminating against them did not publicly announce that they were doing so? The only way we would know is by taking note of the fact that an individual claiming to have been discriminated against belonged to a group whose members were statistically underrepresented.

For instance, let us imagine that a black woman earns more than a comparably qualified white male. Let us suppose further that, had it not been for institutionalized racism, she might have acquired a better job somewhere else and earned even more. We would only be able to determine whether this was so by looking at how other members of her racial group fared in comparison to comparably qualified whites. If the discrepancy in earning power between her racial group and comparably qualified whites was sufficiently greater than might be expected from a purely random, market-based distribution of social inequalities, we would have good reason to believe that she, too, had suffered discrimination. So even if it were true that only individuals suffer discrimination, determination of this fact requires examining discrepancies that appear only at the level of groups. Hence, equal protection against discrimination must apply to groups as well to individuals.

*Equal Protection As a Mandate for Group Preferences*

Now that I have shown that the banned sources—and not the banned classifications—approach is the best interpretation of the Equal Protection

Clause, I am in a better position to analyze some of the debate over the legality of affirmative action. As noted earlier, opponents of affirmative action generally appeal to an originalist or natural law interpretation of the Civil Rights Act (1964). The act implemented an antidiscrimination policy that expressly prohibited the use of race, color, religion, sex, or national origin by employers (of at least fifteen people), employment agencies, and labor organizations *except for legitimate occupational reasons.*[15]

Defenders of affirmative action can argue, on originalist grounds, that the antidiscrimination provision of the Civil Rights Act was not intended to rule out all racial, ethnic, and gender classifictions but only ones that harmed women and minorities. Legitimate occupational reasons sometimes do require using such classifications in order to combat discrimination and redistribute employment opportunities and services to women and minorities. Defenders of affirmative action can also rightfully claim that their interpretation of the Civil Rights Act conforms to the original intent of the Reconstruction Congress that enacted the Fourteenth Amendment—the same Congress, be it noted, that passed the Freedman's Bureau Act expressly entitling former slaves to "forty acres and a mule."

Defenders of affirmative action can further argue, on natural law grounds, that respect for basic human rights requires preferential treatment for persons suffering discrimination. Indeed, the courts have recognized that without preferential treatment the following forms of institutionalized discrimination cannot be rectified:

- the disparate treatment (or classification) of persons who are similar in relevant respects and, conversely, the similar treatment (or classification) of persons who are different in relevant respects;
- the adverse impact of "practices, procedures, or tests neutral on their face, and even neutral in terms of intent," on the educational and employment opportunities of a particular group whenever these are irrelevant to determining requisite performance levels; and
- the perpetuation of the effects of past discrimination into the present.

In sum, originalist and natural law interpretations of the Civil Rights Act do not necessarily speak against affirmative action; in fact, they support it.

## Bakke *Reconsidered*

Justice Powell argued that UC–Davis's minority set-aside violated Bakke's rights for three reasons: Bakke was not judged on the basis of his qualifications; he was not treated as an individual but as a member of a group; and he was wrongly punished for harms perpetrated by others.

The first argument assumes that test scores and grades are the only qualifications for being a successful doctor, but Davis, like most other professional schools, thought otherwise. Davis claimed that race was also a relevant qualification when it came to fulfilling its other obligations as a publicly funded institution: improving health care services in minority communities, producing role models to encourage more minorities to become doctors, and sensitizing the medical profession as a whole to racial discrimination.[16] Surely this qualification is no less valid than some of Davis's other admission criteria, including its preference for in-state over out-of-state residents.

The second argument supposes that it is wrong to judge people on the basis of qualities over which they have no control. If valid, this argument would preclude judging Bakke by the very qualities on which he rests his own claim to superior qualifications, namely his natural intelligence and fortuitous upbringing in Florida's segregated school districts. Only if judging Bakke's racial qualifications prevented judging his intellectual qualifications could he argue that UC–Davis violated his rights. But the university's set-aside program did not prevent the school from fairly evaluating his intellectual qualifications, nor did it demean him as an inferior being.

However, perhaps Bakke unfairly bore the burden of compensating minorities for harms he had nothing to do with. The proper response to this argument is that innocent parties have no right to reap the benefits of injustice. As John Arthur so felicitously puts it:

Bakke's right to an equal opportunity to compete in a fair system cannot be used to justify his taking advantage of the system's unfairness, especially when we know that but for the system's unfairness another applicant would deserve admission. The white applicant is *not* . . . being asked to bear the burden of past injustice; he is being prevented from cashing in on an unfair advantage provided him by the system.[17]

*What Remains of Affirmative Action After Bakke?*

In light of *Hopwood* and the success of California's antiaffirmative action referendum (Proposition 209) in withstanding court challenges, some educators in Texas and California have proposed alternative approaches to achieving some of the same ends formerly accomplished under affirmative action. One proposal, recently passed by the Texas House of Representatives, involves automatically admitting to the best public universities the top 10 percent of each high school graduating class. In the largely segregated school districts of Texas, this proposal might ensure a proportionally representative matriculation of black and Latino students; in the more integrated school districts of California, the result would be less satisfactory. Black and Latino students who attend high schools with mostly white and Asian student bodies might not be among the top 10 percent in their graduating classes, in which case they would not be automatically admitted—even if they were more qualified than the upper 10 percent of those graduating from predominantly black and Latino high schools.

Another proposal, approved by the Texas Senate, would require that only half of university admissions be based on test scores, grades, and class rank. The other half would be based on a combination of academic qualifications and broadly defined economic or social disadvantage (40 percent) and on athletic and musical abilities (10 percent).

Because minorities still score disproportionately lower on test scores and comprise such a small population relative to the white majority (numerically, there are more economically disadvantaged whites than minorities), only one in six students likely to be admitted using this formula will be a minority.[18] These projections conform to results obtained under a similar admissions program that was recently put into effect by the Board of Regents of the University of California. That program required that 50 to 75 percent of all admissions be based exclusively on GPA and SAT scores, with the remainder based on nonacademic criteria. Under this program, the 1998 admissions for UC–Berkeley show a 66 percent decline in African-American admissions from the previous year and a 52 percent decline in Latino admissions (the corresponding statistics for UCLA were 42 and 33 percent, respectively).[19]

In the final analysis, the effectiveness of any alternative to affirmative action is moot; for if such geography- and class-based proposals succeed in racially diversifying university admissions, the current Supreme Court will most likely strike them as racially discriminatory (against whites).

### The Moral Justification of Affirmative Action and the Rights of White Males

I noted that Bakke had no right to be preferred over less qualified persons if he achieved his superior qualifications through a system that gave him an unfair advantage over them. The same kind of argument sometimes applies mutatis mutandis to white male entrepreneurs whose lower bids for government contracts are rejected in favor of higher bids by female or minority entrepreneurs. If a government's past refusal to contract with female or minority entrepreneurs resulted in their having a competitive disadvantage vis-à-vis their white male counterparts, white male entrepreneurs have no right to benefit from that advantage. Had it not been for the government's past discrimination, female and minority entrepreneurs might have had greater working capital, more opportunities to develop a sufficient track record, and so forth, than their white counterparts.

Again, by parity of reasoning, if a company has refused to hire or promote members of a protected class until recently so that they have less seniority than their white male colleagues, it is no obvious violation of the rights of those with seniority if they are laid off ahead of more recently hired members of protected classes or withheld promotion opportunities extended to them. Were it not for the original act of unfair discrimination, members of these protected classes would have had greater seniority.

Furthermore, even younger white males who are now competing with women and minorities for scarce jobs and who did not directly benefit from past discrimination still benefited from it indirectly; they shared in the higher earnings and benefits enjoyed by their forefathers, who did not have to compete with women and minorities. Thanks to these earnings and benefits, they were able to do something their forefathers could only dream of—attend college and aspire to higher paying professions.

White males are also psychologically advantaged by knowing that all careers are open to them and that, through dint of hard work alone, they can achieve anything. This advantage increases relative to the psychological self-doubt plaguing their African-American counterparts. Because their fathers and mothers were denied opportunities to succeed in school and career, they now view higher education and professional life as bastions of white privilege, hence their high college drop-out rate.

Hence, just because the older generation of minorities bore the brunt of discrimination does not mean that their progeny suffered less harm than they did. Just as the progeny of older white males might have benefited the most from past discrimination, so too the progeny of minorities might have suffered the most. Unlike their parents and grandparents, middle-aged blacks who were raised with high expectations must now live with the discomfiting thought that racial barriers will likely remain for some time. For the poorest generation of black urban youth, these expectations have long been dashed.

Yet, as Gertrude Ezorsky points out, many white blue-collar workers also suffered economically from racism—even if they benefited noneconomically from a more pervasive system of white privilege. Employers often replaced (or threatened to replace) white workers with black workers who, intimidated by racism, were willing to work for less under substandard conditions.[20] Faced with these threats, white workers formed unions that protected them from arbitrary hiring, firing, and promotion. In so doing, they also excluded women, blacks, and other minorities from these unions as well as from membership in the trades organized by them. Today, this exclusion proceeds by more subtle means, often by appeal to principles of seniority and merit that dictate that those last hired be the first fired.

Certainly, just because principles of seniority and merit that protect workers from arbitrary hiring, firing, and promotion by their employers have been used to block the entry and promotion of women and minorities into trades and other occupations is no reason to reject such principles out of hand. However, it does show that even just measures taken to combat the adverse impact of white racism on white male workers ultimately harmed blacks (and women) in ways that required remedial affirmative action. Ironically, when such measures are invoked in order to obstruct affirmative action hiring and promotion, they end up undermining their own rationale and, even worse, harm the very group—white male workers—they were intended to benefit.

Ezorsky herself notes that affirmative action indirectly benefits whites as well as blacks. By opening up the pool of qualified candidates for positions, it allows for a more competitive selection of talents based on merit. Likewise, by redistributing minorities and women in higher paying professions, it partly eases the labor glut affecting low-paying, marginally skilled jobs, thereby improving the bargaining position of poor whites. Moreover, some court rulings advancing the cause of affirmative action—such as those striking down irrelevant and excessive job qualifications—also directly benefit some white males.

Second, Ezorsky observes that the principle of merit, which guarantees efficient job performance for employers as well as just distribution of opportunities for job seekers and employees, does not render affirmative action redundant, as many critics maintain. These critics insist that the principle of merit alone compels businesses not to discriminate: if racial discrimination artificially constricts the available pool of qualified candidates (thereby undermining the principle of merit), businesses seeking to maximise job efficiency and profitability will not discriminate.[21] Thus, affirmative action becomes unnecessary.

This argument underestimates the profitability of discrimination. Counterbalancing the loss of job efficiency owing to discrimination are the savings in wages and benefits achieved by threatening to replace white workers with unemployed blacks willing to work for less. And companies might hesitate to integrate their workforce for fear of angering racist patrons.

Third, even if the principle of merit sufficiently motivated businesses to integrate their workforces, it would not protect those last hired (minorities, women, and temporary workers) from being first fired. To abide by the principle of seniority and merit, government should devise affirmative action remedies that disperse the effects of layoffs across groups in ways that do not affect their overall percentage of the workforce, or compensate those who lose jobs or promotions with monetary awards funded by progressive tax revenues. Economic retrenchment can be achieved without layoffs by simply reducing the work hours of each employee. When layoffs are necessary, those laid off should be compensated (the same applies to persons denied promotion because of affirmative action).[22] In general, persons should be compensated in proportion to the benefit denied them, but against this benefit must be charged the benefit unfairly derived from discrimination.[23]

Sadly, consent decrees upheld in lower court decisions establishing compensatory schemes (see *Vulcan Pioneers v. New Jersey Department of Civil Service* [1984]) were later ruled unconstitutional by the higher court (*Firefighters Local Union No. 1784 v. Stotts et al.* [1984]). The courts have ruled against laying off senior personnel for the sake of retaining recently hired minorities and women. But if compensating white males for jobs lost due to affirmative action is now moot, compensating minorities and women for jobs lost to institutionalized discrimination continues to provoke debate.

*Affirmative Action As Compensatory Justice*

Affirmative action is sometimes defended as a way of compensating persons who have been discriminated against for loss of employment opportunities they have suffered in the past. In tort law, a defendant $D$ causes some discrete harm to a plaintiff $P$, for which $P$ is demanding restitution *as a right*. Suppose that $D$ wrongly evicts $P$ from a store $P$ is leasing so that $P$ loses $500. In order that $P$ be restored to his or her prior position, $P$ now demands that $D$ make good the loss of $500.

Something like this defense applies in discrimination suits filed under Titles VII and VIII of the Civil Rights Act. A plaintiff $P$ who was wrongly denied a position because of discrimination can sue to get that position (and perhaps a monetary settlement compensating for lost earnings and benefits).

But here we note a slight disanalogy with the paradigm case, albeit one that is entirely in keeping with medical malpractice suits involving nonrestorative compensation. Compensation will not restore $P$ to the same position $P$ occupied before being denied the job, because $P$ did not already have the job. Instead, compensation will give to $P$ what $P$ *would have had* had $P$ not been discriminated against: namely, a job and a calculable range of lost earnings and benefits.

The tort model can be modified to include class action suits (for instance, besides compensating Native Americans for land stolen from them by previous administrations, the U.S. government also compensated Japanese Americans for damages—loss of property and freedom—incurred when they were interned in concentration camps during World War II). However, more controversially, it can sometimes require innocent beneficiaries of injustice to compensate the victims (or the victim's descendants).

Suppose that the law protecting seniority prohibits laying off person $D$ who currently holds this job, so that compensating plaintiff $P$ will require that $P$ be awarded another position in the company, one that would have been awarded to an even more highly qualified applicant $A$. In this scenario, the company in question makes restitution to $P$ by harming $A$, who—unlike $D$—did not benefit from the company's past history of discrimination. Now it seems as if $A$, who is innocent of any wrongdoing and who has not palpably benefited from the harm caused to $P$ by the company, is being required to pay reparation to $P$.

One can cite numerous examples of innocent persons having to pay for damages caused by others. Stockholders sometimes see their dividends decline after a company is forced to pay restitution for acts of discrimination committed by management. Even if the stockholders did not knowingly collude in the discrimination and did not benefit from it, they are still held responsible for it, since it is they who elected the chief executive officers of the company.

Unfortunately, the analogy between the above case and the one involving $P$ is imprecise on one crucial point: the older generation of employees (like $D$) who receive undeserved jobs as a result of past discrimination are not the ones who now are required to pay compensation by giving up their jobs. Rather, it is the younger generation of job seekers (like $A$) who bear this burden.

There is another disanalogy between tort law and affirmative action. In tort law, as in most civil rights litigation, the plaintiff being compensated is an *individual* who has suffered some discrete harm. In affirmative action, by contrast, the harm being repaired extends to a whole *group*. This difference means that those who receive compensation—the younger generation of women and minorities—might not have experienced as much educational and employment discrimination as the older generation. Thus, the problem of young white males as a group paying restitution for the sins and ill-gotten gains of their forefathers mirrors in reverse the problem of young minorities and women reaping the rewards of compensation that are (it seems) rightly owed their progenitors.

In sum, the argument for affirmative action as compensatory justice is problematic for two reasons: the oppression borne by women and minorities for which affirmative action allegedly provides just compensation is not a discrete harm whose costs can be precisely calculated; and the young white males who pay compensation and the minorities and women who receive it are not obviously equivalent, respectively, to those who have caused (or benefited from) harm and those who have suffered it.

First, the harm caused by the cumulative effects of legally, politically, economically, socially, and culturally institutionalized sexism and racism cannot be traced back to a single, discrete act of discrimination perpetrated by an individual or distinct set of individuals. Institutionalized sexism and racism were not invented and imposed by anyone in particular; their original and primary causes are multiple and complex. Their agents and authors remain either unknown or, if known, ubiquitous—innumerable government agencies who legally maintained slavery and discrimination, and virtually anyone who knowingly benefited from them or tacitly acquiesced in them without offering resistance.

To complicate matters further, there is no direct causal link connecting the economic and educational disadvantages suffered by women and minorities today to the sexist and racist oppression suffered by women and minorities in the past. Having had ancestors who were oppressed is neither necessary nor sufficient for having been oppressed oneself, because statistical probabilities that apply to groups allow for individual exceptions.

These deviations from the classic model of tort liability are not peculiar to affirmative action. Tobacco companies are held liable for increased rates of cancer among smokers and those who associate with them. Although there is no direct causal link connecting tobacco consumption with cancer (some smokers do not develop cancer, while some nonsmokers do), the statistical increase in the risk of cancer associated with smoking is significant enough to establish at least partial liability. Hence, so long as there is significant statistical evidence of heightened employment risk, the absence of any provable causal connection linking past discrimination and present oppression does not absolve the agents of discrimination (businesses and governments) from liability.

The above example also shows that groups suffering heightened risk can be the beneficiaries of liability suits. For example, smokers can initiate class action suits against tobacco companies even if not all individuals within that group have suffered demonstrable heart and respiratory disease. Likewise, all Jews living in Israel benefited from Germany's postwar reparations regardless of whether they or their families were victimized by the Nazis.

Therefore, groups as well as individuals, innocent as well as guilty persons, can be assigned liability (or given compensation) for risks or harms caused (or suffered). In all these cases, something like the principle of shared responsibility (or shared benefit) is at work.[24] But how do we calculate the damages owed to groups, such as African Americans, for the heightened risk of underemployment they suffer as a result of past oppression borne by their ancestors?

It is clear that the damages cannot be accurately assigned and calculated (or fully indemnified). Perhaps for that reason we should, as Cass Sunstein argues, reformulate the question in terms of "risk management" instead of compensation.[25] Women and minorities, as well as many white males, today find themselves disadvantaged with respect to the distribution of basic resources of citizenship. Denied equal opportunity access to education, employment, housing, and health care, they are too immersed in the daily struggles of life to defend themselves politically. Political disenfranchisement, in turn, means loss of influence over the legislative process and the judicial system. Poverty translates into heightened risk for their physical safety. They are more vulnerable to domestic violence and crime; if they happen to be black or Latino, they are more vulnerable to police brutality and a justice system that discriminates against persons of color; if they are poor, they are denied quality legal representation and access to bail. So even if the state were not to pay restitution to blacks for harms they suffered in the past, it would still be obligated—on purely procedural grounds—to "compensate" them for increased risks to their well-being caused by institutionalized racism.[26]

Incredibly, many critics of affirmative action deny that African Americans suffer from heightened risks. Indeed, they argue that, had their ancestors not been enslaved, African Americans today would be much worse off than they are now—starving, perhaps, in some famine-stricken African country.[27] Of course, had European slavery and colonialism never existed, Africa might have blossomed into an affluent economic power in its own right. In that case, the living descendants of African slaves might have been *better* off than they are today—even better off than European descendants, who would have been denied the cumulative benefits of four hundred years of plunder, slavery, and genocide!

Critics of affirmative action also blame the heightened risks of urban poverty on the "pathological communalism" of African culture. Nicholas Capaldi, for instance, insists that African Americans are "incomplete individuals" who lack a sense of autonomy and inner directedness. Because they are not motivated to take individual responsibility for their lives, they acquiesce in welfare dependency and blame whites for their inadequacies. Even their insistence on identifying with one another as an oppressed group betrays their "tribal" thinking.

To begin with, only those who developed within the modern Western European tradition of liberal culture could even become individuals, in the sense of being autonomous and inner directed. . . . In Africa, the relevant locus of identification was and is the tribe. . . . So the second thing I mean by identifying African Americans as incomplete individuals is that given their background in Africa, it was to be expected that they would react to and adapt to their marginal position by developing a culture of poverty. It was not slavery per se that led to the culture of poverty, but the meeting of two different worlds and the lack of resources within their prior world for adapting to their new world. This condition was perpetuated even after slavery was ended.[28]

Capaldi thinks that an African tribal culture valuing passive deference to authority and neglect of family is responsible for creating the black urban underclass. He does not bother to mention the role that European "culture" (capitalism and colonialism) played in destroying the familial integrity and individuality of slaves. He does not bother to justify his one-sided, Eurocentric distortion of African culture or his racist assumption that African culture predestines its practitioners to a status of moral inferiority. Amazingly, he seems unaware of the extent to which African culture was suppressed and eventually fused or assimilated into European and Christian culture. However, the cultural "pathologies" (if we can call them that) exhibited by today's black urban underclass stem predominantly from the latter, not the former.

In the final analysis, Capaldi's blaming African culture for the plight of the black urban underclass is irrelevant. Slavery and discrimination alone are serious harms that merit compensation. The only question is whether affirmative action—a very modest compensation, to be sure—is fair to whites and blacks.

I argued above that even young white males (like *A*) who did not directly collude in or benefit from discrimination still benefited from it indirectly, so much so that their higher qualifications in comparison to minorities and women are undeserved. Hence, it is not unjust that they forfeit some positions to minorities and women. Conversely, I noted that the younger generation of African Americans who did not suffer the blatant discrimination that their forefathers did might have suffered a greater, cumulative harm. Hence, it is not unjust that they be the beneficiaries of positions that should have gone to their forefathers.

But doesn't affirmative action fail to indemnify the poorest blacks who have been most harmed? Arguably, it is not poor, unskilled blacks who are most harmed by discrimination, but middle-class blacks. During Jim Crow, the gap in earnings between poor whites and poor blacks living in the South was much less than that between educated, middle-class whites and educated, middle-class blacks. In 1949 a black college graduate on average made only 68 percent of what a comparably educated white college graduate made, while a black male with a high school diploma made 82 percent of what a comparably educated white male did. The greater gap in earnings between educated whites and blacks continued through the sixties and lessened only with the implementation of antidiscrimination laws and affirmative action policies.

Discrimination, then, not only prevents persons from developing talents, but it also prevents them from exercising the talents they already have. Antipoverty policies and policies aimed at providing equal opportunity public education remedy only some of the effects of past discrimination. Affirmative action remedies other effects; it helps women and minorities who are already talented to develop their talents further and acquire positions commensurate with their training. Albert Mosley puts this point well when he says that

> Providing equal opportunity thus means more than simply moving Black prople above the poverty line, for this would do nothing for those whose ability would likely have placed them far above the poverty line, were it not for the increasing hostility at higher levels of achievement. While it might appear that Black businessmen have been harmed the least by racial discrimination, the fact is that many such individuals may in fact have been harmed most, relative to what they could have achieved if racial discrimination had not impeded their efforts.[29]

Affirmative action thus mainly benefits those who have been harmed the most by past discrimination: younger African Americans who have had to overcome the cumulative burdens of past discrimination in order to make the best of their superior talents.[30] It does no injustice to white males who lose out to lesser qualified women and minorities, since the former have achieved their superior qualifications through the undeserved advantages of past discrimination. Therefore, the analogy with tort law in this respect is again cogent, if not perfect; the group that most benefited from discrimination is now being required to compensate the group that most suffered from it.

### Women and Affirmative Action

Are women as deserving of affirmative action protection as blacks? One might think that they are more deserving, insofar as antidiscrimination laws afford them less protection than blacks. Statutes that treat women differently are held to a modestly higher standard of scrutiny than the "mere rationality" standard accorded most legislation; instead of being narrowly tailored to the satisfaction of a compelling state interest—as in the case of race-conscious legislation—they need be only "substantially related" to satisfying an "important" government interest.

Recent opinions show just how generous the court has been in sanctioning sex discrimination as an important state interest. I noted in Chapter 2 that the Court has permitted states to exclude pregnancy from a list of "disabilities" covered by worker's compensation. It also has allowed them to criminalize sex between female minors and older men while permitting sex between male minors and older women, ostensibly because girls are more vulnerable to harm than boys (*Michael M. v. Sonoma County Superior Court* [1981]).

These decisions testify to the difficulty of eradicating sex discrimination. Although women as well as blacks are discriminated against, women live with their oppressors on intimate terms. Thus, consigning women to the home is seen as a way of protecting them. Again, because women are identified as dependent childbearers (rather than independent workers), courts and legislatures see fit to promote their "natural" chastity, domesticity, and nurturing qualities.

How does the difference between gender and racial discrimination bear on affirmative action? Because women as a group are dispersed across many different regions, classes, and races, it is difficult to gauge the extent of their oppression in simple economic terms. On the one hand, the occupational segregation that traditionally consigns women to part-time, low-paying, low-skill jobs (in combination with the domestic segregation that consigns women to child-rearing) results in women earning substantially less than men (as of 1990, full-time working women in the United States earn 71 cents for every dollar that men earn). On the other hand, domestic home-makers who earn very little still benefit from their husband's income. For these reasons, gauging the monetary impact of sexist oppression for pur-poses of compensation is nearly impossible.

The strongest argument for extending affirmative action to women is pro-cedural: to guarantee them equal opportunity to succeed in professions and trades that have been the exclusive enclaves of men. The impressive strides that white women have made in breaking into these occupations suggests that they soon will no longer need the protection of affirmative action to the degree that blacks will. Women of all races now make up more than half of all college students and generally outperform their male counterparts. They constitute 40 percent of all college professors and 43 percent of all man-agers. They are well represented in the legal profession: fully 39 percent of law firm associates and 67 percent of nontenure-track instructors in law schools are women. They have made significant inroads into the medical profession, where they compose almost a third of all doctors and a third of all scientists.

Despite these advances, however, women have a long way to go before they will achieve full parity with men. Most women are concentrated in largely female (75 percent) occupations; they make up only 11 percent of all law partners and tenured professors and only 9 percent of all judges. They also have less seniority than their male counterparts, a situation only partly explained by their having entered the job market later than men.

Given that continuing gender-based disparities are not solely explicable in terms of late entry into the labor market, I think a strong case can be made for retaining affirmative action for women. Merely closing the income gap between men and women by paying persons in low-paying, female-domi-nated occupations (like teaching, nursing, clerical support, and so forth) wages that are comparable to what equally educated persons in higher-pay-ing, male-dominated occupations receive does nothing to increase the per-centage of women in these other occupations. In order to increase female representation in these occupations, affirmative action is needed.

The Clinton administration agrees and it recently expanded the list of af-firmative action beneficiaries of federal contracts to include small businesses owned by women, the "disabled," and the "socially disadvantaged" (in ad-dition to those owned by blacks, Latinos, Indians, Asians, Eskimos, and Na-tive Hawaiians).[31] By allowing more women and whites to take advantage of affirmative action, the administration hopes to comply with the Supreme Court's ruling in *Adarand Constructors Inc. v. Pena* (1995), which allows affirmative action to remedy non–racially specific "disadvantages."

The Clinton plan may well succeed in generating wide public support for affirmative action. In doing so, however, it will have increased social tension between different groups competing for a diminishing pool of affirmative action contracts. More important, it will have skirted the question of whether all oppressed groups are equally deserving of affirmative action. Expanding the list of affirmative action beneficiaries might be good public relations, but it also might reduce the number of placement opportunities for those groups who are most deserving.

All things being equal, Native Americans and African Americans should be preferred over women and other oppressed groups in affirmative action hiring. To begin with, oppressed groups should be favored over those who are not oppressed. Groups deserving compensation for past harms or special protection against increased risks are to be preferred over groups deserving representation for diversity's sake alone. Unless ethnicity (or special cultural and linguistic compentence) is a job requirement—in which case affirmative action does not apply—considerations of diversity should not take precedence over considerations of procedural and compensatory justice. So long as ethnic groups enjoy equal protection and suffer no discrimination, they should not be favored over women and racial minorities in the granting of government contracts.

With the possible exception of Native Americans and Latinos, blacks still remain more vulnerable to heightened risk than women and other minorities. Women and minorities have faced (and continue to face) discrimination. However, as I noted earlier, it is difficult to gauge the economic impact of discrimination on women. Most white women have benefited from the same racism that has benefited their working husbands. Thus, although the "protective" and paternalistic oppression borne by white women as a class has made possible their disempowerment, exploitation, and vulnerability, such economic effects have been, on the whole, more unevenly dispersed than those associated with the "caste" oppression borne by African Americans. Moreover, because the genocide, enslavement, and legal disenfranchisement visited upon Native Americans and African Americans aimed expressly at expropriating their property and exploiting their labor, its economic damages—concentrated and calculable—are more susceptible to compensatory reparation.

In this chapter I argued that strong affirmative action policies are consistent with the moral principles underlying the Fourteenth Amendment's

Equal Protection Clause and the Civil Rights Act of 1964. Although I interpret these texts and principles as embodying an evolving conception of equal respect and equal concern, more static interpretations—of an originalist or natural law type—also support affirmative action. Finally, I defended affirmative action on grounds of compensatory and procedural justice. This defense is consistent with the possibility that affirmative action unfairly harms some white males. These harms, I suggested, could be compensated or mitigated by dispersing recessionary effects evenly throughout the workforce.

Although participation in affirmative action is entirely voluntary, affecting only institutions that freely accept public tax revenue, implementation of it is not. When a government has legally abetted in the enslavement, exploitation, and oppression of certain of its citizens, it is morally obligated to redress the harm done to them. As I will point out in the next chapter, the same applies to the political disempowerment of minorities by democratic majorities.

# 9

## RACIAL REDISTRICTING
## AND DEMOCRATIC REPRESENTATION

Political equality cannot exist unless all significant political groups are allowed to elect representatives of their choice. In the United States, however, who gets elected is very much determined by the geographical boundaries of electoral districts. Consider the following two cases: Columnist Ray Gonzales reports that, when he served in the California Assembly as a Democratic representative during the seventies, leaders of both parties agreed to a redistricting plan that extended his jurisdiction from Kern County westward across Ventura County to approximately the twelve feet or so of beachhead adjoining the Pacific Ocean. To be more precise, the western border of his district was drawn at the high-tide marker, thereby permitting the district of his Republican neighbor, directly to the south, to extend around his (Gonzales's) district through the narrow corridor of beachhead left exposed during low tide. The reasons for this proposal were patently political: the Republican assemblyman wanted to exclude the Santa Barbara campus of the University of California from his district, which extended down to the high-tide marker, but wanted some way to include the wealthy and conservative beach communities just north of the notoriously radical university.[1]

Here is the second case: The Fourth Congressional District in Illinois connects a Northside Chicago community composed mainly of citizens of Puerto Rican descent with a Southside community composed mainly of Mexican Americans. The odd-shaped district was recently challenged by (among others) a coalition of disaffected politicians from the Puerto Rican community, who argued that there were sufficient cultural and ethnic differences between the two communities to warrant subdividing the district into two separate congressional jurisdictions. The Illinois Supreme Court eventually ruled in favor of the defendants on March 11, 1996, and its decision went unchallenged by the U.S. Supreme Court two years later.[2]

The two cases mentioned above both concern the geographical boundaries of legislative districts, but there is little else that they share in common.
Gonzalez and his Republican counterpart were the beneficiaries of a redistricting scheme designed to ensure that Republican and Democratic candidates would continue to be elected in their traditional partisan strongholds;
more specifically, it protected the Republican incumbent from being voted
out of office. By redrawing his district to include communities likely to vote
Republican and exclude communities likely to vote Democratic, his reelection in the next partisan campaign was virtually assured.

By contrast, creation of the Fourth Congressional District had little or
nothing to do with protecting incumbents. Although some of the plaintiffs
were motivated by personal animus against the current representative of the
district (Luis Gutierrez), others were not. Instead, they were opposed to
the philosophical rationale underlying the creation of the district, which
aimed to ensure that the Latino community in Chicago could elect someone to Congress who would effectively represent its perspective and interests. In short, they argued that the Fourth District was mistakenly premised
on the assumption that, just because Puerto Rican and Mexican-American
citizens share a common linguistic heritage, they also share common political interests.

There is another difference between the two cases: whereas the Supreme
Court has consistently upheld the right of political parties to redraw electoral districts for purposes of protecting incumbents, it has almost as consistently ruled against the right of African Americans and other minorities to
elect representatives of their choice. As I discussed in Chapter 3, conservative members of the Supreme Court believe that racial redistricting stereotypes minorities by presuming that each member of a minority community
thinks alike and has the same interests. This belief also undergirds the plaintiffs' argument against the Fourth District.

The Court's thinking in these two cases might strike us as somewhat
bizarre. Protecting incumbents against being voted out of office by their
constituents—by reshuffling the constituents—seems contrary to the principle of democracy, unless one assumes that doing so promotes the representation of those constituents' interests (broadly construed). But if it is
acceptable to redraw districts for the sake of electing incumbents who represent the partisan interests of nonminority communities, then why isn't it
acceptable to redraw districts for the sake of electing minority candidates
who represent the racial perspectives of geographically segregated minorities? In short, why is it okay to presume that individuals living in wealthy,

white suburbs in Santa Barbara share interests meriting representation by Republican politicians but not okay to presume that individuals living in poor, black (or Latino) communities share perspectives meriting representation by black and Latino (or white) politicians?

My discussion in Chapter 3 of the Supreme Court's opposition to racial redistricting suggests that there is no satisfactory answer to this question. The Court's belief that any affirmation of a common racial identity involves false stereotyping seems mistaken. Members of a given racial or ethnic group often share common perspectives or at least substantial and overlapping interests, which seems to be the case with the Latino community bounded by the Fourth District. Despite their differences, the Puerto Rican and Mexican-American constituencies composing that community probably share overlapping perspectives and interests that merit their being grouped into a single political district.[3] There is no reason why these perspectives and interests are less deserving of representation than the partisan interests of white suburbanites who have been legitimately grouped into political districts.

The Court's opposition to racial redistricting is laced with inconsistencies. However, this does not mean that its opposition is without warrant. After all, racial redistricting might not be the most just and effective method for ensuring the representation of minority interests. Indeed, some progressives have joined conservatives in arguing that racial redistricting diminishes the bargaining leverage of representatives elected from minority districts and encourages an antidemocratic politics of group identity that pits one race against another.

## *Racial Redistricting As a Remedy for Political Discrimination*

Before assessing the merits of racial redistricting as a policy for ensuring minority representation, we need to closely examine its moral and legal rationale. The constitutional guarantee of equal protection under the law embedded in the Fourteenth Amendment clearly prohibits majorities in state legislatures from violating the rights of minorities. Some of these rights are political in nature and specifically include an equal right to vote for representatives.

The right to vote for representatives is subsidiary to a more basic right to participate in the making of decisions that equally affect one's life, especially the democratic ratification of statutes that define and sanction basic rights generally (see Chapter 11). The right to vote for representatives does not guarantee that the representative of one's choice will be elected, but it does presuppose that the equal and unconstrained exercise of that right will be regulated by fair procedures (see Chapter 1).

Constitutional guarantees of pure procedural fairness played a key role in protecting blacks' rights to vote during the civil rights struggles of the sixties and seventies. The right of individuals to vote without fear of constraint underscored the unconstitutionality of poll taxes, property qualifications, and literacy tests aimed at preventing southern blacks from voting during the Jim Crow era. The elimination of these requirements constituted the first wave of civil rights reform. The second wave strengthened the individual's right to cast an equally weighted ballot by rectifying gross numerical disparities between populous black districts and their less populous white counterparts.

Eliminating racial gerrymandering of this sort, however, did not address the problem of black vote dilution caused by another form of gerrymandering.[4] Once they were forbidden to gerrymander boundaries concentrating blacks in overpopulated districts, southern state legislatures sought to gerrymander them in ways that allocated blacks more evenly among predominantly white districts—sometimes by incorporating single-member districts in which blacks composed a majority into larger, at-large districts in which whites constituted a majority—thereby ensuring that blacks would remain a permanent minority within each of those districts. For this very reason, the securing of equal voting rights for blacks as a group required a third wave of civil rights reform.

Given the long history of discrimination against blacks and the well-documented existence of racially polarized voting patterns in key regions of the country, the policy of carving out so-called majority-minority legislative districts (sometimes containing 65 percent or more of some minority population) presented itself as the most viable remedy for ensuring that minorities would have real opportunities for electing representatives who advocated their interests, values, and perspectives.[6]

Clearly, the rationale behind the new form of racial redistricting was very different from the one that motivated southern legislators in the sixties. The new rationale, most famously articulated in the Voting Rights Act (1965) as amended in 1982, prohibits "political processes leading to nomination or election in the State or political subdivision" in which members of a protected class "have less opportunity than other members of the electorate to participate in the political process and to elect representatives of their choice."[7] The observant reader will notice the act's focus on equal opportunity (pure procedural fairness) rather than good outcome (see Chapters 1 and 7). Yet, while the act expressly disavows any "right to have members of a protected class elected in numbers equal to their proportion in the population," it does protect against redistricting proposals that either dilute the concentration of minorities in ways that worsen their prospects for electing representatives of their choice (para. 2) or effect a retrogression in their current prospects for doing so (para. 5).[8]

### Recent Constitutional Challenges to Racial Redistricting

The Court's main precedent on racial redistricting, *United Jewish Organizations v. Carey* (1977), upheld a race-conscious plan designed to maximize black voting strength against a suit brought by a Brooklyn Hasidic community that had alleged that the plan diluted the voting strength of Jews in the community. The Court ruled that the plan neither stigmatized nor discriminated against any race. A decade later, further challenges to racial redistricting forced the Court to define its working definition of vote dilution more narrowly. In *Thornburg v. Gingles* (1986), the Court ruled that statistical evidence of disproportionate underrepresentation of minorities was insufficient to prove vote dilution unless three other threshold conditions were met. First, the minority whose rights were at stake had to be "sufficiently large and geographically compact to constitute a majority in a single-member district." Second, this minority had to be "politically cohesive." Finally, the white majority had to "vote sufficiently as a bloc to enable it . . . usually to defeat the minority's preferred candidate."[9]

Since *Thornburg*, most of the challenges to racial redistricting have focused on the alleged failure to satisfy the first and second conditions (requiring geographic compactness and political cohesiveness, respectively). In order to grasp the legality and morality of these procedural constraints, it is imperative that we understand the Court's position on strict scrutiny oversight of racially motivated legislation.

To begin with, the Court initiates strict scrutiny oversight only after it has been determined that plaintiffs allegedly harmed by a racially motivated statute have demonstrated that they have standing to sue. Once they have demonstrated this, strict scrutiny is automatically triggered if the statute contains racial categories or is expressly motivated by racial considerations. In the case of racial redistricting, strict scrutiny is triggered when one of the *Thornburg* conditions is not met. Finally, in order for racially motivated statutes to withstand strict scrutiny, they must be defensible. Defensible statutes satisfy a compelling state interest *and* are narrowly tailored to achieving this end, such that no less racially motivated schemes will accomplish it as well.

Plaintiffs have standing to sue only if they claim to have suffered a concrete "injury in fact,"[10] one that is not "a generally available grievance about government—claiming only harm to . . . every citizen's interest in the proper application of the constitution and laws, and seeking relief that no more directly and tangibly benefits [the plaintiffs] than it does the public at large."[11] Now, minorities suffer a concrete injury in fact when their votes are diluted by redistricting schemes that favor the majority, for the harm they allege results from a prejudicial application of generally sound constitutional procedures that adversely affects only them. But what about members of the majority who feel that they have been harmed by schemes that empower minorities?

That whites might also have standing to challenge racial redistricting schemes was first announced by Justice Sandra Day O'Connor in her majority opinion in *Shaw v. Reno* (1993). Sharply departing from *United Jewish Organizations,* she noted that racial classifications stigmatize their beneficiaries as inferior and discriminate against those who fall outside their protection. In particular, racial redistricting, she believed, "undermine[s] our system of representative democracy by signaling to elected officials that they represent a particular racial group rather than their constituency as a whole."[12]

Later district court opinions read this passage as implicating two kinds of harms suffered by whites as a result of racial redistricting schemes: the general—but nonjusticiable—harm associated with "undermining our system of democracy" and the individual harm associated with not having one's interests fairly represented on account of one's race. Thus, the only "concrete injury in fact" alleged by white plaintiffs so far has been simply this: a redistricting plan included them in a predominantly black district wherein their chances for electing a white representative (or a nonwhite representative) of their choice were diminished.

Here we see how the question of justification, of compliance with the Equal Protection Clause, indirectly bears on the issue of standing. White plaintiffs argue that they have been discriminated against by redistricting plans that allegedly favor blacks. But why? White plaintiffs do not claim that racial redistricting underrepresents whites *as a group,* because in states where racial redistricting has occurred the percentage of congressional seats represented by whites is in fact greater than the percentage of whites in the total population. Nor can they claim without taint of racism that, as individual members of a white majority inhabiting predominantly minority districts, their interests cannot be adequately represented by a minority representative. Nor, finally, can they reasonably claim that their interests are not being fairly represented because their preferred candidate did not get elected.[13]

Contrary to O'Connor, it would seem that white plaintiffs have not suffered a concrete "injury in fact" entitling them to challenge racial redistricting schemes. Whatever injury is caused amounts, at best, to "a generally available grievance about government." Discounting the fact that white plaintiffs have doubtful constitutional standing for challenging racial redistricting schemes and assuming that such schemes are objectionable on general grounds pertaining to matters of governance, what might these grounds be? The answer can only be that racial redistricting schemes demean *all* individuals, irrespective of race, by segregating them on the basis of stereotypes.[14]

In *Shaw*, O'Connor conceded that all redistricting is race-conscious insofar as "the legislature is always aware of race when it draws district lines." She also recognized that race would have to be factored into court-mandated redistricting proposals aimed at fighting minority vote dilution. What triggers strict scrutiny is not simply the presence of race-consciousness in this sense, but race-consciousness that "cannot be understood as anything other than an effort to separate voters into different districts on the basis of race." The "irregular" and "bizarre" shape of two majority-minority districts provided her with evidence for suspecting that such a proposal might be motivated by such separatist aims.[15] Subsequent opinions by the Supreme Court have held that even when such aims are absent and the districts in question are compact, the mere use of racial factors always triggers strict scrutiny.[16] Thus, while acknowledging that legislators will inevitably be conscious of racial factors in drawing up districts, O'Connor condemns their use of racially indexed demographic data.[17]

In the final analysis, the Court has yet to specify what kind of evidence would show that an irregularly shaped majority-minority district was *not* explicable as an attempt to segregate (in the Court's 1996 ruling in *Shaw v. Hunt*, two North Carolina districts ruled unconstitutional were among the most integrated districts in the state). Nor has much attention been given to the fact that the irregularity and noncompactness of many majority-minority districts often have less to do with empowering nonwhite voters than with protecting white incumbents.

Let us leave aside the problematic procedural requirement (implicit in O'Connor's reliance on *Thornburg*) that politically cohesive communities of interest *must* map onto compact, preexisting political boundaries.[18] Implicated in the Supreme Court's ruling is a more important matter of principle (specifically, of equal protection). The Court continues to allow the creation of irregular, noncompact districts for the benefit of incumbents and nonracial minorities but not for the benefit of blacks or Latinos.[19] In the words of Pamela Karlan, "[this decision] turns the Equal Protection Clause on its head by making the clause's originally intended beneficiaries—African Americans—the one class that cannot draw distinct lines in its favor."[20]

This discussion takes us to the issue of justification. In *Shaw v. Reno*, O'Connor identified several compelling state interests that might justify race-conscious redistricting. Besides compliance with sections 2 and 5 of the Voting Rights Act (prohibiting minority vote dilution and retrogression in minority voting power), these include eliminating the effects of past discrimination and reducing racial polarization. As for the tailoring requirement, the district court in *Shaw v. Hunt* allowed states to draw noncompact districts as long as less race-conscious remedies were not available.[21] Subsequent lower courts, however, have held that irregularly shaped majority-minority districts in and of themselves reinforce racial stereotypes regardless of whether their irregularity was necessitated by nonracial interests in protecting incumbents and partisan shares.

To conclude, the Supreme Court has yet to articulate a middle standard for determining when the three conditions stipulated in *Thornburg* demarcate a clear case of racial injustice mandating racial redistricting. Without such a standard these conditions fail to adequately distinguish racially polarized voting outcomes caused by political differences from those caused by racial prejudice. Neither black minorities in predominantly white districts nor white minorities in predominantly black districts are treated unequally if their disagreement with the majority reflects mutual disagreement in political ideology rather than racial prejudice. The disagreement between whites and blacks over affirmative action might reflect *mostly* differences in political ideology and experience rather than white prejudice. If so, the failure to get black politicians elected who advocate strongly on behalf of affirmative action does not imply that blacks have been denied their right to elect representatives of their choice.

This right would have been denied them, however, if the white majority had dismissed their chosen representative just because he or she were black. Significantly, the Senate Judiciary Committee's report accompanying the 1982 amendment to the Voting Rights Act tacitly endorses this standard in its enumeration of factors that indicate the predominance of racial prejudice in a white majority's voting behavior (including the prevalence of race-baiting political campaigns, the lack of responsiveness of elected white officials to the particular needs of minorities inhabiting their districts, and the extent of past or present officially sanctioned discrimination in the political subdivision under consideration).

Following Andrew Altman, one can therefore conclude that the decisive difference between legitimate versus illegitimate racially polarized voting patterns is at least conceptually transparent if not always empirically demonstrable in the delegitimating role of racial prejudice in the attitudes of the majority.[22] Thus, contrary to the Court, in order to justify racial redistricting, no stereotypical assumption about the shared interests of blacks and other minority groups nor any theory of proportional group representation need be invoked beyond a specific demonstration of racial prejudice.

### Partisan Versus Racial Redistricting

The Court permits redistricting based on partisan but not racial grounds; in doing so, it presumes that partisan loyalty provides a more enduring basis for defining a community's political interests than racial (or ethnic) identification. For example, in *Miller v. Johnson* (1995), Justice Kennedy argued that because Georgia's Eleventh District linked "four discrete, widely spaced urban centers that have nothing to do with each other" and stretched across "hundreds of miles [of] rural counties and narrow swamp corridors," its members could not share any common interests. In his opinion, this district combined black neighborhoods that were "worlds apart in culture" and thoroughly disparate in social, political, and economic interests.[23]

Kennedy's argument can be paraphrased as follows: What representatives represent are their constituents' interests, the most important of which gravitate around geographically bounded economic, political, cultural, and social issues. Voting districts that range over widely diverse economies, polities, cultures, and societies are less efficient in representing interests. Many racially reapportioned districts range over widely diverse economies, polities, cultures, and societies. Therefore, because such districts are inefficient in delimiting a genuine community of interest, their sole effect is to reinforce a false community of interest reflecting racist stereotypes.

In Chapter 3 I argued that it is not necessary for members of distinct groups to share common interests in order to constitute a distinct community of political interest, since they may share overlapping interests that suffice for this purpose. Whether they share common or overlapping interests is irrelevant, however, because what unites members of such communities (and what also merits representation) is often something more general—a perspective, or outlook. The constituents of Georgia's Eleventh District might well share overlapping interests (contrary to Kennedy's asertion),[24] but even if they do not, they share a common perspective: that of having grown up black in a white supremacist state.

Because perspectives are based in experience, it might seem that the view I am defending implies that African Americans can be adequately represented only by African Americans. If this were true, racially polarized voting (blacks voting only for blacks, whites voting only for whites, and so on) would be perfectly proper. On the contrary, persons other than members of an oppressed minority can sometimes understand and effectively represent that group's perspective.[25] The mistaken notion that representatives must identify personally with the experiences and perspectives of their constituents leads to the absurd conclusion that they must exactly mirror the diverse experiential composition of each and every constituent.[26] What I am suggesting, by contrast, is that in order for a minority group to communicate its sufferings and aspirations to the majority in a rhetorically compelling manner—and in order for that group to feel assured that its chosen spokespersons will be fully accountable to it in this regard—it must have some of its own members elected as representatives.[27]

Kennedy is wrong on another point as well. In the United States, race and ethnicity provide more enduring bases for demarcating communities of political interest than partisan loyalty. In white suburban communities especially, voters increasingly identify themselves as independents; in general, these voters tend to cast their ballots for incumbents rather than parties.[28] The more dynamic the community, the more unstable its partisan identification. By contrast, blacks and Latinos are less mobile, tending to gravitate toward (or be concentrated in) more segregated communities. Not only are their partisan loyalties more stable (ranging from weakly to strongly Democratic), but so are their interests and perspectives. Whereas white voters have the luxury of viewing themselves simply as individuals with independent interests, blacks and Latinos cannot help but view their interests in light of a shared experience of discrimination and oppression. Hence, O'Connor's frank admission that "when members of a racial group live together in one community, a reapportionment plan that *concentrates* members of the group in one district and *excludes* them from others may reflect wholly *legitimate* interests."[29]

## Racial Redistricting As Politically Divisive

As I noted earlier, O'Connor and other conservative members of the Supreme Court argue that racial redistricting constitutes more than just a "concrete injury" suffered by whites and minorities. In O'Connor's opinion, it also "exacerbate[s] the very patterns of bloc voting" that undermine our system of representative democracy. Echoing these sentiments, Jean Bethke Elshtain writes:

> To the extent that citizens begin to retribalize into ethnic or other "fixed identity" groups, democracy falters. Any possibility for human dialogue, for democratic communication and commonality, vanishes . . . difference becomes more and more exclusivist. If you are black and I am white, I do not and cannot in principle "get it." . . . Mired in the cement of our own identities, we need never deal with one another. Not really. One of us will win and one of us will lose the cultural war or the political struggle.[30]

If O'Connor and Elshtain are right, avoiding a race war in which one side ends up tyrannizing the other requires that individuals transcend their group identifications (interests, values, and perspectives) and identify themselves simply as citizens who possess abstract rights and duties. In other words, the right to "elect representatives of one's choice" should extend only as far as the right of individuals to cast ballots, leaving untouched the representation of groups.[31] Only in this manner can the content of democratic dialogue, and therewith the content of the law, be impartial with respect to different racial groups. Put in Rousseauian and Rawlsian terms, only if citizens bracket out their contingent social differences and agree on the universal terms of dialogue (perhaps by imagining themselves party to an ideal social contract regulated by a veil of ignorance) can they reach agreement on laws that will equally advance their universal interests.

I have already discussed the limits of this conception of impartial dialogue in Chapters 1 and 6. As effective as the bracketing procedure might be for initially conceptualizing the ideal scope of basic abstract rights (such as the right to immigrate), it cannot be invoked without qualification in resolving real-life political dilemmas. Thus, to take our current example of multiracial democracy, no mere appeal to universal terms of dialogue and universal interests makes it the case that such terms and interests—if they exist—suffice to overcome differences in understanding and social position.

Refusal to acknowledge these differences, rather than their open contestation, is what exacerbates racial polarization. As Lani Guinier rightly observes, "the forces of [racial] silence cede all the space to the forces of bigotry" by ignoring the fact that "the [color-blind] language of universal reform"—of welfare rights, crime, and immigration—is *implicitly* "racialized" and "blackened" by many of those who oppose reform.[32] Here, refusal to discuss reform outside of the sociohistorical nexus linking racial discrimination, economic deprivation, and political powerlessness not only perpetuates public ignorance and ineffectual policy but also alienates racial groups whose voices have been suppressed by mainstream media. However, if blacks and other minorities are to be encouraged to discuss social, political, and economic reform publicly *from their perspectives,* they also must be allowed to do so from within the protected spaces of communities over which they exercise control.[33] This bespeaks less a politics of separatism, although separatism might sometimes be a legitimate response to oppression, than a politics of solidarity and community pride.

### The Radical Critique of Racial Redistricting

Defending a legitimate conception of racial group identity does not seal the argument in support of racial redistricting. As Lani Guinier and others have pointed out, racial redistricting procedures might not be as effective as other, nonracial remedies for combating minority vote dilution, such as the use of plural voting in enlarged, multiseat districts.[34] Indeed, as I argue below, racial redistricting might actually work to disempower minorities, either by marginalizing minority representatives or by increasing the number of hostile representatives. This disempowerment would lend some credence to the charge that majority-minority districts are indeed poorly tailored toward achieving their goals and so fail to pass constitutional muster.

Guinier notes that the real benefits of single-seat black districts in mobilizing the black community quickly diminish once it is understood that representatives of these districts are but tokens who wield little influence in legislatures. Divested of political influence, they end up compromising, selling out to special interests, or succumbing to the perks of patronage;[35] as incumbents virtually reassured of reelection, their interest in the community wanes. Conversely, voter mobilization in support of them ceases to be politically informed and becomes symbolic and routine.

According to Guinier, the very fact that black representatives from majority-minority districts do not have to compete for reelection with representatives from white districts explains why the former are powerless to mitigate racial polarization and effect policy reforms on behalf of their constituents. Because representatives from white districts do not have to compete with representatives from black districts, they can afford to dismiss or ignore them. This "ghettoization" of black representatives in the legislature—what Guinier calls "deliberative gerrymandering"—only reinforces racial segregation and stereotyping and does nothing to advance the black community's political agenda. In order to ensure both equal representation of perspectives and equal satisfaction of interests, representatives of white districts would have to see that it was in their interest to negotiate in good faith with their minority compatriots, and that, Guinier insists, would occur *only if* they were forced to run for reelection in multiseat districts with a substantial minority population. Under these conditions, neither white nor black candidates could take the black community's support for granted, and so members of this community would again have the opportunity to mobilize themselves and become politically educated.

Instead of allowing legislators and judges to draw up single-seat districts that impose stereotypical views about what all African Americans want, Guinier would allow African Americans as individuals to choose which of their social perspectives best articulates their social position, their personal identity and interest.[36] Although we cannot choose the formative experiences that determine our social perspectives, we can choose, given the various types of formative experiences we have had, to identify more with one perspective than another. Using a cumulative voting scheme, of course, would permit even more flexibility in this area. To cite Guinier:

However defined and redefined, contextualized and complicated, the almost irrefutable existence of something like a racial minority group identity suggests that a vital political system must accommodate those who *choose* that identity. To make room, however, does not mean to evict other identities. To this end, a racial minority group identity should be represented to the extent that its members in fact act collectively. Mere assumptions about alleged uniformity should be insufficient to justify measures to ensure group representation. This approach acknowledges that one's racial group is not the only club to which one belongs. Collective group preferences might be measured by using innovative electoral schemes like cumulative voting and proportional representation. In this view, unity is defined as collaboration rather than as sameness.[37]

In this passage, Guinier takes aim at the "alleged uniformity" of minority communities that is often appealed to in justifying court-mandated racial redistricting procedures. Like her conservative opponents, she too objects to the way in which these procedures "impose" a group identity on individuals in an illegitimate, top-down fashion (cf. Chapter 3). Unlike them, however, she emphatically reaffirms the "existence of a racial minority group identity" while conceding that its complexity and contextuality cannot be predefined in terms of a single, essentially unified identity. In her opinion, whatever minority group identity that exists comprises at best a collective, collaborative dialogue of fluid, overlapping, but distinct perspectives and preferences. Hence, any individual member of a racial minority group will "choose" (or interpret) that group's identity in a manner befitting his or her own situated, yet evolving, sense of self. Consequently, representing the distinct individual identities that make up (and extend beyond) any given minority group identity will require more open-ended procedures of representation involving larger, more demographically diverse districts containing multiple seats. By giving voters in these districts the opportunity to vote for many candidates, voters will have a better chance of getting their various group interests (perspectives) represented in proportion to their groups' numbers.

For example, in a four-seat district, an African-American lesbian businesswoman might decide that her interests, values, and perspectives are best spoken for by apportioning her votes among an Anglo-American lesbian, an African-American heterosexual male, and an Asian entrepeneur. In a single-seat district, this kind of flexible representation of identity and interest could not exist and, more important, neither could the dialogical interaction between persons speaking from different perspectives.

Ironically, it is precisely here—in her emphasis on the dialogical transformation of identity—that Guinier's proposal begins to run aground. Besides enhancing possibilities for expanding one's perspective and transforming one's interests, Guinier's proposal also seeks to increase both the representation of blacks in legislatures and, therewith, the satisfaction of the black community's interests. But it is unclear whether the transformative dynamic set in motion by cross-cultural and cross-racial coalition-building will leave intact anything like a distinctly black group identity that could be the subject of representation—a result that, good in the long run, might be bad in the short run.

Before examining this problem further, it is worthwhile noting that racial redistricting, at least as it has been implemented in the United States, has its own shortcomings as a system of representation. Recent studies show that racial redistricting has probably diminished the substantive satisfaction of the black community's interests—even if it has increased their formal representation—simply by reducing the total number of seats held by white Democrats (whom the Leadership Council on Civil Rights rate higher than their Republican counterparts in supporting civil rights measures and redistributive policies targeted toward ameliorating the condition of minorities).[38] In essence, the incorporation of blacks into predominantly black districts has siphoned off black voters from other districts in which they could have contributed to electing white Democratic representatives and thus more Democratic representatives overall. Ironically, then, racial redistricting has increased the number of black representatives voicing black *perspectives* while reducing the number of representatives—black and white—supporting black *interests*, thereby disproportionately underrepresenting the interests of blacks as a whole.[39]

It would appear that the failure of racial redistricting to advance the satisfaction of the black community's interests would lend credence to Guinier's support for open-seat districting. In open-seat districts, blacks could theoretically exercise broader leverage in getting their voices heard and their interests met. However, this result is far from obvious, and for two reasons.

First, it can scarcely be denied that a representative representing a small, single-seat district will more effectively advocate the distinct perspectives, values, and interests of that district's inhabitants than if he or she, along with others, were to represent the perspectives, values, and interests of several different communities composing a large district. Second, the kind of transformative dialogue that Guinier believes open-seat districts will encourage works by destabilizing (or, in her words, disaggregating) the preference rankings of individuals and groups.[40] It accomplishes this goal by provoking critical reflection on the social costs of satisfying our interests, on the worthiness of the core values that anchor them in some preference ranking, and on the expansiveness of social perspectives that ground our affective understanding of them in relation to others' interests. Thus, by setting our identities in motion, mutual criticism destabilizes our interests as well as our group identifications.[41]

Perhaps it is for this reason that Guinier sometimes downplays the importance of representing and satisfying the black community's interest in favor of representing its social perspective, which is arguably less susceptible to radical transformation and individual caprice. Here the focus returns to increasing the number of black representatives, but it remains an open question whether her proposal for open-seat districts would improve upon the remedy of racial redistricting in this respect.

Let us suppose for the sake of argument that Guinier's proposal would increase the number of minority representatives. Would such a proposal, if presently implemented, bring about the kind of transformative, egalitarian dialogue desired by Guinier and other progressives?

There is risk in opening up the political process too quickly. Black as well as white representatives will have to expand their base of support to include each others' primary constituencies. However, as experience all too painfully has shown, in order for impoverished black communities to compete effectively for influence with more affluent (and more numerous) white communities inhabiting the same multiseat district, economic, educational, and perhaps even demographic inequalities between the two would have to be eliminated (as was amply confirmed in cases involving gerrymandering on behalf of southern whites in the sixties).[42] Perhaps I am underestimating the political incentives for black candidates to remain loyal to their minority base and for white candidates (who are more numerous) to reach out to this same group. Still, unless the political "dialogue" in which electoral bargaining occurs is independent of social inequalities and other constraints, it cannot be an effective or legitimate medium by which individuals can freely choose their group affiliations. And, as a matter of related concern, there is no reason to think that representatives from multiseat districts will be any more immune to the corrupting influence of patronage, special interests, and compromise politics than those from single-seat ones.

In conclusion, we seem to be left with two models of democratic political dialogue and no clear criterion by which to choose between them. In fact, the dilemma is strikingly similar to that posed by the separatist black power movement of the sixties and the black identity educational reforms of the nineties.

Guinier's proposal for a system of cumulative voting within multiseat districts would seem to encourage integration, but at the risk of abandoning the notion of a representable identity of interest, if not of perspective, and of forcing minority communities to compete for political influence with better funded and better organized white constituencies. It might bring about immediate dialogue, but under conditions that could well be unequal, and it might not ensure the election of minorities.

By contrast, the strategy of racial reapportionment might better promote the election of minorities who would be more accountable to their constituents and who would gain immediate access to legislative bodies from which to communicate their perspectives.[43] Furthermore, this quasi-separatist strategy might initially promote a healthy sense of community autonomy, pride, and solidarity at the grassroots level. Unfortunately, the quality and efficacy of dialogic participation in governmental forums might be of a marginal nature—in fact, too marginal to adequately advance the satisfaction of minority interests. It also might reinforce patterns of segregation that have for so long worked to the disadvantage of most minorities save, perhaps, Native Americans, who claim limited sovereignty of their tribal lands. Finally, if racial redistricting is implemented by courts and legislatures for paternalistic reasons—because the minority to be protected has yet to organize itself into a politically cohesive group capable of exercising bargaining leverage—this action could appear to be an external imposition rendering the constitution of the group's identity less legitimate than it otherwise might be.

Perhaps neither strategy will suffice to ensure full minority participation in political life. Guinier mentions at least two other conditions that would have to obtain in order for transformative democracy to flourish under her proposal. First, the system of proportional interest representation might have to be supplemented by supermajoritarian parliamentary procedures, including minority veto privileges and office rotation ensuring periodical minority control over governmental agendas.[44] As I noted in Chapter 1, these procedures advance rather than retard the equal treatment of both majorities and minorities when properly applied. Second, in order to ensure that the minority community remains intact as a cohesive political force resisting the disintegrative effects of a pluralistic competition for influence, it would have to revitalize itself as a protest movement.

All things being equal, Guinier's proposal for multiple-seat districts combining cumulative voting procedures constitutes a transformative strategy for reform that will have to be implemented in the long run if racial injustice is ever to be overcome. Racial redistricting, however, may be a worthwhile affirmative (action) strategy to pursue in the short run, as Guinier herself concedes.[45] Indeed, given the above prerequisites for transformative politics (including the revitalization of the black community as a protest movement), one wonders whether Guinier's dismissal of the transformative potential of racial redistricting is not premature. If these prerequisites obtained in the case of racially reapportioned, single-seat districts, including "influence districts" that have around 40 percent minority voter population, they too might become more effective vehicles for racial integration and minority empowerment than they currently are. Certainly, in jurisdictions where minorities are demographically dispersed, the best vehicle for change might well be multiseat districts; such districts would seem to hold more promise for effecting the proportional representation of both minorities and women,[46] if such representation is in fact called for.[47] But where residential segregation is deeply entrenched, single-seat majority-minority districts might well be preferable as short-term strategies for transforming black communities into self-transcending protest movements oriented toward achieving racial integration in the long run.

# PART V.
# GLOBAL AND MULTICULTURAL ASPECTS
# OF EQUALITY AND DIFFERENCE

# 10
## MULTICULTURAL EDUCATION AND RESPECT FOR MINORITIES

Years ago when I was a professor at the University of Northern Iowa, I had the good fortune of befriending an Oglala Sioux Vietnam veteran named Russ who happened to be enrolled in my logic course. He was an enormously talented and bright student, but he had a difficult time handling formal logic. In the course of our weekly tutoring sessions, he finally told me that logical analysis and linear inference were alien to the holistic manner of understanding and problem-solving in which he had been raised. Furthermore, he said that it was because of his intuitive capacity for seeing how foregrounded objects were organically related to one another by way of a totality of background experience that he had been able to survive in combat situations requiring instantaneous decisions. His eloquent testimony on behalf of the advantages of a different kind of reasoning eventually led me to appreciate the way in which even formal logic presupposes a preanalytical understanding of conceptual and experiential relationships.

Russ taught me something about logic—and about cultural bias—about which I had hitherto been ignorant. He also made me appreciate the extent to which Native Americans might be discriminated against in the assessment of their educational achievement (Russ ended up with a C– in my logic course, which he might have failed if someone less open-minded had taught the course). Still, the kind of cultural bias Russ encountered at UNI was nothing compared to the discrimination experienced by Native American children in public schools.

Native American health expert and educator Carol Locust has written poignantly about this discrimination, which invariably stems from failing to sufficiently recognize the different but equally legitimate conception of health and knowledge informing Native American culture.[1] Although we have come a long way since the military-like boarding schools run by the

219

Bureau of Indian Affairs from 1819 until the 1920s (which aimed at extirpating all traces of Native American language and culture),[2] public schools still have difficulty accommodating the spiritual beliefs of Indian children within a secular setting. Teachers express alarm whenever Indian parents remove their children from school because the children complain of suffering from the negative effects of witchcraft or "ghost sickness" (a "malady of lethargy, apathy, and general non-specific unwellness caused by the spirits of dead children calling for them to join them"); conversely, these parents may leave their children in school even if the children display symptoms (fever, vomiting, headache, and so on) that school authorities deem to require medically supervised home care.[3]

Parents also disagree with authorities about requiring their children to shower after physical education (Indian culture forbids common showers or other public acts that violate the sacredness of the body). And they disagree with them about what constitutes a medical handicap meriting special education; what European medicine considers to be a physical or mental disability, Indian culture considers to be a gift. Indeed, in sharp contrast to Western culture, Indian culture reinforces "non-verbal communication and alternative avenues of communication, including visual/spatial memory, visual/motor skills, and sequential visual memory, but not verbal skills."[4] Finally, forcing Indian children to attend classes away from home disrupts the familial and communal bonds cultivated in caring for younger siblings and in helping parents and grandparents with household chores; it is in the carrying out of these tasks that traditions are instilled in children concerning their responsibility to family and tribe. By denying them the opportunity to learn social responsibility at home, Indian children become more vulnerable to delinquency later on in life.

Locust concludes her indictment of public education: "As Native people, we cannot separate our spiritual teachings from our learning, nor can we separate our beliefs about who and what we are from our behaviors. As Indian people, we ask that educational systems recognize our right to religious freedom and our right, as Sovereign Nations, to live in harmony as we were taught. However, non-Indians must be educated about traditional beliefs that Indian people have before they can understand what changes may be needed."[5] Her discussion of the cultural clash between Native Americans and mainstream educators raises fundamental questions about the rights of parents to educate their children as they see fit, even when doing so hinders their children's chances of assimilating to mainstream culture. It also raises questions about how far public schools should strive to accommodate the multicultural differences of their students in the curriculum. Public schools on reservations currently recognize cultural holidays celebrated by Native Americans; should they also teach Native American spiritual beliefs (incorporating, for example, Native American creationist accounts of the universe in discussions of science)? If we answer in the affirmative, while otherwise repudiating the teaching of Christian creationism in public schools,[6] is it because Native Americans have been an oppressed minority threatened with cultural assimilation?

### Historical Background to the Multicultural Debates: Reactions to Assimilation

American debates about multiculturalism center around the ambivalent appeal to cultural assimilation that has marked our nation's treatment of immigrants, blacks, and Native Americans.[7] Until recently, J. Hector St. John de Crevecoeur's famous definition of an American in *Letters from an American Farmer* (1782) as "either a European or the descendant of a European" seemed to aptly describe American political life.[8] Assimilation to the national identity, with its commitment to abstract ideals of liberty, equality, and republicanism, was seen to be naturally attainable by almost "everyone" except blacks, Asians, Jews, and Indians. In fact, the Americanization movement that emerged in the first decades of the twentieth century only begrudgingly conceded that Eastern and Southern European "races" could become good Americans—assuming, of course, that they spoke good English, practiced good hygiene, understood the rules of citizenship, and remained untainted by such "un-American" ideologies as socialism.

The ideal advocated by the Americanization movement could not have been further removed from that promoted by today's multiculturalists.[9] Not only did the movement expressly disdain any gesture appreciative of the intrinsic merit of immigrant cultures, but by 1920 (after having fallen under the sway of the Ku Klux Klan and other nativists), it impelled state and federal lawmakers to restrict immigration, limit the rights of aliens, and ban both foreign language instruction and the teaching of foreign languages in states like Nebraska. This highly restrictive notion of assimilation did not wane in popularity until World War II, when enlisting the aid of blacks, Latinos, Asians, and Native Americans in the fight against fascism became a major priority.

Tragically, the one minority that did not benefit from this change was African Americans. Denied equal citizenship, some of them supported separatist ventures, such as Marcus Garvey's "Back to Africa" program or the American Communist Party's support for a separate black state in the South.

Even in spite of the civil rights movement, support for separatist movements remained strong, especially among groups like the Black Muslims, whose popularity increased as government enthusiasm for integration flagged. The failure of the government's color-blind antidiscrimination policies to address the economic plight of the black urban ghetto only solidified their doubts. As disappointment erupted into violence, black leaders began to plot a new nationalist agenda. Accordingly, advocates of Black Power in the sixties— spearheaded by the Black Panthers and other urban organizations—urged the black community to control its own health, education, welfare, and security needs independently of the white business/government establishment, whose exploitation of the ghetto economy they compared to the worst kind of colonial violence.[10]

Many blacks today still voice separatist sentiments—which just goes to show how a frustrated desire to assimilate can quickly be transformed into a separatist desire to acquire protective group rights.[11] Other minorities, of course, have their own reasons for questioning the ideal of assimilation. As I have already discussed, the assimilation of Native Americans—which might have enhanced the freedom and well-being of some of them (especially women) had it not been carried out so half-heartedly and with total disregard for their rights—was designed to weaken their resolve to resist further exploitation of their lands. The assimilation of handicapped persons—which, by contrast, was motivated by benevolent if at times misguided motives—arguably left some of them, such as the deaf, worse off than they would have been otherwise. Gays and lesbians also rejected assimilation, since their struggle for civil rights has always been premised on gaining acceptance of their distinct lifestyle. Even Asian Americans and Latinos have not unqualifiedly embraced assimilation; their support for bilingual education as a way of instilling pride in their native cultures has also served to remind Americans of the contributions that immigrants with different perspectives and talents bring to the country.[12]

Women's assimilation into the masculine culture of public life merits special treatment, since in some ways it articulates an ambivalence that runs through all marginalized groups. In the sixties, "first-wave" feminists, led by such stalwart activists as Betty Friedan, Shulamith Firestone, and Gloria Steinem, wanted nothing more than to secure for women the same rights enjoyed by men. But assimilation into the hierarchical, competitive, and individualistic ethos of patriarchal business culture often meant forsaking family, friends, and community. By the eighties, "second-wave" feminists like Carol Gilligan, Sara Ruddick, and Nel Noddings had rejected assimilation, arguing that the "ethic of care" that culminated feminine patterns of socialization represented a positive countermodel to a masculine "ethic of justice." "Third-wave" feminists later argued that the "ethic of care" was insensitive to cultural differences between white, heterosexual, middle-class women, on the one side, and minority, lesbian, and working-class women, on the other.[13] Today, feminists increasingly see their criticism of universal cultural norms as decisively rejecting patriarchal hierarchy. In sum, the women's movement culminates a trajectory of political struggle that is common to all oppressed groups: from assimilation to separation and finally multicultural alliance premised on respect for difference.

Today's multicultural "politics of identity" represents both a positive and a negative alternative to assimilation. On the positive side, it refuses to reduce social injustice to economic oppression, acknowledging the different ways in which groups are dominated or denied positive recognition. On the negative side, it encourages persons to identify mainly with a single group, thereby obscuring the overlapping nature of social injustices and group identities. In this regard, the civil rights struggles of the sixties acknowledged an important truth that is sometimes forgotten by multiculturalists: the need to transform oneself in joining together to transform society.

*Multiculturalism and the Academy:*
*Gendered and Racialized Science*

In order for multiculturalism to become an effective vehicle for social transformation, it first had to become a force within mainstream education. Accordingly, multiculturalism first insinuated itself in the academy during the political protests of the sixties and entered the mainstream twenty years later, when many of the movements that had spawned it had all but disappeared.

Initially, multiculturalism was defended as an example of what a genuine liberal arts education ought to be: a form of cultural enrichment enhancing personal growth and correcting racist, ethnocentrist, and sexist bias in the humanities and sciences. In keeping with this modest aim, universities like Stanford expanded their Western Civilization courses to include non-Western or minority materials. Others, like UC–Santa Barbara, added an ethnicity requirement or, following UC–Berkeley, a sequence on American cultures. Colleges and universities further supplemented these curricular changes with new programs focusing on women's and gay/lesbian studies.[14]

Conservatives responded to these modest reforms with alarm, proclaiming that multiculturalism suppressed rather than enhanced an open-minded appreciation of culture. Writing in 1990, Roger Kimball warned that "multiculturalism . . . is about undermining the priority of Western liberal values" on which real pluralism rests.[15] This sentiment was later echoed by Robert Leiken, who proclaimed that multiculturalism's "true ideological forefather is not Gramsci but Mussolini."[16]

Contrary to conservative hyperbole, the modest multiculturalism adopted by institutions of higher education was hardly the assault on academic freedom it was depicted as being. And yet it was not entirely apolitical, as some of its defenders maintained, since it challenged the classist, sexist, racist, and ethnocentrist bias implicit in so-called "objective" science. For example:

- Although modern genetics refutes older biological theories of race, many doctors and public health officials talk as if there existed a causal relationship between being black and being susceptible to sickle-cell anemia.[17]
- Defenders of sociobiology at prestigious universities continue to argue that differences in IQ between whites and blacks are hereditary and resistant to rectification by means of social programs.[18]
- Research on medical problems that mainly afflict poor people and minorities remains underfunded; when conducted, it often manifests the kind of racial bias and discrimination associated with the infamous Tuskegee Study.[19]
- Scientists continue to look for biological explanations for the low incidence of females in the hard sciences as well as for their greater presence in domestic and care-giving vocations.[20]
- Research targeting women's health needs is grossly underfunded in comparison to research targeting men's health needs; furthermore, most research has involved the use of male test subjects, who sometimes respond to experiments and treatments differently than women.[21]
- Biologists and doctors insist on the biological basis of gender, despite the existence of hermaphroditism, transsexualism, and other ambiguities that suggest that gender determinations are at least partly culturally conditioned.[22]
- Applications of science and technology continue to stress an undemocratic and elitist conception of knowledge, the result being that people living in non-Western cultures feel constrained to adopt costly, ecologically maladaptive and socially disruptive, high-tech methods of farming, manufacturing, and healing.[23]

To conclude, multiculturalism politicizes our perception of knowledge and who it serves; it asks us to consider whether education ought to promote the recognition of oppressed and marginalized groups or reinforce the traditional hegemony of the Western canon.

## Multiculturalism As a Liberal Ideal

The liberalism embraced by most American and Canadian educators justifies two different multicultural ideals.[24] The first is the familiar and uncontroversial liberal arts view of education as a "marketplace of ideas" (to use John Stuart Mill's famous phrase). According to this ideal, exposure to different cultures is essential for the attainment of knowledge and personal enrichment. The second is the more controversial ideal of equal opportunity education. According to this ideal, the teaching of marginalized subcultures is essential for extending equal respect to students who identify with them.

It is important to note that neither of these ideals takes cultural diversity to be an end in itself or a good to be pursued aside from its contribution to knowledge, personal enhancement, or social justice. The liberal arts ideal sees cultural diversity as a means for generating the critical reflection necessary for sifting truth from falsehood. Commitment to truth implies nothing about the nature of truth: it might be found in all cultures (either in the same way or in different ways), or it might be found only in one of them. The liberal arts ideal also values diversity in individual lifestyles but not necessarily cultural diversity; as Mill argues, it might be that only one culture—the one associated with Western liberalism—upholds individuality as an end in itself.

Diversity as an intrinsic good finds just as little support from the equal opportunity camp. Equal opportunity multiculturalists frequently say that they want to diversify the curriculum along with diversifying the student body and faculty. But, with the exception of more extreme postmodernists (see below), their reason for doing so is to show equal respect to groups that have either been ignored or misrecognized. Indeed, multicultural justice might require sacrificing diversity in one area—say, foreign language instruction and the teaching of world religions—for the sake of achieving it in another.

As should be apparent by now, liberal arts and social justice ideals of multiculturalism sometimes conflict. Liberal arts education in the United States and Canada has happily encouraged the study of world religions and the high cultures of ancient civilizations while neglecting the study of ethnic groups, women, and gays that compose a substantial portion of the student body. Conversely, although most programs oriented to the study of these groups aim to broaden the understanding of all students, some do not. Some programs devoted to the study of women and minorities often see themselves as catering specifically to the needs of those whose "culture" they specially treat. Indeed, for purposes of extending equal recognition to oppressed minorities and women, it suffices that there be programs with which just these groups will identify.

The distinction between the two ideals mentioned above is basic to understanding current debates over multiculturalism. Many conservative critics are not opposed to multiculturalism in its liberal arts guise, which they generally endorse. Rather, what they oppose is multiculturalism conceived as a social justice agenda, which they feel undermines the aims of a liberal arts education. For them, "politicizing" the curriculum in this way necessarily entails substituting texts articulating local and personal experiences of oppression for texts articulating timeless truths.[25]

Conversely, many supporters of equal opportunity multiculturalism oppose the aims of a traditional liberal arts agenda on the grounds that it fails to respect the lived experiences of oppressed minorities. The founding texts of world religions, to take just one example, seem unrelated to the historically and regionally situated understandings of oppressed minorities. Worse, by presuming that these texts are unproblematic expressions of universal truths, any opportunity to read them as responses to specific historical events and conditions—either as ideological legitimations or as veiled criticisms of social oppression—gets lost.[26]

My own view of the matter is that the two ideals complement one another. Take the liberal arts agenda. There are at least five senses in which this agenda can be said to be political. First of all, the liberal aim of personal enrichment cannot be dissociated from the political aim of securing equal recognition. If individuals are not shown respect and their interests are not acknowledged as objects of concern, their personal growth and enrichment will likely suffer as well.

Second, the liberal arts agenda is political in the sense that it endorses a value intrinsic, and possibly exclusive, to political liberalism: free speech and discussion. In cross-cultural dialogue, the reader approaches a text respectfully, with an open mind and a certain humility. He or she refrains from imposing his or her prejudices willy-nilly on what is read, allowing the text to speak its message freely. In short, the reader treats the text as an equal in dialogue who possesses certain rights.

Third, the expansion of our cultural horizons that comes with a liberal education produces certain political effects. It makes possible a critical distancing from our own taken-for-granted cultural assumptions. Indeed, it resists fetishizing traditional authority of any kind. And so as much as we learn from tradition, we also come to question its claim to offer timeless truth. In short, we learn to think for ourselves, beholden to our own moral lights rather than to the factual powers that be.

Fourth, our questioning of culture can take a more radical turn. So-called "classical" texts reveal their partiality in several ways. Because their authority lives on through the successful reapplication of their meaning to changing historical circumstances, their meaning never remains the same. The reception of a text in countless contexts shows how its meaning can be varied, fragmented, even reversed (think, for instance, of the many opposed ways in which the Bible has been interpreted).

Not only do texts convey different messages to different persons, but the messages conveyed often contain subtle inconsistencies. In close readings of literary masterpieces, we become aware of the depth and complexity of their meaning, which speaks to the unfathomable paradoxes and tensions of the human condition.

Finally, an authentic interpretation of a text requires understanding the historical context in which it was written. However, interpreting a text against the background of the author's own biography and the economic and political forces that shaped it can lead us to appreciate the way in which textual meaning and insight are not universally valid for all classes and generations, even for those numbered among the author's own contemporaries.

Once interpretation goes outside the spoken medium of mutual understanding and becomes causal explanation of concealed motives, the aims of liberal and political education converge; we realize that the production of high culture—of "exemplary truth"—is itself a site of social and political contestation. And so it is perfectly appropriate to question the ideological signification of classical texts as products of social, economic, political, and cultural influences. Having done so, it is appropriate to ask whether the assignation of classical status to these texts has come at the expense of marginalizing other texts within the tradition. Perhaps, as the social justice multiculturalists argue, we must read both "classics" and marginalized (and in some cases suppressed) texts against one another—for instance, Plato's recipe for elite education contained in *The Republic* against Paulo Freire's *Pedagogy of the Oppressed;* James Madison's reflections on the uses and abuses of political factions in *Federalist* 51 against Lani Guinier's subtle critique in "The Triumph of Tokenism" of America's system of majoritarian democracy; and Benjamin Franklin's autobiographical celebration of the enterprising American inventor against Mayan revolutionary Rigoberta Menchú's autobiographical account of the genocidal implications of economic "progress" under Guatemala's U.S.-backed military regime.

I have argued that a liberal education is necessarily political. But is a political education necessarily liberal? Recall that equal opportunity multiculturalism initially began as a liberal endeavor to further knowledge and personal growth. In order to carry out its mission of showing equal respect to minorities and women, it had to correct false characterizations of them as depicted in the canon. Far from treating the canon as mere ideology, it took it seriously and then showed how its falsehoods expressed and supported deeper social structures and institutions. In this way, it advanced the personal growth of all students as liberal—tolerant and enlightened—political agents.

### Liberal Versus Postmodern Defenses of Multiculturalism

Defenses of equal opportunity multiculturalism come in two varieties: liberal and postmodern. The first, exemplified in a recent essay by Charles Taylor,[27] argues that multiculturalism is an outgrowth of a peculiarly modern need for recognition. In the West, the need to be recognized as a free, self-made individual rather than as a generic product of hereditary roles first gained prominence during the Enlightenment. Enlightenment rationalism encouraged emancipation from tradition and social conformity and, along with it, respect for individuals in their universal humanity. Post-Enlightenment romanticism perpetuated the cult of the individual but did so by emphasizing the nonrational (emotional and expressive) side of individual personality. Exemplified in Rousseau's estimation of personal authenticity—or being true to oneself—it called for respecting individuals in their particularity.

Romanticism culminated in the Enlightenment's call for individual emancipation but reversed its privileging of individual over community. How did this transformation happen? Romantics like Wilhelm Gottfried Herder realized that, because an individual's linguistic and cultural affiliations are an important part of his or her particular identity, respecting the latter called for respecting the former.[28] If, for Enlightenment rationalists, respecting the universal humanity of individuals involved endowing them with rights, then respecting their particularity entailed the same for Romantic expressivists; for them, respecting the sovereign rights of the individual qua individual was scarcely conceivable apart from respecting the sovereign rights of the cultural (and racial) nationality to which he or she belonged.

Today, the politics of recognition commonly associated with "identity politics" is much less bound up with the romantic multiculturalism of Herder and Taylor than its advocates seem to realize. As Anthony Appiah notes, there is marked cultural homogenization across the broad spectrum of "identities" competing for recognition in the United States. In comparison to his native Ghana, which "has several dozen languages in active daily

use and no one language that is spoken at home—or even fluently understood—by a majority of the population," almost all Americans (97 percent),
with the sole exception of recent immigrants, speak English fluently.[29] And
just as the vast majority of recent immigrants buy into American popular culture and its symbols, so too do they accept its mainly Protestant separation of
church and state. Indeed, it is precisely in reaction to this cultural homogenization—that is, to the loss of families possessing relatively closed and distinctive ethnic cultures that was so much the product of earlier
antiassimilationist discrimination—that today's youth (mostly college educated) seek to recover a particular "identity" for themselves, sometimes by
cobbling together different cultural strands (as in the case of hyphenated ethnic revivals), sometimes by organizing themselves politically against discrimination by the white male establishment (as in the case of feminist,
African-American, and Latino struggles on behalf of affirmative action), and
sometimes by merely acknowledging something important about themselves
as individuals (as in the case of gays and lesbians who finally come to terms
with their sexuality). And this, Appiah reminds us, is as much an expression
of liberal individualism as it is of communitarian traditionalism.

   Writing with Canada's less assimilationist, bi- or tricultural society in mind
(if one takes into account First Nation peoples as well as French- and English-
speaking Canadians), Taylor's defense of multiculturalism also attempts to do
justice to this modern mélange of liberal individualism and communitarian
traditionalism. This project is easier said than done, however, since Romanticism shares a subjectivist prejudice with its Enlightenment antipode that renders it ill suited for conceptualizing intercultural community. In short, the
Romantic treats every culture as if it were a self-generating spirit, or collective personality, inhabiting each member of a distinct national community.
When set alongside the Romantic's pantheistic penchant for unifying spirit
and nature, subjectivism of this sort dangerously inclines toward racialism (or
the view that each people possesses an innate spiritual genius uniquely determining its destiny and identity).

   Taylor perceives the danger of subjectivism all too clearly, which is why he
insists on treating multiculturalism as an intercultural ideal premised on the
belief that cultures, no less than individuals, draw their sense of identity and
purpose from without. Although cultures do not possess identities and purposes in the same way that individuals do, they do draw spiritual strength in
the course of communicating with one another. More precisely, they do so
inasmuch as their practitioners expand their horizons by familiarizing themselves with other cultures. To the extent that cultural affinities are recognized

and affirmed by individuals in cross-cultural dialogue, cultures, too, acquire a secure "identity" within the cultural community to which they belong.

Despite his cogent critique of subjectivism, Taylor himself occasionally succumbs to it. Thus, he sometimes opposes the rights of individuals to the rights of groups, as if each of these were subjects containing their own exclusive, self-contained source of legitimacy. In his opinion, "one has to distinguish the fundamental liberties, those that should never be infringed and therefore ought to be unassailably entrenched, on one hand, from privileges and immunities that are important, but that can be revoked or restricted for reasons of public policy."[30] The "reasons of public policy" that Taylor had in mind when he penned this comment were those given by the provincial government of Quebec in support of its right to exist as a distinct francophone culture; the "privileges and immunities" he believed could be revoked by them were the nonfundamental rights of francophone and immigrant Quebeckers to send their children to English-speaking schools. This manner of formulating the principle of multicultural rights implies that fundamental individual rights have a meaning, scope, and rationale that transcends group rights to cultural preservation, just as the latter transcends less basic "privileges and immunities." In reality, however, the relationship between individual and group rights is more complicated: the precise scope, meaning, and rationale of individual rights are always conditioned by public policy concerns relating to the ostensible interests of the groups to which these individuals belong, including interests on behalf of preserving legitimate cultures at some minimal level of integrity.

Taylor can be forgiven for succumbing to subjectivism; it is, after all, deeply embedded within the liberal constitutional framework that he, like most multiculturalists, takes for granted. Postmodern critics of subjectivism, by contrast, have found it expedient to dispense with this framework, which they believe vacillates interminably between respecting subjects in their universal humanity (free from groups) and recognizing them in their cultural particularity (free within groups). By taking seriously the idea that cultures are but textures loosely interwoven of indefinite strands of contrasting colors, postmodernists reject even the static "identity politics" advocated by many liberal multiculturalists, preferring instead a dynamic "politics of hegemony" linking overlapping "positions."[31]

Rejecting the possibility of real agreement (unity or identity) between positions, postmodernists do not see truth, self-fulfillment,[32] or moral justice as ideals that can (or should) be redeemed. Reducing linguistic meanings to superficial effects of power relations, they view the academy as but one among many power struggles wherein appeals to dialogue and mutual recognition belie a war of rhetoric and verbal threat.

Postmodern defenses of multiculturalism thus take the following form: If all fields of knowledge reflect but a contingent state of power relations—and if, by parity of reasoning, no field of knowledge can lay greater claim to impartial authority than another—why not confer academic legitimacy on the knowledge proferred by marginalized subcultures as well? If the response to the question is that "their practitioners are not powerful enough to move us (entrenched academic mandarins) to do so," the postmodern multiculturalist can reply in kind—by marshaling his or her own political forces of coercion as evidence to the contrary.

Postmodernists have a point. Appreciating the extent of racial, gender, sexual, and ethnic bias in the academy leads us to understand why gay studies might have as legitimate a claim to academic respectability as physics. But if "multiculturalism" is just a code word for recognizing the marginalized worldviews, experiences, and insights of minority positions (as postmodernists claim), why not include creationism in science, say, or racism in anthropology? Why not simply celebrate cultural diversity for diversity's sake?

In conclusion, none of the three multicultural agendas currently vying for power in the academy are entirely coherent, despite the fact that all accurately lay claim to some aspect of our multicultural condition. Liberal arts and equal opportunity agendas are attractive because they appeal to commonly accepted ideals of truth, justice, and individuality. Unfortunately, these ideals have been largely forged within the crucible of liberalism and romanticism, whose subjectivistic metaphysics—with all its contradictions—is hard to overcome. Postmodern variants of political multiculturalism, by contrast, are more forthright in their rejection of subjectivism, appealing as they do to the relational (dynamic, complex, open-ended, and contestable) nature of culture. This account of culture promises much in the way of a radical transformation of identities. Indeed, those who envisage a utopia wherein differences in sex, gender, and race cease to have any defining significance will doubtless draw inspiration from this brand of multiculturalism. Unfortunately, postmodernism provides no descriptive or normative resources for justifying its commitment to multiculturalism beyond a dubious affirmation of diversity for diversity's sake.

*Multiculturalism Applied*

Foremost among the specific applications of multiculturalism is the determination of what gets taught. This decision depends on at least five factors:

the goals of the school, the programs it sets up to achieve them, the curriculum (or course of studies) internal to the latter, the texts adopted for use in teaching, and the preferences of individual educators.

The goals of the educational institution shape its predilection for one or another set of programs. Private institutions, such as those with strong religious, political, or vocational missions, generally feel less compelled than public ones to offer a fully rounded liberal arts education. Music conservatories and art institutes usually do not offer separate programs for the intensive study of theology or Latin. However, just these latter disciplines will form the core of Catholic seminaries, which may not be much interested in teaching engineering, music, and art. Only private schools that claim to offer a full range of liberal arts instruction typically have programs dealing with all of these subject matters.

Public institutions financed by taxes will define their mission differently. Although most four-year colleges and universities of this type offer a liberal arts education, they also see themselves as fulfilling a public trust to address society's problems. Because public institutions fall under a stronger social justice obligation than private schools, they rightly feel more constrained to embrace multicultural agendas targeting oppressed domestic groups.[33]

However, a stronger obligation to teach multiculturalism may well exist at the level of primary education. Helping children to appreciate their own and other cultures must be undertaken with extreme care.[34] To begin with, appreciating ethnic cultures requires appreciating the ancestor cultures from which they originated. Any adequate appreciation of black ethnicity will encompass understanding both African ancestral cultures and their partial suppression and alteration owing to the legacy of slavery. As the foregoing suggests, appreciating ethnic cultures also requires tracing their genealogies across migrations. Finally, it involves understanding their current status as hybrids combining elements of other cultures.[35] In general, the decision as to which of the many cultures gets taught will vary depending on context. Perhaps, as Anthony Appiah suggests,

> we should try to teach about those many world traditions that have come to be important at different stages of American history. This means that we begin with Native American and Protestant Dutch and English and African and Iberian cultures, adding voices to the story as they were added to the nation. Because different elements are important to different degrees in different places today, we can assume that the balance will be and should be differently struck in different places.[36]

Accompanying any multicultural education should be a liberal respect for persons as individuals, including a respect for diversity and interracial community. Here we encounter some familiar tensions. Multicultural and antiracist agendas differ in important respects. Antiracism views social groups through the lens of racial domination, which indiscriminately privileges whites over nonwhites. Thus, from the standpoint of antiracism, Irish Americans and Polish Americans belong to a single (dominant) white majority, just as Haitian Creoles and African Americans belong to a single (subordinate) black minority. By contrast, multiculturalism views social groups through the lens of culture. From this perspective, Irish Americans, Polish Americans, Haitian Creoles, and African Americans designate four distinct groups whose ethnic contributions to American life are roughly equal.

Antiracism and multiculturalism represent partial if complementary perspectives, which should not surprise us. Group identities are constituted both internally, by their members' cultural affinities, and externally, by relations of racial hierarchy imposed from without. Education should therefore incorporate both antiracist and multicultural perspectives, bearing in mind the following points.

First, multiculturalism and antiracism have different aims: the humanistic universalism that the latter uses to promote integration provides a counterpoint to the cultural particularism that the former uses to promote respect for differences. Second, multiculturalism and antiracism achieve their ends by deploying different strategies: highlighting positive achievements versus highlighting negative handicaps. Both strategies are needed if members of groups are not to be seen merely as passive victims of discrimination or as fully empowered agents of their own destiny. Finally, as my earlier example of Irish immigrants in America illustrates all too well, one must not forget that cultural distinctions frequently function to legitimate racial distinctions and vice versa.

Antiracism and multiculturalism sometimes conflict with the aim of achieving interracial community. Emphasis on racial domination and cultural difference can produce a hyperethnic consciousness preventing persons from viewing themselves as members of a larger interracial community. For example, Afrocentrist education often subordinates teaching respect for interracial community to teaching antiracism. Indeed, militant Afrocentrists believe that fighting white racism requires teaching reverse racism—for instance, teaching (as Leonard Jeffries urges) the depiction of Europeans as "cold, individualistic, materialistic, and aggressive 'ice people'" in contrast to the warm, sociable "sun people" of Africa.[37] Even Afrocentrists who eschew the teaching of reverse racism adopt a questionable reverse ethnocentrism that proclaims ancient Egypt, construed as a sub-Saharan rather than Mediterranean culture, to be the true source of Western science, medicine, mathematics, democracy, and philosophy.

What makes Afrocentricism of this sort objectionable is not its ethnocentrist oversimplification of history—a failing, after all, that is common to most Western Civilization courses—but its tendency to discourage African-American children from appreciating all the complex strands of their multicultural identity. Such ethnocentrism in turn diminishes prospects for achieving interracial community, which is not to say that African-Americans' heightened sensitivity to racial oppression is misplaced. But each of us must be sensitized to the complexity of oppression, as virtually everyone occupies a dominant social position—be it of race, gender, sexual orientation, religious affiliation, or linguistic culture—with respect to some other person.

## *Multiculturalism and Faculty Composition*

Of the diverse factors that determine the content of multicultural education, the choice of instructors ranks among the most important, for they, after all, determine much of what gets taught. Instructors hired to teach Chicano literature may be expected to have a deep familiarity with the language, culture, and experiential perspective of the Chicano community. Moreover, they may be expected to perform educational duties that extend beyond the teaching of literature, such as encouraging Chicano students as role models and through counseling. These latter duties especially suggest that, in some cases, being Chicano might be relevant to teaching.

This impression is further reinforced when we recall that the principle of recognition requires respecting individuals in their cultural particularity as well as in their universal humanity. A student who feels that his or her culture has been ignored or misrecognized by society will surely not want that experience repeated in the classroom. But unless a curriculum exists that treats the positive contributions of that culture—and faculty and students who actively embody and identify with it—this student might not feel accepted as an equal member of the academic community. Lacking the support of faculty and students with whom he or she can identify, this same student might lack the self-confidence necessary to persevere in what otherwise appears to be an alien, if not unfriendly and hostile, environment.[38]

Thus, the principle of recognition seems to compete with, if not contradict, other well-established principles of liberal thought. Preeminent among them is the notion of *meritocracy*. The idea behind meritocracy is that those who are most qualified to perform a certain job—or, more precisely, those who on the basis of past performance can be reasonably expected to perform a certain job most efficiently—ought to be awarded that job regardless of their race, gender, religious affiliation, ethnicity, or any characteristic that seems irrelevant to the actual performance of the job as it is has been technically defined.

In one sense, this idea is clearly progressive, for it prohibits us from discriminating against people on the basis of characteristics that are irrelevant to job performance. However, the mechanism that prevents us from excluding women and minorities from jobs and and other voluntary memberships can sometimes prevent us from including them in these associations as well. As I noted in Chapter 7, testing procedures and job criteria that are otherwise neutral in their formulation can serve racist ends. In educational settings, job qualifications are defined so narrowly as to exclude any consideration of gender, race, and ethnicity as factors contributing to successful job performance.

My example of the Chicano literature instructor shows why such a consideration is sometimes relevant. Is it also relevant to consider gender, race, and ethnicity when these are not directly relevant to job performance, for example, in hiring physics instructors? Women and minorities are not likely to feel welcome in any discipline that is overwhelmingly dominated by white males, especially since feelings of natural inferiority in the hard sciences have been engrained in them since elementary school. Thus, it seems that physics departments should also consider the gender, race, and ethnicity of applicants when filling posts, at least whenever there is serious underrepresentation of women and minorities within the department.

Of course, many will disagree about what constitutes underrepresentation. Should the standard for adequate representation be the percentage of women and minorities in the national or regional population? Should it be the percentage of women and minorities enrolled in the school? Should it be the percentage of women and minorities currently employed in the discipline or the percentage currently available for hire?

Hiring women and minorities in rough proportion to their current representation within a discipline is probably the least that should be aimed for. However, when this percentage is very low in comparison with the percentage of women and minorities enrolled in the school that is hiring, the standard should be the percentage of women and minorities enrolled in the school. Again, stronger standards (indexed to national or regional demographic representation) might be appropriate in cases in which women and minorities have been disproportionately excluded from all institutions of higher education. Thus, in philosophy departments nationwide (whose aggregate faculty composition is about 1 percent black), an ideally adequate representation of black faculty should be no less than 12 percent (the percentage of blacks in the population at large) and possibly larger if the school in question has a very large percentage of blacks in its student body.

As in the case of affirmative action, only qualified women and minority job applicants should be given preferential treatment. In disciplines like the humanities especially, in which measurements of research and teaching qualifications are often highly subjective and of unreliable predictive value, being a woman or minority ought to weigh heavily when coupled with evidence of modestly good teaching and research capabilities.[39]

### Multiculturalism and International Relations: Studying the Western Canon in a Global Context

So far I have focused on the equal opportunity defense of multiculturalism as a way of rectifying social injustice. Now I would like to examine the other defense of multiculturalism—as a vehicle of knowledge and personal growth—by raising the following question: Should a liberal arts education stress the accomplishments of Western civilization, or should it give equal time to the study of non-Western texts?

Conservatives insist that preference should be given to studying just those texts that most scholars have thought worthwhile because of their exemplary value to Western culture, their estimable quality, or their universal wisdom. Now, few would deny that students trained in the liberal arts should have some fairly deep and extensive familiarity with the texts that have exerted so much influence over the cultural traditions shaping their own environment. But how much? To the exclusion of familiarizing these students with the non-Western canon? No defender of multiculturalism could abide such an approach. Whatever its practical merits—which, I submit, are very few—immersion in the dominant culture is no substitute for a liberal education.

To be sure, critics of multiculturalism warn of dire consequences—the imperiling of "democratic, liberal society"—should "Western civilization and culture [not be] placed at the center of our studies."[40] But it is unclear what they really mean. Are the critics worried that multicultural education will dissolve the nation into a state of civil war?[41] Do they think that it will undermine the moral integrity or intelligence of its citizenry? Or are they just worried that the nation's military resolve and global economic competitiveness will be weakened?

Unlike political arguments in support of teaching Western civilization, arguments stressing that civilization's inherent superiority seem somewhat clearer. Yet, as Mill observed in *On Liberty* (1859), whatever superior truth Western civilization might claim to possess could not be demonstrated apart from its having been proven in dialogue with other civilizations and cultures. And even demonstrably superior doctrines lose their strength and vitality unless given the opportunity to defend themselves against challenges by other doctrines.

Taking these objections to heart, more modest defenders of Western civilization will acknowledge the need for some multicultural curricular diversity. Indeed, those who are most modest will simply eschew any overarching claims regarding that civilization's superiority. For them, multicultural dialogue will present an opportunity to discover truth wherever it might be found.

This aim is surely worthwhile but must be qualified by three considerations. First, it is easier to proclaim the universal value (interest, or validity) of some culture or tradition when discussion is not focused on its specific claims. The liberal philosophical tradition of Locke and Mill that constitutes part of the Western canon undoubtedly touches on universal themes concerning social conflict and cooperation. However, its underlying presupposition that all persons naturally pursue their individual self-interest does not.

Second, and related to this point, cultures and traditions are notoriously partial, often mixing what is true and universal with what is merely false and parochial. As I have already discussed, Western science and literature present us with images of women, gays, racial minorities, and non-European colonized peoples that share this defect.

Third, determining which texts within any given culture canonically articulate it is itself problematic. Taking quality as a distinguishing mark of the canonical gets us nowhere. How do we know which texts possess the highest quality? Do we rely on the opinions of scholars? If so, is it because their opinions converge with the opinions of their predecessors? But why should the sheer weight of authority, of countless generations of scholars having been more or less forceably indoctrinated into a literary tradition by their predecessors, inspire confidence in their judgment? Indeed, why should it, once we realize how women and minorities have been excluded from the academy?

In order to avoid misunderstanding, let me emphasize that I am not defending cultural relativism or skepticism regarding universal moral and cultural truths. To begin with, it is likely that most cultural disagreements revolve around facts of one kind or another rather than moral values. Cultures that practiced human sacrifice (the Aztecs), infanticide (the ancient

Greeks), and geronticide (the Eskimos) did not necessarily value human life less than we do. On the contrary, they believed either that those sacrificed would achieve greater glory in the hereafter (Aztecs) or that those left to die (the very young, the very old, and the very sick) would be better off dead or would endanger the survival of the clan if left to live. Hence, cultural relativism in metaphysical belief and factual circumstance need not entail relativism in basic values.

If cultural relativism impacts upon the question of moral truth at all, it is mainly in regard to specific codes, which interpret basic moral values differently. For instance, many people regard liberalism's supreme estimate of individual freedom as but one cultural instantiation of a more universal respect for human life. However, even if it were an integral part of respecting human life, it would not be any more immune to cultural relativity and difference. No matter how universally accepted liberalism becomes, it always will only designate a set of general principles whose particular instantiation in any given legal code will differ depending on local culture and circumstance.

Be that as it may, we must not exaggerate the extent to which particular cultural codes actually differ. Take, for example, the so-called debate between feminists and multiculturalists over female genital mutilation. Some defenders of female genital mutilation wrongly claim that the practice is ordained by the Koran (Qur'ān) or by other religious texts. Or they argue that the practice, however debilitating, painful, and desensitizing it might be, is so firmly embedded in certain Asian, Middle Eastern, and African cultures that if women living in those cultures refuse to submit to it, they would be denying themselves the social recognition of their community, thereby incurring serious damage to their sense of identity and self-respect. Indeed, some defenders go so far as to compare this practice with the fashionable but equally painful and harmful cosmetic surgery endured by many Western women. If we continue to regard these latter practices as legitimate aesthetic preferences, why not, they argue, bestow the same title on female genital mutilation?

The answer, I think, is that none of these surgical practices is specifically endorsed by any religious belief system, and their entrenchment in popular culture is no obstacle to their being eradicated given sufficient medical and moral education. To recall my earlier distinction between cultural practices and doctrines (see Chapter 4), if these practices are mainly endorsed by customs of etiquette, their authority does not rest on firm convictions supported by deep values. Only value judgments and moral duties possessing relatively unconditional religious and metaphysical authority are purported to be true (or in some sense necessary or obligatory).

For example, within Western medicine a growing consensus has emerged that many cosmetic treatments, such as liposuction, breast reduction (or enlargement), and so on, are potentially harmful. Yet there are no religious clerics or cultural guardians rallying to the side of the cosmetics industry in defiance of the medical establishment on this point. These treatments exist because women feel that their self-respect depends on conforming to male-imposed standards of beauty, not because moral or religious doctrines demand them as a matter of true faith. Similarly, within Asian, Middle Eastern, and African cultures, most clerics and doctors oppose female genital circumcision, and even among those who support the subordination of women to men in these societies, there is virtually no support for it. In short, this practice is as little entrenched in the religious worldviews of non-Western culture as is the use of cosmetic treatments in Western culture.

Of course, it may be that value relativism of some sort still exists even if differences in customary practice offer no proof of it. Western feminists, for instance, continue to debate multiculturalists regarding the patriarchal subordination of women in certain non-Western cultures. Whether the subordination of women in illiberal societies and cultures is reflected mainly in superficial popular etiquette or is rooted in deeper religious values—admittedly a difficult determination given the popular reception of the latter as it frequently bears on the former—is a question clearly germane to establishing the extent of a given culture's patriarchal bias and thus its overall legitimacy as a vehicle for personal self-realization. As Susan Moller Okin and other feminists have pointed out, cultures, even very liberal ones that claim a Western pedigree, typically encourage some degree of patriarchal domination in the private sphere even if they should happen to entrench gender equality in the public sphere (in the form of antidiscrimination legislation).[42]

Typically, the more religiously fundamentalist and traditionalist a culture is, the more it subordinates women to patriarchal control in both private and public spheres. This is because women in these cultures are often viewed as the major preservers of family life, patrilineage, and cultural tradition (if not high religious tradition). Hence, unlike boys, girls born into traditional cultures are often confined to their homes, restricted in their choice of dress, occupation, and spouse, and forbidden to participate in extracurricular activities such as dating unless chaperoned, a constraint on self-expression and self-realization that can become unbearable for girls who have immigrated with their families to more liberal societies.

The contradiction between two strands of multicultural identity politics—the liberal, emancipatory strand advocated by feminists on behalf of individual women and the communitarian, tradition-respecting strand advocated by defenders of cultural rights for minority groups—cannot be denied. Resolving it, as we have seen, is made especially difficult by the fact that we are not talking here about the rights of oppressed double minorities (or internal dissidents) that can be secured by granting them rights of exit, but about the rights of children who, like the congenitally deaf children born to deaf culture parents who wish to deny them cochlear implants, have no right of exit.

Now, we could withhold government assistance to cultural groups (such as the Kiryas Joel Hasidim and Old World Amish) that some feel violate the rights of girls and boys to equal opportunity education and citizenship. We could even deny these groups legal permission to educate them in ways that are overly narrow and incapacitating with regard to commonly accepted standards of psychological well-being. However, it is important to note that government intrusion into the private practices of cultural minorities—especially religious fundamentalist sects (Christian, Islamic, Jewish, Hindu, and so forth) that particularly restrict the educational and experiential opportunities of boys and girls—on behalf of protecting the individual rights of all children to equal opportunity education and equal citizenship treads dangerously close to abandoning the liberal principle of religious and cultural toleration. If we go that route (denying group rights to virtually all minority cultures), we will probably have to concede that very few cultures indeed (including those that gravitate around most mainstream Christian denominations) merit toleration, since they, too, inhibit children from questioning their inherited social roles. Even if girls and boys are allowed to question some inherited social roles, they are not allowed to question others (most notably those regarding sexual orientation), which can lead some children who might be inclined to a same-sex orientation to feel oppressed or to have their self-respect and self-esteem stymied.

Perhaps the clash between feminist/gay/lesbian and communitarian strands of multiculturalism is overexaggerated. The presence of women political leaders in such patriarchal societies as Bangladesh, Pakistan, and India suggests that all religions and cultures are susceptible to the effects of scientific and moral enlightenment, with the economic necessity of having fewer but better educated children leading the way to occupational, political, *and* familial liberalization.

Critics of multiculturalism should not take too much comfort in the convergence of Western and non-Western cultures regarding the emancipatory enlightenment of men and women. Convergence of opinion certainly exists in many areas and may well continue to increase owing to further multicultural exchanges. However, convergence of opinion proves nothing about the truth or falsity of cultural belief systems. The global dissemination of Western technology and science says less about its superiority than it does about the powerful influence of Western capitalism.[43] Educators who appeal to the progressive liberalization of the globe to support their belief in the superiority or universality of Western culture thus beg a very important question: Is this convergence a sign of real emancipatory enlightenment or of blind domination?

Short of eliminating all traces of domination in the production of intercultural commerce and dialogue, we will never know.[44] Yet one thing remains beyond doubt. As long as human beings continue to live under diverse conditions that require diverse cultural adaptations, cultural relativism in the application and understanding of general interests, values, and norms is scarcely unavoidable. Granting that, educators should be charitable in teaching any culture—not by uncritically accepting its claim to authority and insight in all matters, but by appreciating its complexity as a source of value and meaning for "them" as well as for "us."

# 11
## GROUP RIGHTS IN A GLOBAL CONTEXT

Rights are entitlements to certain goods that human beings need in order to live minimally decent lives. Many of them are exercised by individuals in their capacity as members of groups. The Universal Declaration of Human Rights adopted by the General Assembly of the United Nations in 1948 mentions some of the most important ones:

- the right to a nationality (Article 15),
- the right to freedom of thought, conscience, and religion (Article 18),
- the right to freedom of peaceful assembly and association (Article 20),
- the right to take part in the government of [the] country (Article 21),
- the right to social security [and] the realization of economic, social, and cultural rights (Article 22),
- the right to work [and] to form and join trade unions (Article 23),
- the right to a standard of living adequate for . . . health and well-being (Article 25),
- the right to education (Article 26), and
- the right to freely participate in the cultural life of the community (Article 27).

These group-specific rights, as I have called them, are distinguishable from individual property rights and civil liberties in that the goods they entitle are those whose enjoyment is mainly contingent upon participating in a particular community or group. Thus, one typically claims a right to nationality, civil association, political participation, union affiliation, and cultural life as a member of some particular group, not merely as a human being.[1] Even freedom of religion, freedom to work, and freedom from insecurity and ignorance are rights whose exercise is seldom exclusively individual.

It may well be, as I shall argue below, that virtually all rights—even the right to be left alone in the individual pursuit of one's aims—are exercised by participating in political communities who protect and enforce them. But this is not the opinion held by most of us, for it goes against the common belief, well established in liberal political thought since Locke, that rights are first and foremost demands that individuals make against the state and community—demands, in other words, to be left alone to go about one's business without interference from others.

Because of the prevalence of this libertarian view of rights in the United States, most Americans do indeed have considerable freedom to be left alone, but at the expense of other freedoms. These other freedoms depend on the positive possession of opportunities, capacities, and resources for choosing and acting that are provided in large part by the state or by groups and communities. Because the individual right to own and exchange property without interference is protected above the right of citizens to control the production and distribution of goods upon which their other freedoms depend, poorer citizens will have fewer opportunities, capabilities, and resources for choosing and acting than their wealthier counterparts. And, just as important, they will have less freedom to be left alone from drug dealers, petty thieves, gang-bangers, nosy social workers, and policemen conducting random raids in their homes.

It is especially disconcerting to note that the U.S. Department of State has promoted this libertarian view of rights in the global arena with the same—or worse—implications. Not only has it been reluctant to accord the positive possession of opportunities, resources, and capacities for choosing and acting the supreme status it accords civil liberties, political rights, rights to protection, and rights to own and exchange private property, but it has even supported governments that undermine these latter rights as well.[2]

Nowhere has this approach been more evident than in its dealings with Central America. Throughout most of this century, the U.S. government has supported the right of American companies to freely transact business in this region. Doing so has enabled them to reap tremendous profits, which in turn have helped subsidize the higher wages, salaries, benefits, and cheap commodities that Americans enjoy. However, with the exception of a very small wealthy elite, few persons in the countries in which these companies have set up business have profited. Indeed, the vast majority, already quite impoverished, often see their standard of living decline.

They also see their civil and political rights decline. The ever-growing gap between rich and poor engenders social conflict: the poor seek to organize themselves into unions and political parties in order to raise wages and redistribute land and wealth, policies that directly interfere with the profit-taking of U.S. companies and their foreign clients. Hence, preserving "business as usual" invariably requires the use of government terror (torture, imprisonment, assassination, and the like) in destroying labor unions, peasant associations, student organizations, and opposition political parties and newspapers.[3]

One might object that doing "business as usual"—that is, allowing U.S. companies to acquire, own, and exchange property without impediment—need not have such an effect. But that supposition would ignore the reality of today's global economy. Economic development in the Third World depends upon foreign investors (banks and companies based in rich industrialized nations) who expect a return that is anywhere from two to four times their capital outlay (including foreign aid and loans). The net drain of wealth from poor to rich countries is abetted by the fact that rich countries typically purchase raw materials from poor countries in exchange for finished manufactured products. Rich countries encourage poor countries to become suppliers of a single raw material or export crop, whose price is then determined by the rich countries; the difference in price between raw materials (whose prices are often artificially depressed) and finished products (whose prices are often artificially elevated) yields an imbalance in trade between rich and poor countries.[4]

Compounding the imbalance of trade are structural distortions induced in Third World economies as a result of their financial dependency on world banking institutions, lack of control over technologies, patents, licensing, and royalty arrangements, and the inability of local enterprises and banks to compete with more powerful multinationals for scarce markets and credit. Because imbalances in trade increase the indebtedness of Third World countries, their governments are required to restructure their economies in order to increase exports.[5]

On one hand, productive capacities used for satisfying local subsistence needs—for instance, small family farms that produce corn, beans, and other low-cost staples—are sold to foreign multinationals and reoriented toward satisfying a luxury export demand for cash crops such as exotic flowers, avocados, bananas, and the like. Not only does this process result in raising the cost of staples (which in many cases must now be imported from abroad), but the introduction of high-tech methods of farming in the export economy also robs workers and peasants of their former jobs.

On the other hand, because the importation of goods from abroad is costly, those goods that are imported tend to be luxury items consumed by the country's wealthy elite. The net result is starvation and unemployment,[6] government indebtedness (with its corresponding cutbacks in public health, education, and welfare), economic anarchy and fragmentation (with domestic production units being tied to foreign multinationals rather than to one another), political powerlessness (with foreign ownership of land, industry, and basic infrastructure),[7] and environmental degradation and pollution.[8]

Given the U.S. State Department's insistence on defining human rights in terms of individual rights—including the right to transact business without government interference—it is not surprising that many persons in Third World countries claim to have little use for rights. In the words of Claude Ake, a professor of political science at the University of Port Harcourt, Nigeria:

> The Western notion of human rights stresses rights which are not very interesting in the context of African realities. There is much concern with the right to peaceful assembly, free speech and thought, fair trial, etc. The appeal of these rights is socially specified. They appeal to people with a full stomach who can now afford to pursue the more esoteric aspects of self-fulfillment. The vast majority of our people are not in this position. They are facing the struggle for existence in its brutal immediacy. Theirs is a totally consuming struggle. They have little or no time for reflection and hardly any use for free speech. They have little interest in choice for there is no choice in ignorance. There is no freedom for hungry people or those eternally oppressed by disease. It is no wonder that the idea of human rights has tended to sound hollow in the African context.[9]

Despite his skepticism about the worthiness of applying the Western notion of rights in an African context, Ake is not opposed to realizing the ideal of human rights as such. Indeed, he is all too cognizant of how political authoritarianism, abetted by progressive liberal defenders of "benevolent" colonialism like John Stuart Mill, has prevented economic progress in his own country and brutalized its citizens.[10] His point is rather different: if human rights are to have currency in Africa, they must be reconnected to the egalitarian impulse, concretely institutionalized in a social democracy wherein—to cite Article 29 of the UN Declaration of Human Rights—the exercise of rights is linked to "duties to the community."[11]

In order to "domesticate" and "re-create" the notion of human rights within an African context, Ake urges that we appreciate the communal nature of African society. Most people in Africa are still locked into traditional economies marked by cooperative economic ventures and collective property relations. They view themselves less as individuals needing recognition than as members of families, clans, lineages, and ethnic groups. Hence, if the ideal of human rights is to have any purchase in this context, it will have to lose its abstract, individualistic connotation. In short, the rights that apply here will apply first and foremost to groups and will aim at the positive provision of goods (work, shelter, health, education, and so forth) necessary for satisfying basic human needs.

Ake's proposal sounds good, but does it really make sense? Can we defend a coherent conception of rights that is not individualistic and mainly oriented toward procuring the unfettered freedom of acquiring and exchanging property?

*Basic Rights in a Global Context*

One way to begin to answer this question is by recalling the close connection between rights (justice) and impartiality (rationality) discussed in Chapter 6. There I noted that an impartial consideration of what is owed to anyone by right (as a matter of justice) would have to bracket out (or abstract from) all those things that are undeserved—things like natural endowments and fortuitous social circumstances. Appealing to Rawls's hypothetical model of social contractors trying to reach unanimous agreement on basic principles of justice, I further observed that, under conditions of uncertainty, in which persons were ignorant of the particular facts concerning their social status and identity, such contractors would choose principles that maximized the well-being of the most unlucky among them. These principles would provide a right to liberty, including a right to immigrate, qualified only by a respect for others' rights to self-preservation.

Would they include other rights as well? Besides a principle of liberty, Rawls believes that impartial contractors would also endorse a "difference principle," stipulating that any increase in economic inequalities works to the advantage of the least well-off. Suppose instituting capitalism increases the inequality between rich and poor far beyond what it currently is under some communal arrangement; so long as the poor saw their basic standard of living rise, they would (according to Rawls) consent to it.

Leaving aside both the fact that global capitalism has worsened the condition of the world's poorest fifth and the assumption (implicit in Rawls's defense of the difference principle) that rational, impartial people would trade social equality for a bare increase in their standard of living, would any reasonably sane person accept an arrangement that did not first guarantee his or her basic subsistence? Would merely improving that person's chances of survival—for instance, by replacing acute starvation with severe, chronic malnutrition—sufficiently motivate him or her to abide by the new economic arrangement? Or would chronic desperation motivate—and even entitle—that person to steal from the rich?

In his book *Basic Rights: Subsistence, Affluence, and U.S. Foreign Policy,* Henry Shue criticizes the inadequacy of Rawls's difference principle and defends the priority of communities' *basic* subsistence and security rights over less basic rights of individuals to acquire and exchange property. Indeed, according to Shue, subsistence and security rights are essential to the meaning of any right whatsoever.[12]

Shue begins his argument by breaking down the distinction between subsistence and security rights as well as the distinction between negative and positive freedom. As he understands it, rights are reasonable demands made on others to provide socially guaranteed protection against standard threats on one's basic self-esteem as a human being.[13] Because rights are not freedoms exercised by individuals in the abstract but are permissions and entitlements obligating others, they are inherently *relational,* presupposing social guarantees (often legally enforced) and other positive enabling conditions.

Take the so-called negative freedom to engage in unrestricted activity. The freedom not to be acted upon by some external agent cannot exist as a right unless some agency acts to secure it through provision of some positive means, which in our society typically assumes the form of police-enforced legal sanction. Such security rights—which are as positive (enabling) as they are negative (permitting)—in turn are integral, and not merely instrumental, to the meaningful exercise of any other right.[14]

The same applies to subsistence rights. Without provision of basic food, shelter, clothing, and health care, the right to engage in unrestricted activity is meaningless. Naked, starving, homeless, or incapacitated people cannot be free to act, because the necessary conditions for action are absent. Just as important, persons who are this helpless are more vulnerable to coercive threats on their freedom to act, since they are less able to take advantage of whatever security apparatus happens to be in place.[15]

Just as security rights cannot be fully implemented without subsistence rights, so subsistence rights cannot be fully implemented without security rights. In some cases, merely providing people with food, clothing, and shelter—in short, the subsistence on which they can build strength and stamina for resisting potential aggressors—suffices to guarantee most of their security rights. Conversely, merely protecting people's security—without government

provision of food, clothing, and housing subsidies—sometimes suffices to
guarantee most of their subsistence rights. (For example, allowing peasants
and workers to organize themselves politically without fear of repression
might be the first step toward electing leaders who will enact laws prohibiting multinationals from buying up productive capacity geared toward the
satisfaction of local subsistence needs.) Indeed, it has not been lack of U.S.
foreign aid that has prevented poor Central American countries from satisfying the subsistence needs of their citizens, but its unwanted presence, in
the form of military assistance, which usually works to shore up oppressive,
undemocratic oligarchies.

Concerns about moral relativism do not undermine Shue's argument.
Reasonable persons might disagree about what specific rights individuals in
any given society have. However, any just society will acknowledge that its
members are entitled to at least some share of goods by right, nonpossession
of which renders them unacceptably vulnerable to the depredations of others. Rights to such goods will be meaningless apart from the satisfaction of
more basic security and subsistence rights.[16]

But surely, the libertarian will object, freedom to be left alone to go
about one's business is just as necessary to the enjoyment of any right as
are security and subsistence. Indeed, imprisonment threatens a person's
security and subsistence, as do other restraints on his or her freedom to
speak and associate. External impediments to action, however, are not the
only deprivations of freedom that compromise one's dignity as a human
being. Political powerlessness also threatens a person's basic security and
subsistence.

Of course, dictators can provide their subjects subsistence and security.
However, they cannot provide them a *right* to subsistence and security.
Rights are demands for social guarantees against standard threats to security
and subsistence, and political powerlessness is undoubtedly such a threat.
Hence, some basic level of effective democratic participation in the political
and economic institutions of our society is necessary both for protecting our
rights as well as for articulating and channeling the public sentiment that justifies them.[17]

Therefore, the individual right to be left alone is basic too, but only if it
is protected by law and defined by legislators in a manner compatible with
each person's equal exercise of all of his or her rights. Contrary to the libertarian view, the right to go about one's business without external interference is not absolute; it can be limited by democratic majorities for the sake
of ensuring the satisfaction of the community's subsistence and security

rights. So, as paradoxical as it might sound, the negative freedom to go about one's business unhindered by state interference cannot be fully exercised as a right unless it is limited and protected by a democratic state in which one participates as a political equal.

This is all well and good, but how does Shue's model relate to the other category of rights mentioned by the UN Declaration: the rights of groups to maintain their cultures? Shue subordinates the enrichment of culture to the fulfillment of both basic and nonbasic rights, including the right of individuals to engage in profitable market transactions.[18] He is correct in insisting that the right of individuals to own, acquire, and exchange private property ought not take precedence over basic rights to subsistence and security: no one can reasonably demand that unemployed starving persons desist from taking superfluous food from the wealthy. However, he is wrong to argue that culture is not a basic good, since its absence can cripple an individual's capacity to lead a meaningful, dignified life.

Shue admits that cultural enrichment has priority over the satisfaction of individuals' accidental preferences. More important, he concedes that if the attainment of rights can only be secured through cultural enrichment (including moral education about basic rights), cultural enrichment, too, is a basic right.[19] This acknowledgment partially captures my earlier point that culture—no less than security, subsistence, and liberty—is a necessary condition for the exercise of rights.

Still, Shue's weak admission that an individual right to cultural enrichment might be integral to the exercise of any right whatsoever fails to address the importance of a specific group's right to its own culture. The force and justification of this latter right surely differs depending on whether the group exercising it is monocultural or multicultural. As I argued in Chapter 6, the right to preserve and maintain a specific culture is largely indefensible when extended to multicultural societies and therefore cannot be used to justify denying the security and subsistence rights of would-be immigrants. By contrast, this very same right (to maintain a specific culture) might be invoked with greater justification by Indian tribes. Not only are tribal reservations typically small or impoverished in comparison to the states in which they are incorporated (and so are less obligated on economic grounds to open their territories to settlers), but the peculiar relationship between religion and land upon which their sovereignty is based adds a further cultural dimension (the free exercise of religion) missing from the multicultural state's (economically and politically based) right to exclude.

## Rights and Duties

Regardless of whether we are talking about an individual right to cultural enrichment (moral education) or a group-specific right to practice a specific culture, these are rights claims that impose obligations on persons to ensure their fulfillment. Following Shue, these obligations can be broken down into three categories: the duty to avoid depriving a person of a right; the duty to protect against the deprivation of a right; and the duty to aid the deprived.[20]

As Shue notes, no specific right can be neatly correlated with any simple duty. In fact, the determination of who is obligated to do what is highly contextual and depends a great deal on determining the complex causes of deprivation as well as which agencies can most efficiently remedy it. Furthermore, our obligations are always qualified by our limited capacities, resources, and opportunities. If local institutions that would normally assume primary responsibility for rectifying rights violations are too powerless to act, the responsibility shifts to more distant agencies that can (including foreign countries).[21] At the same time, no one should be expected to shoulder unfair burdens and make unreasonable sacrifices.[22]

This last point bears some elucidation. One of the advantages of a libertarian conception of rights is that it defines our duties in terms we can easily accept: a natural duty to forbear from interfering with others combined with a conventional duty to fulfill contracts voluntarily entered into. Forbearing from interfering imposes no burden on us, since we are not required to do anything but desist from acting in certain ways. A related advantage of this conception is that it makes the determination and assignment of rights violations a relatively straightforward matter: we know who it is that has interfered (or broken their agreement) with us, even if we do not always know their names or the identities of their superiors.

The libertarian conception of rights, which limits natural rights to the single negative right to noninterference, is no doubt indefensible. It cannot account for strong duties owed to strangers in dire distress,[23] let alone its own possibility, which tacitly presupposes a positive democratic mechanism of legislation and enforcement. Most important, it neglects the essential complementarity of rights to liberty, subsistence, security, and culture.

Admittedly, the burdens imposed on us are greater, and the determination and assignment of violations murkier, once we expand our conception of rights to include subsistence, security, cultural rights, and political rights. Given that qualification, it might be useful to think of Shue's tripartite schema as designating three "successive waves of duty," to use Jeremy Waldron's phrase.[24] To begin with, we are obligated to avoid depriving others of their rights, which often can be accomplished by simply omitting to act in a harmful way toward others (for example, I refrain from stealing your basic allotment of food). However, when following this duty fails to protect against the deprivation of a right (because others are stealing your food), I am obligated, along with my fellow citizens, to set up an effective protection agency (say, a legally sanctioned police force) to discourage further violations of it. If this institution fails to deter depredations (for example, because of desperation born of widespread starvation), we are then obligated to design institutions that will eliminate this incentive (e.g., by controlling market-based inequalities, redistributing wealth through progressive taxation, counteracting the natural causes of famine, and so on).

At the outermost fringe of this second wave of duty, we have an obligation to elect politicians who will enact and execute policies favorable to the protection of rights. Politicians are obligated to establish international tribunals, economic structures, and security forces to ensure that rich countries do not exploit poor countries and to prevent isolated countries from gravely violating the rights of their own citizens (as occurred in the genocidal massacre of civilians in Rwanda and the former Yugoslavia).[25] Ideally, our policies should be aiming at the creation of a global federation of constitutional republics whose external as well as internal relations are governed by principles of democratic and social equality.[26] However, international legal and economic guarantees will not automatically secure the fulfillment of rights. In cases of natural disaster, for example, we have an additional obligation to aid those in distress.

In some respects, the "waves of duty" metaphor is misleading. For example, we have duties to aid those over whom we exercise social responsibility (our children and parents, for example) that are relatively permanent and unconditional regardless of how well their rights are institutionally protected. Moreover, we have to acknowledge that, in default of adequately protecting the rights of persons through appropriate political and economic institutions, we might still have obligations to provide aid. Simply because someone else (say, a corrupt dictator) is to blame for starvation in a particular country does not relieve me of my obligation to provide aid. If an international agency like the Red Cross or the United Nations fulfills this obligation adequately, so much the better. If it does not, I must consider what duty I have, both as a citizen of an affluent democracy and as a fellow human being.

What I have said about duties in general applies to duties applicable to culture. Society has an obligation to protect the rights of individuals to culture

by providing them with an education. More specifically, it has an obligation
to protect their rights to practice the particular culture of their choice. But
just how far should such protection extend? Are all cultures equally worthy
of protection? In an ideal world, which cultural identifications would pass
away and which would remain?

### Rights to Cultural Preservation

In Chapters 3 and 4, I argued that the right of cultural groups to preservation is bounded by two sorts of considerations: their legitimacy and their inevitable contamination by other cultures. I further argued in Chapter 6 that
this right can (with few exceptions) be overridden by the right to subsistence
(especially as it pertains to starving immigrants). I will now address these
considerations separately.

Cultural groups whose members share affinities that have arisen (or been
maintained) through external imposition or constraint are less legitimate, on
the whole, than those whose affinal bonds are voluntarily constituted. Of
course, within any group there will be affinities that have been more or less
externally imposed and constrained. Likewise, within any group some persons will have interpreted their affinities with more freedom and consciousness than others.

I have argued that racial groups have arisen and been maintained through
external imposition and constraint in a manner that renders them illegitimate, at least in the long run. Even if we imagine race as designating cultural (or ethnic) affinities instead of biological and moral ones, it is still the
case that what we call "African-American" culture (to take just one example) depends on racial "caste" segregation. Eliminating this injustice and
bringing about full racial integration will doubtless result in black and white
Americans identifying with a common American culture containing African
as well as Latino, Asian, and European aspects. In other words, along with
increased racial intermarriage we can also expect cultural fusion to continue
apace. And we can further hope that such fusion will not involve assimilating differences to one preferred racial or ethnic way of life.

Thus, in an ideally nonracist society, differences in skin pigmentation
would probably cease to be relevant in the choice of conjugal partner, and
skin coloration would gradually become dissociated from cultural affinity.
The same applies to differences in gender. Even if we were to leave aside the
growth in sex-change operations, the loosening of established (heterosexual)
gender roles will likely continue in an emancipated society that allows indi-

viduals greater freedom to choose their identities. It cannot be argued that this trend is unnatural, since it reflects a thoroughly human tendency compatible with respecting social obligations to family, friends, and strangers.

A nonracist and nonsexist society would thus be largely blind with respect to color and gender. Differences in skin pigmentation and sexual anatomy (or sexual orientation) would not affect enjoyment of basic political rights and obligations; access to governmental and nongovernmental institutions guaranteeing employment, housing, and marriage opportunities; and cultivation of preferences, social roles, and so on.[27] Differences in skin pigmentation and sexual anatomy in such a society would still exist, despite the increasing prevalence of interracial coupling and bisexuality, as would diversity in individual characteristics, attitudes, and ways of life. But such differences would no longer determine or correspond to these dimensions of cultural diversity.

The color- and sex-blind ideal seems an appropriate goal to strive for. Canada and the United States have largely approximated it at the level of basic rights and have striven to realize it at the level of institutional access despite continuing legal obstacles preventing the implementation of homosexual marriage and affirmative action. Only at the third level (of cultural preferences) do we find racial and gender distinctions predominating, but these appear to be on the wane (perhaps more so in the case of race than in the case of gender).

I have argued in Chapter 3 that blindness with respect to difference is also a desirable ideal to pursue in areas of national loyalty. All things being equal, it is preferable for citizens of a state to identify themselves first and foremost as bearers of basic human rights rather than as biologically related kin possessing special moral qualities and privileges. If national identifications are to persist in an ideal society, they will do so as ethnic identifications, shorn of any racial manifestations.

The ideal of difference-blindness seems more questionable, however, when applied to most cultural distinctions of a religious or ethnic nature. Even if the ideal society would not take into account ethnic and religious affiliation in allocating basic political rights and duties, it very likely would do so in distributing institutional benefits and burdens and cultivating personal preferences. For instance, parochial schools would take the religion of applicants into account when making hiring decisions; and government might subsidize religious communities, like the Kiryas Joel, with special housing and educational facilities. Religion and ethnicity would also determine a person's cultural preferences, including his or her choice of associates, friends, and mates. Whether religion and ethnicity also would be allowed to perpetuate the patriarchal subordination of women in an ideal society seems unlikely (it is certainly to be hoped that antiracism and antisexism will be diffused throughout all religious and ethnic subgroups).

A culturally pluralist society in matters of race and gender might seem to have one drawback that a culturally pluralist society in matters of religion and ethnicity does not: it is more difficult to determine which rights, institutions, and preferences are racist and sexist. However, this view is mistaken. Although it is true that a society characterized by racial and gender pluralism in any of the three dimensions cited above has this drawback, a similar problem arises with respect to religiously and ethnically diverse societies, as my discussion of the Kiryas Joel case amply attests. In other words, the question inevitably arises whether the protection of some religious or ethnic minority does not cross over into favoritism (and by implication, discrimination against those who are not favored).

Unless simplicity and lack of ambiguity are the only criteria for evaluating societal ideals, we cannot conclude that pluralistic societies are inherently less desirable than nonpluralistic ones. I have given independent reasons for believing that difference-blindness is desirable in areas of race, sex, and nationality. Difference-blindness is also appropriate for religious and ethnic groups, at least at the level of basic rights.[28] However, I would now like to adduce further reasons for believing that difference-sensitivity—rather than difference-blindness—is the ethnic and religious ideal to be striven for in terms of institutional access and cultural preference.

Let me begin by qualifying my argument with a point made earlier in Chapter 4. It is virtually impossible (if not undesirable) for any culture to so completely differentiate itself from other cultures that communication and contamination are precluded. Cultures survive and adapt by absorbing (learning from) other cultures. Furthermore, it sometimes happens that cultures fuse with one another or become assimilated to a dominant culture. There are no general rules for determining when fusion or assimilation is good (or bad). In general, we look to the specific context of a culture and its adherents in making this judgment. For example, if a cultural group originates and sustains itself in a manner that is legitimate and does not violate the rights of its own or other groups' members, and if furthermore its adherents seek to preserve their way of life against tangible external threats without depriving others of their basic subsistence, then its demand for special group rights protecting against such threats might well be warranted.

There is no general decision procedure (beyond that cited above) for determining whether a given cultural group's demand for special legal protection is warranted or not. Above all, we are not entitled to say that just any cultural group has a right to be protected against cultural fusion. However, we can at least show that global cultural assimilation represents an undesirable extreme.

While we can expect that cultural mixing will accelerate as a result of increased global migrations, we should harbor no illusions about the equality of the exchange. Throughout most of the Third World today, the increasingly pervasive, mass-produced and mass-marketed culture that so many associate with the American lifestyle—fast-food chains, large discount stores, strip malls, rock and roll, MTV, Hollywood action cinema, pop fashions and designs, high-tech production and delivery systems—is quickly replacing local cultures. This preference is partially based on envy: if one cannot live in the lap of luxury, one can at least adopt its outer trappings of success. However, it is also shaped by years of cultural imperialism, in which colonial peoples were taught to believe that their ways of life were inferior to those imposed upon them by the "advanced" civilization of the West.

It remains a hotly debated issue whether the expansion of unregulated markets in goods, services, and labor will result in assimilating local cultures to the dominant, global culture of American capitalism or fusing them to it in ways conducive to the promotion of environmentally more adaptive lifestyles.[29] Evidence indicates that if consumer culture does not replace local culture, it at least undermines it, which becomes especially apparent when we see how the traditional meaning of local culture is crassly reappropriated and distorted for purposes of local advertising.

Defenders of globalization will doubtless find something positive in this destruction of tradition. With their caste structures and gender roles, traditions can be oppressive to poor people, women, and outsiders. Liberated from oppressive traditions, individual consumers can simply pick and choose which cultural fragments they want to incorporate into their personal identities. Although postmodernists and feminists are certainly right to celebrate the liberation of persons from oppressive traditions, it is worthwhile asking whether there are any anthropological limits to the emancipation from tradition. Does there ever come a point when emancipation from tradition is unhealthy and destructive of a genuinely human form of existence?

To answer this question, consider the Ik, an African tribal people who inhabit a mountainous region in northern Uganda. Until they were forceably expelled from their native hunting grounds in the late forties in what is today known as the Kidepo wildlife preserve, the Ik were a warm, friendly, and close-knit people. The expulsion uprooted them from their hunter-gatherer

lifestyle, subjected them to great famine, and utterly undermined their religious culture, which had been based on ancestor worship and ties of kinship.
What remained of them was a collection of individuals who had largely lost
any sense of value and purpose, save for their selfish desire to survive at all
costs. Predisposed to lying and cheating and almost totally bereft of familial
love, the Ik show us that tradition is a luxury, necessary for human decency,
perhaps, but dispensable as a means of survival.

The Ik represent an extreme example of an individualism that has increasingly come to the fore in our own profit-oriented society. The economically and culturally impoverished lifestyles of inner-city youths mirror
the cynicism of the Ik, whose wisdom consists in knowing that justice cannot be expected from one's fellow citizens, least of all from government and
corporate bureaucracies.

Therefore, one should not wax too triumphant in the face of growing individualism—especially one that is so defined in terms of the bottom line—
unless pampering one's narcissistic needs through wasteful consumption
paid with long hours of alienated labor strikes one as inherently worthwhile.
But perhaps I am too pessimistic. After all, is it not true that globalization
offers prospects for greater international cooperation and world peace?

Defenders of Western rationalism often assume that the roots of violent
conflict lie mainly in cultural differences—or rural "tribalism." Unfortunately,
they ignore the violence unleashed by the "civilizing" forces of so-called rational economic development, urbanization,[30] and bureaucratic governance.
Global capitalism consolidates local economies into a mass system of standardized consumption and production. It replaces low-tech, labor-intensive
forms of domestically diversified production aimed at satisfying local subsistence needs with high-tech, standardized forms of export production aimed
at producing profits for a privileged few. The spread of a global monoculture
of mass-produced and mass-consumed commodities not only promotes the
homogeneity of lifestyles, but it also incapacitates our biological adaptability.
A consumer monoculture geared toward endless economic growth portends
disastrous consequences for a global environment that has already exhausted
its capacity to absorb greenhouse emissions. Just as important, it eliminates
the biological diversity required for long-term adaptation.

Geographical diversity has forced people to cultivate diverse cultures,
both figuratively and literally. To take just one example, the subsistence
lifestyle of the inhabitants of Chloe Island off the coast of Chile led them to
develop several thousand varieties of potato. Now, thanks to global capitalism, they cultivate just three, all mainly for export. Unfortunately, standard-

ized strains of wheat, rice, maize, and potato generally resist local pest problems for only five or six years, and even then only with the help of ecologically unsound pesticides. Seed companies like Cargill and W. R. Grace must therefore genetically engineer new artifical strains. But the "credits built up in the gene banks by traditional, location-specific farming will be exhausted" once the local habitats have lost their diversity.[31]

Cultural diversity, then, is not simply a spiritual and existential issue but a matter of physical survival. While we can debate the good or bad effects of cultural homogeneity from a spiritual or existential point of view, there is little debating its biological impact, which is surely bad.[32] Export economies deprive local habitats of resources that could be used for satisfying local subsistence needs. The only question that remains to be answered is whether global exchanges might somehow reverse this trend, replacing export-induced homogeneity with local, community-based diversity. In this philosopher's opinion, it all depends on whether exchange is conducted as a democratic dialogue that is respectful of difference or as an elitist appropriation that assimilates everything to the law of the market.[33]

# NOTES

## INTRODUCTION

1. Lawrence Blum, "Antiracism, Multiculturalism, and Interracial Community: Three Educational Values for a Multicultural Society," in *Social Justice in a Diverse Society*, ed. Rita C. Manning and René Trujillo (Mountain View, Calif.: Mayfield, 1996), p. 377, cites the tragic case of a Chinese immigrant who was killed by a white Texan, who mistakenly identified his victim as "just another Japanese person out to take away his job." The example illustrates the way in which racial identifications transcend ethnic distinctions.

2. From a speech delivered by Bob Dole on October 28, 1996, in San Diego, where he endorsed a California ballot initiative (Proposition 209) barring all state-sponsored affirmative action programs.

3. Those who want a more in-depth view of my thinking on foundational matters should consult *Reason, History, and Politics: The Communitarian Grounds of Legitimacy in the Modern Age* (Albany: State University of New York Press, 1995).

4. A comprehensive discussion of disability rights can be found in Anita Silvers, David Wasserman, and Mary B. Mahowald, *Disability, Difference, Discrimination: Perspectives on Justice in Bioethics and Public Policy* (Lanham, Md.: Rowman and Littlefield, 1998).

## 1. EQUALITY AND DIFFERENCE IN DEMOCRACY AND LAW

1. Cited in John Arthur, *The Unfinished Constitution: Philosophy and Constitutional Practice* (Belmont, Calif.: Wadsworth, 1989), pp. 133–34.

2. Cf. *Grumet v. Board of Education*, 81 NY2d 518 (1993); *Grumet v. Cuomo*, 90 NY2d 57 (1997); and *Grumet v. Pataki* (1998), index no. 5648-97.

3. In 1993 Congress passed the Religious Freedom Restoration Act, which prohibited government from "substantially burdening" a person's religious practices through laws never intended for that purpose. The law was passed in response to the Supreme Court's ruling in a 1990 Oregon case that rejected claims of religious bias by two drug counselors who were denied unemployment benefits because they used a hallucinogenic drug during Native American religious rites. Although in 1997 the Court ruled that the act was overly broad and hence unconstitutional, a more narrowly

focused reformulation of it—the Religious Liberty Protection Act—is expected to be passed into law by 2000. This new version of the law allows some restrictions of religious practice, provided they are the "least restrictive" means for advancing a compelling state interest, such as health or commerce.

4. The concept of right is ambiguous between legal right and moral right. The position maintained in this book is that these rights are fundamentally distinct but interrelated. By "moral rights" I do not mean all that morality permits and expects of us, but just those basic *entitlements* to goods (security, subsistence, liberty, and cultural attainment) that persons claim just because they participate in cooperative social structures of mutual recognition and mutual concern that are "natural" to the human species (and thus necessary for living a minimally decent and dignified life). By "legal rights" I mean the positive guarantees, or *enforceable sanctions,* that persons and their appointed representatives have chosen to make good these *and other claims.* Legal rights are not to be understood as mere derivations of moral rights, and for two reasons. First, although some legal rights directly instantiate moral rights (such as the right not to be wrongfully harmed), others do not. For example, parking laws make our lives more convenient by coordinating traffic, but their absence would not jeopardize our basic moral rights. Again, many legal rights emanating from civil (property, contract, and tort) law exist for the sake of resolving social conflicts rather than for safeguarding basic moral rights. Here, the expectation is that legal rights should conform to moral rights but not necessarily instantiate them. Second, moral and legal rights have different justifications, the former being grounded in nature, the latter in procedures of democratic legislation. Because moral rights have their basis in nature rather than legislation, they provide a relatively independent standard for critically assessing the justice (or moral conformitivity) of legal rights.

5. However, some utilitarians—most notably Peter Singer—argue that we ought to extend rights to animals as well. Because we normally extend rights to infants and mentally defective persons, Singer insists that our possession of rights ought not to be made contingent on our possession of reason, but on our capacity to feel pleasure and pain, a capacity that many animals possess to a very high degree. Others, like Michael Tooley, propose a somewhat different argument for extending rights to animals. Arguing that consciousness ought to be the basis for ascribing rights, he concludes that the right to X depends on possessing certain desires with respect to X. Because highly conscious animals (such as cats, for example) want to avoid suffering, they have a prima facie right not to undergo suffering. However, because neither newborn infants nor most animals are conscious enough to desire their own existence as continuous subjects of experiences, Tooley reasons that they do not have a right to life. Contrary to Singer and Tooley, I argue that possession of rights is conceptually connected to membership in a species whose normal functioning involves a minimum threshold of moral reasoning (see below). This qualification virtually precludes the possibility of any nonhuman animal possessing rights. However, it does not preclude the possibility of their being an object of moral concern. This explains why we have a prima facie obligation not to harm them—an obligation, I might add, that should not be overridden as often or as easily as it currently is in the food and science industries. Cf. note 6 below and Peter Singer, *Animal Liberation* (New York: Random House, 1975), and Michael Tooley, "Abortion and Infanticide," *Philosophy and Public Affairs* 2, no. 1 (1972): 37–65.

6. The idea that rights and norms follow from the peculiar, *relational* nature of human existence finds early support in Aristotle's definition of human beings as in-

herently political *(zoon politikon)*, and later reappears in Hegel's identification of human spirit *(Geist)* with mutual recognition *(Anerkennung)* and in Ludwig Feuerbach's and Karl Marx's definition of the human person as a self-conscious species-being *(Gattungswesen)*. More contemporary attempts to ground universal moral rights in communicative and other forms of interrelatedness can be found in the writings of Jürgen Habermas and Alan Gewirth.

Critics have objected to such relational theories of rights on two major grounds: conceptual and moral. Conceptual objections point to the incoherence of deriving a normative rights claim of the form "P ought to have X" from a factual or metaphysical claim about what is or must be the case regarding human beings and other intelligent social creatures. Defenders of any such theory of natural rights typically respond to this objection by arguing that the unavoidable conditions of sociality—for instance, the necessity of exchanging speaker and listener roles—directly presuppose expectations of mutuality (reciprocity) that already instantiate very general rights and duties. Critics, however, then go on to argue that the sheer generality of such "natural" rights and duties deprives them of the concrete, prescriptive meaning and force inherent in the very concept of right. Defenders respond to this objection by pointing out that natural rights and duties are not totally indeterminate in meaning and force (despite their abstractness and generality), and so can be used to criticize particular laws.

The moral objection against relational theories of rights focuses on the moral irrelevance (and arbitrariness) of designating any specifically human capacity as a prerequisite for full moral consideration. Animal rights activists like Peter Singer argue that assigning privileged rights to human beings simply because of their membership in the human species (what he calls speciesism) is analogous to racism. In his opinion, membership in a species, like membership in a racial group, is morally irrelevant for purposes of drawing moral distinctions. However, defenders of a relational theory of rights rightly argue that assigning a privileged status to the human species *because* of the peculiar social and rational manner by which that species procures its self-preservation is *not* speciesist, since it allows that nonhumans (intelligent extraterrestrials, say) might also possess this status.

7. Racists, of course, believe otherwise: racial differences designate cognitive and moral differences that in turn justify unequal rights.

8. I borrow the following distinction between oppression and domination from Iris Marion Young, *Justice and the Politics of Difference* (Princeton: Princeton University Press, 1990).

9. Cf. Lisa Newton, "Reverse Discrimination As Unjustified," in *Moral Controversies: Race, Class, and Gender in Applied Ethics,* ed. Steven J. Gold (Belmont, Calif.: Wadsworth, 1994), pp. 478–81.

10. The close connection between moral equality (justice) and impartiality informs one procedure for thinking about universal rights. This procedure, famously deployed by John Rawls in *A Theory of Justice* (Cambridge: Harvard University Press, 1971), is discussed in greater detail in Chapter 6.

11. Here I have in mind Ronald Dworkin's understanding of the principle of equal respect and equal concern as set forth in *Law's Empire* (Cambridge: Harvard University Press, 1986).

12. Although the wording of the Fourteenth Amendment makes it seem as if equal protection guarantees the personal rights of individuals taken as individuals, the original intent of the post–Civil War Reconstruction Congress in drafting the amendment suggests a somewhat different interpretation: the protection of individuals

taken as members of discriminated groups. The Equal Protection Clause provided constitutional support for the 1866 Civil Rights Act, which was designed to protect newly freed slaves from the racist decrees of the southern "Black Codes." Indeed, the Supreme Court in the latter half of the nineteenth century narrowly interpreted the amendment to apply only to (in the words of Justice Miller's opinion in the *Slaughter-House Cases* of 1873) "the slave race" and "the newly-made freeman and citizen." Only with *Lochner v. New York* (1904) did the high court begin to explicitly include all citizens among the amendment's beneficiaries. In doing so, however, it has consistently compared the equality of treatment meted out to individuals in their capacity as members of oppressed groups. By contrast, the right to privacy that the Supreme Court adduced in *Griswold v. Connecticut* (1965) from its reading of the Fourth Amendment's stricture against unreasonable searches does not invite us to compare the equal treatment of different groups of individuals, but simply requires that each individual be protected in his or her privacy.

13. For example, federal mandatory sentencing guidelines for possession of crack-cocaine, which is principally consumed by minorities, are much harsher than those for possession of pure cocaine, which is mainly consumed by whites.

14. Not surprisingly, discrimination against women plaintiffs in rape cases, where consent to engage in intercourse has been understood in terms of what a typical man (rather than a woman) might reasonably infer, has led to some modifications in the difference-blind processing of criminal cases. In some jurisdictions women are no longer forced to endure brutal cross-examination regarding the reliability of their testimony as evidenced by their past sexual history, and the standard of voluntary consent has been modified to include women's different understanding of what reasonably counts as consent. Likewise, law professor Paul Butler has argued that jurors (especially black jurors) have a moral obligation to not convict black defendants who are plainly guilty of having committed nonviolent offenses (such as possession of narcotics) on the grounds that the American criminal justice system as a whole discriminates unfairly against blacks, as witnessed by their higher rate of incarceration. In Butler's opinion, such jury nullification (as in the acquittal of Washington, D.C., mayor Marion Barry of criminal drug use and possession) allows African Americans to determine for themselves what sorts of antisocial conduct in their communities must be exempted from criminal liability in order to further the interests of their community. Although the right of jurors to determine the justice of laws—and not merely the facts regarding their application—through nullification has been upheld by the courts (despite the fact that jurors are not informed of this right by judges), the racial partiality of Butler's recommendation for invoking it appears to constitute a more radical departure from difference-blind due process (and one that eerily parallels the refusal of white jurors in the South to convict white plaintiffs who were plainly guilty of having murdered blacks). Cf. Paul Butler, "Racially-Based Jury Nullification: Black Power in the Criminal Justice System," *Yale Law Journal* 105 (1995): 677, 679, and Douglas E. Litowitz, "Jury Nullification: Setting Reasonable Limits," *CBA Record* (Sept. 1997): 16–21.

15. Who is to count as a member of a protected class requiring special treatment will depend on context; elderly persons will not require special legal provisions to ensure against vote dilution, but they might require provisions guaranteeing income, health care, and continued employment (e.g., by requiring employers to provide flexible conditions of employment). Blacks, whose political rights are threatened by vote dilution, will not require special legal provisions guaranteeing flexible working conditions, but parents, pregnant women, and elderly persons will. Optimally, the decision

about which classes of persons ought to be protected and in what manner should be left to the citizens and their elected representatives. However, the risks associated with this approach might have to be balanced against those associated with top-down judicial paternalism. The history of oppression meted out to the descendants of black slaves would have warranted the Supreme Court's reversal of legal segregation even in the absence of a national consensus in support of such an undertaking.

16.  The conflict between liberal values of freedom and equality and communitarian values of traditional authority and fixed identity is especially pronounced in Israel, in which ultra-Orthodox Jews and their political party (Sephardic Torah Guardians, or Shas) have gained control of the Interior Ministry and enforced strict rules over how Israelis are married and buried, who can convert to Judaism, what consumer items need rabbinical certification, and so on. Not only does the Israeli government subsidize schools run by Shas, but it grants Orthodox yeshiva students exemptions from military service. The problem with this kind of state-religion involvement is that Israel claims to be a liberal, multicultural democracy in which non-Jews have the same rights as Jews (excluding special military exemptions for Arabs) and in which women have the same rights as men.

17.  Locke's arguments in *A Letter Concerning Toleration* (1685) are not, oddly enough, based on classical liberal assumptions regarding the fundamental freedom and equality of all persons that inform his own contractualist theory of rights. Rather, they are based on the weaker assumption that the state is not more likely to succeed in making a person believe the right thing than if that person is left to do so on his or her own. Because nothing in this argument speaks against the state for censoring doctrines that it believes weaken public order, Locke did not propose to extend religious freedom to Catholics (who profess loyalty to the pope) or atheists (who recognize no enduring obligations bound by divine oath).

18.  For a good discussion of the racial underpinnings of the real-life social contract that united "civilized" Europeans in their oppression and domination of non-Europeans, see Charles Mills, *The Racial Contract* (Ithaca: Cornell University Press, 1998).

19.  Since Kant, philosophers have distinguished between two kinds of freedom: negative freedom (or freedom from constraint) and positive freedom (or freedom to act). Generally, both kinds of freedom complement one another. Free action depends on absence of constraint, in which constraint can take the external form of physical coercion or the internal form of passive hindrance (for example, lack of money can constrain my choice of activities); conversely, absence of constraint depends on free action (avoiding criminal assaults or possessing enough money requires that I do something). I discuss this distinction in greater detail in Chapter 11. See also Isaiah Berlin, *Four Essays on Liberty* (Oxford: Oxford University Press, 1969), and Joel Feinberg, *Social Philosophy* (Englewood Cliffs, N.J.: Prentice Hall, 1974), pp. 9–11.

20.  Justice Powell noted that the "Rotary Club is not the kind of intimate or private relation that warrants constitutional protection" because the bylaws of the organization explicitly assert that its purpose "is to produce an inclusive, not exclusive, membership . . . enabling the club to be a true cross section of the business and professional life of the community" (cf. *Board of Directors of Rotary International et al. v. Rotary Club of Duarte et al.*, no. 86-421, *Supreme Court of the United States*, 95 L. Ed. 2s 471 [May 4, 1987]).

21.  In August 1999, the New Jersey Supreme Court unanimously ruled (in direct opposition to the 1998 California decision) that the Boy Scouts of America is a "public accommodation" on par with restaurants, libraries, schools, and theaters and as such is covered by state antidiscrimination law. The ruling denied the legality of

the organization's expulsion of James Dale, a gay assistant scoutmaster who had earned more than twenty-five merit badges and scouting's highest rank and honor during twelve years of involvement. In effect, the New Jersey ruling implied that excluding gays from Scout membership might deprive them of their civil right to participate in organized, extracurricular activities, especially in locations lacking comparable alternatives.

22. Cf. chapters 1 and 3 of David Ingram, *Reason, History, and Politics: The Communitarian Grounds of Legitimacy in the Modern Age* (Albany: State University of New York Press, 1995), for a critical assessment of the communitarian views of Michael Sandel, Michael Walzer, Charles Taylor, and Alasdair MacIntyre.

23. Admittedly, the Greeks were less troubled by the democratic tyranny of the group over the individual since they did not conceive of the good or freedom of the individual as something apart from the good or freedom of the state, nor did they believe in the universal equality of all human beings as embodiments of universal reason. They neither included all members of the state as full-fledged citizens (slaves, resident aliens, and women were all denied this privilege) nor granted inalienable rights to those that were (as evidenced by Socrates' condemnation for blasphemy).

24. I discuss various versions of the economic justification of democracy in chapters 1 and 5 of Ingram, *Reason, History, and Politics*.

25. The economic model also mistakenly assumes that a single-rank ordering of preferences will emerge when voters are presented with more than two options; indeed, in bipartisan contests revolving around multiple issues, winners are seldom in a position to infer a clear "mandate from the people" to pursue one policy over another. For further discussion of these decision-theoretical problems, see chapters 1 and 5 of Ingram, *Reason, History, and Politics*.

26. Legal philosophers disagree about what these limits are. Some, like Robert Bork, argue that the courts should avoid inventing new rights by striking only laws that the Founding Fathers would have thought violated a right. Others hold that laws that violate basic political rights (John Ely) or that violate political rights *and* basic social entitlements (Ronald Dworkin) as conceived by contemporary moral philosophy can also be nullified. Still others (Jeremy Waldron) argue that allowing courts to nullify any democratic legislation amounts to sanctioning judicial tyranny. For a rich discussion of this problem as it applies to interpreting the equal protection clause of the Fourteenth Amendment, see Chapter 8 and Ingram, *Reason, History, and Politics*, chapter 6. See Robert Bork, *The Tempting of America: The Political Seduction of the Law* (New York: Simon and Schuster, 1990); John Ely, *Democracy and Distrust* (Cambridge: Harvard University Press, 1980); Ronald Dworkin, "Equality, Democracy, and the Constitution: We the People in Court," *Alberta Law Review* 28 (1990): 324–46; and Jeremy Waldron, "A Rights-Based Critique of Constitutional Rights," *Oxford Journal of Legal Studies* 13 (1993): 18–51.

27. What rights guarantee is a matter of some dispute. They do not all guarantee freedom of choice (children, for example, cannot choose to waive their right to an education) or simple benefits (the right to ingest harmful quantities of a given substance yields no tangible good). Their differences aside, however, all of them seem to guarantee at least this much: the *equal* treatment of individuals and groups by the government.

28. Rights are liberties that we attribute to persons, but they are also duties (constraints on liberties) that bind them. Reason can perhaps inform us about what general sorts of liberties persons must have in order to live minimally decent and fulfilling lives, but it cannot establish the precise nature of the corresponding duties.

Because duties are mutually binding, rights necessarily take the legal and social form of political agreements between persons. For more on the relational nature of rights, see Chapter 11 and Martha Minow, *Making All the Difference* (Ithaca: Cornell University Press, 1990).

29. See Chapter 7 for a discussion of perfect, imperfect, and pure proceduralism.

30. See Chapter 9 for further discussion of democracy and redistricting.

31. For a critical assessment of this objection, see Chapters 3 and 9.

32. See Chapter 9 for an analysis of Guinier's proposal.

33. Cf. Jürgen Habermas, *Between Facts and Norms: Contributions to a Discourse Theory of Law and Democracy*, trans. Bill Rehg (Cambridge, Mass.: MIT Press, 1996). For a critical assessment of Habermas's position, cf. Ingram, *Reason, History, and Politics*, chapters 5 and 6.

34. For Habermas, cross-cultural dialogue is possible because every culture uses some concept comparable to what we mean by "truth," or reference to an intersubjectively shared "reality" distinct from mere subjective "appearance." Although different cultures sometimes appeal to different methods and criteria for establishing the truth (or validity) of factual (moral) claims, the fact that they understand the world in different ways is no hindrance to their capacity to translate claims into their own language. And despite the fact that some premodern cultures do not include everyone as equal participants in discussions, they all implicitly understand the difference between rational persuasion and rhetorical manipulation.

35. Cf. John Rawls, *Political Liberalism* (New York: Columbia University Press, 1993).

36. Rawls insists that each person need only convince himself or herself of the validity (or "truth") of a constitutional framework from the standpoint of that *particular* comprehensive worldview which he or she happens to share with other *like-minded* folk. Habermas, however, argues that this conviction is not sufficiently rationality, since it cannot be tested in dialogue with persons sharing *different* comprehensive doctrines. In Rawls's theory, persons sharing different comprehensive doctrines can agree on a constitutional framework *in dialogue,* but only if they voluntarily refrain from appealing to the particular truth-grounding reasons emanating from their conflicting belief systems and practices. In Habermas's theory, by contrast, full trust in the constitutional framework can only be had if all can agree on it for roughly the *same* reasons, *which reasons strike them as true and convincing relative to each of their comprehensive doctrines.* My view of the matter lies somewhere in between these extremes: persons must be convinced *publicly* of the validity of the constitutional framework from the standpoint of *each* of their comprehensive doctrines as long as their rationales agree metaphorically rather than (as Habermas insists) literally. Cf. Habermas, *The Inclusion of the Other: Studies in Political Theory,* ed. Ciaran Cronin and Pablo De Greiff (Cambridge, Mass.: MIT Press, 1998), pp. 59ff, and Ingram, *Reason, History, and Politics,* chapter 7.

37. For a discussion of the kind of injustice that occurs "whenever a plaintiff is deprived of the means of arguing and by this fact becomes a victim," as in the case where the settling of a conflict between two parties "is made in the idiom of one of them in which the wrong suffered by the other signifies nothing," see Jean-Francois Lyotard, *Le Différend* (Paris: Les Editions de Minuit, 1983), pp 24–25. For an edifying application of Lyotard to the problem of settling Native American claims, see John William Sayer, *Ghost Dancing the Law* (Cambridge: Harvard University Press, 1997).

2. Differences Made Legal: Oppression and Domination

1. Writing for the majority in *Michael M v. Sonoma County Superior Court* (1981), Justice William Rehnquist explicitly notes that "the Equal Protection Clause does not 'demand that a statute necessarily apply equally to all persons' or require 'things which are different in fact to be treated in law as though they were the same'" (cited in John Arthur, *The Unfinished Constitution: Philosophy and Constitutional Practice* [Belmont, Calif.: Wadsworth, 1989], p. 262).

2. I owe this distinction to Iris Young. As Nancy Fraser notes, mainstream "liberal" political theorists like John Rawls do not adequately acknowledge the distinction. They and their Marxist counterparts tend to view domination as a species of oppression, thereby closely linking the attainment of recognition and respect with the attainment of a just distribution of basic goods. Conversely, Hegelian political theorists like Axel Honneth tend to view oppression as a species of domination, thereby reducing moral and political struggle to a struggle for recognition rather than to a struggle for self-development. See Iris M. Young, *Justice and the Politics of Difference* (Princeton: Princeton University Press, 1990); Nancy Fraser, *Justice Interruptus: Critical Reflections on the Postsocialist Condition* (London: Routledge, 1997); Axel Honneth, *The Struggle for Recognition: The Moral Grammar of Social Conflicts*, trans. Joel Anderson (Cambridge, Mass.: Polity Press, 1995); and John Rawls, *A Theory of Justice* (Cambridge: Harvard University Press, 1971).

3. Power, in fact, only functions relationally, often—but not always—between persons, such that one exercises it over another. Even when exercised in this manner, power need not constitute domination (e.g., it can be exercised in a manner that is democratically accountable). However, power most often functions as a relational constraint that conditions (and disciplines) our behavior in ways that are largely impersonal. Systemic structures (market, bureaucratic, ideological, and so on) function this way. See Michel Foucault, "The Subject and Power," in *Critical Theory: The Essential Readings*, ed. David Ingram and Julia Simon-Ingram (New York: Paragon House, 1991), pp. 310–19.

4. The distinction I am making here roughly corresponds to the distinction between (political) *action* and (consumptive and productive) *labor* drawn by Hannah Arendt in *The Human Condition* (Chicago: University of Chicago Press, 1958).

5. These last points converge in rape law, where female consent is defined in terms of what any "reasonable man" might have taken as consent. Rape trials also highlight the paradox that women who do not violently resist sexual advances are seen as complicitous, while those who do are perceived as being less (passive) victim than (active) agent of their suffering. This dilemma also explains why women's testimony is not taken seriously; either it is too emotional and subjective (the result of trauma), or it is too rational and objective (the result of not having suffered trauma). For an excellent discussion of this point, see Laura Hengehold, "An Immodest Proposal: Foucault, Hysterization, and the 'Second Rape,'" *Hypatia* 9, no. 3 (1994): 88–107.

6. See Cass Sunstein's critique of the Court's reasoning in *The Partial Constitution* (Cambridge: Harvard University Press, 1993), p. 77.

7. For example, under Illinois' Work First program, companies hiring public aid recipients receive up to $2,100 annually in tax credits in addition to the recipient's cash and food stamp allotment. Work First recipients who are unable to find work after six months can be required to take a "work experience" job, where they will work twenty hours per week for no wages at all as a condition for continuing to receive aid. Taking advantage of Illinois' Earnfare program, which provides free labor

to corporations—with taxpayers subsidizing each aid recipient's $410 in monthly alotments ($120 in food stamps and $290 in cash stipends) in return for eighty hours of work—Walgreen's has significantly reduced its full-time staff and posted a record $232 million in profits for the first half of fiscal year 1998, up 16 percent from the previous year. Moreover, as the Walgreen case well illustrates, despite workfare's being touted as a way to provide welfare recipients with job training and regular employment, very few workfare recipients are hired on as full-time employees by the companies they work for (ironically, employees replaced by workfare recipients are often forced back onto public assistance). Not surprisingly, given its failure to restore working dignity to the lives of its beneficiaries, many critics have concluded that in practice workfare is little more than a governmental scheme designed to provide large corporations with free and heavily subsidized labor.

8. Identity-based injustices such as racism and sexism, however, reinforce and maintain both systemic deprivation and political domination.

9. For a theoretical defense of justice as equality of resources, see Ronald Dworkin, "What Is Equality? Part 2: Equality of Resources," *Philosophy and Public Affairs* 10, no. 4 (1981): 283–345; and my discussion of Dworkin in *Reason, History, and Politics: The Communitarian Grounds of Legitimacy in the Modern Age* (Albany: State University of New York Press, 1995), pp. 252ff.

10. Cf. Fraser, *Justice Interruptus.*

11. For a defense of workplace democracy, see David Schweickart, *Against Capitalism* (Cambridge: Cambridge University Press, 1993), and Ingram, *Reason, History, and Politics,* chapter 6.

12. Cf. Chapters 3 and 4.

13. Cf. Deborah Rhode, *Justice and Gender* (Cambridge: Harvard University Press, 1989); and Jodi Dean's review essay, "Beyond the Equality/Difference Dilemma," *Philosophy and Social Criticism* 20, no. 1–2 (1997): 155–70.

14. Because persons straddle different social groups, it is not unusual to find one person suffering multiple sorts of injustice or suffering one kind of injustice while benefiting from another. A gay businessman might profit from exploiting his heterosexual employees, just as they might benefit from cultural discrimination preventing gays from adopting children. Hence, membership in oppressed and oppressor groups is often complex.

### 3. Groups and Individuals: The Race Controversy

1. Cornel West, *Race Matters* (Boston: Beacon Press, 1993), pp. 26–27.

2. *Shaw v. Reno,* U.S. Supreme Court Reports, 125L Ed 2d, no. 1 (1993): 529.

3. *Miller v. Johnson,* U.S. Supreme Court Reports, 94-631 (1995): 9.

4. Marx's distinction between an economic class whose members are conscious of their unique class interests and one whose members are not (the distinction between a class existing in itself and a class existing for itself) parallels my distinction between aggregate and affinal groups.

5. In commenting on the arbitrariness of what is taken to be a racial characteristic by scientists, Henry Louis Gates Jr. notes that "we could differentiate humans along countless axes, such as height, weight, and other physical features. If we assigned racial categories to groups of humans with different heights—for example, every foot of height from four feet up determines a new race—we would be more biologically precise than the usual racial designation by skin color. For no fixed biological boundary exists between Asian and Caucasion, black and Indian, whereas a

fixed boundary does exist between those who are shorter than five feet and those who are between five and six feet" ("Critical Remarks," in *Anatomy of Racism*, ed. David Theo Goldberg [Minneapolis: University of Minnesota Press, 1990], p. 332).

6. Test scores from the 1993 SAT showed that out of 1,600 possible points, blacks averaged 741 compared with whites at 938. Although scores improve with income, blacks from the highest income bracket still score less on average (871) than whites from the lowest income bracket (874). See Andrew Hacker, *Two Nations: Black and White, Separate, Hostile, Unequal* (New York: Ballantine, 1995), pp. 146–48.

7. I assume that possession of property *P* is essential to being a member of race *R* if all and only members of *R* possess *P*.

8. I am indebted to Iris Young, *Justice and the Politics of Difference* (Princeton: Princeton University Press, 1990), for this distinction.

9. Among the many excellent studies of socially conditioned racial embodiment are Frantz Fanon, *Black Skin, White Masks*, trans. Charles Lam Markmann (New York: Grove Press, 1967); Lewis Gordon, *Bad Faith and Antiblack Racism* (Atlantic Highlands, N.J.: Humanities Press, 1995); Michael Omi and Howard Winant, *Racial Formations in the United States: From the 1860's to the 1980's* (New York: Routledge, 1986); Gail Weiss, *Body Images* (London: Routledge, 1998); and Linda Alcoff, "Towards a Phenomenology of Racial Embodiment," *Radical Philosophy* 95 (May/June 1999): 15–26, and "Philosophy and Racial Identity," *Radical Philosophy* 75 (January–February 1996): 5–14.

10. The analysis presented here responds to some objections put forth by Anthony Appiah in "Race, Culture, Identity: Misunderstood Connections," in *Color Consciousness: The Political Morality of Race*, ed. A. Appiah and A. Gutmann (Princeton: Princeton University Press, 1996), pp. 34ff.

11. Jean-Louis Flandrin, *Families in Former Times: Kinship, Household, and Sexuality in Early Modern France*, trans. Richard Southern (Cambridge: Cambridge University Press, 1979); Ann Stoler, "Making Empire Respectable: The Politics of Race and Sexual Morality in Twentieth Century Colonial Cultures," *American Ethnologist* 16 (1989): 634–60.

12. Anthony Pagden, *Lords of All the World: Ideologies of Empire in Spain, Britian, and France c. 1500–c. 1800* (New Haven: Yale University Press, 1995), pp. 1–2, divides the era of conquest into periods: the colonization of the Americas from 1492 to 1830, which involved the subordination of Native Americans and African slaves, and the colonization of Asia, Africa, and the Pacific from 1730 to the period after World War II.

13. Robert A. Williams Jr., *The American Indian in Western Legal Thought: The Discourses of Conquest* (New York: Oxford University Press, 1990).

14. Robert A. Williams Jr., "The Algebra of Federal Indian Law: The Hard Trail of Decolonizing and Americanizing the White Man's Indian Jurisprudence," *Wisconsin Law Review 1986* (1986): 230–33.

15. See Pagden, *Lords of All the World*, chapter 1, and Pierre van den Berghe, *Race and Racism: A Comparative Perspective* (New York: Wiley, 1978).

16. Cf. Kant's ranking of Europeans, Asians, Africans, and Native Americans, in descending order of innate talent, in "On the Different Races of Mankind," as well as his infamous remark that "so fundamental is the difference between [the black and white] races of man . . . it appears to be as great in regard to mental capacities as in color," both contained in *Observations on the Feeling of the Beautiful and Sublime*, trans. John T. Goldthwait (Berkeley: University of California Press, 1960), pp. 111–13.

17. See L. C. Dunn and Theodosius Dobzhansky, *Heredity, Race and Society* (New York: Mentor, 1960), pp. 114 ff; and L. C. Dunn, "Race and Biology," in *Race, Science and Society,* ed. Leo Kuper (New York: Columbia University Press, 1965), pp. 61–67.

18. N. P. Dubinin, "Race and Contemporary Genetics," in Kuper, *Race, Science and Society,* pp. 68–94. Barely 0.012 percent of an individual's genetic endowment accounts for racial differences.

19. Defending W. E. B DuBois's thesis that racial identifications can sometimes express nonracist affinities that merit conservation—especially against the overwhelming desire among many racial minorities to shed their color and assimilate to the dominant (usually white) race—African-American philosopher Lucius Outlaw, "On Race and Philosophy," *Graduate Faculty Philosophy Journal* 18, no. 2 (1995): 175–99, has recently challenged the view that racial as well as ethnic groups arise solely from an unnatural history of legally sanctioned discrimination. Outlaw's "third path between racism and anti-racism," which attempts to circumvent biological (essentialist) accounts of race without endorsing extreme "social constructivist" reductions of race to unreal and wholly illegitimate ideological fictions, explains the formation of groups whose members distinguish themselves by reference to their physical appearance and culture (what he calls raciation and ethnicization) in terms of "natural-social evolution" (p. 179). According to Outlaw, although particular racial groupings can originate, either partly or entirely, in racist constructions (and, historically speaking, typically have done so in the West), the "anthropological necessity" for individuals to procure their preservation by gathering into groups on the basis of distinctive physical and cultural similarities can scarcely be denied, for the survival of the group on which the lives of its constituent members depend is only enhanced by maintaining its solidarity against outside threats. In the words of Outlaw, "It is through the choosing of partners . . . for the physical reproduction of descendants through which, to paraphrase Aristotle, humans satisfy their desire to achieve relative immortality by leaving someone behind after their death who looks and carries on like themselves" (p. 192). Outlaw thus concludes that, however much the basic parameters of racial and cultural diversity can be altered through contingent interracial and intercultural couplings, the fact remains that such diversity is both "natural" and desirable and as such unlikely to be eliminated.

I think Outlaw's and DuBois's nuanced attempts to defend races and ethnicities as "social-natural kinds" are laudable to the extent that they seek both to acknowledge the reality of race in the embodied self-understanding of individuals and to retrieve a positive, nonracist (nonethnocentrist) conception of race (ethnicity) for critical purposes. However, these attempts fail to distinguish clearly the naturalness of physical differences from the naturalness of cultural differences. Even though both races and ethnicities gravitate around relatively closed breeding populations, races (genetically construed) refer to statistical probabilities associated with *heritable* physical (visible) traits, whereas ethnicities refer to statistical probabilities associated with *learned* cultural habits and ways of understanding. Although social groupings gravitating around perceived physical resemblances may have evolved in response to the survival needs of social groups generally, there is no evidence that such social groupings are still adaptive (the heightened frequency of interracial couplings and adoptions as well as the increasing growth of multicultural and multiracial communities suggest that they are not). Even if members of racial and ethnic groups continue to resist mixing for the reasons mentioned by Outlaw, this tendency, however "natural," need not be desirable ideally and in the long run. In response to the argument that physical differences in skin pigmentation are adaptive relative to geographical and climatalogical variations, one need only note that global environmental changes, combined with the invention of protective skin treatments, clothing, and modern (confined) modes of lifestyle, have rendered such differences less important than they once were. In contrast to physical differences, cultural (ethnic) differences compose multiple repositories of knowledge that continue to prove themselves valuable for adaptation (as I argue in Chapter 11). Hence, whereas racial homogenization is not contrary to natural-social evolution and indeed may well be an ideal to be striven for, the same cannot be said of cultural homogenization (although extreme ethnic fragmentation is probably not beneficial to the survival of the species either).

20. The poor Irish who immigrated to the United States in the 1820s and 1830s frequently lived among (and married with) free black Americans in the cities of the North and South. These groups were so closely identified with one another that the mainstream Anglo population came to refer to the Irish as "white Negroes" and African Americans as "smoked Irish." In 1841 an Irish leader urged his American kinsmen to join the abolitionists in the name of racial solidarity—a plea that, as the New York City draft riots in 1963 sadly attests, went unheeded. See Noel Ignatiev, *How the Irish Became White* (London: Routledge, 1995).

21. The differences between North American and Latin American racism merit considerably more attention than can be given here. Spanish and Portugese colonists appropriated the New World and its inhabitants by way of absorption and assimilation, intercoupling with slaves imported from Africa as well as with indigenous natives. The *casta* system, which endowed specific groups with hierarchies of rights and privileges depending on the quantity and quality of their racial mixing *(mestizaje)*, could not have evolved into the sort of racially segregated societies typical of North America simply because so few persons (in some countries, less than 5 percent) were *not* mixed *(mestizo)*. The willingness of Spanish and Portugese colonists to mix with Africans and natives may well reflect their Catholic and Roman heritage (ancient Rome also chose the path of assimilation in its absorption of conquered peoples). By contrast, the refusal of North American colonists to do the same might be explained by their Protestant and Germanic heritage, which gravitated around a concern for maintaining purity of descent and belief. See Carlos A. Fernandez, "La Raza and the Melting Pot: A Comparative Look at Multiethnicity," in *Racially Mixed People in America,* ed. Maria P. P. Root (Newbury Park, Calif.: Sage, 1992), pp. 135–37; Linda Alcoff, "Mestizo Identity," in *American Mixed Race: The Culture of Microdiversity,* ed. Naomi Zack (Lanham, Md.: Rowman and Littlefield, 1995), pp. 257–78; and Carl N. Degler, *Neither Black Nor White* (Madison: University of Wisconsin Press, 1986), pp. 19–20, 39–47, 61–67, 105–7.

22. Charles Mills, *The Racial Contract* (Ithaca: Cornell University Press, 1998), p. 76.

23. Naomi Zack, "Black, White, and Gray: Words, Words, Words," reprinted from *Race and Mixed Race* (Philadelphia: Temple University Press, 1993), in *Social Justice in a Diverse Society,* ed. Rita C. Manning and René Trujillo (Mountain View, Calif.: Mayfield, 1996), p. 114.

24. W. E. B. DuBois, *Dusk of Dawn: An Essay Toward an Autobiography of a Race Concept* (Milwood, N.Y.: Kraus-Thomson, 1975), pp. 116–17.

25. Tommy Lott, "DuBois on the Invention of Race," in Manning and Trujillo, *Social Justice in a Diverse Society,* p. 106.

26. W. E. B. DuBois, "The Conservation of Races," in *Negro Social and Political Thought, 1850–1920,* ed. Howard Brotz (New York: Basic Books, 1966), pp. 486–87.

27. Ibid., p. 485.

28. By the time he wrote *Dusk of Dawn,* DuBois understood full well that African-American racial identification is culturally and geographically hybrid in ways that resist reduction to any single cultural-historical locus. In "The Conservation of Races" (1897), by contrast, he thought that African-American racial identification could be defined in terms of an "authentic" African-American (or even Pan-African) culture. For a critique of this view, see Bernard R. Boxill, *Blacks and Social Justice* (Totowa, N.J.: Rowman and Littlefield, 1992), pp. 182ff.

29. Lott, "DuBois on the Invention of Race," in Manning and Trujillo, *Social Justice in a Diverse Society,* p. 105; Anthony Appiah, "The Uncompleted Argument: Du Bois and the Illusion of Race," in *Race, Writing, and Difference,* ed. Henry Louis Gates Jr. (Chicago: University of Chicago Press, 1986), p. 32.

30. Cf. G. Doppelt, "Is There a Multicultural Liberalism?" *Inquiry* 41 (1999): 244.

31. Frantz Fanon, *Black Skin, White Masks,* trans. Charles Lam Markmann (New York: Grove Weidenfeld, 1968), pp. 228–29.

32. Ignatiev and Garvey's journal *Race Traitor* and their coauthored book bearing the same title (New York: Routledge, 1996) have become icons in "whiteness studies" programs on many college campuses today. Although Garvey and Ignatiev argue that white racial identifications are illegitimate in a way that black racial identifications are not, their argument partly relies on the fact that white racial identifications really serve only the interest of upper-class whites (see Chapter 8 for the details of this argument). Hence, they believe that most whites can and should dissociate themselves from this identity as something that has oppressed them as well. Against their recommendation for conscious dissociation, Linda Alcoff argues that all whites, regardless of economic class, benefited from white racial identification in that it gave them a clear sense of their own superiority and entitlement, however unconscious it might have been. Because racializing effects are inscribed in embodied self-images, habits, and modes of perception, they cannot be consciously renounced in the easy manner prescribed by Ignatiev and Garvey. Cf. L. Alcoff, "What Should White People Do?" *Hypatia* 30, no. 3 ((Summer 1998): 6–26.

#### 4. CULTURES AND GROUP AFFINITIES

1. Cf. Edward Dolnick, "Deafness as Culture," *Atlantic Monthly* (September 1993): 37–53; and Maria Arana Ward, "As Technology Advances, a Bitter Debate Divides the Deaf," *Washington Post,* May 11, 1997, p. A1. Dolnick notes that the "average deaf sixteen-year-old reads at the level of a hearing eight-year-old. When deaf students eventually leave school, three in four are unable to read a newspaper. Only two deaf children in a hundred (compared with forty in a hundred among the general population) go on to college" (p. 40). In other studies, teachers of the deaf judged that two-thirds of their students were hard to understand or unintelligible. As Ward observes, "One in three [deaf students] drops out of high school. Only one in five who starts college gets a degree. Deaf adults make 30 percent less than the general population. Their unemployment rate is high, and when they are employed, it is usually in manual jobs such as kitchen workers, janitors, machine operators, tailors, and carpenters, for which a strong command of English is not required."

2. In response to a *60 Minutes* segment presented in fall 1992 highlighting the accomplishments of seven-year-old Caitlin Parton, a beneficiary of implant technology, DEAF activists charged that implants were "child abuse," "pathological," and "genocide" (Dolnick, "Deafness as Culture," p. 43).

3. Northeastern University linguist Harlan Lane and other defenders of DEAF culture challenge the success rate of implants and argue that deaf children should learn the language that comes natural to them—ASL. To assume that medical specialists know better than deaf parents what is best for their deaf children is, he notes, the height of arrogance. See Harlan Lane and M. Grodin, "Ethical Issues in Cochlear Implant Surgery: An Exploration into Disease, Disability, and the Best Interests of the Child," *Kennedy Institute of Ethics Journal* 7, no. 3 (1997): 231–51.

4. Cf. Chief Justice Warren Burger's Supreme Court ruling in *Wisconsin v. Yoder* (1972) upholding the right of the Amish to limit their children's formal education to eight years on the grounds that sending them to high school would expose them to a "worldly" influence in conflict with maintaining their "Amish way of life." For a summary account and critique of this decision, see John Arthur, *The Unfinished Constitution: Philosophy and Constitutional Practice* (Belmont, Calif.: Wadsworth, 1989), pp. 142ff. In an earlier landmark case (in re *Gault* [1967]), the Supreme Court recognized that neither the Fourteenth Amendment nor the Bill of Rights applies solely to adults alone. Thus, when children have been committed to mental health facilities against their own wishes or have been subjected to life-restricting (or life-endangering) medical treatments (or the refusal of such treatments, including abortion), government agencies have overridden parental wishes on the grounds that such decisions severely endanger or restrict the life and freedom of the child. Similar arguments could apply in the case of parental decisions restricting the educational opportunities and physical capacities of deaf children.

5. Dolnick, "Deafness as Culture," p. 46. On June 21, 1999, the Supreme Court ruled in a 7 to 2 decision that persons with correctable physical impairments, including deafness, do not suffer a disability (defined as a "substantial limitation to a major life activity") entitling them under the Americans with Disabilities Act to anti-discrimination protection against unfavorable hiring and retainment decisions. Henceforth, whatever employment discrimination befalls congenitally deaf children who might have benefited from cochlear implants had their parents not refused them this treatment will no longer be clearly illegal.

6. "Those born deaf deride those who become deaf six or twelve years later . . . ASL-users who do not use lip movements scorn those who sign with mouthed English," notes Gallaudet psychologist Larry Stewart (Dolnick, "Deafness as Culture,"p. 53).

7. Cued speech uses eight hand signals to help deaf persons distinguish words (like "bat" and "pan") that look alike when read from lip movements. Total communication, the method favored at most schools for the deaf, combines speech, writing, ASL, and finger spelling. DEAF proponents, by contrast, favor a bilingual-bicultural approach in which English is taught as a second language. Needless to say, all of these approaches have limited success in bridging the deaf-hearing divide; see Dolnick, "Deafness as Culture," p. 48ff).

8. Excerpt from *Domination et colonisation* (1910), trans. and reprinted in Philip D. Curtin, ed., *Imperialism* (New York: Walker, 1971), pp. 294–98. Also cited in Charles Mills, *The Racial Contract* (Ithaca: Cornell University Press, 1998), p. 25.

9. E. B. Tylor, *Researches into the Early History of Mankind and the Development of Civilization* (1878; reprint, Chicago: Chicago University Press, 1964; Ruth Benedict, *Patterns of Culture* (1934; reprint, Boston: L. Houghton Mifflin, 1989); Franz Boas, *The Mind of Primitive Man* (New York: Macmillan, 1938).

10. Non-Europeans have also appealed to race in justifying their superiority. The Japanese, for example, have long considered themselves a superior "race" with re-

spect to the Ainu in their own country. Beginning in the 1930s, Japanese propagandists argued that white and black races were inferior to the yellow races, of which they above all others exemplified. One Japanese policy statement dating from World War II (entitled *An Investigation of Global Policy with the Yamato Race as Nucleus*) actually outlines the racial caste system—based on "natural" racial hierarchies and maintained by eugenics—that the "victorious" Japanese would have imposed on their Pacific empire. This virulent form of racism, however, was not entirely home-grown; it both responded to preexisting Eurocentric racism and mimicked the latter's ideology of colonial empire. Cf. John W. Dower, *War Without Mercy: Race and Power in the Pacific War* (New York: Pantheon Books, 1986), pp. 262–90.

11. The unavoidably coercive nature of any process of adolescent acculturation need not render a culture illegitimate, so long as such acculturation enables the maturation of capacities for free rational choice later on in life.

12. According to the Mayan leader and Nobel Prize winner Rigoberta Menchú, "The justification for our struggle was to erase all the images imposed on us, all the cultural differences, and the ethnic barriers, so that we Indians might understand each other in spite of different ways of expressing our religion and beliefs. Our culture is still the same. I discovered that all Indians have a common culture in spite of linguistic barriers, ethnic barriers, and different modes of dress. The basis of our culture is maize" (*I Rigoberta Menchú: An Indian Woman in Guatemala*, ed. and intro. by Elisabeth Burgos-Debray, trans. Ann Wright [London: Verso, 1984]), p. 169.

13. This, at any rate, has been my personal experience working in Guatemala with representatives from different Mayan and refugee groups.

14. See Judith Butler, *Gender Trouble: Feminism and the Subversion of Identity* (New York: Routledge, 1990). Most doctors view the thirty different varieties of intersex condition as birth defects meriting surgical correction on the assumption that people must be clearly male or female to function in our society. Interestingly, since John Money's experiments with intersex children in the early sixties, standard medical opinion has (at least until recently) converged with Butler's own view that sexual and gender identity are more a product of socialization (voluntary and involuntary construction) than biology. That thesis is now being challenged by Milton Diamond and other reproductive biologists. Customarily, genetically male babies born with androgen insensitivity syndrome (AIS), a condition in which the body's cells cannot absorb male sex hormones, and genetically female babies born with congenital adrenal hyperplasia (CAH), a disorder in which the fetus overproduces male hormones, have both been surgically assigned female genitalia on the assumption that being a male with an abnormal or nonexistent penis is psychologically intolerable for most males. Recent studies, however, show that surgically corrected AIS females are often sexually attracted to other females, suggesting to some researchers that male genetic dispositions outweigh female socialization patterns in the determination of sexual identity. CAH females also confirm the powerful impact of biology on sexual orientation, since most of them are attracted to other females as well. Today, many intersex adults refuse to categorize themselves as simply male or female, heterosexual or homosexual, but instead regard themselves as sexually complex. In keeping with this view, many pediatricians are now heeding the advice of the Intersex Society of America to refrain from performing corrective surgery (unless required for health reasons) until intersex children are old enough to decide their own sexual fate. See "In Intersex Cases Gender Is a Complex Question," *Chicago Tribune*, June 20, 1999, pp. 1 and 9.

15. Will Kymlicka, *Multicultural Citizenship* (Oxford: Oxford University Press, 1995), p. 76.

16. A federal task force has recently recommended that respondents be allowed to check more than one category, even while it rejected the addition of a new category, "multicultural," as being hopelessly vague, confusing, and useless for policy planning.

17. William Julius Wilson, *The Truly Disadvantaged* (Chicago: University of Chicago Press, 1990); excerpted in Rita C. Manning and René Trujillo, eds., *Social Justice in a Diverse Society* (Mountain View, Calif.: Mayfield, 1996), p. 156.

18. Ibid., p. 157.

19. Cf. Glen Loury, "The Need for Moral Leadership in the Black Community," *New Perspectives* 16 (Summer 1984): 14–19.

20. Wilson, *Social Justice in a Diverse Society*, p. 164.

21. Conservatives like Lawrence Mead argue that the problem of nonwhite unemployment is *not* lack of jobs but a high turnover rate caused by the poor's impatience with working menial jobs that pay little. In his opinion, their search for better employment is undisciplined because they wish to forgo the burden of what it takes to get better jobs: acquiring skills, arranging child care, finding jobs, and so forth. While there may be some truth to Mead's diagnosis of poor minorities' negative attitudes toward menial work (after centuries of doing menial work for white men, it is understandable that blacks might loathe these jobs), his own solution to the problem of nonwhite unemployment is seriously flawed. Contrary to Mead's view, there are few economically viable jobs in the ghetto, and scaling back welfare payments in favor of mandatory work fare does not discourage welfare dependence. As Wilson notes, "The greatest rise in black joblessness and female-headed families occurred during the very period (1972–80) when the real value of AFDC plus food stamps plummeted because states did not peg benefit levels to inflation" (*Social Justice in a Diverse Society*, p. 165). See Lawrence M. Mead, *Beyond Entitlement: The Social Obligations of Citizenship* (New York: Free Press, 1986), pp. 73, 80, and Michael Sosin's critical review of *Beyond Entitlement* in *Social Service Review* 61 (March 1987): 156–57.

22. Stephen Steinberg, *Turning Back: The Retreat from Racial Justice in American Thought and Policy* (Boston: Beacon Press, 1995), pp. 142–55, 195–98, for example, cites Norman Fainstein's data showing that blacks were never heavily represented in the industrial sector as Wilson suggests, and that blacks have encountered occupational discrimination at all levels of employment. As for the migration of the black middle class from the ghetto and its integration into businesses and professions, he notes (following the research of Sharon Collins and others) that black entrepeneurs and professionals continue to work and reside in or around urban ghettos, that they mainly serve black clientele, and that educated blacks are typically hired to mediate between white corporations and black communities. Educated blacks, he adds, are also segregated into marginalized, dead-end positions with little power and job security; those who are luckier are almost entirely concentrated in government employment (which, however, also evinces considerable race-based occupational segregation). Also see Norman Fainstein, "The Underclass/Mismatch Hypothesis as an Explanation for Black Economic Deprivation," *Politics and Society* 15 (1986–1987): 379–80; and Sharon Collins, *The Making and Breaking of a Black Middle Class* (Philadelphia: Temple University Press, 1997).

23. This point is forcefully argued by Hans-Georg Gadamer in *Truth and Method* (New York: Seabury Press, 1975). For my critique of Gadamer's account of interpretation, see *Reason, History, and Politics: The Communitarian Grounds of Legitimacy in the Modern Age* (Albany: State University of New York Press, 1995), pp. 130–33.

24. Alasdair MacIntyre, *Whose Justice? Which Rationality?* (Notre Dame: University of Notre Dame Press, 1988), p. 398. For my critique of MacIntyre's account of cross-cultural translation, see *Reason, History, and Politics*, pp. 127–30.

25. For a discussion of power and domination, see Michel Foucault, "The Subject of Power," in *Critical Theory: The Essential Readings*, ed. David Ingram and Julia Simon-Ingram (New York: Paragon House, 1991), pp. 310–19.

26. The question of whether communication can be unconstrained by the effects of power and domination was the subject of a famous debate between Jürgen Habermas and Michel Foucault. See my discussion of this debate in *Reason, History, and Politics*, pp. 178ff.

27. Cf. Ofelia Schutte, *Cultural Identity and Social Liberation in Latin American Thought* (Albany: State University of New York Press, 1993), especially chapter 2.

28. Matthew Arnold, *Culture and Anarchy*, ed. Samuel Lipman (New Haven: Yale University Press, 1994), p. 95. Also cited in Anthony Appiah and Amy Gutmann, eds., *Color Consciousness: The Political Morality of Race* (Princeton: Princeton University Press, 1996), p. 58.

29. For a defense of moderate patriotism (and moderate racial identification) compatible with the views expressed here, see Stephen Nathanson, *Patriotism, Morality, and Peace* (Totowa, N.J: Rowman and Littlefield, 1993), "Is Patriotism Like Racism?" *APA Newsletter* 91, no. 2 (Fall 1992): 9–12, and "Race, Racism, and Racial Loyalty: A Reply to Steve Martinot," *APA Newsletter* 95, no. 1 (Fall 1995). For a critque of Nathanson, see Paul Gomberg, "Patriotism is like Racism," *Ethics* 101 (1990): 144–50.

30. John Rawls, "The Law of Peoples," *Critical Inquiry* 20 (1993): 36–68, and Jürgen Habermas, *Inclusion of the Other* (Cambridge, Mass.: MIT Press, 1998), have each sketched distinctive models for conceiving Kant's vision of a federation of constitutional republics under the rule of law. For Rawls, the kind of overlapping consensus requisite for maintaining a global rule of law would not necessarily require that each state adopt democratic institutions; for Habermas, it would.

5. LIBERALISM AND THE RIGHT OF
INDIGENOUS PEOPLES TO SELF-GOVERNANCE

1. For example, Rigoberta Menchú explicitly criticizes biological theories of race based on blood descent and ridicules Ladinos (the offspring of Spanish and Indians who speak Spanish), who rank themselves according to the purity of their Spanish blood. She herself equates "being Indian" with living in accordance with the traditions of one's Indian forebears. (*I Rigoberta Menchú: An Indian Woman in Guatemala*, ed. and intro. by Elisabeth Burgos-Debray, trans. Ann Wright [London: Verso, 1984], p. 167). Menchú's account is also in keeping with the well-known Native American practice of adopting "whites" into the tribe.

2. Ibid., pp. 170–71.

3. Middlebury College anthropologist David Stoll has recently challenged the accuracy of Menchú's claims about her father's meager landholdings, her brother's brutal execution in the central square of Chajul, and her own lack of education at an early age. For her part, Menchú declared in 1997 that the autobiography she dictated to Burgos-Debray contained so many editorial distortions (and provided her with so few profits) that she felt it did "not belong to me morally, politically, or economically." More recently, Menchú modified some of the biographical details of her earlier account in *Crossing Borders: An Autobiography* (London: Verso, 1998). Missing

in this exchange is the fact that Stoll acknowledges the accuracy of most of Menchú's story, and that his own "fact-finding" methods (interviewing frightened Mayans in public places with the use of translators) are highly questionable. Also missing is the political aim of Stoll's book: to demolish Menchú's vision of her people as having a distinctively premodern Mayan identity prevailing above and beyond their local linguistic and community attachments, which they were willing to defend independently of any political coaxing by outside agitators and urban revolutionaries. Cf. David Stoll, *Rigoberta Menchú and the Story of All Poor Guatemalans* (Boulder, Colo.: Westview Press, 1998), and Hal Cohen's insightful diagnosis of the controversy, "The Unmaking of Rigoberta Menchú: An Anthropologist Takes on a Legend—and Puts His Own Reputation on the Line," *Lingua Franca* (July–August, 1999): 48–55.

4. *I Rigoberta Menchú*, p. 205.

5. Ibid., p. 15.

6. Ibid., p. 67.

7. Ibid., pp. 8, 166, and 167.

8. Ibid., p. 49.

9. Ibid., pp. 221–23.

10. *Acuerdo sobre Identidad y Derechos de los Pueblos Indígenas: Suscrito en la Ciudad de Mexico por el Gobierno de Guatemala y La Unidad Revolucionaria Nacional Guatemalteca (31 de Marzo de 1995)*, Art. IV.E.3 (p. 23). On May 16, 1999, the popular referendum held to ratify multicultural provisions of the treaty was defeated, along with fifty other amendments to the constitution concerning electoral and judicial reforms. Interestingly, in a vote marked by extreme political cynicism (barely 18 percent of the registered voters cast ballots), all but one of the departments heavily populated by Indians (the department of Quiché) voted in favor of it.

11. Ibid., Art. I.

12. Ibid., Art. IV.F.3-7.

13. Ibid., Art. III.1.

14. Ibid., Art. IV.E.1-6.

15. Michael Walzer, *On Toleration* (New Haven: Yale University Press, 1997).

16. Ibid., p. 23.

17. John Stuart Mill, *Considerations on Representative Government,* reprinted in *John Stuart Mill: Three Essays,* ed. Richard Wollheim (Oxford: Oxford University Press, 1981), p. 385.

18. Ibid., p. 382

19. Charles Taylor, "A World Consensus on Human Rights?" *Dissent* 43, no. 3 (Summer 1996): 15–21.

20. The Supreme Court's decision to let Georgia's antisodomy statute stand in *Bowers v. Hardwick* (1985) reinforced the secondhand citizenship of gay couples in many regions of the United States.

21. The most obvious exceptions to this rule are the large concentrations of Latin American immigrants in Chicago, Miami, New York, Los Angeles, and Houston. Retaining close ties to their countries of origin (maintained by close geographical proximity), they often feel less compelled to assimilate than Asian Americans (who also feel linguistically and culturally estranged from the dominant Anglo culture). Subsequently, their demands for political representation (limited political sovereignty) in the eighties has led to the creation of a number of Latino-majority municipal, state, and federal voting districts.

22. Of course, some immigrants also support bilingualism as a way of transmitting their native language to their children.

23. Joseph Carens, "Dimensions of Citizenship and National Identity in Canada," *Philosophical Forum* 28, nos. 1–2 (Fall–Winter 1996–97): 111–24.

24. Ibid., p. 118.

25. The following account is based on Ward Churchill's synopsis of treaty history in "Perversions of Justice: Examining the Doctrine of U.S. Rights to Occupancy in North America," in *Radical Philosophy of Law*, ed. David S. Caudill and Steven Jay Gold (Atlantic Highlands, N.J.: Humanities Press, 1995), pp. 200–220.

26. Locke is inconsistent on the property rights of Indians. In chapter 5, paragraph 26, of the *Second Treatise of Government*, reprinted in *John Locke: Two Treatises of Government*, ed. Peter Laslett (New York: New American Library, 1965), he observes that the "wild Indian, who knows no inclosure . . . is still a tenant in common" of tribal hunting and foraging grounds; and, having "mixed his labor" in "the fruit or venison" located on these grounds, shares an exclusive property right to these grounds, along with other members of his tribe. However, in paragraph 32 he makes land ownership dependent on an act of *private enclosure*. The implicit suggestion that Indians do not have rightful title to their common hunting and foraging grounds is corroborated by his reference to the "vacant places of *America*" (paragraph 36) and "the wild woods and uncultivated waste of America left to Nature, without any improvement, tillage, or husbandry" (paragraph 37).

27. Cited in Churchill, "Perversions of Justice," in Caudill and Gold, *Radical Philosophy of Law*, p. 205.

28. Adolf Hitler, *Hitler's Secret Book* (New York: Grove Press, 1961), pp. 44–48.

29. The organization Women of All Red Nations (WARN) estimated that upwards of 42 percent of all native women of childbearing age had been sterilized without their consent by 1972, a statistic whose accuracy was later supported by a GAO study of 3,406 sterilizations that had been performed over a three-year period in just four hospitals. See M. Annette Jaimes and Theresa Halsey, "American Indian Women: At the Center of Indigenous Resistance in Contemporary North America," in *Dangerous Liaisons: Gender, Nation, and Postcolonial Perspectives*, ed. Anne McClintock, Aamir Mufti, and Ella Shohat, vol. 11 of *Cultural Politics* (Minneapolis: University of Minnesota Press, 1997), pp. 298–328, esp. p. 312.

30. According to one report, "since 1988, when Congress passed the Indian Gaming Regulatory Act, about 200 tribes have entered the field [of gambling]. Revenues have grown from $570 million in 1990 to $7 billion last year, representing about 10 percent of legalized gambling in America. Some tribes have done well for themselves with gambling, yet a 1996 GAO report found that tribal governments received only about one third of post-prize revenues from their casinos, and much of that money is hoarded by Indian elites" (Ken Silverstein, "Cashing In: An Annotated Guide to Indian Gambling," *The Nation* [July, 6, 1998]: pp. 20–21).

31. The Supreme Court recently upheld the right of the Skokomish and Elwha Klallam tribes in Washington State to harvest 50 percent of the salmon and shellfish from their former fishing areas (now converted to private property). The legal battle between the tribes and the property's current tenants was solved by allowing the tribes to enter the property five days a year to satisfy their quotas (*Chicago Tribune*, July 5, 1998, sec. 1, p. 5).

32. The Muckleshoot Indians of Enumclaw, Washington, have recently suspended construction of their 20,000-seat amphitheater in the face of opposition from surrounding communities, who claim that the theater will clog traffic, attract

unruly crowds, and spoil the rural charm of this western Washington hamlet.

33. The Goshute tribe of Skull Valley, Utah, are encountering resistance from state authorities to their proposal to build a waste dump for radioactive materials on their reservation, despite the fact that the area is already home to four such facilities, all run by state and federal agencies.

34. The strongest opposition to tribal immunity comes from Republican senator Slade Gorton of Washington, who in 1997 introduced legislation that would end such immunity.

35. Thanks to this ruling, former governor Pete Wilson of California signed a compact on April 25, 1998, with the Pala Band of the Mission Indians that allows them to purchase up to 199 slot machines. Since then, he has threatened to confiscate the slot machines of other tribes if they do not sign on to the compact within sixty days. Although Wilson's proposal would allow each tribe to acquire up to 975 machines by purchasing other tribes' allocations, it would create bidding wars between tribes in which the more powerful would win. For California Indians, Wilson's plan stands in direct violation of the IGRA (which requires that compacts be negotiated on a tribe-by-tribe basis) and reflects the "sign or starve" mentality of the land expropriation treaties Native Americans were forced to sign in the 1800s.

36. The interesting case involving Russell Means (a Sioux actor, activist, and cofounder of the American Indian Movement [AIM] who led the 1973 uprising at Wounded Knee, South Dakota) might well decide whether tribes can continue to claim judicial sovereignty. Means, who is accused of beating his father-in-law in 1997 in Arizona's Navajo Nation, is standing trial before the Navajo Supreme Court (recently convened at Harvard University in February 1999). Although federal law now permits Indian tribes to prosecute nonmember Indians, the law contradicts a U.S. Supreme Court ruling delivered a year before the law was passed. Appealing to this latter ruling, Means argues that his right to equal protection will be violated if the Navajo Supreme Court is allowed jurisdiction over his case, since this court will be partial toward his father-in-law. Advocates for Navajo sovereignty, however, argue that with intermarriage and intermingling—as well as violent crime—on the rise, tribal officials need more control over their territories.

37. In Canadian law, Section 37 of the Indian Act of 1876 declares that such lands are "for the use and benefit in common" of the tribe and can therefore only be sold, alienated, or leased by it collectively.

38. For a discussion of the sorts of misunderstandings that frequently arise in the context of education, see Carol Locust, "Wounding the Spirit: Discrimination and Traditional American Indian Belief Systems," in *Social Justice in a Diverse Society*, ed. Rita C. Manning and René Trujillo (Mountain View, Calif.: Mayfield, 1996), pp. 313–24.

39. Leslie Green, "Internal Minorities and Their Rights," in *The Rights of Minority Cultures*, ed. Will Kymlicka (Oxford: Clarendon Press, 1995), p. 264.

40. Chandran Kukathas, "Are There any Cultural Rights?" in Kymlicka, *The Rights of Minority Cultures*, p. 242. In 1967, Senate hearings were held to determine whether a special exemption to the Bill of Rights would be granted to the New Mexican Indian Pueblos. Unlike other Native American cultures, Pueblo culture is quasi-theocratic; tribal leaders are elected by elder religious figures; government is run by consensus; and anyone who benefits from communal property, such as threshing machines, must participate in communal religious rites. Protestant dissidents who refused to participate in such rites were subsequently ostracized from social affairs and denied use of these machines. Interpreting this response as a violation of equal pro-

tection under the law, the Senate denied the Pueblos their exemption. Cf. Frances Svensson, "Liberal Democracy and Group Rights: The Legacy of Individualism and Its Impact on American Indian Tribes," *Political Studies* 27, no. 3 (1979): 421–39.

41. Green, "Internal Minorities and Their Rights," in Kymlicka, *The Rights of Minority Cultures,* p. 270.

42. Kymlicka's half-hearted defense of group rights is reflected in his incoherent belief that illiberal national minorities who deny equal educational opportunities to girls, require young women to undergo genital mutilation, and suppress dissident subminorities should not be forceably compelled to change, even though they have no right to legitimate protection, but instead should be encouraged to change through rational persuasion. As G. Doppelt, "Is There a Multicultural Liberalism?" *Inquiry* 41 (1994): 234–36, notes, Kymlicka's suggestion (see *Multicultural Citizenship,* [Oxford: Oxford University Press, 1995], pp. 165–67) that nonintervention in these cases is analogous to nonintervention in cases involving illiberal nation-states ignores the fact that subnationalities do not enjoy the same unlimited legal jurisdiction over their members that nation-states have hitherto been accorded (with the recent NATO intervention in Serbia having shown just how limited even that jurisdiction is). Indeed, allowing illiberal groups to oppress subgroups goes against the grain of the liberal argument Kymlicka gives in support of granting groups special rights in the first place, namely that doing so protects cultural practices that are freedom-enhancing for all their practitioners.

43. Will Kymlicka, *Liberalism, Community, and Culture* (Oxford: Oxford University Press, 1989), p. 198.

44. Jaimes and Halsey, "American Indian Women," in McClintock, Mufti, and Shohat, p. 304.

45. Ibid., p. 303.

46. See Eleanor Burke Leacock, "Montagnais Women and the Jesuit Program for Colonization," in *Myths of Male Dominance: Collected Articles* (New York: Monthly Review Press, 1981), pp. 43–62, and Paula Gunn Allen, *The Sacred Hoop: Recovering the Feminine in American Indian Traditions* (Boston: Beacon Press, 1986), p. 40.

47. Jaimes and Halsey, "American Indian Women," in McClintock, Mufti, and Shohat, *Dangerous Liaisons,* p. 308.

48. Doppelt, "Is There a Multicultural Liberalism?" p. 236.

49. In contrast to liberalism, which views democracy as a contest for power between competing factions and political interests, native cultures view democracy as a form of power-sharing oriented toward doing what is best for the community. Whereas the former sanctions majority rule subject to the protection of minority rights, the latter sanctions a process of consensus-building in which everyone is supposed to win.

50. Evangelical Native Americans inhabiting tribal reservations could voluntarily agree to stop proselytizing and to conceal their religious services in exchange for full tribal membership and tolerance.

### 6. Citizenship and the Rights of Immigrants

1. In 1854 the California Supreme Court ruled in *People v. Hall* that new Chinese immigrants were to be officially classified as "Indians." See Michael Peter Smith and Joe R. Feagin, eds., *The Bubbling Cauldon: Race, Ethnicity, and the Urban Crisis* (Minneapolis: University of Minnesota Press, 1995), p. 7.

2. Cf. Vernon M. Briggs, "Immigration Policy and the U.S. Economy," *Journal of Economic Issues* 30, no. 2 (June 1, 1996): 379ff.

3. The percentage of foreign-born adults (twenty-five years and older) who had less than a ninth grade education was 25 percent compared to 10 percent for native-born Americans; however, the percentage of foreign-born adults with college graduate degrees was 3.8 percent versus 2.4 percent for native-born Americans.

4. George J. Borjas, "The Economics of Immigration," *Journal of Economic Literature* 23, no. 4 (December 1994): 1667–1717.

5. Cf. Ana Mendieta, "Restricciones a la inmigracion," *Exito* (March 28, 1996): 3.

6. A recent Roper survey showed that 70 percent of all Americans supported limiting annual immigration to less than 300,000 (among registered Republicans the percentage is 95 percent). Cf. Roy Beck, "Republicans Against Reform," *National Review* 48, no. 6 (April 8, 1996): 21–22. Despite public furor over the number of women who immigrate illegally in order to bear children in the United States or who immigrate in order to receive public assistance for the children they already have, a recent study of Hispanic women in California hospitals shows that, among these women, probably no more than one in sixteen immigrates in order to acquire citizenship status for their children, while only one in seven do so to acquire benefits for children born outside the United States. See Peter Brimelow, *Alien Nation: Common Sense About America's Immigration Disaster* (New York: Random House, 1975).

7. In truth, both Republicans and Democratics were divided on the issue of immigration reform. Libertarian-minded Republicans representing business interests supported a lax immigration policy while their nativist and protectionist counterparts, spearheaded by Pat Buchanan and Lamar Smith, did not. Opinion within the Democratic Party was split as well, with labor leaders, civil rights activists, and environmentalists supporting restrictive immigration policy and ethnic democrats mainly opposing it. See Lowell Sachs, "Treacherous Waters in Turbulent Times: Navigating the Recent Sea Change in U.S. Immigration Policy and Attitudes," *Social Justice* 23, no. 3 (Fall 1996): 125ff.

8. The Immigration Act of 1990 actually increased the ceiling of immigration from 500,000 to 675,000; while it sought to reduce the number of unskilled laborers, it permitted entry of 140,000 immigrants who made special contributions to the economy and reserved 65,000 slots for workers with "specialty occupations," who then could qualify for six-year H-1B visas.

9. These statistics appear in *Migration World Magazine* 24, nos. 1–2 (February 1997): 42–44.

10. INS interviewers read the following statement to persons with insufficient documentation: "U.S. law provides protection to certain persons who face persecution, harm, or torture upon their return to their home country. If you fear, or have a concern about, being removed from the United States or about being sent home, you should tell me so during this interview because you may not have another chance." Critics of the INS procedure claim that it intimidates some persons, especially if they come from countries with repressive regimes. As of July 1997, only 5 percent of the 14,400 immigrants processed according to this procedure have been granted formal hearings about their fear of returning to their country. Cf. Vincent J. Schodolski, "New INS Rules Worry Immigrant-Rights Advocates," *Chicago Tribune*, July 10, 1997.

11. Public Law 104-193; 110 Stat. 2105 (August 22, 1996).

12. Legal immigrants and their children can still take advantage of the Job Training Partnership Act of 1982 (sec. 403[c]) and the Head Start program (sec. 505).

However, selected postsecondary educational grants will no longer be available to them.

13. Under section 403(c) of the welfare reform law, legal immigrants will still be eligible for emergency medical assistance, emergency disaster relief, certain child nutrition prorams, foster care and adoption assistance, and student assistance programs (Head Start, federal job training, and so forth). They also will be eligible for more local types of aid, much of it charitable, in the form of clothing, food, shelter, and medical aid as well as the usual forms of police, fire, sanitation, and transportation services.

14. Section 435 stipulates that these quarterly contributions include the contributions of both spouses and parents (prior to the applicant's eighteenth birthday).

15. At least twelve states—including Texas, California, New York, Illinois, and Florida—are using their own tax revenues for compensating children, the elderly, and disabled immigrants for losses in medicaid coverage, SSI benefits, food stamps, and cash assistance.

16. Michael Walzer, *Spheres of Justice: A Defense of Pluralism and Equality* (New York: Basic Books, 1983), pp. 37–38.

17. Ibid., p. 36.

18. Ibid., p. 38.

19. By contrast, Canada's admissions policy, which stresses economic contribution, favors applicants who are young, reasonably affluent, and college-educated, regardless of whether they are related to Canadian nationals.

20. Walzer, *Spheres of Justice*, p. 41.

21. John Rawls, *A Theory of Justice* (Cambridge: Harvard University Press, 1971), p. 115.

22. Ibid., p. 33.

23. Ancient Athens, for instance, embodied what many people have regarded as the highest level of participatory democracy and cultural achievement ever attained; yet the benefits of this achievement, which mainly accrued to male citizens, depended on slavery, the exploitation of foreign laborers *(metics)*, the domination of women, and imperialism.

24. Joseph Carens, "Aliens and Citizens: The Case for Open Borders," in *The Rights of Minority Cultures*, ed. Will Kymlicka (Oxford: Clarendon Press, 1996).

25. I discuss this point further in Chapter 11.

26. It is sometimes argued that rights violations only occur when persons undertake some action that directly harms someone else. On this view, refraining from acting—for example, by refusing to help someone who is drowning or starving to death when it is within one's capacity to do so—does not involve the commission of a crime or rights violation. Against this view I would argue that "omissions" are themselves "commissions." For example, there need be no morally relevant distinction between knowingly refraining from providing food assistance to anonymous starving persons in a foreign country and knowingly sending them poisoned food. In both situations, the agent can behave in a way that he or she knows will likely result in the death of another person. Furthermore, in some instances—say, in situations involving natural famine and political anarchy—the principal responsibility for saving lives *and* the principal cause for letting them die may devolve upon foreign strangers (or their respective governmental and nongovernmental agents) rather than upon the immediate kin and consociates of the victims. Admittedly, this approach presupposes that persons can incur responsibility for maintaining the lives of others even if they have not voluntarily assumed such responsibility—an assumption that, at first glance,

seems to extend our obligations to others in ways that are unacceptably indeterminate and indefinite. However, while our strong obligations to others are not wholly indeterminate and indefinite, they are not always easily discernible, often requiring a great deal of information regarding context-specific factors concerning the causes of life-endangering conditions and their most direct and effective remedies. For further discussion of this problem, see Chapter 11 and note 27 below.

27. The principle of mutual aid, as distinct from the principle of impartial justice, is typically interpreted as a principle of charity (the so-called "Good Samaritan" principle). While failure to fully do one's duty as a Good Samaritan may convict a person of being uncharitable, selfish, and otherwise morally vicious, it cannot convict him or her of being unjust or of violating the basic rights of others. Once we assume that persons can involuntarily assume responsibility for the lives of others—for example, by innocently benefiting from unjust economic arrangements that endanger their lives—their duty to provide aid (in whatever form) ceases to be merely a matter of virtuous charity and becomes a matter of justice. For further discussion of this point, see Chapter 11 and note 26 above.

28. One potentially problematic implication of treating natural talents and environmentally conditioned social status as "undeserved" is that one might be tempted to treat dispositions, character traits, actions (conditioned by such dispositions and traits), and consequences that flow from such actions as equally undeserved, in which case most (if not all) actions would cease being objects of blame or praise. For purposes of my argument, it suffices to classify place and family of birth as undeserved, leaving open the deserved or undeserved status of talents, dispositions, and character traits.

29. This argument appeals to the principle of marginal utility, which assumes that additional increments of a given good beyond a basic threshold yield decreasing increments of utility. For example, giving a single loaf of bread to a starving person—the difference between life and death—will be more valuable than giving him just half of a loaf. But each loaf of bread he consumes beyond the basic minimum necessary for survival will provide him with less value, so that the 100th loaf of bread he receives will mean very little in comparison to the first, life-saving one. Theoretically, an equal distribution of the world's population (combined with an equal distribution of the world's resources) could be maximally efficient (or valuable), assuming that each person's baseline survival needs were met; the decrease in value consumed by the richest 20 percent of the world's population (their being deprived of the gadgets and comforts of a luxurious, middle-class lifestyle) will be more than compensated for by the increase in value consumed by the poorest 20 percent (their being saved from starvation and severe malnutrition). Practically, of course, it is debatable whether a system (like capitalism) that produces an unequal distribution of resources improves (or maximizes) the condition of the worst-off better than any other, more egalitarian system. My own view is that the most efficient—if not perfectly egalitarian—distribution of resources would be attained under some system of market socialism. For a defense of this view, see David Schweickart, *Against Capitalism* (Cambridge: Cambridge University Press, 1993).

30. Neo-Malthusians like Garrett Hardin criticize lax immigration policies and famine relief programs on the grounds that equalizing access to vital resources will promote unsustainable population growth leading to economic and environmental crises. Developmentalists like myself disagree; sustainable economic development abroad (including the provision of social and educational support systems) removes the primary incentive for immigrating *and* having large families. See Garrett Hardin,

"Living on a Lifeboat," in *Managing the Commons*, ed. G. Hardin and John Baden (San Francisco: W. H. Freeman, 1977), pp. 261–79, and note 29 above.

31. For the importance of democracy in procuring basic rights to subsistence and security, see Chapter 11.

32. Utilitarianism (the doctrine that equates justice with maximizing the overall well-being of the most people) has sometimes been invoked to support the view that human lives can be expended for the sake of perfecting a civilized way of life. According to this argument, overall well-being is best achieved by satisfying the "highest," spiritual needs of "cultivated" persons—those involving the enjoyment of art, literature, intellectual achievement, the contemplation of unsullied nature, and the like—even if it means sacrificing the lives of "uncultivated" persons. Utilitarianism informed by marginalist thinking would reject this argument on the grounds that additional increments of utility (food, shelter, culture, and so on) beyond a basic threshold yield progressively diminishing returns of satisfaction. Therefore, equalizing living conditions for all persons, which is what unrestricted immigration encourages, might well be the best way for maximizing the greatest happiness for the greatest number. Cf. note 29.

33. Carens, "Aliens and Citizens," in Kymlicka, *The Rights of Minority Cultures*, p. 344.

34. For further discussion of this point, see Chapter 11.

35. The United Nations Development Program's *Human Development Report* for 1999 notes that 20 percent of the world's population inhabiting the richest countries receive 86 percent of the world's income, 82 percent of its exports, and 68 percent of foreign direct investment, while those inhabiting the poorest 20 percent barely receive 1 percent of each. The combined incomes of the richest 20 percent are almost seventy-four times greater than those of the bottom 20 percent. Indeed, the three richest officers of Microsoft—Bill Gates, Paul Allen, and Steve Ballmar—have more assets than the combined gross national product of the forty-three least-developed countries and their 600 million inhabitants. While the two hundred richest people have more than doubled their income between 1994 and 1998, half of the world's countries have seen their citizens' per capita incomes fall below where they were ten or twenty years ago (in sub-Saharan Africa, per capita income has fallen from $661 in 1980 to $518 in 1999). As for the concentration of power, the report notes that ten countries (including the United States) account for 84 percent of global research and development spending and control 95 percent of all patents. The top ten corporations control 86 percent of telecommunications, 85 percent of pesticides, 70 percent of computers, and 60 percent of veterinary products. These figures were cited in the lead story of the *Chicago Tribune*, July 12, 1999.

36. My own view, which I cannot defend here, is that the best alternative to the system currently in place would be a global economy combining regulated markets, communal control of productive assets, democratically structured workplaces and profit sharing, and international democratic federations ensuring equitable, environmental development for all countries. Cf. note 29 above and Chapter 11.

37. Even Cubans, who once were automatically admitted as political refugees, are now routinely denied entry to the United States and returned to Cuba on the grounds that they are "only" economic refugees. But these refugees, most of whom suffer less economic deprivation than many inhabitants of our own cities, are fleeing economic hardships that are at least partly created by the U.S. trade embargo against Cuba (in place since 1962). As of May 20, 1999, the Nicaraguan Adjustment and Central American Relief Act of 1997 (NACARA) was changed so that Salvadorans

and Guatemalans living in the United States for seven years could also suspend deportation proceedings by showing that returning them to their country of citizenship gravely endangers their lives. Specifically, the new rules presume that most Salvadorans and Guatemalans would suffer from extreme penury as a result of economic and social devastation wrought by armed conflict if forceably returned to their native countries. The changes, however, do not exempt from deportation the children of Salvadorans and Guatemalans who entered the United States within the last seven years. To rectify this problem, the Clinton administration is expected to support legislation backed by Representative Luis Gutierrez that would enable immigrants from Guatemala, Honduras, Haiti, and El Salvador who entered the United States by December 1995 eligible for permanent residency.

38. American agribusiness played no small role in converting vast labor-intensive farming operations in Mexico into mechanized ones, thereby throwing out of work hundreds of thousands of campesinos.

## 7. Affirmative Action and the Legacy of Racism

1. Cited in Jonathan Kozol, *Savage Inequalities: Children in America's Schools* (New York: Crown, 1991), pp. 7–8.

2. Ibid., pp. 7–9.

3. Ibid., p. 20.

4. Ibid., p. 8.

5. Ibid., p. 15.

6. Ibid., p. 18.

7. *Report of the U.S. National Advisory Commission on Civil Disorders* (New York: Bantam Books, 1968), p. 1.

8. The 1996 report issued by the Joint Center for Political and Economic Studies, a Washington group that tracks trends among African Americans, indicates that in 1995 the black teenage birth rate fell by 9 percent (17 percent since 1991), the average life expectancy for black men rose to 65.4 years (thanks in part to a 17 percent decline in the murder rate), and the median income for black households rose by 3.6 percent (higher than the 2.2 percent registered by white households), with black married couples now earning 87 percent as much as their white counterparts. The proportion of black adults, age twenty-five to twenty-nine, who have completed high school has equaled that of white adults in the same age bracket, and black students are showing more improvement than white students on the SAT verbal examination and other national tests. Although these statistics are encouraging, William Julius Wilson, a professor of social policy at the John F. Kennedy School of Government at Harvard University, notes that they largely reflect improvements in the overall economic prosperity of the country and—most important—do not count the 800,000 black men in prisons when computing unemployment and high school completion rates. Furthermore, the apparent success of blacks in comparison with whites is somewhat misleading, since Latinos—who earn and achieve considerably less than whites on average—were counted among the white population in the statistics cited. See "Quality of Life Is Up for Many Blacks, Data Show," *New York Times,* November 18, 1996, p. A13.

9. It should be noted that the poverty rate among Latinos (28 percent) is also high.

10. Cf. "Education Gap Between Races Closes," *New York Times,* September 6, 1996, p. A8. Also see Chapter 3, note 6.

11. See Tom Wicker, *Tragic Failure: Racial Integration in America* (New York: William Morrow, 1996), p. 131; Donald Kinder and Lynn Sanders, *Divided by Color: Racial Politics and Democratic Ideals* (Chicago: University of Chicago Press, 1996), p. 286.

12. A recent controlled study shows that whites are three times more likely to receive job offers than equally qualified blacks—and this despite affirmative action. The study, involving matched pairs of white and black job applicants, showed that 20 percent of the former group advanced beyond initial interviews, while only 7 percent of the latter did. Among those who advanced, whites received 15 percent more job offers than blacks, who bested their white competitors in only 5 percent of the audits. Cf. Margery Turner, Michael Fix, and Raymond Struyk, *Opportunities Denied, Opportunities Diminished: Racial Discrimination in Hiring* (Washington, D.C.: Urban Institute Press, 1991); also cited by Albert G. Mosley in A. G. Mosley and Nicholas Capaldi, *Affirmative Action: Social Justice or Unfair Preference* (Lanham, Md.: Rowman and Littlefield, 1996), p. 41. Job discrimination results in some surprising racial imbalances in occupations such as athletics in which minorities actually predominate. Although the percentage of minority coaches in *professional* baseball (14 percent), basketball (24 percent), and football (10 percent) pales in comparision with the percentage of minority athletes represented in these occupations (well over 55 percent), the percentage is even lower in the *college* ranks. The Center for the Study of Sport in Society at Northeastern University recently reported that college teams lag far behind their pro counterparts in hiring minorities. Although blacks constitute a majority of college football players (52 percent) and basketball players (61 percent), only 7 percent of all football coaches and 17 percent of all basketball coaches in Division 1-A are black (more disturbing still, only 2.4 percent of all Division 1 baseball coaches are Latino or black).

13. The practice of increasing qualifications for mortgage loans in specified (redlined) minority districts continues to be a chronic problem. A 1996 study of 561 Chicago lending institutions conducted by the nonprofit Association of Community Organizations for Reform Now (ACORN) showed that upper-income blacks were seventeen times more likely to be rejected than whites with similar incomes and were one and one-half times more likely to be denied loans than whites who earned half as much. In general, it showed that blacks were three times as likely to be turned down for loans as whites. One of the worst offenders, Marquette National Bank, has its main and branch offices located in minority and median-income white areas. It rejected loan applications from minorities ten times more frequently than those from whites. Indeed, only 1.5 percent of its loans went to minority neighborhoods (10 percent of its loans went to poor white and minority tracts, while nearly half went to affluent white suburban and city neighborhoods). These shocking results are confirmed by other studies. A 1989 study by the Federal Reserve Board of loaning practices in the Boston area showed that banks extended loans to black applicants half as often as they did to white applicants. Other studies in New York and Ohio replicated this result for less qualified white and minorities (blacks and Latinos), while showing greater parity between well-qualified applicants of all racial backgrounds. Cf. "Bank Given Poor Mark on Lending," *Chicago Tribune*, January 23, 1998; *New York Times*, July 13, 1995, p. D1; and *Columbus Dispatch*, February 14, 1995, p. 4C, which included a report by Ohio Commerce Director Nancy Chiles (the *Times* and *Dispatch* items are cited in Mosley and Capaldi, *Affirmative Action*, p. 41).

14. Studies show, for example, that black athletes are consistently paid less than similarly skilled and experienced white athletes. See Lawrence Kahn and Peter Sherer,

"Racial Differences in Professional Basketball Players' Compensation," *Journal of Labor Economics* 6 (1988): 40–61; also cited in Mosley and Capaldi, *Affirmative Action*, p. 40.

15. In 1987, the Department of Housing and Urban Development estimated that every year there were two million instances of housing discrimination against minorities. Cf. "Stepping Up the War on Discrimination," *New York Times*, November 1, 1987.

16. Ian Ayres, "Fair Driving: Gender and Race Discrimination in Retail Car Negotiations," *Harvard Law Review* 104, no. 4 (February 1991): 817–72.

17. Howard Schuman, Charlotte Steh, and Lawrence Bobo, *Racial Attitudes in America* (Cambridge: Harvard University Press, 1985), pp. 73–82; also cited by Gertrude Ezorsky, *Racism and Justice: The Case for Affirmative Action* (Ithaca: Cornell University Press, 1991), p. 13.

18. Wicker, *Tragic Failure*, p. 95.

19. For a more balanced view of poor urban communities than that given by Wilson, *The Truly Disadvantaged* (Chicago: University of Chicago Press, 1990), and one in particular that positively stresses their unique organizational strengths, see Larry Bennett and Adolph Reed Jr., "The New Face of Urban Renewal: The Near North Redevelopment Initiative and the Cabrini-Green Neighborhood," in *Without Justice for All: The New Liberalism and Our Retreat from Racial Equality*, ed. Adolph Reed (Boulder, Colo.: Westview Press, 1999), pp. 175–211. According to Bennett and Reed, Wilson's traditional view that physically concentrated poverty produces "deviant" behavior has led to the adoption of scattered housing urban renewal projects that seek to integrate low-income and middle-income households (e.g., in accordance with a 30/70 percent ratio, as in the Chicago Housing Authority's plan for Cabrini-Green). The problem with many of these plans is that they presume that physical design (low-rise and single-family low-income units scattered throughout middle-income neighborhoods) will automatically generate community esprit de corps across races and income levels, thereby altering the "deviant" behavior of poor blacks and Latinos—a presumption that has yet to be borne out.

20. Wicker, *Tragic Failure*, pp. 141–51.

21. These findings were reported in a 1996 University of Michigan School of Public Health study of Harlem, published in the *New England Journal of Medicine* (cited by Bob Herbert in the editorial section of the *New York Times*, December 2, 1996, p. A13).

22. Kinder and Sanders, *Divided by Color*, pp. 12–34.

23. Ibid., pp. 92–127.

24. Ibid., pp. 136–37.

25. Cf. Andrew Hacker, "Black Crime, White Racism," *New York Review of Books* (March 3, 1988): 36–41. Of course, the fears and suspicions that many whites direct toward blacks are recounted by nearly all blacks as almost constant parts of their daily experience of never feeling, to quote Toni Morrison, "as though I were an American" (p. 41).

26. For a thorough documentation of the overtly racist and white supremicist research sources on which Murray and Herrnstein based their conclusions, see Charles Lane, "The Tainted Sources of 'the Bell Curve'," *New York Review of Books* (December 1, 1994): 14–19. For criticisms of their selective use and interpretation of data, cf. Russell Jacoby and Naomi Glauberman, eds., *The Bell Curve Debate: History, Documents, Opinions* (New York: Random House, 1995).

27. Steven A. Drizin, "Race Does Matter in Juvenile Justice System," *Chicago Tribune*, May 13, 1999, sec. 1, p. 23.

28. The study, by Dorothy Hatsukami and Marian Fischman, appeared in the fall 1996 issue of the *Journal of the American Medical Association*. Both researchers—psychologists who specialize in drug addiction—suggest sharply reducing the disparities in cocaine sentencing from a 100 to 1 to a 2 to 1 ratio. See "Study Poses a Medical Challenge to Disparity in Cocaine Sentences," *New York Times*, November 20, 1996, pp. A1 and A11.

29. New Jersey recently attempted to forestall a federal civil rights lawsuit by negotiating a consent decree to settle allegations that state police had deployed racial profiling in pulling over an overwhelmingly disproportionate percentage of black and Latino drivers (similar consent decrees have been negotiated by police departments in Pittsburgh and Steubenville, Ohio). The ACLU has filed a civil rights lawsuit against the Illinois State Police, arguing that their policy of stopping rental vehicles and cars with license plates from six states (New York, Arizona, California, Florida, New Mexico, and Texas) is a thinly veiled justification for racial profiling (although Latinos make up just 2.7 percent of Illinois drivers, they constitute nearly one-third of all drug inspection stops). See "Report on Police Stops Adds to Fire," *Chicago Tribune*, June 9, 1999, sec. 2, p. 1.

30. See Thomas Sowell, *The Economics and Politics of Race* (New York: William Morrow, 1983), and *Civil Rights: Rhetoric or Reality?* (New York: William Morrow, 1984), especially pp. 77 and 130–31.

31. Nicholas Capaldi, "Affirmative Action: Con," in Mosley and Capaldi, *Affirmative Action*, p. 99.

32. Nancy Foner, "New Immigrants and Changing Patterns in New York City," in *New Immigrants in New York*, ed. N. Foner (New York: Columbia University Press, 1987), p. 11.

33. Ezorsky, *Racism and Justice*, p. 60, cites an unpublished manuscript by Reynolds Farley ("West Indian Success: Myth or Fact?" Population Studies Center, University of Michigan, 1987) which states that in New York City a native white male college graduate can expect to earn 50 percent more than an equally educated black male of West Indian ancestry.

34. Ezorsky, *Racism and Justice*, pp. 59–60.

35. This report comes from Kathleen Parker of the National Center for Career Strategies, cited in *Executive Edge* (August 1990).

36. "Study Finds Segregation in Cities Worse Than Scientists Imagined," *New York Times*, August 5, 1989.

37. Lester Thurow, *Generating Inequality* (New York: Basic Books, 1975), p. 197.

38. For a discussion of class-based differences in voter participation and class biases in voter registration, see Sidney Verba and Norman H. Nie, *Participation in America, Political Democracy, and Social Equality* (New York: Harper and Row, 1972), and Richard A. Cloward and Francis Fox Piven, *Why Americans Don't Vote* (New York: Pantheon, 1987).

39. During the height of desegregation efforts (between 1963 and 1971) the number of black high school principals in ten southern and border states decreased by two-thirds. Cf. John W. Smith and Bette M. Smith, "Desegregation in the South and the Demise of the Black Educator," *Journal of Social and Behavioral Sciences* 20, no. 1 (Winter 1974): pp. 33–40.

40. Jennifer L. Hochschild, "Race, Class, Power and the American Welfare State," in *Democracy and the Welfare State*, ed. Amy Gutmann (Princeton: Princeton University Press, 1989), p. 169.

41. Andrew Hacker, "Goodbye to Affirmative Action," *New York Review of Books* (July 11, 1996): 29.

42. Andrew Hacker, *Two Nations: Black and White, Separate, Hostile, Unequal* (New York: Ballantine Books, 1995), p. 118.

43. Hacker, "Goodbye to Affirmative Action," p. 27.

44. Ibid., p. 21.

45. Linda F. Wightman, "The Threat to Diversity in Legal Education: An Empirical Analysis of the Consequences of Abandoning Race as a Factor in Law School Admission Decisions," *New York University Law Review* 72 (April 1997): 1–53.

46. "Minority College Applications Rise," *Chicago Tribune,* January 29, 1998, sec. 1, p. 12. Although select minority applications to the University of California system for 1998 increased by 3 percent for blacks and about 10 percent for Native Americans and Mexican Americans after recording a two-year decline, applications from other Hispanic students continued to fall (by 3 percent), and the apparent decline in white and Asian-American applicants by about 10 percent and 2 percent respectively could not be confirmed owing to a 200 percent increase in the number of students who declined to state their ethnicity.

47. Hacker, "Goodbye to Affirmative Action," p. 25.

48. Ibid., p. 24.

49. As for the problem of competition, Hacker, "Goodbye to Affirmative Action," p. 26, mentions the suit, brought by some black-owned companies seeking a share of government contracts, against the state of Ohio for its decision to include companies owned by immigrants from India on its eligibility list for state contracts expressly set aside for beneficiaries of Ohio's affirmative action mandate. The judge ruled in favor of the state on the grounds that the affirmative action mandate indirectly included immigrants from India among its beneficiaries since it expressly targeted "Orientals" as well as blacks.

50. Using academic criteria alone, Asians would have constituted 51.1 percent of all students admitted to UCLA in 1994; with affirmative action, they in fact constituted only 42.2 percent—a large percentage when one considers that Asians make up only about 7 percent of California's population. Despite their overrepresentation in the University of California's student body, many believe that Asians have been discriminated against by the admissions officers of that institution and its Ivy League counterparts. Statistics for 1984 showed that Asians were admitted to these campuses at a rate of only 82 percent of that of comparably qualified whites. Noting that both whites and Asians experienced somewhat lower admission rates due to affirmative action policies, administrators at these schools nonetheless denied that such policies were to blame for the discrepancy between white and Asian admission rates. Instead, they pointed out that admissions are contingent on other nonacademic factors—such as ensuring that students are drawn from geographically diverse regions and are evenly distributed across major disciplines—that favor whites and work against Asians, who tend to be disproportionately concentrated in certain geographic regions and academic fields (most notably the natural sciences). For a discussion of this issue, see Don Toshiaki Nakanshi, "A Quota on Excellence? The Asian American Admissions Debate," *Change* (November/December 1989): 39–47.

51. I am assuming here that providing decent services to some Asians will sometimes require possessing a deep familiarity with Asian languages and customs that only a person of Asian background might possess.

52. According to the Green Book, a compilation of data by the House Ways and

Means Committee, the percentages of whites, blacks, and Hispanics receiving welfare are 38.9, 37.2, and 17.8, respectively.

53. The statistical correlation between racial discrimination, economic deprivation, and political powerlessness testifies to a "causal" connection at least as strongly confirmable as that between cigarette smoking and lung cancer. In both cases, exceptions to the rule do not disprove causal links between hazardous lifestyles and increased risk of mortality. For a more detailed discussion of causation in science, see chapter 2 of David Ingram, *Reason, History, and Politics: The Communitarian Grounds of Legitimacy in the Modern Age* (Albany: State University of New York Press, 1995).

54. For example, Nicholas Capaldi argues that it is dangerous to substitute "sociological principles that are extraneous to the law and highly controversial if not downright false" for "certain moral principles and traditional practices" (Mosley and Capaldi, *Affirmative Action,* p. 129). His belief in the falsehood of social science stems from its supposed resistance to "empirical confirmation" and its proliferation of competing theories and languages. Capaldi does not try to defend this (in my opinion) erroneous view of social science (as contrasted with natural science). Nor does he seem bothered by his own highly speculative and problematic moral principles (derived from Lockean natural law theory), whose divine cosmology sanctifies individualism and free will while denigrating communalism and environmental conditioning (pp. 96ff.). For a refutation of the naive view of science espoused by Capaldi, see my *Reason, History, and Politics,* chapter 2.

55. For a sampling of the literature espousing the "dysfunctional culture" and "cognitive inferiority" hypotheses respectively, see Sowell, *The Economics and Politics of Race,* and Richard J. Herrnstein and Charles Murray, *The Bell Curve: Intelligence and Class Structure in American Life* (New York: Free Press, 1994).

56. Increased representation of blacks in the skilled professions, however, may benefit unemployed or underemployed blacks by providing them with the services of professionals who live and work in their communities.

57. By its very nature, capitalism exacerbates economic inequalities and limits the capacity of the welfare state to increase employment, raise minimum wages, and siphon off investment capital (through borrowing and taxing) for purposes of eliminating systemic poverty.

58. A recent study by Derek Bok and William G. Bowen, *The Shape of the River: Long-Term Consequences of Considering Race in College and University Admissions* (Princeton: Princeton University Press, 1998), shows that more than 75 percent of black affirmative action beneficiaries who scored higher than 1300 on the SAT believe colleges and universities should use race-sensitive policies to increase racial diversity (see note 59).

59. A recent study conducted by Drs. Robert C. Davidson and Ernest L. Lewis of the University of California–Davis School of Medicine and published in the *Journal of the American Medical Association* shows that there is no difference between special-admission students and regular-admission students in completing residency training and performance and obtaining board certification. Examining files of students admitted at the institution from 1968–1987 and questionnaires sent to graduates and directors of their residency programs, the authors concluded that special-admission students do almost as well as regular-admission students. Constituting 20 percent of total admissions, about 8 percent of whom were minorities covered by affirmative action while the remainder were persons who either had unique skills (e.g., bilingualism), displayed exemplary leadership qualities, or had overcome

physical and economic barriers, special-admission students had a 94 percent graduation rate compared with the 98 percent graduation rate for regular-admission students. Another study conducted by Derek Bok and William G. Bowen, the former presidents of Harvard and Princeton, disproves the claim by some opponents of affirmative action that black students with low test scores who attend the most selective institutions of higher education would be better off at less selective institutions. The study, which tracked 45,184 students who entered twenty-eight selective institutions in 1976 or 1989, shows that black students at these institutions graduated at twice the rate of their counterparts in less selective institutions (75 percent versus 40 percent) and were more likely to earn a graduate degree than white graduates (40 percent versus 37 percent). However, Shelby Steele and other critics of affirmative action note that 33 percent of the black graduates who went on to earn doctorates ended up doing low-paying community work rather than establishing lucrative practices in places like Beverly Hills. See Bok and Bowen, *The Shape of the River,* and Ben Gose, "A Sweeping New Defense of Affirmative Action," *Chronicle of Higher Education,* September 18, 1998, pp. A46ff.

60. This amount is based on the cumulative value (with compound interest) diverted from black families from unpaid labor (slavery) prior to 1863, underpaid labor and labor discrimination since 1863, and denial of educational and commercial opportunities. The value diverted from black families during a forty-year period of employment discrimination (1929–1969) has been calculated at $1.6 *trillion;* a similar figure for the period of slavery (1790–1860) is $4.7 *trillion.* See David H. Swinton, "Racial Inequality and Reparations," p. 156, James Marketti, "Estimated Present Value of Income Diverted During Slavery," p. 107, and Robert S. Browne, "Achieving Parity Through Reparations," p. 204, all in *The Wealth of Races: The Present Value of Benefits from Past Injustices,* ed. Richard F. America (New York: Greenwood Press, 1990).

61. John Rawls, *A Theory of Justice* (Cambridge: Harvard University Press, 1971), pp. 83ff.

62. Given their legal sanctioning of past discrimination, governments might feel compelled to sacrifice efficiency for justice; but profit-oriented businesses—which voluntarily elect to contract with government agencies under affirmative action guidelines—will not.

63. Hacker, "Goodbye to Affirmative Action," p. 27.

64. *Washington v. Davis,* 426 U.S. 229 (1976).

65. Studies show that black pupils constitute almost 40 percent of those classified as mentally retarded, disabled, or deficient, even though they constitute only 16 percent of the public school student population. Once they are tracked into special education classes for slow learners, few of them later get retracked into college-prep classes. Thus, while segregated schools have been declared illegal, segregated education within schools continues unabated. See Hacker, *Two Nations,* p. 169.

66. See note 59.

## 8. THE LEGALITY AND MORALITY OF AFFIRMATIVE ACTION

1. John Arthur, *The Unfinished Constitution: Philosophy and Constitutional Practice* (Belmont, Calf.: Wadsworth, 1989), p. 244.

2. The application of strict scrutiny to racial classifications first emerged in *Korematsu v. United States* (1944), in which the high court upheld the forced relocation of Japanese Americans in concentration camps on grounds of public security.

Justice Hugo Black's opinion expressly linked the violation of equal protection as it applies to racial and ethnic minorities to governmental actions that do not simply have a disparate impact on them but also are intended to perpetuate racist discrimination against them. Black's emphasis on discriminatory intent continues to guide the Court's interpretation of equal protection violations, with conservative members rejecting all race-conscious statutes as racist and discriminatory even if their discriminatory intent is to eradicate racism.

Instead of interpreting strict scrutiny to imply the unconstitutionality of all race-conscious legislation, some conservatives on the high court (most notably Sandra Day O'Connor) have elected to interpret it less strictly, permitting some remedial race-conscious legislation. Of course, the high court could have subjected racial classifications to even lower standards of scrutiny, with the lowest permitting unequal treatment of racial and ethnic groups so long as such treatment was "rationally related" to a "legitimate" governmental end. Following this reading, a segregation statute that rationally (i.e., effectively) preserved racial harmony (certainly a legitimate governmental end) could pass constitutional scrutiny. A more demanding, intermediate level of scrutiny—currently applied to gender classifications and briefly adopted by the high court in its 1990 ruling in *Metro Broadcasting, Inc. v. FCC* upholding racial set-asides in federal broadcast licensing regulations—has been strenuously advocated by more liberal members of the Court. This level of scrutiny demands that racial classifications be "substantially related" to an "important" governmental end. Following this reading, a segregation statute, unlike an affirmative action policy, would be regarded as substantially unrelated to preserving racial harmony or to attaining an even more important governmental end, such as racial justice in the distribution of educational and employment opportunities. For a critique of the high court's insistence on using strict scrutiny instead of intermediate scrutiny in evaluating the constitutionality of race-conscious legislation, see Justin Schwartz, *A Not Quite Color-Blind Constitution: Racial Discrimination and Racial Preference in Justice O'Connor's "Newest" Equal Protection Jurisprudence,* 58 Ohio State Law Journal 1055 (1997).

3. Cf. *Firefighters Local Union No. 1784 v. Schotts* (1984) and *Wygant v. Jackson Board of Education* (1986).

4. Upholding a lower court's decision, the Third District Court of Appeals ruled in 1996 that diversity alone—in the absence of any demonstration of past discrimination and severe underrepresentation—constituted just cause for laying off Sharon Taxman, the white plaintiff. Although the media presented the case as if Taxman and Debra Williams, the black teacher who was retained ahead of her, possessed *equal* credentials because they were hired to teach high school business on the same day in 1980 and were judged equal in ability in subsequent evaluations, Williams in fact was arguably more certified because she possessed a more advanced master's degree. Had the school board given this reason as the deciding factor instead of its desire to promote racial diversity, the suit would never have come up. Incidentally, Taxman was reinstated in 1992 but sued the Piscataway School Board for $144,000 in lost income dating back to 1989, the year she was laid off. The suit was eventually settled out of court in 1997, when the NAACP agreed to pay Taxman's back pay.

5. Albert G. Mosley and Nicholas Capaldi, *Affirmative Action: Social Justice or Unfair Preference* (Lanham, Md.: Rowman and Littlefield, 1996), pp. 20–21.

6. *Hopwood v. State of Texas,* WL 121235 (5th Cir).

7. Mosley and Capaldi, *Affirmative Action,* p. 5.

8. John David Skrentny, *The Ironies of Affirmative Action: Politics, Culture, and*

*Justice in America* (Chicago: University of Chicago Press, 1996). However, Nixon's plan was inspired by less enlightened motives as well. Although Nixon wanted to respond to the problem of urban black unemployment—one of the chief sources of black discontent that fueled the riots in the late sixties—he also wanted to undermine the Democratic Party by implementing a strategy designed to splinter that party's white labor unions (which were still largely segregated) and black workers seeking entry into organized trades.

9. In 1971 the Department of Labor issued Order 4, which extended the provisions of Executive Order 11246 to include women. This order mandated that employers with at least fifty employees and $50,000 in government business develop "specific goals and timetables" for hiring underutilized women and minorities at levels that "would reasonably be expected by their availability." The order was later followed by the Equal Employment Opportunity Act of 1972, which extended the EEOC's oversight to labor organizations and businesses with over fifteen members and to all municipal, state, and federal employees. Unions and companies not doing business with the government were encouraged to enter into voluntary consent decrees establishing mechanisms for ameliorating chronic minority underrepresentation as a way of avoiding costly class action lawsuits.

10. Gertrude Ezorsky, *Racism and Justice: The Case for Affirmative Action* (Ithaca: Cornell University Press, 1991), pp. 116–17.

11. Cf. *Local 28, Sheet Metal Workers' Intern. Assn. v. EEOC* (1986), *Local 93, International Association of Firefighters v. City of Cleveland* (1986), *United States v. Paradise* (1987), and *Metro Broadcasting Inc. v. F.C.C.* (1990).

12. For a critique of originalism, see Ronald Dworkin, *Law's Empire* (Cambridge: Harvard University Press, 1986), chapter 6, and David Ingram, *Reason, History, and Politics: The Communitarian Grounds of Legitimacy in the Modern Age* (Albany: State University of New York Press, 1995), chapter 6.

13. The idea that laws are more than just concrete rules, constituting as well a (more or less) coherent system of moral principles requiring philosophical interpretation, has been most ardently expounded in Anglo-American legal philosophy by Ronald Dworkin in *Law's Empire*.

14. This line of reasoning is exemplified in Justice Henry Brown's landmark opinion in *Plessy v. Ferguson* (1896) upholding the doctrine of "separate but equal." For Brown, southern states had reasonably concluded that the "public good" for both whites and blacks could best be achieved through segregation. Weighing the interests of whites and blacks equally, he concluded that "legislation is powerless to eradicate racial instincts or to abolish distinctions based upon physical differences, and the attempt to do so can only result in accentuating the difficulties of the present situation. . . . If one race be inferior to the other socially, the Constitution of the United States cannot put them upon the same plane" (Arthur, *The Unfinished Constitution*, p. 219).

15. The act does *not* "require any employer to grant preferential treatment to any individual or any group because of the race, color, religion, sex, or national origin of such individual or group on account of an imbalance which may exist with respect to the total number of percentage of persons of any race, color, religion, sex or national origin employed by any employer" (Title VII, sec. 703[j]).

16. Studies show that "each ethnic group of patients [is] more likely to be cared for by a physician of their own ethnic background than by a physician of another ethnic background" (Gang Xu, Silvia Fields, et al., "The Relationship Between the Ethnicity of Generalist Physicians and Their Care for Underserved Populations," Ohio

University College of Osteopathic Medicine, Athens, p. 10; cited in Mosley and Ca-paldi, *Affirmative Action,* p. 52).

17. J. Arthur, *The Unfinished Constitution,* pp. 251–52.

18. In his book *The Remedy: Class, Race and Affirmative Action* (New York: Basic Books, 1996), Richard Kahlenberg defends class-based remedies as a good method for achieving racial diversity. However, William Forbath and Gerald Torres, "The 'Talented Tenth' in Texas," *The Nation* (December 15, 1997): 20, point out that none of the class-based remedies proposed so far will likely have that desired effect. Cf. Peter Applebome, "Seeking New Approaches for Diversity," *New York Times,* April 23, 1997, p. B7.

19. The number of 1998 African-American admissions for UC–Berkeley and UCLA declined from 562 and 488 to 191 and 280, respectively. The number of 1998 Hispanic admissions for these same institutions declined from 1,266 and 1,497 to 600 and 1,001, respectively. See "After Proposition 209: Fewer Minorities Get into UCLA and Berkeley," *Chicago Tribune,* April 1, 1998, sec. 1, pp. 1, 28.

20. Ezorsky, *Racism and Justice,* pp. 81–84.

21. See Jan Narveson, "Politics, Ethics, and Political Correctness," in *Political Correctness: For and Against,* ed. J. Narveson and Marilyn Friedman (Lanham, Md.: Rowman and Littlefield, 1995), pp. 78–79.

22. Cf. Ezorsky, *Racism and Justice,* pp. 84–88, for a discussion of these remedies.

23. A white male who lost a position to a less qualified minority worker might be monetarily compensated for loss of earnings, benefits, and so on, but that portion of his past earnings and benefits stemming from institutionalized racism should also be progressively taxed to fund the affirmative action compensation scheme.

24. For a good discussion of group responsibility, see Larry May, *Sharing Responsibility* (Chicago: University of Chicago Press, 1992).

25. Cf. Cass Sunstein, "The Limits of Compensatory Justice," *Nomos* 33: *Compensatory Justice,* ed. John Chapman (New York: New York University Press, 1991), pp. 281–310.

26. Note that persons are made vulnerable by economic recessions, partly instigated by the Federal Reserve Bank, that unfairly burden them with the costs of sustaining a stable process of profit-taking in which they derive little or no benefit.

27. Mosley and Capaldi, *Affirmative Action,* p. 78.

28. Ibid., p. 103.

29. Ibid., pp. 30–31.

30. In fact, affirmative action has mainly benefited blacks in blue-collar trades. Although blacks modestly doubled their low representation in the legal profession (from 1.3 percent in 1960 to 2.7 percent today), their representation among doctors has declined from 4.4 percent in 1960 to 3.7 percent today, while the representation among college teachers has remained about the same (4.8 percent). By contrast, blacks now occupy 21.0 percent of all telephone operators (up from 2.6 percent in 1960), 26.4 percent of all police officers (up from 8.0 percent in 1970), 7.5 percent of all firefighters (up from 2.5 percent in 1960), 6.1 percent of all electricians (up from 2.2 percent in 1960), 7.7 percent of all secretaries (up from 2.0 percent in 1960), and 9.7 percent of all retail salespersons (up from 2.4 percent in 1960). See Andrew Hacker, *Two Nations: Black and White, Separate, Hostile, Unequal* (New York: Ballantine Books, 1995), pp. 118, 135–38.

31. In 1996, all but 27 of the 6,115 companies awarded federal contracts under affirmative action program 8(a) were owned by ethnic and racial minorities (blacks, Hispanics, Indians, Asians, Eskimos, and Native Hawaiians), which the law *defines* as

"socially disadvantaged," or qualified. Under the old law, white applicants had to provide a "preponderance" of evidence showing social disadvantage; now they need only provide "clear and convincing" evidence (*Chicago Tribune*, August 15, 1997, sec. 1, p. 6).

### 9. RACIAL REDISTRICTING AND DEMOCRATIC REPRESENTATION

1. See Ray Gonzales, "Decisión del Tribunal, una burla para la justicia," *La Raza*, July 20, 1995, p. 34.

2. The reactions of the Latino community to this debate are documented in December 25, 1995, and March 14, 1996, editions of *La Raza*.

3. Unlike Mexican Americans, Puerto Ricans are citizens of the United States and so do not share the former's concerns about immigration and naturalization. However, both groups do share overlapping interests, ranging from the provision of bilingual education to the prevention of drug trafficking, gang-related crime, unemployment, poverty, unsanitary and unsafe habitats, and so on.

4. The term *gerrymander* was originally applied to a salamander-shaped district that was designed to consolidate the political power of Elbridge Gerry, the governor of Massachusetts from 1810 to 1812. The application of the term to majority-minority districts created in the last decade is misleading, however, in that, unlike politically gerrymandered districts, these districts were *not* created by a majority to consolidate its power.

5. In a landmark case, *Allen v. State Board of Elections* (1969), the Supreme Court ruled that Mississippi's provision for holding at-large elections for each county board of supervisors had the effect of denying blacks the right to elect representatives of their choice.

6. By redistricting I mean the redrawing of political boundaries designed to secure something approximating proportional group representation. So construed, redistricting is distinct from matters pertaining to apportionment, which establishes a uniform numerical allocation of voters across districts so as to ensure equality of voting impact. Sometimes the distinct aims of apportionment and redistricting overlap, as was demonstrated in the landmark decision of *Baker v. Carr* (1962). Here the Supreme Court upheld a suit by Tennessee city dwellers complaining that inequalities between less populated (white) districts and more highly populated (black) districts resulted in the underrepresentation of (black) urban dwellers' interests.

Ironically, the current system, which permits each state to elect two senators (originally designed to strengthen the political clout of sparsely populated states comprising farming and grazing communities), dilutes the voting impact of racial minorities concentrated in urban regions. As Senator Daniel Patrick Moynihan recently discovered when working with Harvard's Kennedy School of Government, the most populous states receive about $1,000 less a year per capita (in terms of taxes paid out versus federal benefits received) than less populated states. The numerical dominance of sparsely populated states in the Senate also has enabled a relatively small number of ranchers and farmers to successfully lobby for the giveaway of federal grazing and mineral rights. See Daniel Lazare, *Frozen Republic: How the Constitution Is Paralyzing Democracy* (New York: Harcourt Brace, 1996).

7. Voting Rights Act of 1965, Public Law 89-110, para. 2, 79 Stat. 445. The citation is from the act as amended in 1982, Public Law Nos. 97-205, 96 Stat. 134. The Act of 1965 stipulated that voting districts in seventeen states and jurisdictions had to be cleared by the Justice Department or the D.C. District Court to prevent

retrogression of minority voting power in areas with a history of vote discrimination. In 1975 the provisions of the act were extended to protect Hispanics, American Indians, Alaskan Natives, and Asians as well.

8. As formulated, the act seems to mandate two conflicting courses of action: *maximizing opportunities* for fair representation and *correcting retrogression* in current opportunities. Legislatures have sometimes designed their districts to accord with the former interpretation, but since the late eighties there has been a gradual shift in favor of the latter. In *Miller v. Johnson* (1995), the Supreme Court struck down a "max-black" plan that reconfigured three of Georgia's eleven districts— comprising almost the exact percentage (27 percent) of Georgia's black population—as majority-minority districts. By contrast, the "ameliatory" plan that the Court preferred, which was designed to rectify demonstrable "retrogression," would have contained two majority-minority districts. In the latest round of decisions handed down by the Supreme Court in June 1996, the majority ruled that Congressional District 18 in Texas, which recorded a declining share of African-American population from 41 percent in 1980 to 35 percent in 1990, could not be reconfigured to ensure the continued election of that minority's chosen representative, even when that minority had maintained or increased its share of the total population in the immediate region. See Sandra Day O'Connor's majority opinion in *Bush v. Vera*, 116 Sup. Ct. 1969 (1996).

9. Confirmation of a statistical correlation between voting and race has been well documented. See Stephen Feldman, "Whose Common Good? Racism in the Political Community," *Georgia Law Journal* 1835 (1992): 1848.

10. *Association of Data Processing Orgs. v. Camp*, 397 U.S. 152 (1970).

11. *Lujan v. Defenders of Wildlife*, 1992, 112 Sup. Ct., 2143 (1992).

12. *Shaw v. Reno*, 509 U.S. 648 (1993).

13. O'Connor's concern that racial redistricting encourages the underrepresentation of whites inhabiting minority districts seems at odds with her earlier opinion in *Davis v. Bandemer* (1986), where she argued that the supporters of a losing candidate are generally adequately represented by the winning candidate. Worse, while expressing concern about harms visited upon whites inhabiting predominantly black districts, she said nothing about the harms suffered by blacks inhabiting predominantly white districts.

Incidentally, although it is *not* true that representatives "virtually" represent the interests of all of their constituents—on the contrary, they advocate most strongly on behalf of those core constituents who got them elected—the Court has been reluctant to concede this point *except* in cases involving racial gerrymandering schemes that relegate blacks to the status of permanent minorities. For this reason, the Court has intervened cautiously in cases involving partisan gerrymandering, refusing to define this violation in a way that would clearly distinguish it from politically motivated redistricting. In the 1970s it upheld politically motivated, bipartisan plans designed to protect incumbents, especially those that conformed to results obtained in the three previous elections. However, in *Davis v. Bandemer* and in *Badham v. Eu* (1989), the Court moved closer to defining a violation. In the latter case it intimated that a partisan gerrymander would obtain only if the plaintiff showed that he or she suffered discrimination comparable to that experienced by racial minorities. Given the improbability of any well-represented party being systematically excluded from the entire political process in a manner comparable to that experienced by blacks in the South during Jim Crow, the Court's refusal to overturn any partisan plan is likely to continue into the future.

14. Conservatives argue that the harms caused by racial redistricting as a form of forced *segregation* are similar to those caused by affirmative action as a form of forced *integration* in that both involve set-asides that violate the equal rights of individuals to be treated as individuals. Cf. Abigail Thernstrom, *Whose Votes Count? Affirmative Action and Minority Voting Rights* (Cambridge: Harvard University Press, 1987), pp. 237–38.

15. The two districts that triggered strict scrutiny in *Shaw* were North Carolina's First and Twelfth Districts—the former having been likened to a "bug splattered on a windshield," the latter to a snake whose 160-mile-long stretch along the corridor of Interstate 85 is so narrow at points that, as one state legislator remarked, "if you drove down the interstate with both car doors open, you'd kill most of the people in the district" (*Shaw v. Reno*, 521, 649).

16. In *Miller v. Johnson* ([1995], pp. 11, 14), Justice Anthony Kennedy held that, even when compactness requirements are satisfactorily met, evidence of racially motivated legislative *intent* taken separately suffices to justify a strict scrutiny challenge.

17. O'Connor later qualified her views about the appropriateness of race-conscious redistricting in *Bush v. Vera* (1996). There she asserted that it would be permissible for persons engaged in politically motivated redistricting to be "conscious . . . of the correlation between race and party" so long as they did not rely mainly on race data to achieve their purposes. According to O'Connor, by relying on a computer program designed to represent and model different racial compositions—a database that was more sophisticated in its block-by-block analysis than the "political" data obtained by precinct tabulations of party registrations and past voting statistics—the Texas legislature's plan for District Thirty ostensibly showed that it had subordinated incumbency protection to the aims of ensuring the election of a black representative (*Bush v. Vera*, 1947, 1950). However, as Justice John Paul Stevens noted in his sharp dissent, the initial motivation for redrawing District Thirty *was* to protect an incumbent. Since this incumbent happened to represent a predominantly black democratic constituency, he wondered what harm could be perpetrated on the blacks of that district by making use of the fact that 97 percent of them voted for the incumbent whose reelection was now being politically reassured through redistricting. Indeed, requiring the state to ignore the association between race and party affiliation, he added, could be "potentially as harmful as it would be to prohibit the Public Health Service from targeting African-American communities in an effort to increase awareness of sickle-cell anemia" (*Bush v. Vera*, Stevens dissenting, 1974).

18. Politically cohesive communities of interest do not always map neatly onto geographically compact territories. In the days when regional sentiments were stronger than they are today—and when cultures, polities, and economies were more segregated and localized—this mapping was less problematic. Perhaps that explains why the single-seat system of apportioning congressional districts appealed to the Founders. Be that as it may, dynamic demographic shifts and the dispersion of diverse interest groups across the political landscape have rendered the geographical conception of political community in many instances less relevant, if not otiose. Compounding this trend is the fact that in modern societies the traditional, geographically discrete communities of interest that once served as a locus of personal identity—family, neighborhood, church, and so on—are being uprooted, or supplanted, by voluntary associations that range across older political boundaries. Perhaps one ought to conclude from these demographic trends that the single-seat method of redistricting has outlived its usefulness. However, the fact remains that a substantial portion of what constitutes one's political interests is a function of one's

location—a location, I might add, that for blacks and many other minorities has seldom been freely chosen and socially unconstrained.

19. Cf. Justice John Paul Stevens's dissents in *Miller v. Johnson* and in *Bush v. Vera.*

20. Pamela S. Karlan, "Apres *Shaw* le deluge?" *PS: Political Science and Politics* (March 1995): 52.

21. Less race-conscious remedies involve (1) fewer majority-minority districts or smaller black majorities within individual districts, (2) less rigid quotas, (3) shorter durations, (4) better relationships between the plan's goal and the overall percentage of minorities in the plan's jurisdiction, and (5) greater respect for third parties, such as incumbents, state jurisdictions, and the like.

22. Andrew Altman, "Race and Democracy: The Controversy over Racial Vote Dilution," *Philosophy and Public Affairs* 27, no. 3 (1998): 175–201.

23. *Miller,* 6.

24. Nothing I have said so far speaks against the existence of overarching interests within the black community that ought to be represented. These favor enacting and strengthening civil rights and affirmative action laws; improving schools and health care delivery systems; increasing the minimum wage; providing jobs and job training for those who are unemployed (or underemployed); maintaining federal and state funding for AFDC, food stamps, Medicaid, and public housing; and enforcing antigun and antigang statutes.

25. Cornel West, *Race Matters* (Boston: Beacon Press, 1992), chapter 2, for one, has argued strenuously against a politics of black authenticity that presumes that blacks ought to support blacks simply because of their skin color. Although I share West's disdain for a politics that subordinates differences in ideological commitment and economic interest to a racial "closing of ranks" of the sort that prevailed when liberal blacks rallied around arch-conservative Clarence Thomas during his Senate confirmation hearing, I do not wish to discount, as he does, the idea of a black perspective born of racial discrimination. Without this notion, progressives would be hard-pressed to plead for the election of more blacks (as distinct from white liberals, who could just as persuasively and accountably represent black interests and values).

26. For a discussion of the paradoxes besetting "mirroring" conceptions of proportional representation as inadequate models of accountability, and the relative merits of defining representation in terms of thresholds, see Will Kymlicka, *Multicultural Citizenship* (Oxford: Oxford University Press, 1995), pp. 138ff; H. Pitkin, *The Concept of Representation* (Berkeley, Calif.: University of California Press, 1967), chapter 4; and Ann Phillips, "Democracy and Difference: Some Problems for Feminist Theory," *Political Quarterly* 63/1 (1992): 79–90.

27. Ensuring that members of an oppressed group have a chance to elect representatives who share their perspective provides legislatures with firsthand information about what it is like to be a member of such a group, information that is vital to the legislative process and difficult to obtain otherwise. However, even if white representatives can obtain secondhand information about what it is like to be one of the oppressed, it is important that such information also be articulated by representatives who actually have that perspective, because this symbolically shows that the majority respects the minority as an equal and autonomous advocate for its own perspective.

28. For a statistical demonstration of the instability of partisan voting trends in comparison to racial voting trends, see Mark E. Rush, *Partisan Representation and Electoral Behavior* (Baltimore: Johns Hopkins University Press, 1993).

29. *Shaw v. Reno,* 656; emphasis added.

30. Jean Bethke Elshtain, *Democracy on Trial* (New York: Henry Holt, 1995), p. 36.

31. In *Holder v. Hall,* 114 Sup. Ct. 2581 (1994), Justice Clarence Thomas argued (with Justice Scalia concurring) that the "terms of [the Voting Rights Act] reach only state enactments that limit citizens' access to the ballot" (p. 2592) and thus do not entitle the government to intervene when "numerical minorities lose" (p. 2596). This opinion sought to dismiss or reinterpret the amended version of the Voting Rights Act, especially paragraph 2 (1982), that explicitly defines the right of members of a protected class (specifically those individuals who have been discriminated against on account of color or race) to "elect representatives of their choice," which the accompanying House report identified as "minority candidates or candidates identified with the interests of a racial or language minority" (H. Rept. 227, 97th Cong., 1st sess., 1981, 30). Thomas argued that this interpretation of the act's 1973 mandate to ensure "all action necessary to make a vote effective" (para. 19731[c][1]) merely reflected a "series of partisan statements about purposes and objectives" that arbitrarily identified "effective" with "the capacity to control single-member districts" (*Holder,* 2596). While not expressly denying the existence of groups as such, Thomas insisted that no correlation between race and voting behavior establishes the existence of a *racial* group interest (p. 2598 n. 13). Concurring with Justice O'Connor's earlier opinion that the very idea of a group interest stereotypically presumes that all blacks think and act alike, he concluded that the protection of such a presumed interest by means of racial redistricting would discriminate against "double minorities," or *individual* members of a racial minority that hold views that deviate from the majority of persons within said minority. Although this view does not explicitly reject the existence of group identities as such, the argument against stereotyping would seem to have this implication, since it identifies individuals—not groups—as the locus of genuine "symbolic" representation. For a critique of Thomas's position, see Lani Guinier, "[E]racing Democracy: The Voting Rights Cases," *Harvard Law Review* 108/109 (1994): 109–37, esp. 118ff..

32. Lani Guinier, "The Miner's Canary: Race and the Democratic Process," *Dissent* 42, no. 4 (Fall 1995): 524.

33. According to Guinier, "The goals of the Voting Rights Act can and should be defended by framing them philosophically within a theory of group representation" ("[E]racing Democracy," p. 113). Instead of offering "a theory of exit for minority group members who choose to emphasize their individual identity," she proposes a theory that will "empower those whose *chosen* identity is group-based" (p. 123).

34. Lani Guinier, "The Triumph of Tokenism: The Voting Rights Act and the Theory of Black Electoral Success," *Michigan Law Review* 89 (1991): 1077–1154.

35. Ibid., p. 1111.

36. For Guinier, "The goal of a genuine, multiracial democracy should be to maximize participation by individuals and groups, without requiring monological group identities" ("The Miner's Canary," p. 521).

37. Guinier, "[E]racing Democracy," pp. 131–32.

38. Cf. Carol Swain, *Black Interests: The Representation of African Americans in Congress* (Cambridge: Harvard University Press, 1993). Not surprisingly, the impulse behind the racial redistricting policies of the eighties was strategically abetted by the Rose Institute (a conservative think tank) and aggressively implemented by the Justice Department during the administrations of two Republican presidents who were arguably hostile to the interests of most blacks and Hispanics.

39. Among the interests cited by Guinier, "The Triumph of Tokenism," p. 1134,

NOTES TO PAGES 209–16

that are largely shared by most blacks are interests in civil rights enforcement, government intervention on behalf of the poor, and increased opportunity for equal education and social advancement.

40. As Guinier notes (citing Young), "Interests are not necessarily descriptive of an essentialist concept of group identity but are fluid and dynamic articulations of group preferences" (ibid., p. 1136 n. 287).

41. According to Guinier, "Participation, which involves the ability to take part in the formal electoral process by casting a ballot, is individualistic, symbolic, and outcome-independent. The aggregation interest, which means having one's preferences taken into account in choosing public officials, is collectivist, instrumental, and outcome-dependent" ("[E]racing Democracy," p. 126 n. 113). It is odd that Guinier would defend interest aggregation as a way of constituting individuals into groups, since groups that are constituted through passive plebiscitary mechanisms (voting) lack precisely the sort of affinal dialogic group identity that she seeks to defend as warranting representation.

42. Guinier, "The Triumph of Tokenism," p. 1142. More recently, lack of accountability to the black community was one of the reasons why black plaintiffs challenged Durham, North Carolina's multimember state district, which had had a ten-year history of electing a black representative.

43. Guinier herself notes that, given the majoritarian and territorial tradition underlying single-seat districts, "interest proportionality may not be most viable as a litigation strategy" (ibid., p. 1137 n. 290).

44. Ibid., p. 1140. A consensus-building, minority veto rule was ordered as part of the remedy for structural vote dilution in the city of Mobile, Alabama (see *City of Mobile v. Bolden*, 446 U.S. 55 [1980]). In Selma, Alabama, the city council agreed to appoint five white and five black voting members to the school board, with a chair rotating annually between the two racial groups. Guinier also cites John Calhoun's supermajoritarian proposal requiring a concurrent majority of minority representatives (in this case, southern legislators) in the ratification of federal legislation (pp. 302–3).

45. For a discussion of the distinction between transformative and affirmative strategies of reform, see Chapter 2.

46. Racial reapportionment schemes almost invariably dilute the strength of minority votes, since the percentage of the minority population within a subdivision invariably exceeds the percentage of its representation. As a rough approximation, for a minority community to merit just one of three seats in a subdivided area, it would have to comprise no less than 33 percent and no more than 65 percent of the total population inhabiting said area. Any percentage falling between these limits would designate excess minority population and therefore potentially wasted (or diluted) minority voting strength. By contrast, if the jurisdiction in question were not subdivided into single-seat districts but were instead reconfigured as a multiseat district with single-shot or cumulative election procedures, excess minority strength beyond what was required to elect a single minority representative could be used to influence the election of other candidates. Of course, under single-shot voting schemes of the sort that recently existed in Durham, North Carolina (where citizens were allowed to vote for only one candidate within a multiseat district), the potential for exercising influence normally would be somewhat compromised. In a five-member race for three seats, a cohesive minority subcommunity constituting 25–30 percent of the district's population might be able to pool its votes to ensure the election of a lone minority candidate. However, by restricting its influence in this way, it would not be

exercising any political leverage with respect to other, nonminority candidates. (See Guinier, "The Triumph of Tokenism," p. 1142 n. 307).

47. However, as Iris Young, *Justice and the Politics of Difference* (Princeton: Princeton University Press, 1990), p. 187, notes, "Proportional representation of group members may sometimes be too little or too much to accomplish that aim [of representing group experiences, perspectives, and interests]," for if it were implemented in the United States, American Indians and other small groups would still be without representation while women, who constitute more than 50 percent of the population, might be represented at the expense of other minority groups.

## 10. MULTICULTURAL EDUCATION AND RESPECT FOR MINORITIES

1. See Carol Locust, "Wounding the American Spirit: Discrimination and Traditional American Indian Belief Systems," in *Social Justice in a Diverse Society*, ed. Rita C. Manning and René Trujillo (Mountain View, Calif.: Mayfield, 1996), pp. 313–24.

2. Native Americans were not granted religious freedom until passage of the American Indian Religious Freedom Act of 1978.

3. Locust, "Wounding the American Spirit," in Manning and Trujillo, *Social Justice in a Diverse Society*, p. 318.

4. Ibid., p. 322.

5. Ibid., p. 323.

6. The reason for repudiating the teaching of creationism in high school science courses is that scientific theories of cosmology and evolution are grounded in a method of experimental self-criticism that is alien to the religious apologetics founding creationism. The teaching of creationism is appropriate, however, in the study of religious worldviews.

7. Debates about multiculturalism have been influenced by cultural tensions peculiar to Canada and the United States. These tensions, in turn, partly stem from extracultural conflicts, such as the growing competition between immigrants and natives for scarce blue-collar jobs. By contrast, the problem of multiculturalism facing sub-Saharan African states in forging national and transnational loyalties out of diverse cultural identities is very different. Here, instead of fostering respect for cultural differences, African leaders struggle to construct new, postcolonial African identities to offset the genocidal tribal factionalism encouraged by former European colonizers. See K. Anthony Appiah, "The Limits of Pluralism," in *Multiculturalism and American Democracy*, ed. Arthur M. Melzer, Jerry Weinberger, and M. Richard Zinman (Lawrence: University Press of Kansas, 1998), pp. 37–54; and Jon Cruz, "From Farce to Tragedy: Reflections on the Reification of Race at Century's End," in *Mapping Multiculturalism*, ed. Avery F. Gordon and Christopher Newfield (Minneapolis: University of Minnesota Press, 1996, pp. 19–39.

8. As quoted in Nathan Glazer, "Is Assimilation Dead?" in Melzer, Weinberger, and Zinman, *Multiculturalism and American Democracy*, p. 16.

9. Multiculturalism comprises a complex set of strategies for compensating oppressed groups and combating cultural prejudices. The teaching of Afrocentrist historical perspectives to African-American kids in primary and secondary schools or the expansion of area specialties in institutions of higher learning focusing on women, African Americans, Hispanic Americans, Asian Americans, gays, and lesbians are two of the more prominent strategies. Another involves replacing the Western canon (written mainly by white European men) with recent narratives written by members

of oppressed groups. Still others go even farther, requiring the hiring of women and minority faculty as supportive role models.

10. In *Black Power: The Politics of Liberation in America* (New York: Random House, 1967), pp. 44–47, Kwame Toure (formerly known as Stokely Carmichael) and Charles Hamilton summarized the aim of Black Power as a struggle for black community empowerment premised on the democratic ideal of equal power-sharing within a pluralistic context.

11. The leader of the Nation of Islam, Louis Farrakhan, supports "black capitalism" and other conservative separatist solutions, while the Reverend Jesse Jackson advocates "self-help" combined with government aid.

12. The status of Latino (and possibly Asian-American) immigrants with regard to assimilation is complicated by the fact that they often retain strong identifications with their native cultures. As political and economic refugees, many expect to return to their native countries. See Roberto Suro, *Strangers Among Us: How Latin Immigration Is Transforming America* (New York: Knopf, 1998).

13. Important "third-wave" feminists include bell hooks, Maria Lugones, and Sarah Hoagland, all of whom explicitly criticize the ethic of care from a multicultural perspective.

14. Cf. Christopher Newfield and Avery Gordon, "Multiculturalism's Unfinished Business," in Gordon and Newfield, *Mapping Multiculturalism*, pp. 76–115.

15. Roger Kimball, *Tenured Radicals: How Politics Has Corrupted Our Higher Education* (New York: Harper Perennial, 1990), p. 193.

16. Robert Leiken, "O Their America," *Times Literary Supplement,* May 22, 1992, p. 6.

17. See Sandra Harding, "Introduction: Eurocentric Scientific Illiteracy—A Challenge for the World Community," in *The "Racial" Economy of Science: Toward A Democratic Future,* ed. S. Harding (Bloomington: Indiana University Press, 1993), p. 8.

18. For a critique of racist biases in IQ testing, see R. C. Lewontin, Steven Rose, and Leon J. Kamin, "IQ: The Rank Ordering of the World," in Harding, *The "Racial" Economy of Science,* pp. 142–60.

19. From 1932 until 1972, the U.S. Public Health Service conducted experiments on black men suffering from advanced stages of syphilis. The so-called Tuskegee Study allowed as many as one hundred of these men to die as a result of complications stemming from their condition—without treating them with available cures—simply in order to determine the impact that race played in the evolution of the disease. The men, overwhelmingly poor and uneducated, were never fully informed about their condition, their treatments, or the purpose of the study. See James Jones, "The Tuskegee Syphilis Experiment: A Moral Astigmatism," in Harding, *The "Racial" Economy of Science,* pp. 275–86. On a more positive note, the Physicians Committee for More Responsible Medicine, a vegetarian and animal-rights group, has recommended that the U.S. Department of Agriculture revise its food pyramid (which emphasizes the consumption of milk and meat) in order to take into account that African Americans and Latinos, who suffer from diabetes, hypertension, and other diet-related conditions in higher proportions than whites, should be encouraged to reduce their consumption of milk, meat, and other fatty foods. See "Dietary Guidelines Need More Cultural Diversity," *Chicago Tribune,* June 24, 1999, sec. 1, p. 20.

20. Studies on brain lateralization, hormones, and brain anatomy have sought to link differences in male and female visiospatial ability, verbal ability, and aggression.

For a critique of these studies, see R. Bleier, *Science and Gender: A Critique of Biology and Its Theories on Women* (New York: Pergamon Press, 1984).

21. Eileen Nechas and Denise Foley, *Unequal Treatment: What You Don't Know About How Women Are Mistreated by the Medical Community* (New York: Simon and Schuster, 1994), pp. 21–37.

22. See Judy Butler, *Gender Trouble: Feminism and the Subversion of Identity* (New York: Routledge, 1990), and Chapter 4, note 14.

23. Cf. Vandana Shiva, "Colonialism and the Evolution of Masculinist Forestry," pp. 303–14; Richard Levins and Richard Lewontin, "Applied Biology in the Third World: The Struggle for Revolutionary Science," pp. 315–25; Karl Grossman, "Environmental Racism," pp. 326–34; Donna Haraway, "The Bio-Politics of a Multicultural Field," pp. 377–97; and Sharon Traweek, "Cultural Differences in High-Energy Physics: Contrasts Between Japan and the United States," pp. 398–407, all in Harding, *The "Racial" Economy of Science*.

24. This distinction was suggested to me by my colleague Tom Wren, "The Concepts of Culture and Multiculturalism," in *Philosophy and Multiculturalism*, ed. Paul Churchill (New York: Humanities Press, forthcoming).

25. See Allan Bloom, *The Closing of the American Mind: How Higher Education Has Failed Democracy and Impoverished the Souls of Today's Students* (New York: Simon and Schuster, 1987), pp. 336ff.; Roger Kimball, "The Periphery v. the Center: The MLA in Chicago," in *Debating P.C.*, ed. Paul Berman (New York: Dell, 1992), pp. 62ff.; and Dinesh D' Souza, *Illiberal Education: The Politics of Race and Sex on Campus* (New York: Random House, 1992).

26. This is a prevailing theme among many liberal and radical critics of the traditional arts approach. Indeed, many radicals chide advocates of multiculturalism for focusing too excessively on culture, as if cultural oppression were not *primarily* a manifestation of deeper economic and political oppression. For a good sampling of the radical perspective on multiculturalism, see Gordon and Newfield, eds., *Mapping Multiculturalism*, especially the contribution by Jon Cruz, "From Farce to Tragedy," pp. 19–39.

27. Charles Taylor, *Multiculturalism and the Politics of Recognition: An Essay by Charles Taylor* (Princeton: Princeton University Press, 1992).

28. See Wilhelm Gottfried Herder, *Ideen zur Philosophie der Geschichte der Menschheit* (*Ideas for the Philosophy of the History of Mankind*, published in four parts between 1784 and 1791).

29. K. Anthony Appiah, "The Multiculturalist Misunderstanding," *New York Review of Books* (October 9, 1997): 30–36.

30. Taylor, *Multiculturalism and the Politics of Recognition*, p. 59.

31. The politics of hegemony is inspired by the thought of Italian Marxist philosopher Antonio Gramsci (1891–1937).

32. Postmodern political multiculturalism owes much to the post-Enlightenment, Nietzsche-inspired critique of subjectivism that insinuated itself into many English and modern language departments following their favorable reception of such French poststructuralists as Jacques Derrida, Michel Foucault, Jean-François Lyotard, and Gilles Deleuze. This critique advances a very different account of the relationship between culture and individual identity than that proffered by Taylor and other liberals. While postmodernists and liberals both agree on the social and cultural situatedness of the "self," only the latter describe this in terms of a dialogue of mutual recognition tending toward higher levels of meaningfulness and integrity.

33. Because women constitute a ubiquitous and numerous group, many (perhaps

most) public colleges and universities have established womens's studies programs. Demographically concentrated ethnic minorities, Native Americans, and gays and lesbians, by contrast, have not acceded to the same status. As one might expect, institutions located in urban settings with large concentrations of ethnic minorities devote more resources to their study, as do institutions located near sizable concentrations of Native Americans and homosexuals.

34. L. Blum, "Anti-Racism, Multiculturalism, and Interracial Community: Three Educational Values for a Multicultural Society," in Manning and Trujillo, *Social Justice in a Diverse Society*, pp. 370–82. Blum notes that it is neither appropriate nor particularly meaningful for white students to value the contributions of white leaders, thinkers, and artists in the same way that black students value the contributions of black leaders, thinkers, and artists. White leaders, thinkers, and artists are more than adequately honored in our society for their contributions; and while the concept of black ethnic culture as locus of appreciation is acceptable (if problematic), the same idea applied to white culture is both unacceptable and even incoherent. None of this, however, speaks against white students appreciating the contributions of their own and other European ethnic cultures to American society.

35. The current status of a culture would include "family ethnic rituals, foods, customs regarding family roles and interactions, values, musical and other cultural preferences, philosophies of life, and the like" (ibid., p. 375).

36. Appiah, "The Limits of Pluralism," in Melzer, Weinberger, and Zinman, *Multiculturalism and American Democracy*, p. 51.

37. Leonard Jeffries, quoted by Joseph Berger, "Professors' Theories on Race Stir Turmoil at City College," *New York Times*, April 20, 1990.

38. In fact, as of 1996, the completion rate (around 13 percent) among Latino and African-American college students was half that of whites, a fact that is not entirely explicable on the basis of poor academic preparation. Cf. Willie M. Legette, "The Crisis of the Black Male," in *Without Justice for All: The New Liberalism and Our Retreat from Racial Equality*, ed. Adolph Reed (Boulder, Colo.: Westview, 1999), p. 311.

39. Objectively ranking job candidates assumes that (a) sufficient evidence of past performance is available, (b) such evidence can form the basis for reliable predictions of future performance, (c) common standards exist for comparing the diverse approaches and styles of scholarship informing the evidence, (d) application of such standards is not subjective, and (e) significant discrepancies in performance capability can be discerned upon applying them. In many academic hiring cases, the five conditions mentioned above are not satisfiable with any reliable degree of certainty. Past publication record is a highly uncertain basis for predicting the future scholarly performance of specialists at the entry level. Teaching, therefore, probably ought to weigh more heavily (assuming student and peer evaluations of classroom performance are on average a more reliable predictor of future teaching performance than writing samples and presentations are of scholarly performance). Whenever there are no significant discrepancies among applicants in scholarship and teaching (which is to say that all of them are judged reasonably competent in these areas), the job ought to go to the woman or minority candidate.

40. Donald Kagan, "Western Values Are Central," *New York Times*, May 4, 1991, p. A23; also cited by Marilyn Friedman in M. Friedman and Jan Narveson, *Political Correctness: For and Against* (Lanham, Md.: Rowman and Littlefield, 1995), p. 8.

41. It is far from clear whether (and if so, to what extent) cultural conflict is bad. The fact that a society like Japan is lacking in cultural antagonism may make it less

congenial to sustaining robust levels of public debate requisite for counteracting a paternalistic despotism of technical elites. Of course, the fact that a country like Bosnia is wracked by multicultural antagonism between its Muslim, Croat, and Serb factions may make it less congenial to sustaining the kind of constitutional consensus requisite for maintaining a stable democracy. Bosnia-Herzegovina's federal parliament mandates equal representation among its three ethnic groups, each of which elects an executive leader to a three-member presidency. Each half of the country—the Serbs and the Muslim-Croat Federation—has its own ethnically based parliament as well. According to a recent study by the International Crisis Group, this arrangement frustrates the achievement of a unified constitutional democracy: "Politicians only have to seek support from one ethnic group to win office. . . . as a result, it will always be easier and more rewarding for politicians to outbid each other on ethnic issues rather than to preach reconciliation" ("Nationalists Lead Bosnia Vote Despite U.S. Coaxing," *Chicago Tribune,* September 20, 1998, p. 6).

42. Susan Moller Okin, "Feminism and Multiculturalism: Some Tensions," *Ethics* 108 (July 1998): 661–84.

43. The linkage of multiculturalism and postcapitalism is forcefully made by Martin Matustik, *Specters of Liberation: Great Refusals in the New World Order* (Albany: State University of New York Press, 1998), chapters 3 and 9.

44. The possibility that Western rationality (emancipatory enlightenment) inherently inclines toward technological domination and hierarchy rather than democratic equality has been broached by philosophers since Nietzsche. For a classic statement of this thesis, see Theodor Adorno and Max Horkheimer, *Dialectic of Enlightenment* (1947; reprint, New York: Herder and Herder, 1972); for a criticism of it, see David Ingram, *Reason, History, and Politics: The Communitarian Grounds of Legitimacy in the Modern Age* (Albany: State University of New York Press, 1995), especially chapter 2.

## 11. GROUP RIGHTS IN A GLOBAL CONTEXT

1. Rights to assembly, association, and freedom of thought, conscience, and religion are perhaps best thought of as civil liberties that devolve upon individuals rather than groups. But even if they are claimed on behalf of one's humanity rather than on behalf of one's membership in particular groups, their exercise typically occurs within the context of religious communities and the like whose maintenance may require special exemptions, privileges, protections, and other group-specific rights. Thus (to cite an example from Chapter 1), my right as an individual human being to practice my Orthodox Jewish faith might require that the government exempt me from certain work days and dress codes and provide my children with special education benefits within the context of parochial schools designed to protect them against harassment from members of mainstream denominations.

2. The State Department urged that the Universal Declaration of Human Rights be split into two independently ratifiable treaties: the International Covenant on Civil and Political Rights and the International Covenant on Economic, Social, and Cultural Rights. While supporting the former covenant, the State Department has refused to endorse the latter on the grounds that these rights are less genuine and binding. Clearly, the department's division of rights is arbitrary and incoherent (some rights, like the right to join labor unions, straddle the distinction, while most rights that fall under one covenant are ineffectual apart from being conjoined with rights falling under the other). Even as a marker of priorities, the distinction fails to

take into account that *within* each division there are rights that are more basic (meriting greater protection) than others. Thus, the economic right to acquire land and productive capacity for profit is less basic than the economic right to bare subsistence, just as the political right to contribute money to political campaigns and parties is less basic than the political right to vote. By not taking into account the priority of subsistence over market freedom, the State Department has condoned the violation of subsistence rights in the name of economic freedom.

3. In response to the standard U.S. policy during the 1970s and 1980s of sending military weapons and training personnel to any anti-Communist government regardless of its flagrant violations of human rights, Congress passed the Foreign Assistance Act, which prohibits foreign aid to excessively brutal regimes.

4. Martin Khor notes that "prices of Southern commodities have been plummeting while the prices of manufactured goods imported from the North continue to rise. According to the United Nations, the prices of commodities other than oil fell by an average of 52 percent between 1980 and 1992. . . . In the period from 1986 to 1989, sub-Saharan Africa suffered a total loss of $56 billion due to the decline in the purchasing power of its exports" ("Colonialism Redux," *The Nation* [July 15/22, 1996]: 19).

5. In 1996, the IMF established the Heavily Indebted Poor Countries initiative, which provides minimal debt relief for the few countries that qualify in exchange for their adopting grueling "structural adjustment" policies that slow growth, reduce spending on education and health care, and—most ironically—increase debt burdens.

6. Cf. Chapter 6, note 35.

7. The U.S. bailout of the Mexican economy following the devaluation of the peso in 1994 and the international bailout of the Russian and Southeast Asian economies in 1998 following similar currency crises underscore the great extent to which Third World economies have become dependent on outside investors. The increasing control over domestic economies exercised by international financial institutions—ranging from the regulatory offices of the European Union to the World Trade Organization, the World Bank, and the International Monetary Fund—also illustrates the degree to which national democratic sovereignty has become a victim of economic growth. Popular demonstrations in Italy and France against the Maastricht Treaty (imposing reductions in benefits, wage ceilings, and public expenditures on the member nations of the EU) and in Brazil and Mexico against similar reductions as well as the foreign buyout of domestic land and resources (all imposed by international lending institutions) are largely a response to this attack on democracy.

8. The environmental destruction unleashed in the Amazon region since the seventies (involving the unprecedented burning and flooding of millions of acres of forest for strip-mining, cattle grazing, and electrification) is the most frequently cited example of failed free-market policies. Projects funded by the World Bank and Inter-American Development Bank (IDB), such as the Electro Norte Dam project, are costly, not only in terms of financial losses but also in terms of lost human and animal life, widespread water and air pollution (with its catastrophic "greenhouse" effect), and destruction of indigenous cultures. Because of Brazil's foreign indebtedness, which ranks at the top, and because of new free-market, financial, and trade agreements imposed on that country by its creditors, it cannot reject foreign investment. Hence the government is granting concessions to foreign timber interests to log more than six million acres of virgin forest located in the Amazon. The first concession, entitling twenty-two Malaysian logging outfits to cut twelve thousand

acres in the Tapajos National Forest in 1997, has been especially controversial given their awful environmental record in their own country and elsewhere. Although IBAMA (Brazil's poorly funded and poorly staffed environmental agency) lobbied in 1998 to secure passage of a new bill that makes such activities as illegal logging and dumping of pollutants a crime, key provisions of the bill that would have made setting runaway fires a felony were vetoed by President Ferdinand Cardoso under pressure from ranching and sugarcane interests. (As of May 1999, the Brazilian government had already suspended implementation of its environmental crimes bill for six years and revoked the ban on new Amazon clearing despite the fact that last year alone seventeen thousand square miles—more than 2.5 times the official Brazilian estimate—had been deforested.) Elsewhere, the Brazilian government—on the advice of the IDB and the UN Development Agency—has decided to push ahead with its alteration of the Paraguay and Parana Rivers (the so-called hydrovia project) despite forecasts by the Environmental Defense Fund and U.S., Brazilian, Argentine, and Paraguayan university researchers that doing so will destroy the Pantanal (the world's largest wetland), hurt fishing, and fail to significantly increase soybean and iron ore exports as projected. See "Pirates Leave Mark on the Heart of the Amazon," *Chicago Tribune,* August 27, 1997, sec. 1, p. 20; "South American River Project Is Criticized," *Chicago Tribune,* August 20, 1997, sec. 1, p. 10; and "Brazil Passes Package of Environmental Laws," *Chicago Tribune,* February 17, 1998, sec. 1, p. 8.

9.  Claude Ake, "The African Context of Human Rights," *Africa Today* 34, no. 142 (1987): 5–13.; reprinted in Larry May, Shari Collins-Chobanian, and Kai Wong, eds., *Applied Ethics: A Multicultural Approach* (Upper Saddle River, N.J.: Prentice Hall, 1998), p. 84.

10.  For an excellent discussion of how the truncated economic and political modernization imposed on Nigeria and other African colonies by European powers actually undermined a modern respect for liberal rights, see Olufemi Taiwo, "Running Aground on Native Shores: The Saga of Colonialism and Modernity" (unpublished manuscript), and "Reading the Colonizer's Mind: Lord Lugard and the Philosophical Foundations of British Colonialism," in *Philosophy and Racism,* ed. Susan Babbit and Sue Campbell (Ithaca: Cornell University Press, forthcoming). Today, as Nigeria nudges toward its first democracy in decades, foreign oil companies like Shell and Chevron continue to take advantage of corrupt government military leaders to suppress environmental movements and other popular efforts to gain control of some of the massive wealth generated by oil revenues (very little of which remains in the country, with virtually nothing trickling down to the poorest and most numerous people). See Paul Salopek, "A 'Pearl' Keeps Nigeria Poor," *Chicago Tribune,* February 26, 1999, pp. 1, 14.

11.  Most of Africa's leading political leaders have espoused a conception of democratic socialism or social democracy that is deeply imbued with communitarian thinking. Some, like former Tanzanian president Julius Nyerere, have defended a single-party political system on the grounds that all Tanzanians (regardless of tribal affiliation) converge toward socialist goals (a similar view, I might add, was defended by the first president of Ghana, Kwame Nkrumah, who tried to reconcile nationalism with Pan-African collectivism). Others, like President Nelson Mandela of South Africa, have instead defended a social democratic vision that respects cultural and social differences. For a good sampling of their writings, see Parker English and Kibujo M. Kalumba, eds., *African Philosophy: A Classical Approach* (Upper Saddle River, N.J.: Prentice Hall, 1996).

12.  Henry Shue, *Basic Rights: Subsistence, Affluence, and U.S. Foreign Policy,* 2d

ed. (Princeton: Princeton University Press, 1996), pp. 26, 31; for his critique of Rawls, see pp. 127–29.

13. Ibid., p. 13. Rights are here understood as demands that override personal preferences and lesser moral duties (to bring about the good, for example).

14. Ibid., pp. 37ff.

15. Ibid., pp. 22ff.

16. Ibid., p. 31. Shue's defense of basic universal rights is conditional with respect to the fact that any minimally decent society, premodern or modern, will endow its citizens with at least some rights (basic or nonbasic). However, it is not conditional with respect to citizens' beliefs about which specific rights persons ought to have, because such beliefs can be mistaken. For Shue, "which rights, and correlative duties, people have is determined by the weight of reasons" (p. 73). However, since the "weight of reasons" (or "the quality of reasoning") is at least partly determined by the extent to which *all* concerned parties could be rationally persuaded in an unlimited, inclusive dialogue, it is (contrary to Shue) also partly measured by "the quantity of belief." Hence, the universal validity of basic rights is less dependent on the existence of some belief-independent moral reality than it is on our idealistic expectations that all participants in a truly unlimited, rational dialogue would unanimously endorse such rights in the long run.

17. Ibid., pp. 74–78. Shue admits that we can theoretically conceive the "abstract possibility of a rule of law protecting rights without any genuine influence by those with the right on fundamental decisions about the institutions embodying the rule of law or the implementation of the institution's policies" (p. 84). This suggests that the necessary (essential) interdependence of subsistence, security, and political rights only obtains in practice (as a matter of contingent fact) and not in theory. However, if we accept the argument advanced by Rousseau, Habermas, and others that the rule of law acquires its legitimacy (morally binding force) *only* through genuinely democratic participation (see Chapter 1), the theoretical possibility of an undemocratic legal regime that adequately protects the subsistence and security rights (and nonpolitical civil liberties) of its citizens ceases to make sense.

18. Ibid., p. 118.

19. Ibid., p. 117. Shue's inconsistency regarding culture as a basic right is reflected in his attitude toward education. In the first edition of his book, he explicitly states that the right to publicly supported education is *not* basic since no rational person would choose it over a right to security. However, in the afterword to the second edition, he concedes that "the route to physical security against inhumane or degrading treatment often runs through primary education" (p. 163). People must be taught their rights and how to defend them, which usually requires first learning to read and write.

20. Ibid., pp. 52ff.

21. Ibid., pp. 160ff. Shue insists that Americans assume more responsibility for the disastrous effects of their leaders' foreign policies abroad (especially in Latin America, where our support for brutal military regimes in Guatemala, Honduras, and El Salvador led to gross violations of human rights).

22. It is possible that the most efficacious route to ensuring the subsistence rights of poor people might involve shifting responsibility to third parties in ways that are patently unfair to these third parties. This occurs most often when foreign volunteers sacrifice their time, energy, and resources in order to compensate for the harmful omissions and acts of others. As Shue notes, an *institutional* understanding of rights that assigns duties on the basis of a maximally efficient determination of remedies

must be mutually qualified by an *interactional* understanding of rights that assigns duties on the basis of a just distribution of individual responsibilities and burdens (ibid., p. 165).

23. On the libertarian account, so long as I have not voluntarily and expressly assumed responsibility for the well-being of someone (say, an infant stranger swimming in the pool beside me), my refusal to lend that person positive assistance (to pull him out when he is drowning) constitutes no violation of his basic right to live. At most, refusing to lend assistance in this case would convict me of moral baseness for failing to live up to my minimal Good Samaritan duties. By contrast, the conception of positive rights that I (along with Shue) defend entails that we sometimes incur strong obligations to provide assistance to strangers in need, even if we have not voluntarily assumed responsibility for them. The danger that our responsibility to others is so indeterminate and indefinite—extending to the millions of anonymous starving people throughout the world—as to be impossible to fulfill is, however, wildly exaggerated. The assignment and extent of responsibility are both determinable—more or less precisely, given sufficient information about the causes of and remedies for grievous harm—and limited by available capacities and resources. For further discussion of related issues pertaining to immigration, see Chapter 6, notes 26 and 27.

24. Jeremy Waldron, *Liberal Rights: Collected Papers, 1981–1991* (Cambridge: Cambridge University Press, 1993), p. 25. For further discussion of the assignment of duties, cf. note 16 above and Chapter 6, notes 26 and 27.

25. The recent example of Kosovo shows just how perilous "humanitarian" military intervention in the domestic affairs of a rogue state that is systematically violating the rights of some of its citizenry can be. Such military intervention should never be ruled out in principle, but its legitimate use as a measure of last resort must be based on a frank assessment of probable costs and benefits. The recent NATO intervention (ostensibly in the name of protecting Albanian Kosovars from Serb repression) was of questionable legitimacy, not the least because it followed upon NATO's refusal to grant reasonable concessions (such as the use of UN occupational forces in Kosovo) to Serbian president Slobodan Milosevic during the Rambouillet negotiations leading up to the crisis. Indeed, all things being equal, it would have been better had international intervention been cleared by a general session of the United Nations and members of the Security Council in a manner that could have elicited the approval of Milosevic and his two major allies on the council, Russia and China. As it was, NATO's unilateral decision to force Milosevic's hand (which was already severely constrained by his hypernationalist Serb opponents) by bombing Serbia and Kosovo precipitated his decision to kill and expel Albanian Kosovars on an unprecedented scale. Aside from the huge loss of life and destruction of property, this use of force has further alienated Russia and China from the West and has embittered all sides, Serbs and Albanian Kosovars in particular, in a manner that is almost certain to produce another round of ethnic strife in the future.

26. See Jürgen Habermas, *The Inclusion of the Other: Studies in Political Theory*, ed. Ciaran Cronin and Pablo De Greiff (Cambridge, Mass.: MIT Press, 1998). The only example of transnational democracy currently in existence is the European Parliament, whose 626 delegates have recently acquired the power to reject nominees of member governments for president of the European Commission (the EU's executive body), amend or reject the EU's $135 billion-a-year budget, and share with the commission powers over European legislation in thirty-eight areas. The only other significant transnational legal body is the International Court located in The Hague, whose judicial authority until very recently (thanks to the new War Crimes Tribunal) has been quite weak.

27. Cf. Richard Wasserstrom, "Racism and Sexism," in *Social Justice in a Diverse Society*, ed. Rita C. Manning and René Trujillo (Mountain View, Calif.: Mayfield, 1996), pp. 430–44.

28. This does not preclude the use of group-specific rights as means for protecting basic rights. Exercising the same basic rights to religious, economic, and political freedom, for example, may require instituting schemes of proportional group representation, exemptions for religious minorities, and special entitlements to disabled people. However, unlike disability entitlements and religious exemptions, which are relatively permanent means for realizing individual civil liberties and the like, group rights that grant limited sovereignty over language, education, and other aspects of a societal culture (in Kymlicka's sense) are provisional with respect to real threats of racial and cultural domination.

29. For a discussion of the difference between fusion and assimilation, see Chapter 4.

30. Urbanization has increased in Third World countries as a result of industrial development and the displacement of peasants caused by the introduction of labor-saving technology in large-scale agribusiness. Although a recent UN report praises urbanization as an efficient way of expending fewer resources per capita, this is not true. Cities are resource-intensive: they require the long-distance importation of basic resources and exportation of waste; the concentration of large numbers of persons in densely overcrowded spaces drives up the cost of basic goods (which, like concrete, steel, and other building materials, have to be provided by a global market whose demand for mass-produced and mass-consumed commodities is already stretched to the limit). See Helena Norbert-Hodge, "Break up the Monoculture: Why the Drive to Create a Homogenized World Must Inevitably Fail," *The Nation* (July 15/22, 1996): 21.

31. Ibid.

32. My argument assumes that local resistance to environmental homogenization is deep and ineradicable. Should this resistance be overcome, biological and cultural homogenization would then become adaptive. However, absence of diversity could still pose a problem to survival should the monoenvironment suddenly diversify because of endogenous or exogenous factors. None of these economic considerations, of course, address the spiritual downside of a monoculture that unleashes oppressive conformity.

33. As I stated in Chapter 6, note 29, only a global market economy premised on some kind of international federation of collectively financed, democratically (and community) controlled co-ops will ensure an equitable and environmentally sound distribution and consumption of basic resources.

# INDEX

Adorno, Theodor W., 304n44
Affirmative action
  and *Adarand Constructors, Inc. v. Pena,*
    176, 197
  alternatives to, 186, 293nn18,23
  and Asian-Americans, 159–63, 174, 185,
    196, 288nn46,49,50, 293n31
  and *City of Richmond v. Crosen,* 176
  and Clinton administration, 196–97
  as compensation, 161, 163, 167, 173,
    178, 185, 189–95, 192
  and dependency, 166
  and equal protection, 174, 180–83,
    296n14
  and *Firefighters Local Union No. 1784 v.
    Stoots et al.,* 189
  and *Fullilove v. Klutznick,* 178
  generational impact of, 190, 194–95
  and *Griggs v. Duke Power Co.,* 178
  groups benefited by, 161, 288nn49,50,
    294n31
  and higher education, 160–62, 171–76,
    185–86, 234–36, 288nn46,50,
    289nn58,59, 293nn18,19
  and hiring and retaining, 167, 176,
    187–89, 234–36, 300n9
  history of, 177–79
  and *Hopwood v. State of Texas,* 176,
    185
  and Indian immigrants, 288n49, 294n31
  as inefficient, 166–67, 171–73, 188
  and Latinos, 160–61, 174, 176, 185,
    196–97, 229, 288n46, 294n31
  and Local 28, *Sheet Metal Workers Intern.
    Ass. v. EEOC,* 292n11
  and *Local 93, Int'l Assoc. of Firefighters v.
    City of Cleveland,* 292n11
  and merit principle, 189, 235

  and *Metro Broadcasting Inc. v. F.C.C.,*
    291n2, 292n11
  moral justifications of, 186–95
  and multicultural diversity, 161, 173,
    175–76, 197, 288n49
  and Native Americans, 161, 174, 196–97,
    288n46, 294n31
  and opposition to, 161, 259n2, 296n59
  and Philadelphia Plan, 177, 292n8
  and Piscataway School Board, 176,
    291n14
  and procedural justice, 168
  and Proposition 209, 129, 138, 176, 185,
    259n2
  and qualifications, 171–73, 185–86, 195,
    234–36
  quotas and set-asides, 162, 169, 175–76,
    179, 185, 291n2
  and racial resentment, 161, 163, 166,
    292n8
  and recruitment of minorities, 177,
    234–36
  and *Regents of the University of California
    v. Bakke,* 174–76, 179, 184–85
  as remedying inequality, 165, 169
  and role models, 167, 170, 185, 234,
    300n9
  as stigmatizing benefactors, 166
  and training programs, 178
  and underrepresentation in trades, 163,
    170, 178, 291n4, 292n9
  and *United States v. Paradise,* 292n11
  and *United Steelworkers v. Weber,* 178
  as victimizing white males, 163, 168,
    174–76, 180, 184–89, 195, 198,
    293n23
  voluntary participation in, 177, 198,
    290n62